# REPUBLICS OF LETTERS
## LITERARY COMMUNITIES IN AUSTRALIA

Edited by Peter Kirkpatrick and Robert Dixon

SYDNEY UNIVERSITY PRESS

Published 2012 by SYDNEY UNIVERSITY PRESS
University of Sydney Library
sydney.edu.au/sup

© Peter Kirkpatrick and Robert Dixon 2012
© Individual contributors 2012
© Sydney University Press 2012

**Reproduction and Communication for other purposes**

Except as permitted under the Act, no part of this edition may be reproduced, stored in a retrieval system, or communicated in any form or by any means without prior written permission. All requests for reproduction or communication should be made to Sydney University Press at the address below:

Sydney University Press
Fisher Library F03
University of Sydney NSW 2006 AUSTRALIA
Email: sup.info@sydney.edu.au

**National Library of Australia Cataloguing-in-Publication entry**

Title: Republics of Letters: Literary Communities in Australia / edited by Peter Kirkpatrick and Robert Dixon
ISBN: 9781920899783 (pbk.)
Notes: Includes bibliographical references and index.
Subjects: Communication and the arts--Australia.
Popular culture and literature--Australia.
Literary movements--Australia.
Influence (Literary, artistic, etc.)
Other Authors/Contributors:
Peter Kirkpatrick
Dixon, Robert
Dewey Number:
700.1

Cover design by Miguel Yamin, University Publishing Service, based on the frontispiece of *The Bulletin Reciter* (1901) by Livingston Hopkins.

## Contents

Introduction: Republics of Letters and Literary Communities   v
*Peter Kirkpatrick and Robert Dixon*

PART 1: SITES OF SOCIABILITY, SCENES OF READING   1

1. Literary Community, Cultural Hierarchy, and Twentieth-Century American Readers   3
*Joan Shelley Rubin*

2. The 'Federation of Literary Sympathy': The Australasian Home Reading Union   17
*Kylie Mirmohamadi*

3. Communities of Readers: Australian Reading History and Library Loan Records   27
*Julieanne Lamond*

4. Pacifying Brisbane: *The Muses' Magazine* and the 1920s   39
*Patrick Buckridge*

5. Books and Debate About the Australian Government's Policies Towards Asylum Seekers   53
*Jan Zwar*

PART 2: REPUBLICS OF LETTERS: LOCAL, NATIONAL AND INTERNATIONAL LITERARY COMMUNITIES   69

6. Scenes of Reading: Is Australian Literature a World Literature?   71
*Robert Dixon*

7. Modernising Anglocentrism: *Desiderata* and Literary Time   85
*David Carter*

8. Jindy Modernist: The Jindyworobaks as Avant Garde   99
*Peter Kirkpatrick*

9. *Bobbin Up* in the *Leseland*: Australian Literature in the German Democratic Republic   113
*Nicole Moore and Christina Spittel*

10. An American Introduction: Perfect Readers, Unread Books and Christina Stead's *The Man Who Loved Children*   127
*Fiona Morrison*

11. Connectivity, Community and the Question of Literary Universality: Reading Kim Scott's Chronotope and John Kinsella's Commedia   137
*Philip Mead*

PART 3: SOCIALITY, GENDER AND GENRE — 157

12. The Great Parenting Tradition: Charting a History of Parenting-Book Writers and Readers in Colonial Australia — 159
    *Michelle De Stefani*

13. Reading Publics, Watching Audiences: *Lady Audley's Secret* in Nineteenth-Century Melbourne — 171
    *Susan K. Martin*

14. 'I Must Be My Own Director': Cynthia Reed, Elisabeth Lambert, and Reed & Harris, Publishers — 183
    *Jane Grant*

15. 'Opposing All the Things They Stand For': Women Writers and the Women's Magazines — 195
    *Susan Sheridan*

16. Seven Writers and Australia's Literary Capital — 205
    *D'Arcy Randall*

PART 4: UNSETTLEMENTS: EMERGING LITERARY COMMUNITIES — 217

17. 'Networking, Bumping into, Sucking up to, Catching up with, Meeting, Greeting, Chatting, Joking, Criticising': The Emerging Writers' Community as *Respublica Literaria* — 219
    *Keri Glastonbury*

18. An Unsettled Community: Harpur's Carnival, Harris' Assonance, Mackellar's Code — 227
    *Michael Farrell*

19. The Beginner's Guide to Being an Australian: John O'Grady's *They're a Weird Mob* — 239
    *Lindsay Barrett*

20. 'He Lacks Almost All the Qualities of the Novelist': G.M. Glaskin and his Australian Contemporaries — 249
    *Jeremy Fisher*

21. Anthologies and the Anti-Republic of Australian Gay and Lesbian Poetry — 257
    *Ann Vickery*

22. 'All the Village was Running': Some Voices from Young Refugees in Western Sydney — 267
    *Lachlan Brown*

23. Distance — 279
    *Bonny Cassidy*

Contributors — 293
Index — 297

INTRODUCTION
REPUBLICS OF LETTERS AND LITERARY COMMUNITIES

*Republics of Letters: Literary Communities in Australia* is the first book to explore the notion of literary community or literary sociability in relation to Australian literature in a thematic and comprehensive way. It brings together twenty-four scholars from a range of disciplines – literature, history, cultural and women's studies, creative writing and digital humanities – to address some of the key questions about Australian literary communities: how they form, how they change and develop, and how they operate within wider social and cultural contexts, both within Australia and internationally. If there can be no single set of answers to the research questions that organise the essays in this book, this is perhaps because of the slippage between the two concepts that have deliberately been chosen for its title and subtitle: the 'republic of letters' and the 'literary community'.

The notion of a 'republic of letters', as David Carter observes, has been widely taken up in literary scholarship internationally since the English translation of Pascale Casanova's *The World Republic of Letters* in 2004.[1] One reason for its 'seemingly irresistible attraction', he suggests, is that it captures the interest common among a range of contemporary approaches to the study of literature in cultural institutions – and of the function of intermediaries in those institutions, including writers and readers, editors and critics – in producing literature and literary value. What these different approaches have in common is that they all treat culture as a field, a structure or an economy. Yet Carter goes on to make an important distinction between different ways in which the dynamics of the literary field might be conceived. While the term 'community' suggests aspects of literary sociability, the idea of a community built around shared values and interests, the 'republic of letters' draws on the language of politics, reminding us that this is a field constituted by power and competition. For Casanova, the world literary system is a hierarchical structure, not the level playing field some of the more euphoric accounts of globalisation seem to imply.

Carter usefully describes the 'literary community' and the 'republic of letters' as the 'weak' and 'strong' understandings, respectively, of the dynamics of the literary field: one is built around ideas of community and sociability, of shared interests and values; the other around the dynamics of competition, position taking and symbolic violence both within national literary spaces and across international boundaries. Our title, *Republics of Letters: Literary Communities in Australia*, is meant to invoke both the strong and weak versions of this idea of literary communities, which are variously taken up, in turn, by the contributors.

By focusing on literary *sociability*, we mean to shift attention from individual writers and great books to examine the various forms of community that facilitate and sustain writing and reading, and also the kinds of communal identities that are formed *by* the practices of writing and reading. These include, for example, the networks of writers and readers

---

1 Pascale Casanova, trans. M.B. DeBevoise, *The World Republic of Letters* (Cambridge, Mass. and London: Harvard University Press, 2004 [1999]).

that cluster around literary journals and little magazines, literary 'schools' or movements, reading groups and book clubs, writers' festivals, and the various forms of sociability generated by institutions such as libraries, schools, universities and writers' associations. Though interest in Australian literary communities has grown in recent years – principally through the rise of book history, the history of reading, and print culture studies – it remains a loosely defined, relatively untheorised area in need of a more systematic approach, and drawing on an innovative range of case studies such as those provided here.

Among Australian scholars to date, interest in literary sociability has been confined mainly to studies of late eighteenth- and early nineteenth-century British Romanticism, where it has had radically energising effects. A leading example is Gillian Russell and Clara Tuite's innovative and influential collection, *Romantic Sociability: Social Networks and Literary Culture in Britain, 1770–1840* (2002). This book was designed as an intervention in the received history of British Romanticism, which had been shaped by the English translation in 1989 of Jurgen Habermas' *The Structural Transformation of the Public Sphere*. Habermas' 'two-phase' model sees a decline from the empathic sociability of the early eighteenth-century bourgeois public sphere, a space of conviviality where ideas circulate freely among supposed equals, to the Romantic moment of solitude and disinterestedness, which now become the grounds of the poet's claim to critical authority.[2] Russell and Tuite argue that by reinstating the idea of 'romantic sociability' as an analytical category we are able to rediscover the late eighteenth-century heterogeneous forms of sociality, thereby shifting the traditional focus from the lone writer and the private scene of writing to public 'sites of sociability'; from the authentic to the performative self; from canonical genres like the novel and lyric poetry, to the essay, diaries and letters. In this sense, sociability is not just the context for the writer's work but 'a kind of text in its own right', 'a form of cultural work'.[3] In addition to the early eighteenth-century classic sites of sociability – the tavern, the coffee shop, the theatre and the debating club – the late eighteenth century includes sites of 'private sociability', including walking, home visiting, shopping, private dinners, and radical dining circles, often under the auspices of publishers.[4] One consequence of this re-engagement with Habermas is also to foreground the gendered nature of his model, supplementing masculine forms of sociability with others that reinstate women's historical agency. As an analytical category, then, sociability cannot be treated ahistorically, as a given that does not require explanation. It is, rather, a 'heavily contested' term; it is both 'a practice and a value' that is implicated in specific cultural politics that change historically and have 'highly unstable meanings'.[5]

Although it is located within studies of British Romanticism, Russell and Tuite's work has affinities with that of the American social historian Joan Shelly Rubin. In her three major books, *Constance Rourke and American Culture* (1980), *The Making of Middlebrow Culture* (1992) and *Songs of Ourselves* (2007), Rubin has made a sustained and influential

---

2 Gillian Russell and Clara Tuite, 'Introducing Romantic Sociability', in Gillian Russell and Clara Tuite, eds, *Romantic Sociability: Social Networks and Literary Culture in Britain, 1770–1840*, (Cambridge: Cambridge University Press, 2002), pp. 12–14.

3 Russell and Tuite, p. 6.

4 Russell and Tuite, p. 17.

5 Russell and Tuite, p. 9.

contribution to both theoretical and empirical approaches to the study of literary sociability.[6] In her essay for this volume, she defines the idea of literary sociability succinctly as 'an invitation to contemplate texts as sources of relationships'. She also reasserts the insight that has been fundamental to the histories of books and reading: that 'texts arise from as well as create social networks'. The central assumptions driving Rubin's research are her rejection of the idea that 'alienation was a prerequisite for artistic achievement', and that literature is both the 'source' and the 'product' of social interaction. Her work is typified by its richly researched case studies of the specific 'scenes of reading' that generate literary sociability in America. Both conceptually and through its detailed evidence, her essay offers a productive unpacking of the concept of 'community', which is too often taken for granted as a commonplace, ahistorical term – as Russell and Tuite also observe. Rubin demonstrates that the communities created by what she calls 'scenes of reading' are at once singular and heterogenous, local and national, 'coercive or arbitrary as well as liberating and life-enriching'. In this essay, Rubin offers case studies of three such scenes of reading: the Great Books movement, which began at Columbia University during the Great War; the speaking choir movement, which was imported from Britain in the 1920s; and an example of the text-setting of poetry to music for choral performance during the Cold War. At all times she observes the 'politics of culture' at play, including the fine grain of local engagement with and distinction from 'national politics'. Rubin's idea of the literary community is therefore that it is fundamentally diverse, constituted as much by internal tensions and differences as it is by the experience of commonality: 'Each of these collectivities brought together actual readers in physical space, each rested on an ideology about the benefits of participation in the group', yet, importantly, 'each also simultaneously sustained and challenged elements of cultural hierarchy and critical authority'.

The historically specific cases of literary sociability offered by Rubin, and by Russell and Tuite, are of course distinct from the history of Australian literature over the 200 years from 1788 to 2011 although, as Russell and Tuite's reference to the correspondence between Leigh Hunt and Barron Field in New South Wales indicates,[7] there are significant connections between them. Yet collectively they provide a set of concepts and methodologies that can be adapted to the history of other literary polities that have also privileged the writer, the sole-authored book and the nation at the expense of these other categories. In adapting some of their key concepts, especially the argument that sites of sociability are more than just the context for literary production but 'kinds of texts' that require reading and interpretation, and which produce their own forms of gendered literary subjectivity, the essays in *Republics of Letters* suggest some of the ways in which the concept of literary sociability can be used to map out a new field of inquiry in Australian literary history – or at least ways of reimagining existing accounts of that history. The sites of sociability examined here include literary journals and little magazines, literary societies, women's magazines, writers' friendship groups and workshops, libraries and their borrowers, institutions of

---

6  Joan Shelley Rubin, *Songs of Ourselves: The Uses of Poetry in America* (Cambridge, Mass.: Harvard University Press, 2007); *The Making of Middlebrow Culture* (Chapel Hill: University of North Carolina Press, 1992); and *Constance Rourke and American Culture* (Chapel Hill: University of North Carolina Press, 1980).

7  Russell and Tuite, pp. 19–20.

middlebrow culture, bohemias and bohemianism, literary avant-gardes, literary schools or movements, letter writing and epistolary communities, generationalism in Australian writing, readerships of crime fiction and other popular genres, poetry networks, gay and lesbian literary communities, the role of digital technologies in forming new kinds of community, communities of reading and recitation, and the significance of overseas readerships for Australian fiction.

In Australian humanities research, the 2000s have therefore seen the adoption of significant new methodologies that allow us to better appreciate the historically specific nature of the institutional, intellectual and social formations that support and enable literary culture. It is now accepted, for example, that literature, and texts in general, rather than merely reflecting the social conditions of their production, actively generate new forms of sociability. These innovations in methodology include the literary sociology of Pierre Bourdieu, with its central concepts of habitus and the field of cultural production; the rise of the history of the book, print culture studies, and the history of reading, with their stress on rigorous archival research into the materiality of print cultures and of social and intellectual formations, which are specific to particular kinds of institutions and locations.[8] These approaches have the capacity to shift our thinking about literary culture from the exclusive attention to individual books and great writers, apparently living and working in splendid isolation, to the historically constituted social and intellectual formations that sustain literary culture at levels of description both beyond and below that of the nation.

Still more recently, as we have seen, literary scholars have been challenged to place such richly informed studies of literary sociability at the local and national levels within the broader context of what Casanova calls 'world literary space'.[9] *The World Republic of Letters* takes a global perspective by stating that 'national literary space must not be confused with national territory'. After all, 'the legend of the nineties' in Australia happily excluded the nation's cities in order to celebrate the bush as a national signifier, just as it ignored the complex relations between Australian literary culture and the wider context of what historian Linda Young has usefully termed the 'Anglo-sphere' – the intricately connected literary cultures of Australasia, North America and the United Kingdom.[10] Casanova's point of departure is that, historically, the study of literature in the modern era has been dominated by nationalism. She attributes this to the rise of nationalism in Europe in the nineteenth century. Casanova believes that while we have been encouraged to think of literature exclusively in terms of national literatures, this is increasingly unrelated to the

---

8  Examples include David Carter and Anne Galligan, *Making Books: Contemporary Australia Publishing* (St Lucia: University of Queensland Press, 2007); Tim Dolin, 'First Steps toward a History of the Mid-Victorian Novel in Colonial Australia', *Australian Literary Studies* 22.3 (2006): 273–293; Martyn Lyons and John Arnold, eds, *A History of the Book in Australia 1891–1945* (St Lucia: University of Queensland Press, 2001); Martyn Lyons and Lucy Taksa, *Australian Readers Remember: An Oral History of Reading 1890–1930* (Melbourne: Oxford University Press, 1992); and D.H. Borchardt and Wallace Kirsop, eds, *The Book in Australia: Essays towards a Cultural and Social History* (Melbourne: Centre for Bibliographical and Textual Studies, Monash University, 1988).

9  See Robert Dixon, 'Australian Fiction and the World Republic of Letters', in Peter Pierce, ed., *The Cambridge History of Australian Literature*, (Cambridge: Cambridge University Press, 2009).

10  Linda Young, *Middle-Class Culture in the Nineteenth Century: America, Australia and Britain* (Basingstoke: Palgrave Macmillan, 2003).

realities of a globalising world. Her book is dedicated to moving beyond nationalism in literary study, and looking instead at how all books and authors participate in what she thinks of as a world literary system. For much of the last twenty-five years, work on such concepts as 'invented traditions' and 'imagined communities' has been driven by the conceptually strong category of the nation. In his influential book *Imagined Communities* (1983), Benedict Anderson argued that textual forms such as the newspaper and the novel offered important ways of 'imagining' the modern nation state by creating powerful representations of community and national distinction.

For much of its history, Australian literature has been studied as a *national* literature: that is, as an expression of the national character or way of life developed through the shared experience of place; as an organic tradition of books and authors developing through time. This model of the imagined community has influenced all of the major histories of Australian literature: from H.M. Green's *A History of Australian Literature* (1961), through such keynote edited volumes as Leonie Kramer's *Oxford History of Australian Literature* (1981), Laurie Hergenhan et al.'s *Penguin New Literary History of Australia* (1988), Bruce Bennett and Jennifer Strauss' *Oxford Literary History of Australia* (1998), Elizabeth Webby's *Cambridge Companion to Australian Literature* (2000), and Peter Pierce's *Cambridge History of Australian Literature* (2009), to the *Macquarie Pen Anthology of Australian Literature* (2010) under the general editorship of Nicholas Jose. When imagined communities other than the nation have been considered, they have typically been at the level of large political and social units just below the level of the nation, such as the city or the state, but rarely smaller, more contingent social and intellectual formations.[11]

As Carter reminds us, however, Casanova's world republic of letters is not a benign space, but is structured in conflict, competition and dominance, with some national literatures being older, richer and more powerful than others. While the richest literatures, the ones with the most cultural capital, are the oldest, newer literatures like those of nineteenth-century America and Australia are relatively impoverished; their cultures are thin. What makes the older literatures stronger, Casanova argues, is that they have risen above merely national considerations. In the oldest nations, literature has become 'autonomous' – that is, it is recognised as being of 'universal' value and not merely an expression of the national culture. In Casanova's view, the country in which literary autonomy has been most strongly achieved is France, and, as the spatial centre of the modern world of letters, Paris sets the standards of taste in the same way that time is taken internationally from the Greenwich Meridian in London:

> At stake in the competition ... is mastery of just this measure of time (and space), which is to say the power to claim for oneself the legitimate present of literature and to canonize its great writers ... If modernity is the sole present moment of literature, which is to say what makes it possible to institute a measure of time, the literary Greenwich Meridian makes it possible to evaluate and recognize the

---

11  For examples of city and state-based histories see John Docker, *Australian Cultural Elites: Intellectual Traditions in Sydney and Melbourne* (Sydney: Angus & Robertson, 1974); Delia Falconer, *Sydney* (Sydney: University of New South Wales Press, 2010); and Patrick Buckridge and Belinda McKay, eds, *By the Book: A Literary History of Queensland* (St Lucia: University of Queensland Press, 2007).

quality of a work or, to the contrary, to dismiss a work as an anachronism or to label it 'provincial'.[12]

Although she has been criticised for being too French-centred,[13] Casanova does concede that, in addition to Paris, the world literary system also has other centres that set standards, and that are dominant in their own way. These include London and New York, which dominate the English-speaking world in the same way that Paris does world literature as a whole. By implication, the closer a writer is to one of these great centres, the closer he or she is to modernity and to the present. To be in a rich metropolitan community like London or Paris or New York is to be modern and up to date; to be of the present in terms of time and at the centre in terms of space. To work in a new national literature like Australia's is to be belated or old fashioned in terms of time and provincial in terms of space; it is to belong to the literary suburbs.

In Casanova's model, then, the world is organised into richer and poorer cultural spaces that are in competition with each other. National literary communities are inward looking and backward: they are, in a word, provincial. They show a lack of interest in translation and the literatures of other countries. Writers have a choice of either remaining inside such inward-looking cultures and being recognised as national writers, or aspiring to write in the style of international modernity – to be guided by the Greenwich Meridian of literature. To do this they must leave home, read widely in other literatures, learn other languages, and sometimes become expatriates. To become a citizen of Casanova's world republic of letters is therefore a kind of treason against one's national literature:

> World literary space is ... organized in terms of the opposition between, on the one hand, an autonomous pole composed of those spaces that are most endowed in literary resources, which serves as a model and a recourse for writers claiming a position of independence in newly formed spaces (with the result that Paris emerged as a 'denationalized' universal capital and a specific measure of literary time was established); and, on the other, a heteronomous pole composed of relatively deprived literary spaces at early stages of development that are dependent on political – typically national – authorities.
>
> The internal configuration of each national space precisely mirrors the structure of the international literary world as a whole. Just as the global space is organized with reference to a literary and cosmopolitan pole, on the one side, and a political and national pole on the other, each of its constituent spaces is structured by the rivalry between what I shall call 'national' writers (who embody a national or popular definition of literature) and 'international' writers (who uphold an autonomous conception of literature).[14]

Casanova's own values are explicitly in favour of international writers. These are the ones who are discontented with their provincial culture, who are not happy to live in

---

12  Casanova, p. 90.

13  For a wide range of responses to Casanova's book, many critical, see Christopher Prendergast, ed., *Debating World Literature* (London: Verso, 2004).

14  Casanova, p. 108.

the literary suburbs and be recognised merely as national writers, but who want to test themselves in the great centres of international literary space. This requires a break with the past and with the community of the nation. For Casanova, the great heroes of world literature include exiled and expatriate writers like Henry James, Joseph Conrad, James Joyce, Samuel Beckett and Salman Rushdie.

An alternative to the hard binary oppositions that appear to organise Casanova's thinking – national versus international literary space, the metropolis versus the literary suburb – can be found in the work of American critic Wai Chee Dimock, which provides a more nuanced way of imagining the relations between national and international communities of reading. Like Casanova, Dimock is concerned with developing new forms of literary history that move beyond the nation as an imagined community; but, where Casanova is a true comparativist, Dimock is a specialist in American literature whose interest is in opening up the study of national literatures to transnational perspectives. In *Through Other Continents*, she describes the 'playing field' of literary culture as a transnational, even 'planetary', community that is 'brought into being by that most minute, most intimate of acts, the act of reading', which 'generates relational ties that can ... extend for thousand of miles and thousands of years'.[15] Dimock goes on to develop both a theory of the text and a phenomenology of reading, which she calls 'proximate' reading, in which citations within the apparently bounded, national text are traced like threads into transnational space and what she calls 'deep time':

> what we called 'American' literature is quite often a shorthand, a simplified name for a much more complex tangle of relations. Rather than being a discrete entity, it is better seen as a crisscrossing set of pathways, open-ended and ever multiplying, weaving in and out of other geographies, other languages and cultures. These are input channels, kinship networks, routes of transit, and forms of attachment – connective tissues binding America to the rest of the world.[16]

Dimock's argument therefore has the potential to break down Casanova's seemingly hard opposition between national and international communities of reading. As a crisscrossing set of pathways, a national text can also belong to a wider world. In her later book, *Shades of the Planet*, Dimock draws on mathematical set theory to describe the volatile relation between apparently hierarchical concepts like the local, the national and the transnational. Instead of thinking of such terms as being in an ascending vertical scale that is fixed or rigid, she argues that we can think of them as sets of nested categories that are unstable and recursive. She calls these reversible hierarchies *heterarchies*, using this notion to explain the manifold relations that are possible between local, pre-national, national, transnational and planetary communities of reading. Where Casanova implies that the relation between them is hierarchically arranged – Paris always prior or superior to the province in space and time – Dimock suggests ways in which, in our own reading practice, they can become productively unstable. This can happen in our reading especially at moments when literary

---

15 Wai Chee Dimock, *Through Other Continents: American Literature across Deep Time* (Princeton and Oxford: Princeton University Press, 2006), p. 8.

16 Dimock, p. 3.

citations act like 'a kind of switch mechanism ... in the reversible hierarchy between the local and the global'.[17]

As a number of the case studies in this volume indicate, the implications of these approaches for our thinking about Australian literature and Australian writers can be quite profound. What does it mean, for example, for a writer to identify as 'Australian', and yet to have their formative experiences in specific avant-garde networks in London and New York, as was the case for Patrick White? What does it mean for a writer to be described as 'Australian', and yet live and work for the bulk of their career abroad, as was the case for Christina Stead? What kinds of social and intellectual networks sustained such careers in writing across a series of levels – the local, the national, and the international? What kinds of connections exist between those levels to sustain and make possible the phenomenon of an Australian career that takes place on the international stage? And what kinds of differences exist across those levels to produce distinct communities of reading for each of which such a writer's work may have fundamentally different meanings? Casanova's concept of 'the republic of letters' and Dimock's concepts of 'deep time' and 'heterarchy' are stimulating to literary historians precisely because they enable us to think of both writing and reading as being conducted across a spectrum of imagined communities or networks of sociability. Casanova's literary 'republic' is both flexible and scalable, allowing us to view literature as a semi-autonomous transnational space that is the product of specific national and even local histories, and yet not governed by them but rather by its own laws and politics: the literary 'republic', she writes, is

> a world in which the ways and means of literary art are argued over and decided; ... a world that has its own capital, its own provinces and borders, in which languages become instruments of power.[18]

While acknowledging Casanova's influence in our own title, *Republics of Letters* takes her work as a point of departure rather than a conceptual focus. Her book is about literature as a global polity rather than about what she calls the literary 'province' or 'suburb'. Our book, by contrast, is very much concerned with more local, even avowedly provincial, forms of literary polity: some of the towns and villages and nomad tribes of the world republic of letters, albeit in relation to world literary space – how they evolve, how they structure themselves, how they have been enabled by evolving forms of communications technologies, from print to the internet, and how they view themselves in relation to Australia as a national, and indeed international, space. The essays collected here explore a variety of networked relationships among writers, readers and texts, with an emphasis on processes of literary sociability that often elide or exceed the 'imagined community' of the nation.

The essays in *Republics of Letters* are divided into four thematic groups: 'Part 1 – Sites of Sociability, Scenes of Reading'; 'Part 2 – Republics of Letters: Local, National and

---

17  Wai Chee Dimock, 'Introduction: Planet and America, Set and Subset', in Wai Chee Dimock and Lawrence Buell, eds, *Shades of the Planet: American Literature as World Literature* (Princeton and Oxford: Princeton University Press, 2007), p. 13.

18  Casanova, p. x.

International Literary Communities'; 'Part 3 – Sociality, Gender and Genre'; and 'Part 4 – Unsettlements: Emerging Literary Communities'.

Those in 'Part 1 – Sites of Sociability, Scenes of Reading' explore or exemplify key definitions in the relationship between writing, reading and sociality in what Joan Shelley Rubin calls 'text-centred communities'. In Australian scholarship, there is already a strong tradition of this kind of research on nineteenth-century literary culture, perhaps because in pre-Federation literature, as Andrew McCann observes, the nation functions as an *absence*.[19] The importance of private patronage, private libraries, and the enabling role of personal correspondence among intimate though often far-flung networks of writers and readers can be glimpsed, for example, in Ann-Mari Jordens' account of man of letters Nicol Drysdale Stenhouse and his circle in Sydney in the 1850s, and Eileen Chanin's account of the life and times of nineteenth-century book collector David Scott Mitchell.[20] This work is extended into the early twentieth century in Drusilla Modjeska's and Carole Ferrier's accounts of the loosely affiliated network of Australian women writers centered on Nettie Palmer, and in Peter Kirkpatrick's study of bohemian circles in Sydney in the 1920s.[21]

Among the new case studies offered here, Kylie Mirmohamadi's discussion of the Australasian Home Reading Union suggests that even in the 1890s, on the eve of Federation, there was considerable uncertainty about how such reading communities might be mapped onto established or indeed emerging political entities, including empire, state and nation. Julieanne Lamond examines how we might best use library loans records to describe and define local reading communities. Using innovative digital modelling, she shows that, contrary to nationalist literary histories that saw forms of vernacular realism supplanting the British–Australian romance fiction of authors such as Rosa Praed, 'realist' and 'romance' writers were in fact 'part of the same literary culture, and read by the same people' a century ago.

Patrick Buckridge reveals the extraordinary number of literary and cultural societies that flourished in Brisbane in the 1920s, contributing to what he describes as 'the active creation of a liberal polity' during the otherwise turbulent interwar period. Despite this apparently local focus, many, indeed most, of these societies, as their names indicate, were affiliated with wider forms of imagined community: *L'Alliance Francaise*, the Brisbane Shakespeare Society, *Der Brisbane Goethe Bund*. The power of book publishing on the wider Australian polity in the twenty-first century is the subject of Jan Zwar's chapter. She uses 'empirical mapping' – data from Nielsen BookScan, Factiva and parliamentary records – to examine the impact of books on the asylum-seeker debate of the 2000s. Patterns of reviews, media mentions, academic citations and references in parliament can indicate

---

19  Andrew McCann, *Marcus Clarke's Bohemia* (Carlton: Melbourne University Publishing, 2004), p. 7.

20  Ann-Mari Jordens, *The Stenhouse Circle: Literary Life in Mid-Nineteenth Century Sydney* (Carlton: Melbourne University Press, 1979); Eileen Chanin, *Book Life: The Life and Times of David Scott Mitchell* (Melbourne: Australian Scholarly Publishing, 2011).

21  Drusilla Modjeska, *Exiles at Home: Australian Women Writers 1925–1945* (Sydney: Angus & Robertson, 1981); Carole Ferrier, ed., *As Good as a Yarn with You: Letters Between Miles Franklin, Katharine Susannah Prichard, Jean Devanny, Marjorie Barnard, Flora Eldershaw and Eleanor Dark* (Cambridge: Cambridge University Press, 1992); Peter Kirkpatrick, *The Sea Coast of Bohemia: Literary Life in Sydney's Roaring Twenties*, 2nd edn (Curtin University of Technology: API Network, 2007 [1992]).

in what ways books, and those who write and publish them, remain 'actively part of the democratic process'.

In 'Part – 2 Republics of Letters: Local, National and International Literary Space', a number of contributors take up the problem of thinking about how Australian literary space and time relate to international literary space and time. In the concluding chapter of *The Cambridge Literary History of Australia* (2009), Philip Mead expresses this two-way flow between the global and the local in the following way:

> Generally speaking, post-national Australian literary studies have been moving in two directions: towards transcultural comparisons and contexts, and towards readings of the local. These different spatial turns may appear antithetical – global or transnational versus regional or local – but in critical practice they are complementary. Much work in contemporary literary studies is an attempt to understand and articulate the complexities of the imaginary places, locales, districts and regions of literary texts and their recursive relations to the multi-faceted experience of actual, lived places.[22]

In moving toward such a 'post-national' formation, however, there is a danger of evacuating the space at the centre that was formerly occupied by the nation. As American literature specialist Paul Giles argues, the reason for introducing transnational perspectives into the study of national literatures is not to transcend national cultures, as if that were either possible or desirable, but to provoke discussion on 'the meaning of the "national" today'.[23] For other contributors to this volume, including Rubin, Robert Dixon, and Nicole Moore and Christina Spittel, the nation remains one among the numerous and recursively articulated categories of imagined community; it retains a spectral presence as a fundamental category of cultural policymaking, literary marketing, readership and affect.

In light of renewed interest in the concept of world literature by Casanova, Franco Moretti, David Damrosch and others,[24] Robert Dixon explores how Australian literature – as a disciplinary formation and as an imagined community of writers, readers and critics – can negotiate between provincial, national and world literary space. At what appears to be a time of unprecedented internationalisation, can Australian literature be considered a world literature, or does it remain a relatively minor national literature embedded uncertainly in world literary space? Dixon welcomes the turn toward transnational comparativism as a way of opening up the national literature, of seeing a national literature simultaneously from close up and from far away. But he is sceptical of a tendency in much of the rhetoric about world literature to place national and world literature in a relation of 'sublimation': that is, a preference for the transnational above the local; 'deep time' and the *longue durée* above 'local irregularities'; expansion rather than contraction of the frame of reference. In close readings of Joseph Furphy's *Such is Life* (1903) and Henry Handel Richardson's *Maurice Guest* (1908), he resists, like Carter, the tendency toward hard binaries, seeing a

---

22  Philip Mead, 'Nation, Literature, Location', in *The Cambridge History of Australian Literature*, p. 551.

23  Paul Giles, *Virtual Americas: Transnational Fictions and the Transatlantic Imaginary* (Durham: Duke University Press, 2002), p. 17.

24  See David Damrosch, *What is World Literature?* (Princeton and Oxford: Princeton University Press, 2003); and Franco Moretti, 'Conjectures on World Literature', *New Left Review* 1 (2000): 55–67.

recursive relation between the metropolitan and the provincial as characteristic of the way national literatures are embedded in international literary space.

In his case study of *Desiderata*, a literary journal published in Adelaide from 1929 to 1939, David Carter studies the cross-currents of literary modernism's reception among elite and middlebrow circles in this provincial city. On the basis of fresh archival research, he proposes an elegant model of the relations between local and international literary space, extending from Anglocentrism at one end to provincialism at the other, reflecting Casanova's distinction between national and international orientations. But in an innovative turn that resists and complicates her often hard binaries, he suggests that we can distinguish provincial and modernising forms of cultural identification at both ends of the spectrum. *Desiderata* illustrates 'that cultural nationalism was not the only alternative to the colonial condition and … that British cultural domination was not simply domination but involved a complex network of attachments and transfers of value that could be worked in both directions'. In an analogous way, in his chapter on the Jindyworobak poets, Peter Kirkpatrick shows how that movement's seemingly narrow cultural nationalism is in fact complicated by its international affinities with modernist primitivism and the avant-garde. In Casanova's terms, although their founder Rex Ingamells insisted on the 'centrifugal' primacy of national space, in their appropriation of Aboriginal culture they were nonetheless bound up with 'the centripetal forces that strengthen the autonomous and unifying pole of world literary space'.[25]

The reading nation, the *Leseland* – or at least distinct reading formations within two separate national polities – remains an important determinant in Nicole Moore and Christina Spittel's comparative study of the reception of Dorothy Hewett's novel *Bobbin Up* (1959) in Australia and the German Democratic Republic. These distinct reception histories work 'as revealingly transposed opposites', as between 1949 and 1990 Australian titles published in East Germany formed 'an alternative canon, a shadowy literary archive that rewrites Australia's post-war cultural history from behind the iron curtain'. In Australia, the networks of production and reception for *Bobbin Up* were focused on the Australian Book Society, and in the GDR on that nation's centralised cultural administration. This meant that its readerships in Australia were at once nationally distinctive but internally marginal within the wider culture of the Menzies era. Moore and Spittel's case study is also sensitive to the discursive frames – humanist, universalist, socialist and feminist – which allowed for the transnational mediation of meanings between these two distinct though internally diverse national cultures of reading. They argue that 'Eastern Bloc editions … formed threads along which literary realisations of intensely localised expressive identity, as *Bobbin Up* so thoroughly is, travelled beyond themselves and their reading worlds'.

Fiona Morrison treats the reception history of Christina Stead's once neglected masterpiece *The Man Who Loved Children* (1940) as a case study in the complex relations between the centres of international literary space and the literary province. This difficult and anomalous book was written by an expatriate Australian about her Australian childhood, but the setting was transferred to America during the Depression years of the 1930s at the behest of her American publisher, Simon & Schuster. Focusing on the two introductions to

---

25  Casanova, p. 109.

the novel by American authors Randall Jarrell (1965) and Jonathan Franzen (2010), which were instrumental in its periodic revival, Morrison describes them as

> cosmopolitan intermediaries translating and ushering a peripheral Stead into American centres of literary value ... [and] play[ing] a central role in what Casanova suggests is a contemporary transnational literary field magnetised to vectors of value, dominance, circulation and reputation.

Taking account of the impact of new social networking technologies, Philip Mead begs the question of how 'literary versions of human collectivity' might now be understood in a world where '[c]onnectivity is rapidly evolving in a posthuman world, replacing community'. In suggestive readings of two recent works with strong local focuses – Kim Scott's *That Deadman Dance* (2010) and John Kinsella's *Divine Comedy: Journeys through Regional Geography* (2008) – Mead models a critical practice that overrides Casanova's binarisms by attending to the multiple possibilities of time, space, identity and collectivity that these textual spaces bring into being. As he writes: 'Communities are dimensional in the way space is: they exist in time, in historical incarnations, but also in the existential constellations of individual consciousness. Multiple and virtual, they are always expanding and shifting'.

The essays in 'Part 3 Sociality, Gender and Genre' trace the dynamic social interface between these three terms, re-engaging, as did Russell and Tuite in their work on British Romanticism, with the gendering of literary sociality and the access of women to creative agency. Michelle De Stefani's study of Hannah Boyd's *Letters on Education* (1848) exemplifies Rubin's understanding of literary sociability as an invitation 'to contemplate texts as sources of relationships'. As a study in colonial readerships, it also connects with Russell and Tuite's work on gendered networks of romantic sociability, confirming their argument that sociability is best conceived as both a practice and a value. Using aspects of narratological and reader-response theory, De Stefani demonstrates how this early example of parenting literature interpellates the individual reader into a wider community of parent-readers in both space and time through its metacommentary on literary tradition, while at the same time generating a new and distinctive community of readers in the specific context of mid nineteenth-century New South Wales: 'For the first time the rural mothers of Australia were directly addressed by parenting literature specific to their individual circumstances and predicaments'. In creating a series of communal relationships between the author and reader, between the reader and other colonial mothers, and also with 'expert authors and parents everywhere', Boyd's *Letters* demonstrate how Rubin's 'everyday reading practices' generate multiple forms of engagement: 'the physical object' of the book 'creates for readers a shared community with the present, and also, with the past'; with the immediate context of rural New South Wales but also with parent-readers 'everywhere'.

Susan K. Martin reconstructs the emerging colonial readership for British sensation fiction, complicating her account of gendered sociability by contrasting the reception of Mary Braddon's novel *Lady Audley's Secret* with spectatorship of its stage adaptation in Melbourne in the early 1860s. She draws here on one of the classic models of eighteenth-century sociability, which John Dwyer refers to as the theatrical, performative or 'spectatorial' model of sociality.[26]

---

26  John Dwyer, 'Enlightened Spectators and Classical Moralists: Sympathetic Relations in Eighteenth-

As the publishers of the avant-garde journal *Angry Penguins*, the small firm of Reed & Harris is well known in the history of Australian literature. What is less well-documented is its dealings with the women writers Cynthia Reed (later Nolan) and Elisabeth Lambert. Jane Grant looks at the company's correspondence, 'a far-flung epistolary community', and traces the fortunes of Cynthia's first two novels, in order to recover these two neglected figures for Australian modernism during its most tumultuous period.

In her essay on mid twentieth-century women's journalism, Susan Sheridan considers some of the strategies that women writers used to bridge the gap between their hard-earned place in the literary field and their bread-and-butter work for popular women's magazines. Her case studies of Kylie Tennant, Charmian Clift and Barbara Jefferis suggest that writers must negotiate different forms of professional identity as they move from one literary institution to another – from the novel to women's magazines – each of which has its unique networks of sociability and values. When Tennant began writing for the *Woman's Mirror* in 1961, for example, she felt that she had made her name as a novelist by 'opposing all the things' the women's magazines stood for. Jefferis dealt with the problem by adopting the pen-name 'Margaret Sydney' and assuming the persona of 'an everywoman'. While writing for the women's pages created 'a fragile community of women writers and readers', Sheridan argues that it was too bound up with the gendering of the domestic sphere to constitute 'a positive counter-public sphere', which was not achieved until the rise of women's presses, like Virago, in the 1970s.

D'Arcy Randall's essay on the Seven Writers group in Canberra in the 1970s and 1980s is a case study of literary sociability richly informed by both archival and oral history. It explores the internal dynamics of this group who worked collaboratively for a generation to nurture and critique each others' writing, publishing both individually and collectively while resisting becoming a 'school'. Meeting in each others' homes to workshop manuscripts and discuss the business of publication, Seven Writers are an example of what Russell and Tuite describe as a site of private sociability: writer Sara Dowse speaks of '"a room of her own" … crowded with seven writerly spirits'. Randall explores the complex and fruitful interaction between the more formal and informal parts of the workshops, describes both the internal dynamics of the group and its relations with outsiders, and considers the role of gender in this 'Australian women's literary community' at a time when other writers' networks, especially in the major cities, were overwhelmingly masculine, and located in other sites of sociability, such as the pub and the writers' festival.

As we have seen, networks of literary sociability are partly cultural and social, but they are also enabled by broader developments in the fields of communications technology and intellectual property associated with the phenomena of globalisation. *Republics of Letters* therefore also situates itself within recent 'new modernism' studies, and in particular those involved with 'vernacular modernities'; that is to say, the impact of increasingly rapid technological changes upon the material culture of everyday life and its social formations.[27]

---

Century Scotland' in John Dwyer and Richard B. Sher, eds, *Sociability and Society in Eighteenth-Century Scotland* (Edinburgh: Edinburgh University Press, 1993), p. 96.

27  See Robert Dixon and Veronica Kelly, 'Australian Vernacular Modernities: Peoples, Sites and Practices', in Robert Dixon and Veronica Kelly, eds, *Impact of the Modern: Vernacular Modernities in Australia 1870s to 1960s* (Sydney: Sydney University Press, 2008), pp. xiii–xiv.

'Part 4 – Unsettlements: Emerging Literary Communities' examines some of the ways in which new forms of literary sociability come into being – sometimes through generational change or the global movement of people, sometimes stimulated by new communications technologies, and sometimes in response to government policy. The essays in this section remind us of Russell and Tuite's foundational definition of literary sociability as both 'a practice and a value', a 'heavily contested term' that is implicated in specific cultural politics.

This section begins with Keri Glastonbury's forward-looking account of how newly imagined communities might be at play in contemporary digitised literary cultures. As Michael Farrell observes, a textual community is conventionally defined as people brought together by shared texts or reading practices, though 'such a bringing together may be virtual, through online networks'. Recognising that imagined communities, even in Anderson's classic formulation, are indeed 'imagined', papering over forms of difference and inequality, Farrell examines a seemingly disparate group of texts by Charles Harpur, Norman Harris and Dorothea Mackellar that betray the 'plural knowledges of the past', forms of poetry that do not support the settlement upon which the imagined community of the nation depends. These are works that by virtue of their aberrant style and form and stance have been left to one side of the cultural nationalist canon, even when written by poets like Harpur and Mackellar, who otherwise have been enlisted into that settlement. They form, he argues, a community of 'wild' or 'fugitive' texts distinguished by 'their disinterest in building a national literature'.

Lindsay Barrett interrogates the remarkable effectiveness of John O'Grady's *They're a Weird Mob* – Australia's most popular novel of the 1950s – in negotiating for middlebrow Australian readers the tensions that had arisen between an older version of the 'imagined community' and the new, physical community brought into being by postwar migration. In this sense, Barrett argues, it was 'an intensely ideological work of fiction'.

In contrast to O'Grady's local popularity, Jeremy Fisher questions why G.M. Glaskin, whose books sold well in Europe and America, failed to find critical acclaim and a substantial audience here. Beyond some influential mentors in his hometown of Perth, Glaskin 'never seemed to fit in to the Australian literary community'. His international standing may not have helped, but neither did his homosexuality, and his frank writing about same-sex desire at a time when such themes were still taboo. Ann Vickery, on the other hand, traces how, since the 1980s, periodicals and anthologies have enabled a protean space in which forms of gay and lesbian poetic community have come into being. Historically, queer subcultures have been 'hermetic', lacking an open speaking position within heteronormative society, and Vickery proposes that this place of negativity in relation to the straight world 'may find affinity with poetry's notorious obscurity'.

Lachlan Brown's account of a writing workshop for young refugees in the western suburbs of Sydney, sponsored by the Australian Literacy and Numeracy Foundation in 2009, is a vivid example of Rubin's axiom that texts both produce networks of sociality and are produced by them. The pieces by refugee writers also confirm her argument that sociability is heterogeneous and unstable, embracing both engagement with and subtle resistance to or difference from dominating forms of identity, including narratives of national belonging. Brown notes a distinct and recurring ambivalence about 'Australia' that unsettles the writing by refugees: Tamil, Afghan or Iraqi identities are withheld and 'in play', always ready to 'overshadow any sense of Australian nationality or citizenship, and those sets of "values" that are required or promoted by the government'.

Bonny Cassidy brings this volume to a lyrical close with an account of a journey through outback New South Wales and South Australia that generates a very different form of literary sociality by 'discover[ing] an infinite community of distance and scale'. In seeking connection with the various landscapes she encounters – 'the grammar in being here' – Cassidy considers the relationship between painting and poetry, while locating her own writing process within a neighbourhood of influences that includes Fred Williams, Rover Thomas, Barry Hill, Jennifer Rankin and Charles Buckmaster.

The essays in *Republics of Letters* were first presented as papers at the international symposium, 'Republics of Letters: Literary Communities in Australia', convened by the editors at St Andrew's College at the University of Sydney on 13–14 January 2011. The conference was hosted by the Australian Literature program at the University of Sydney. We wish to acknowledge the intellectual generosity and enthusiasm of delegates to the conference. In particular, we thank Joan Shelley Rubin and Philip Mead for their keynote presentations; Lachlan Brown for research assistance and graphic design; Georgina Loveridge, Stephen Mansfield, Patrick Marland, Lydia Saleh Rofail and Liliana Zavaglia for various forms of research and administrative assistance; and Susan Murray-Smith, Agata Mrva-Montoya and Bronwyn O'Reilly at Sydney University Press for editing and production.

Peter Kirkpatrick and Robert Dixon
University of Sydney
December 2011

# Part 1

# Sites of Sociability, Scenes of Reading

# 1

## Literary Community, Cultural Hierarchy, and Twentieth-Century American Readers

*Joan Shelley Rubin*

Picture a group of mid twentieth-century Chicago business leaders seated around a table in a panelled library arguing about 'great books', or a classroom of schoolchildren fidgeting during a poetry recitation, or a group of women gathered for a monthly book club meeting who discover that the novel they are discussing mirrors their own experience. Those scenes, all of which I have written about over the past thirty years, underscore the power of reading to create literary sociability.[1] In the American context, the historical – and ongoing – connections among individuals that book clubs and recitation practices foster stand in sharp contrast to jeremiads such as Robert Putnam's *Bowling Alone* (2000), which posits a trend in the United States toward isolation and alienation; they contradict as well the recent reports of the National Endowment for the Arts that correlate a decrease in reading with a decline in civic engagement. Thus the impulse to celebrate shared encounters with printed texts as sources of community is understandable and appropriate.

Yet this essay offers a somewhat different response to the abundant evidence of collective reading in the United States since 1900: it both affirms the bond between reading and community and suggests how collectivities of readers invoke or undermine literary judgments, cultural hierarchy and critical authority. That is, I am interested not simply in documenting forms of literary sociability but also in discerning the contributions that such institutions and practices make to understandings of what constitutes 'good reading'; to the location of a text within, or outside of, a high culture canon; and to the degree of deference accorded professional expertise. Along the way, I want to interrogate the idea of community itself – a word that, as Raymond Williams observed, seems 'never to be used unfavourably'. It is my unhappy duty to remind *my* readers that 'community', while typically connoting less formality and greater immediacy than ties between the state and its citizenry (as Williams noted), can be coercive or arbitrary as well as liberating and life-enriching.[2]

---

[1] One of the great rewards of attending the 'Republics of Letters' conference was the opportunity it gave me to discern the themes unifying my work since the late 1970s. This work includes *Songs of Ourselves: The Uses of Poetry in America* (Cambridge, MA: Harvard University Press, 2007); *The Making of Middlebrow Culture* (Chapel Hill: University of North Carolina Press, 1992); and *Constance Rourke and American Culture* (Chapel Hill: University of North Carolina Press, 1980). In most cases, I have cited below the original documents I used for those books so that interested readers may recover the full context of my remarks.

[2] Raymond Williams, *Keywords: A Vocabulary of Culture and Society* (New York: Oxford University

Because the idea of 'literary sociability' captures so much of what I have investigated during the course of my career, however, let us first consider some of the implications that phrase carries. Fundamentally, it invites us to contemplate texts as sources of relationships. But it is worth mentioning the insight, now commonplace among scholars in the history of the book, that texts arise from as well as create social networks. One of the links I recently noticed between my first book, a study of the critic Constance Rourke, and my later work as a historian of reading, is that Rourke emphatically made that point long ago. In the early 1900s, she had been schooled at Vassar College in what the English Department faculty there called 'social criticism' – an approach that excavated 'the social forces beneath rhyme and rhythm and metaphor' and that seems incredibly prescient in its insistence that the value of literature 'depends primarily not on what is read, but on how it is read'.[3] Hence, in the 1920s, when she began delineating an American literary tradition on which artists of the future could draw, she located its origins in the American propensity for creating mythic figures like the Yankee and the backwoodsman. 'Once again', she wrote in her classic *American Humor* (1931), 'personal emotion was submerged in a coarse and crescent patterning of communal emotion; and the flight was toward legend'.[4] From the social creation of shared myths, Rourke further argued, came the 'groundwork' for literature. American novelists, dramatists and poets, she asserted, showed the same self-consciousness, tendency to abstraction, and preoccupation with inward feeling evident in the tall tale or the minstrel show.[5]

Rourke's primary purpose in making these claims was to refute the charges of Van Wyck Brooks and other contemporary intellectuals that the United States possessed no distinctive cultural heritage, that it had produced nothing that could compare favourably to European aesthetic achievements. We might detect defensiveness and even provincialism in that position, and discard it as overly nationalistic (the subtitle of *American Humor* is 'A Study of the National Character'). But Rourke's insistence on the social sources of the American literary tradition led her to a corollary that possesses enduring value: the idea that high art could not be separated from popular expression. In other words, early on she derived from an exploration of literary sociability an awareness of the pitfalls of maintaining a rigidly hierarchical view of culture.

In addition to addressing the relationship between the high and the popular, Rourke's work also rejected the idea that alienation was a prerequisite for artistic achievement; instead, she assigned to the critic the responsibility for ensuring that artists experience the sense of 'belonging' on which the creative expression of the future depended.[6] But it is to literature as the source rather than as the product of social interaction that I now want to turn. I propose to explore three major examples of text-centred communities in twentieth-century America: the Great Books movement; verse speaking choirs; and choruses

---

Press, 1983), pp. 75–76.

3  Gertrude Buck, *The Social Criticism of Literature* (New Haven: Yale University Press, 1916), p. 48.

4  Constance Rourke, 'Vassar Classrooms: "English J" and "Romanticism"', in Elizabeth Woodbridge Morris, ed., *Miss Wylie of Vassar*. (New Haven: Yale University Press, 1934), p. 72.

5  Constance Rourke, *American Humor: A Study of the National Character* (New York: Harcourt Brace Jovanovich, 1959), pp. 135–36, 162.

6  Rourke, *American Humor*, p. 302.

performing poetry set to music. Each of these collectivities brought together actual readers in physical space; each rested on an ideology about the benefits of participation in the group; each also simultaneously sustained and challenged elements of cultural hierarchy or critical authority. In addition, I include a brief discussion of two fictive communities: the Book-of-the-Month Club, a 'club' in name only that nonetheless traded on reading as a social activity, and the readers of the *Saturday Review* in the late 1950s.

Initially conceived of as a way of reforming the undergraduate curriculum at Columbia University, Great Books was the brainchild of John Erskine, a poet and member of the Columbia English Department in the years just before and after World War I. In 1916, Erskine responded to the widespread conviction that students' knowledge of Western literature was in decline by devising a list of around seventy-five 'great' works that undergraduates were to master in a course spanning their first and sophomore years. His syllabus concentrated on the Greeks in the first half-year, moving on to the Romans and Aquinas in the second semester. The third and fourth terms ranged over European history, literature and philosophy, encompassing, among many others, Dante, Shakespeare, Voltaire, Milton, Goethe, Descartes, Mill and Kant.[7] It is easy now for us to see the severe limitations of this exercise in canon formation: no women, black or non-Western authors appeared on Erskine's list, and even male modernists were absent. Yet, within the context of American college education in the early twentieth century, Erskine's proposal was a radical one because it challenged a number of entrenched pedagogical practices. First, Erskine licensed reading non-English works in translation, thereby undermining the ethos of specialisation that was becoming dominant at the nation's newly reconfigured research universities. More importantly, in contrast to the standard lecture format, Erskine called for small discussion groups meeting under the guidance of two instructors, with each session focused on a different book. The instructors were 'not to lecture nor in any way to behave like professors' but only to keep ideas flowing by asking questions and prompting debate'.[8] In that way, Erskine eliminated what he understood as a barrier to the reader's perception of the qualities that defined 'greatness': the ability of a text to speak across time and place, remaining 'true' to diverse readers in variable circumstances.[9]

As an ideology of reading, Erskine's approach to 'great books' contained an element of individualism. Removing the obstacle of the professor as expert heightened the ordinary reader's autonomy by transforming literary interpretation from a passive, mechanical process into one Erskine called 'human, natural, and direct'.[10] Yet he conceived his curriculum to be inherently social in two respects. First, readers who studied the classics would, in Erskine's resonant phrase, 'free themselves from the prison of egotism' and take part 'in the complete citizenship of mankind' by acquainting themselves with widely shared human dilemmas.[11]

---

7 Joan Shelley Rubin, *The Making of Middlebrow Culture* (Chapel Hill: University of North Carolina Press, 1992), pp. 164–78.

8 'Preliminary Report of Committee of Instruction', *Columbia College Gazette*, December 1916, pp. 1–7.

9 John Erskine, *The Delight of Great Books* (Indianapolis: Bobbs-Merrill, 1927), pp. 21–22.

10 John Erskine, unpublished, 'Outline of Great Books', p. 3, quoted in Rubin, *Middlebrow Culture*, p. 168.

11 John Erskine, *Prohibition and Christianity and Other Paradoxes of the American Spirit* (Indianapolis: Bobbs-Merrill, 1927), p. 250.

This universalist perspective had the incidental benefit of solving the problem of discerning an American tradition that Constance Rourke had addressed; Erskine simply asserted that Western literature *was* the American heritage. More concretely, Erskine hoped that the discussion sessions would give students the basis for fellowship outside the classroom. As Erskine put it, 'Here would be, I believed, the true scholarly and cultural basis for human understanding and communication'.[12]

The Columbia faculty implemented Erskine's curricular design, which, over the years, went through a number of modifications but still remains the basis for the university's general education requirement. It was the next iteration of the Great Books idea, however, that more completely realised the potential for literary sociability. In 1926, Mortimer Adler, Clifton Fadiman, and other graduates of the Columbia course brought a version of the class to 134 adult education students at New York's People's Institute. In 1943, after Adler had sold Robert M. Hutchins, the newly appointed president of the University of Chicago, on implementing the Great Books curriculum there, the adult education component of the plan took shape as a seminar that Adler ran for prominent Chicago executives. The nickname for this group, the 'Fat Man's class', tells us that the particular version of sociability that reading Aristotle and Shakespeare created in this context was male, clubby joviality.[13] But the publicity the group garnered led to the enrollment of 80 000 Americans across the nation in Great Books seminars by the end of 1948. The Great Books Foundation, still in existence, arose to handle the demand.[14]

In the immediate postwar period, reading the classics of Western civilisation offered participants a new appreciation of what they regarded as a recently endangered heritage. Moreover, Great Books discussion groups kept alive Erskine's communal vision and underscored his message about the accessibility of culture to the non-expert. In the period of the 'organisation man' beholden to conformity, some class members sought the groups' congeniality as an antidote to anonymity, finding comfort in the fact, as one promotional announcement stated, that here 'you will meet your minister, banker … grocery clerk, and your neighbors'.[15] Mortimer Adler's vision of authors of the classics joined with readers in what Adler called the 'great conversation' nicely encapsulates the promise of the seminars, and of the act of reading *per se*, to create a self-made whole through connection to tradition and to a community linked by its shared interest in what contemporaries called *Good Reading*.[16]

There is, of course, no question that the Great Books movement shored up an entrenched understanding of the Western humanistic tradition as the essence of high culture. (The alternative view of high art as modernist experimentation was inadmissible.) That this

---

12  John Erskine, *The Memory of Certain Persons* (Philadelphia: J.B. Lippincott, 1947), p. 343.

13  Rubin, *Middlebrow Culture*, p. 191.

14  James Sloan Allen, *The Romance of Commerce and Culture: Capitalism, Modernism, and the Chicago-Aspen Crusade for Cultural Reform* (Chicago: University of Chicago Press, 1983), pp. 105–06.

15  Ben Ray Redman, 'No: Not Without Socrates', *Saturday Review of Literature*, 9 December 1950, pp. 32, 34.

16  *Good Reading* was the title of a pamphlet issued between 1932 and 1947 by the National Council of Teachers of English. In the postwar period, an expanded version became first a book published by Pelican/Penguin and then a serial publication of the R.R. Bowker Company.

conservative perspective coexisted with commitments to the creation of community should caution us against romanticising the communal as invariably a source of resistance to dominant values. At the same time, it is important to recognise that the emphasis within the Great Books ideology on dethroning the expert, and on active readers who could extract a text's meaning with no more equipment than the 'power' of their own minds, constitutes a democratic dimension of this form of literary sociability – an aspect that our current antipathy to a rigid canon may obscure. That is, the assertion of cultural hierarchy here licensed the dismantling of critical authority.

Or at least critical authority diminished in theory. The greater the dissemination of Adler's rules for running the seminar, the more Great Books came to resemble a standardised commodity, a kind of prefabricated culture that could be packaged, purchased and displayed. 'It is absolutely essential', a 1946 training manual declared, 'that all the participants face each other, and that they have a table of some sort in front of them to lean on'.[17] This commodification actually enhanced the status of those who promulgated the rules. At the same time, it well served a social purpose at odds with both egalitarianism and community: the creation of a successful personality who, by acquiring the right things, stood to win out in competition with others for the rewards of capitalism. Moreover, the combined effect of disregard for aesthetics and a persistent drive for relevance that Adler inherited from Erskine could lead to discussions that one observer characterised as 'a muddle of blind-alley arguments, profitless repetitions, irrelevant remarks, silly opinions, and fundamental misunderstandings'. A rejoinder to that comment reveals the potential of literary sociability to fuel rather than to offset competitive individualism: the goal of reading great books, an advocate of the community movement explained, was not to study works exhaustively but rather to improve one's 'ability to communicate by learning how to read, speak, and listen more effectively'.[18] Texts here created relationships, but they could be relationships of the sort enshrined in Dale Carnegie's *How to Win Friends and Influence People* (1936). The logical extension of this aspect of the Great Books movement was the publication, in 1952, of the Encyclopedia Britannica's fifty-four volume *Great Books of the Western World* (currently available for purchase in Australia), with its indexed 'Syntopicon', which the advertising whiz William Benton touted as a way to 'save time' and be 'popular and successful'.[19]

The same tendency to bolster the values of American consumer culture is evident in the early history of another institution, the Book-of-the-Month Club, although the potential to create community was present as well. In contrast to the actual groups the Great Books movement generated, the Book-of-the-Month Club fostered literary sociability that was primarily fictive, or at least at one remove from the operations of the club. When the advertising copywriter Harry Scherman perceived the opportunity in the mid 1920s to sell books using direct-mail techniques, he relied on the construct of a 'club' to help make the venture profitable. In fact, the 'club' conceit masked the fact that anyone was

---

17 'Manual for Discussion Leaders', quoted in Rubin, *Middlebrow Culture*, p. 192.

18 Redman, pp. 33, 35; 'Manual for Discussion Leaders', quoted in Rubin, *Middlebrow Culture*, p. 192; Milton Mayer, 'Great Books', *Life*, 28 October 1946, pp. 2–8.

19 William Benton to Robert Maynard Hutchins, 18 October 1949, quoted in Rubin, *Middlebrow Culture*, p. 196.

making money, allying the enterprise instead with other sites of literary sociability such as women's study clubs and societies devoted to rare manuscripts. The appropriation of 'club' thus amounted to a recreation, in language, of a relationship that entailed face-to-face contact and shared interests – qualities at odds with the magnitude and impersonal nature of the actual Book-of-the-Month Club operation as well as of American society at large. Scherman and his associates banked as well on faith in critical expertise by entrusting its authoritative Board of Judges to identify the best new publications: works that had the prospect of becoming the 'great books' of the future rather than those without lasting value. 'There is an overpowering fascination', a 1927 advertising brochure explained, 'about good new books … [I]n reading them, in enjoying them, in talking with others about them, we feel the new thought of our day actually taking shape, and we participate in its formation'.[20]

But if 'talk with others' about literature was an element of the Book-of-the-Month club's appeal, the stronger angle in its initial advertising campaign was an emphasis on social disgrace and isolation. Literary community of the sort marketed by the Book-of-the-Month Club depended on the successful self-presentation that familiarity with recent books permitted; the hapless individual who had to confess, 'in a group of bookish people', that he had 'never got around to reading' a book suffered exclusion and embarrassment.[21] So here again we have literary sociability predicated on received aesthetic standards and entangled with consumer culture, because the remedy for the reader's deficiencies was to purchase the Club's automatic service, by which the choice of the expert judges would arrive unless the subscriber cancelled the delivery. This was not the whole story of the Book-of-the-Month Club – there were appeals to autonomy and genteel culture as well – but it reminds us again that community could coexist with and even underwrite competitive individualism and therapeutic consumption.

Let us now turn back to an actual collectivity, and to the phenomenon of the verse speaking choir, a British import of the 1920s. Shortly after World War I, the poet John Masefield founded the Oxford Recitations, a verse speaking contest for adults, in order to enhance appreciation for the 'British poetic inheritance'. Around the same time, speech teachers in Britain were encouraging choral recitation at national music festivals. American educators got wind of the idea and started so-called speaking choirs themselves. The institution found an especially congenial home at women's colleges and civic venues such as settlement houses.[22] Participants recited poems as if they were singing together under the leadership of a conductor, with antiphonal passages, unison sections, solos, and the like.

The ideology attending the speaking choir movement had many strands: in part, the venture served to shore up the authority of the speech professionals who were insisting on the legitimacy of their academic discipline; in part, it reflected an interest in assimilating immigrants by eliminating the ostensibly detrimental influence of foreign, lower-class, or pronounced local accents. But speaking choir advocates also argued that group poetry

---

20 *The Book-of-the-Month Club* (New York: Book-of-the-Month Club, 1927), pp. 2–3.
21 *The Book-of-the-Month Club*, pp. 2–3, 5.
22 'Settlement houses' refers to institutions such as Toynbee Hall in London and Hull House in Chicago that were founded in the late nineteenth century by reformers who strove to assist the poor residents of surrounding neighbourhoods by stressing the interdependence of social classes.

reading could enable shy participants to gain self-confidence and to experience, in the pop-Freudian language of the time, the therapeutic benefits of 'release' from complexes and inhibitions. By appreciating and reliving release in poetic expression, readers gained heightened 'power' that allowed them to substitute 'unity' for frustration, routine and 'the boredom that comes from emotional poverty'. Here was literary sociability linked to individual growth, much the way the Book-of-the-Month Club promised individual success.[23]

Yet, in addition, the proponents of choric speech endowed the practice with the potential to promote social as well as psychic harmony, especially in the climate of the Great Depression. As the psychologist H.A. Overstreet declared in his 1934 volume *A Guide to Civilized Leisure*, 'to join with others in the rendering of a great poetic experience' as a choir member was 'to feel oneself swept into a oneness of life that is well worth the having'. Overstreet actually used the word 'sociability' in connection with 'communal reading', positing that the practice was an alternative to the 'frenetic demands' of 'our economic civilization'.[24] One hears in that remark the voice of left-leaning commentators who, perceiving the Depression as a crisis of capitalism, connected an interest in the art of the 'people' to a renewal of American life. Like folk dancing, the speaking choir thus took on a broad social purpose, and became worthy of federal aid. As other observers noted, it promised to eradicate class difference, 'stimulate' and unite both the employed and the unemployed, and, as one proponent noted, 'live equally well within a fashionable club or in a settlement house, in urban or rural districts'.[25] The greatest benefit of this text-centred community was a sense of belonging, an antidote to the loneliness and isolation that economic catastrophe arguably brought in its wake. Yet group reading even promised transnational unity. One speech teacher pointed to a performance at the foot of the Acropolis, by the speaking choir of the University of Berlin, as evidence that the 'welding influence of mass artistic achievement' could create international understanding. Unfortunately she made this remark in 1937, so her timing now seems a little off.[26]

In terms of the texts that bound these readers, the speaking choir provides a nice contrast to the Great Books movement because it illustrates canon formation on the basis of principles that had little to do with the criteria promulgated by academics or 'men of letters' either in the interwar period or subsequently. That is, the test of whether a poem was 'good' was neither that it conveyed purportedly timeless insights nor that it was a specimen of modernism. Instead, choric speech advocated privileged works with 'a robust and definite beat' and those that avoided 'purely personal' emotion; their compilations of suitable pieces invoked distinctions between 'objective' poems and inferior 'subjective'

---

23 Joan Shelley Rubin, *Songs of Ourselves: The Uses of Poetry in America* (Cambridge: Harvard University Press, 2007), pp. 136–45; Bonaro Wilkinson, *The Poetic Way of Release* (New York: Knopf, 1931), pp. 17, 51, 70–76, 112.

24 H.A. Overstreet, *A Guide to Civilized Leisure* (New York: Norton, 1934), pp. 48–50. Overstreet was the husband of Bonaro Wilkinson, cited above.

25 Marguerite E. DeWitt, 'Shall We Recite as Groups?', in Marguerite E. DeWitt, *Practical Methods in Choral Speaking* (Boston: Expression Co., 1936), p. 62.

26 Cecile de Banke, *The Art of Choral Speaking* (Boston: Baker's Plays, 1937), p. 11.

ones.²⁷ The result was an eclecticism that spanned poetic structure as well as chronology, while amalgamating the high and the popular, the modern and the sentimental. Thus the speaking choir reminds us that various communities support various hierarchical schemes at a given historical moment, that multiple canons are always present and always provisional, that the authority to certify 'good reading' depends on the particular site at which experts and readers convene.

That point holds as well with respect to instances involving readers who coalesce around opposition to experts. In 1957, when John Ciardi, the poetry editor of the *Saturday Review*, pronounced Anne Morrow Lindbergh's *The Unicorn and Other Poems* 'an offensively bad book – inept, jingling, slovenly, illiterate even',²⁸ he effectively strengthened a literary community united in disagreement with both the substance of his judgement and the language in which he had cast it. Ciardi's adherence to New Critical principles of close reading produced in the majority of *Saturday Review*'s vocal readers (that is, those who wrote letters to the magazine's editor) responses such as the following:

> I am sure that to many these poems express what Mrs. Lindbergh intends them to without using a lot of double talk and futile phrases that mean nothing either to the reader or the writer. Why not take this book of poems for what it is, an expression of Mrs. Lindbergh's own thoughts [?] Don't dissect it for techniques.²⁹

This comment reflects the suspicion of science that was one response, in the postwar period, to the possibility of nuclear annihilation. Other readers zeroed in on Ciardi's unconcealed misogyny: 'Why take a baseball bat', one reader wrote, 'to club a butterfly?'³⁰ Eventually some correspondents came to Ciardi's defence, praising his courage and standards.

In the context of the history of literary sociability, the controversy that Ciardi himself named a 'dialogue with an audience' is striking for the way it reveals two phenomena. First, Lindbergh's champions exhibited no hesitation in dismissing Ciardi's assessment as merely the tirade of a cruel egotist, who deserved little if any deference because of his standing as a cultural authority. 'Why don't you find a new poetry editor?', one woman queried. Another letter-writer stated, 'I cannot imagine [his comments] as legitimate criticism'.³¹ Here, then, is an early example of the public's sense of entitlement to its opinion, an echo of Erskine's empowerment of the reader and a foreshadowing of the situation today when, as Rachel Donadio put it in a recent essay, 'everyone's a critic'.³² Moreover, the Ciardi–Lindbergh affair is notable for the fact that critic and readers alike (as well as *Saturday Review*'s editor Norman Cousins) imagined themselves as a community linked by shared tastes. Ciardi pejoratively labelled his audience a vestige of the 'genteel tradition', a judgment laden with

---

27  Elizabeth E. Keppie, *The Teaching of Choric Speech* (Boston: Expression Co., 1939), pp. 16, 37; Rubin, *Songs of Ourselves*, p. 142.

28  John Ciardi, *Dialogue with an Audience* (Philadelphia: J.B. Lippincott, 1963), pp. 74–79. I have discussed the Ciardi–Lindbergh controversy in Joan Shelley Rubin, 'The Genteel Tradition at Large', *Raritan* (Winter 2006): 70–91.

29  Ciardi, *Dialogue*, p. 79.

30  Ciardi, *Dialogue*, p. 86.

31  Ciardi, *Dialogue*, p. 81.

32  Rachel Donadio, '1958: The War of the Intellectuals', *New York Times Book Review*, 11 May 2008, p. 39.

irony because the so-called genteel critics of the nineteenth century in the United States had seen themselves as upholding standards.[33] But affronted *Saturday Review* subscribers expressed a similar belief that their loyalty to a shared set of values constituted a violation of trust between them and the periodical's editorial staff: 'Why should a magazine that goes to a reading group of kind people', a California woman declared, 'have ignored us in favor of one horrid person?'[34] Cousins replied by defending Ciardi's right to his views but averring that 'he also dismisses too lightly ... the protests involving the question of good taste in the manner of his attack'. The concluding line in Cousins' editorial about the controversy signals his understanding of the fictive communal bonds Ciardi's review had jeopardised. Noting the staff's admiration for Ciardi's forthrightness and energy, he hopefully remarked, 'We believe that in the months and years ahead his relationship with our readers will be no less rewarding to them and to him'.[35]

Although the liberal tolerance that characterised the political outlook of the *Saturday Review* spilled over into readers' aversion toward Ciardi's blustering incivility, that dimension of the Ciardi–Lindbergh contretemps was largely below the surface – or between the lines. The political aspect of the activity that furnishes my final example of literary sociability, however, is highly visible (even more than in the Great Books or speaking choir movements). That example concerns the transformation of a poem into a song for solo voice or chorus by means of what musicologists call text-setting. This is a practice that creates a text-centered community through the act of musical performance – a type of literary sociability that it is easy to overlook, but one that remains common throughout the United States at sites encompassing not only concert halls but also churches, schools, and civic venues. Because the subject of text-setting is so vast, and because generalisations about it must be advanced with caution, I will focus on a single piece, a choral work that I had remembered singing myself as a high school student: the composer Howard Hanson's setting of lines from Walt Whitman that Hanson called 'Song of Democracy'. Examining the history of the ways in which Hanson's piece lent itself to collective expression allows for a close mapping of the intersection between ideology and community; it permits us to see the composer as a reader and a mediator who fosters the social life of a text and thereby helps to create the place of the author within cultural hierarchy.

Howard Hanson was a composer, conductor, music educator, and director, for forty years, of the Eastman School of Music at the University of Rochester. Born in 1896 to Swedish Lutheran immigrants, he had a rapid rise to prominence, winning the first Prix de Rome from the American Academy in Rome in 1921 and snagging the Eastman position three years later. His success fed his belief in the American myth of unlimited opportunity, which in turn contributed to the conservative politics he espoused throughout his life. Hanson's activities at Eastman, which included annual festivals of American music, earned him a reputation as an educational reformer; by the 1930s, he had extended his efforts to the promotion of music in the public schools in order to strengthen what he called the 'spiritual development' of the nation as a whole. In 1946, Hanson began a long affiliation with the international cultural exchange programs sponsored by UNESCO, a connection

---

33 John Ciardi, 'The Reviewer's Duty to Damn', in Ciardi, *Dialogue*, p. 92.

34 Ciardi, *Dialogue*, p. 82.

35 Norman Cousins, 'John Ciardi and the Readers', in Ciardi, *Dialogue*, pp. 84–87.

that encumbered music with the potential to bring about what we might see as community writ large: 'the promotion of human brotherhood and world peace'.[36]

But the UNESCO affiliation entailed more than what its official statements labelled 'the intellectual and moral solidarity of mankind',[37] because liberals within the United States Department of State harnessed the agency to assist with the containment of the Soviet Union and the spread of American democracy. Hanson's assignment to compose two pieces for a UNESCO conference in 1949 thus further implicated him in Cold War anti-communism. The same stance defined the politics of the National Education Association (NEA), the organisation of American teachers that had been instrumental in UNESCO's founding. In 1955, when the NEA sought a composer to create a choral work commemorating its one hundredth anniversary, Hanson was perfectly situated ideologically to accept the commission. Hanson's musical style also contributed to his suitability: although he began his career thinking of himself as a 'modern', his championing of new music did not extend to works he judged excessively dissonant, harsh, formless or decadent. While his pieces incorporated some modernist elements, he is usually considered a neo-Romantic – or what one of his obituaries called a 'conservative modern'.[38]

The text Hanson and an NEA committee selected for the occasion consisted of excerpts from two Whitman poems. One was 'An Old Man's Thought of School'; the other was 'Thou Mother with Thy Equal Brood', which contained the lines 'Sail, sail thy best, ship of Democracy'. Both were products of the 1870s, by which time Whitman's earlier persona as a free-spirited lyricist in search of the perfect self had evolved into an outlook both more nationalistic and more universal.[39] The first set of lines likens young students to ships preparing 'to sail out over the measureless seas,/on the Soul's voyage'. The poem instructs an 'America' seeking the 'real reckoning' for its present and future (would they hold 'good or evil'?) to 'girlhood, boyhood look – the teacher and the school'. The original context for 'An Old Man's Thought of School' was the precarious state of the newly reassembled nation following the Civil War. In 1956, however, for large numbers of Americans, and for Hanson himself, the uncertainty about a good or evil future for the United States arose not from the internal strife of the Reconstruction period but instead from the question of whether or not capitalism would prevail over communism. The second, sometimes separately published part of 'Song of Democracy' lent itself even more readily to that reading. A meditation on the passing of the Old World and the dawn of a distinctively American civilisation, this second poem recapitulated themes that Whitman had articulated most famously in 'Democratic Vistas', published in 1871. But Hanson used only the section of this work that

---

36  On Hanson's life see Andrea Sherlock Kalyn, 'Constructing a Nation's Music: Howard Hanson's American Composers' Concerts and Festivals of American Music, 1925–71', PhD thesis (University of Rochester 2001). The Hanson Papers at Sibley Music Library, Eastman School of Music, University of Rochester, contain a draft autobiography and other relevant primary materials. They are hereafter cited as Hanson Papers. The phrase 'spiritual development' comes from Howard Hanson, 'The Music Supervisor and His Mission', *Musician* (May 1935), p. 8. On brotherhood and peace see Howard Hanson, 'The Scope of the Music Education Program', *Music Educators Journal* (July–August 1948), p. 57.

37  *UNESCO and You*, United States Department of State Publication 2904 (1947), p. iii.

38  'Composer-Educator Howard Hanson Dies', *Chicago Tribune*, 28 February 1981.

39  Richard Chase, *Walt Whitman Reconsidered* (New York: William Sloane, 1955), pp. 79–82, 153.

implores the 'Ship of Democracy' to 'Sail, sail thy best' because its 'freight' includes the heritage not just of America but of all humanity: 'Venerable, priestly Asia sails this day with thee/And royal feudal Europe sails with thee'. Again, this idea, and the injunction that the helmsman should 'steer' with a 'wary eye', could seem more about containing the Soviet threat (the liberal position in the Cold War) or defeating it (the agenda of conservatives within the State Department) than about inspiring Whitman's 'ideal equalitarian planet'.

Hanson's interventions extended the long tradition of Whitman as 'the good gray poet' that was already a popular possession, in part because of propaganda in both world wars.[40] But the composer altered and amplified, so to speak, the nationalistic Whitman in two respects: first, through a set of compositional choices and, second, by the performance of Whitman's texts at sites that enhanced their Cold War utility. In terms of sound and structure, Hanson strove to create 'a setting which would be direct and technically suitable' for schoolchildren and other amateur musicians.[41] Thus he relied on the repetition of a single tone by the chorus for several measures, placing more complex musical passages in the accompaniment. This device made the piece easy to sing, but it also permitted dramatic upward surges that conveyed an upwelling of patriotic fervour: the 'Sail, sail thy best' stanza accents the '-moc-' in 'democracy'; the section departs from Whitman's text by repeating the first lines and imploring the ship of Democracy to stay afloat, enhancing that sentiment with sacralising phrases sung on 'Ah!'. Moreover, Hanson's political and cultural location meant that 'Song of Democracy' acquired Cold War overtones in the process of its dissemination. The unofficial premiere in March 1957 involved a performance for President Eisenhower by the African-American chorus from Howard University, which also sang the piece in Washington's Constitution Hall a month later. Those concerts transmitted an American commitment to tolerance and civil rights: precisely the message that the State Department was then promoting in order to counteract international condemnation of American racial discrimination and a consequent growth of communism.[42]

After the official premiere of Hanson's piece at the NEA convention in June, Hanson's version of Whitman spread across the nation, distributed in print form by the educators' organisation. 'Song of Democracy' was a particular favorite of all-city high school choruses, which, because of their size, increased the volume and impact of the music. In that respect, Hanson's adaptation of a literary text created new, if temporary, communities of readers who, in the act of singing, created shared experiences and memories. Furthermore, the piece found a niche among adult amateur chorales, where the ideal of an inclusive democracy that Whitman's text could support accorded nicely with the non-sectarian ethos typical of such ensembles. 'We have Catholics, Protestants, Jews, Mormons and even some agnostics', explained the conductor of 'a group of local doctors, lawyers, mechanics and housewives' in suburban Los Angeles who sang the work in 1965.[43] Yet along with these examples of

---

40 Charles B. Willard, *Whitman's American Fame: The Growth of His Reputation in America after 1892* (Providence, RI: Brown University Press, 1950), pp. 93, 225–26; 'Walt Whitman's Songs of Democracy', *New York Times*, 16 June 1918.

41 Howard Hanson draft autobiography, chapter 6 fragment, pp. 5–6 (in folder 'Early Version'), Hanson Papers.

42 Mary L. Dudziak, *Cold War Civil Rights* (Princeton: Princeton University Press, 2000).

43 'Valley Chorale Has Doctors, Lawyers, but No Indian Chiefs', *Los Angeles Times*, 13 May 1965.

locally based collectivities, two episodes in the career of 'Song of Democracy' during the late 1950s and 1960s especially emphasise its usefulness in fostering – rather than 'eliding' – a community of the nation, united by putative faith in an 'American way of life'.

The first episode was the European premiere of the piece at a music festival sponsored by the United States Army, the State Department, and local government officials in Nüremberg, Germany, in 1959. The Deutsche Rundfunk and the Voice of America (VOA) taped the performance; the VOA planned to broadcast it 'with commentary in 42 languages'. To Hanson, the conductor of the piece expressed his awareness of the work's political value with pointed sarcasm: he wrote, 'The Russians should love it!'[44] The culminating event in the Cold War appropriation of Whitman's text occurred in 1969 at the festivities surrounding Richard Nixon's inauguration. 'Song of Democracy', performed by the National Symphony Orchestra and the Mormon Tabernacle Choir, was the last number on a concert consisting entirely of American music. As the somewhat snotty *New York Times* reviewer Harold Schonberg noted, 'Mr. Nixon listened intently, but grinned his way between numbers. At the end of the Hanson work, he was determined to be the first to applaud. He brought his fist down in a great downbeat, anticipating the conductor's by a good half measure'.[45]

The personal enrichment that such performances created for participants cannot be ignored, as well as the possibility that individuals rejected the Cold War smugness that Hanson's setting endorsed. Composers can no more encumber their creations with fixed meanings than can poets themselves, as the performance of 'Song of Democracy' in 1991 by the Gay Men's Chorus of Washington makes clear. Nevertheless the history of Hanson's work demonstrates the overarching proposition that text-setting, as a cultural practice, casts composers as agents of literary sociability and as makers of meaning whose creation of new forms constrains as well as liberates readers' interpretive options. Furthermore, like Great Books groups, the Book-of-the-Month Club, and the speaking choir, text-setting is a form of mediation that affects the position of an author within cultural hierarchy. Hanson's decision to devise what he called 'a direct setting' rested on his assumption – one shared by proponents of literary modernism – that complexity and obscurity were beyond the capacities of the average listener or reader. Yet, in theory, composers and their literary counterparts might have striven for greater appreciation of 'difficult' texts by promoting exposure to them. That move would have challenged the artist's investment in the stance of alienated genius. It would have blurred the line between high and popular culture, and, in terms of music, the boundary between the professional and the amateur performer. In the absence of such a challenge, however, the diffusion of 'Song of Democracy' solidified the identification of Hanson's 'conservative modernism' with amateurism, and helped to relegate both the style and the performers to a devalued middlebrow status, vulnerable to the contempt of a Harold Schonberg. In addition, Hanson's sound and choice of texts reinforced the middling position of Whitman himself for a wide swathe of American readers, at precisely the moment when academic critics were trying to move the poet up in the ranking of American authors. New Critics in the mid twentieth century reversed

---

44  Max T. Krone to Howard Hanson, 1 June 1959, box 22, folder 14, Hanson Papers. Programs from the German performances are in this folder as well.

45  Harold C. Schonberg, 'Inaugural Concerts: Americana vs. All-American', *New York Times*, 20 January 1969, p. 32.

Whitman's declining fortunes by reconstituting him as a lyric poet. But to make that case, such critics argued that Whitman's later work – including the texts constituting 'Song of Democracy' – was inferior to his earlier output. Thus Hanson's setting not only furnished the American public a Cold War Whitman but also sustained and perhaps widened a dichotomy between the popular and the scholarly Whitman. And therein lies the irony that, for all of its utility in promoting the hegemony of American capitalism, 'Song of Democracy' literally did give voice to ordinary people by simply bypassing the judgment of academic authorities.[46]

There are of course examples of literary sociability in which questions of cultural hierarchy and critical authority are not much in evidence. With respect to the recitation of poetry in school or at home, for instance, often the intrinsic qualities of the text were not as important as the act of reading aloud. That is, within the community of the classroom, or among family, friends, and lovers, the meaning of a poem turned out to be inextricably linked to, and sometimes overshadowed by, the relationships it evoked among its readers, regardless of the work's canonical status. Consider the remarks of a woman recalling her schoolgirl days:

> I remember coming home from the fourth grade determined to memorize the poem about Columbus that begins, 'Behind him lay the gray Azores … ' As I was stumbling through the first few lines, my father began saying the poem, and said it to the end. With feeling. That glimpse of continuity and linkage between my father and me has stayed with me these fifty-six years.[47]

Perhaps Joaquin Miller's text made it easier for the father to muster feeling. But the 'continuity and linkage' this reader felt arguably would have developed if she had voiced any number of the poems in the schoolroom repertoire. In fact, the disappearance (until recently, anyway) of memorisation and recitation from American classrooms has created a sense of community among older individuals who regard their youthful poetry performances as a sign that they belong to a vanishing era: although a shared familiarity with Longfellow or Wordsworth may contribute to that awareness, the more powerful source of connectedness is the now-outmoded reading practice itself.

One can extend this point even to the social relationships governing silent reading. My favorite example comes from a remarkable late nineteenth-century diary of an Iowa woman who eventually became a Baptist missionary. As a teenager in the 1880s, Clara Holloway repeatedly fended off bouts of depression and loneliness. The erratic attentions of Addie Groesbeck, the young man who eventually became her husband, heightened her propensity for self-blame, leaving her to wonder repeatedly whether she had imagined or caused his ill humor. When Addie failed to appear at Clara's eighteenth birthday party, she was devastated: 'I am reckless tonight', she wrote in her diary, 'and would like to do something dreadful'. After three days, however, Addie made amends, giving her a book of Wordsworth's poems as a birthday present. Proffering a slim volume of verse as a gesture of

---

46 Scott Macphail, 'Lyric Nationalism: Whitman, American Studies, and the New Criticism', *Texas Studies in Literature and Language* 44.2 (2002): 133–60; Chase, *Walt Whitman Reconsidered*, p. 133.

47 Mary Bingham, quoted in Rubin, *Songs of Ourselves*, p. 153.

affection or desire was timeworn, predictable, even trite. Yet those qualities did not detract from (and possibly enhanced) the import of the practice for individuals engaging in it anew. In any case, of more interest than the gift was Clara's response to it. 'I was very much surprised', she wrote confessionally, 'and I know I made him mad. Such a time as I do have. But the book is lovely, and I shall "prize it for the giver's sake", more than for anything else'.

Furthermore, when Clara turned to the poems themselves two weeks later, her sense of her literary preferences was inseparable from her romantic hopes and anxieties: 'I have been reading Wordsworth and like it better all the time. Addie must have known my taste pretty well, when he selected that'. As her dark mood returned over the next few days – 'In the afternoon I was nearly sick with loneliness' – she recorded that she 'settled myself with Wordsworth to comfort me', as if the book as object were a substitute for Addie's physical presence. Although, over the next few months, their relationship reassuringly evolved toward commitment, Clara still measured Addie's seriousness not only by his stolen kisses but also by the number of books (including Whittier's *Poems*) that he lent her. In August, she acknowledged his twentieth birthday by giving him a collection of Bryant's poetry, which she thereafter read herself for the first time – a fact that suggests, again, that she chose the volume for its symbolic weight, rather than for any particular sentiment it contained. When she finally recorded in her diary that Addie had 'asked me if I would take him for life', she captured both the emotional burden this social use of books bore within their relationship and, in a sense, the uncertainty that books' symbolic value helped assuage: 'He ordered me a book for a birthday present but hasn't got it yet'. It is certainly possible – even likely – that the position of Wordsworth, Whittier and Bryant in the schoolroom canon, if not the high culture panoply, enhanced the significance of the texts this young couple exchanged. But Clara's resonant phrase – actually a line from Whittier – 'I shall prize it for the giver's sake, more than for anything else' – is a clear instance of literary sociability that generates greater meaning for a reader because of the personal interaction it involves than because of the words on the page.[48]

Yet with respect to the self-conscious collectivities devoted to 'great books' or verse performance, the politics of culture (to say nothing of national politics) were always in play. We cannot sort out those politics without divesting ourselves of our own assumptions – or our own hopes, really – about community. The human connections that most of us presumably value may arise in settings that are in other respects intolerant of difference or predicated on competition. Despite our own predilection for one or the other, we need to see that literary community can support individual autonomy, deference to authority, or both simultaneously. I would even venture that any history of literary sociability, in the United States or in Australia, demands sensitivity to cultural tension – in us as well as in our subjects.

---

48  Rubin, *Songs of Ourselves*, pp. 277–78.

# 2

## The 'Federation of Literary Sympathy':[1] The Australasian Home Reading Union

*Kylie Mirmohamadi*

When Bishop Montgomery of Tasmania took the stand at the 1892 Hobart meeting of the Australasian Association for the Advancement of Science to advocate the formation of a Home Reading Union in Australia (AHRU), he drew a vivid picture of the need for a body devoted entirely to literary education in the Australian colonies. Prompted by the disbanding of the Literature and Fine Art Section of the Association, Dr Montgomery called for this section, which was 'doomed to extinction', to be allowed to 'live again in a new form by giving birth to a union which may become a great educating power'.[2] Despite this natal moment of confidence in renewal, the trajectory of the union so formed was one of waning fortunes. With declining membership from its early years, it limped to its demise around 1913, although this fate had perhaps been inevitable since 1898.

Others have reflected upon the causes of the Australasian Home Reading Union's decline: Martyn Lyons mentions the conflicting class messages of the union, and John Jenkins its 'over-ambition'.[3] My intention here is not so much to tell the story of the Australasian Home Reading Union (AHRU), but to consider how, at an important juncture in Australian history, this organisation drew upon, illuminated and developed significant ideas about the social and educational functions of reading. In the years leading up to the federation of the colonies, it grappled with the tyranny of cultural distance even as it nurtured an awareness of the specific requirements and responses of Australian reading communities.

This chapter examines the AHRU, and especially the language that was used to represent it and promulgate its message of directed home reading, in the light of this book's emphasis on collective reading experiences in Australia. Recognising that colonial readers, in consonance with the bulk of colonial society, saw themselves simultaneously as British readers, displaced, and Australian readers, in place, it explores the ways in which

---

1 *West Australian*, 18 April 1892, p. 8.

2 'Upon the Formation of a Home Reading Union: A Paper Read by the Bishop of Tasmania before the Literature Section of the A.A.A.S., 1892', *A.H.R.* 1.1 (1892), p. 8. Although the Union included New Zealand, and its journal regularly contained information about activities in this colony, my observations in this chapter are limited to the Australian colonies.

3 Martyn Lyons, 'The Australasian Home Reading Union, 1892–97', in Martyn Lyons and John Arnold, eds, *A History of the Book in Australia 1891–1945: A National Culture in a Colonised Market* (St Lucia: University of Queensland Press, 2001), p. 388; John Jenkin, 'The Australasian Home Reading Union: Spectacular Rise, Precipitous Fall', *Journal of the Historical Society of South Australia* 38 (2010): 58. These sources provide overview histories of the AHRU.

the Australian colonial context shaped the ideas and rhetoric surrounding the antipodean movement for literary education and sociability.[4] At the same time, it acknowledges the union's imported values, methods and structures, from organisations in the Northern Hemisphere. In this way, the AHRU is a fruitful subject in which to apply Martyn Lyons' stipulation that

> any account of reading practices which attempts to identify what was individual about the Australian reader must acknowledge all the ambiguities of a colonial society, the characteristics it shared with the rest of the western world, together with its local peculiarities.[5]

Tracking the AHRU's negotiation of its Old World origins and its pressing New World needs and desires, I argue that the union's antipodean context coloured its literary attitudes and activities in a number of ways. These included the assertion of the need for specifically Australian material, a preoccupation with the bush and reference to Australian landscape in its supporting literature, the reflection of colonial anxieties about reading, and an insistence upon a specifically Australian experience of, and response to, literary texts. I also suggest that the framework of empire, and the politically and culturally charged environment of Federation, shaped the AHRU's project and strivings.

Bishop Montgomery, as well as those who came after him, took pains to emphasise that the AHRU modelled itself on initiatives from other places – namely, the National Home Reading Union (NHRU) in England and the Chautauqua movement in America. The Australian and English Unions, especially, encountered similar issues of gender, genre and class in their endeavours to bring together individuals to form a community of readers.[6] The stronger English antecedent was evident in the structure adopted by the Australasian union, in which reading circles, organised into groups and sections for administrative and reporting purposes, were formed to study set texts, chosen from a predetermined list. Individual members were encouraged to complement their own literary impressions and judgments with those of experts (published in the union journal) and peers (at circle meetings). Emphasis was placed on literary sociability and, although it was not mandatory, belonging to a circle and regularly gathering together was, as in the NHRU in England, strongly encouraged. Lady Jersey, writing publicly to resign as President of the Union in 1893 due to her impending departure from the colony, praised the social benefits of literary association, and reiterated that

> the Union, whilst offering every encouragement to the student, solitary from choice or necessity, specially desires to promote the formation of Circles linked together by common literary pursuits and intellectual pleasure.[7]

---

4  See Lyons, 'Reading Practices in Australia', in Martyn Lyons and John Arnold, eds, *A History of the Book in Australia 1891–1945: A National Culture in a Colonised Market* (St Lucia: University of Queensland Press, 2001), p. 344, for displacement in twentieth-century reading identities.

5  Lyons, 'Reading Practices in Australia', p. 335.

6  For an overview of the Home Reading Union in England see Robert Snape, 'The National Home Reading Union 1889–1930', *Journal of Victorian Culture* 7.1 (2002): 86–110; and Felicity Stimpson, 'Reading in Circles: The National Home Reading Union 1889–1900', *Publishing History* 52 (2002): 19–82.

7  *A.H.R.* 2.1 (1893), p. 7.

Like the English organisation, the Australasian union concerned itself with the question of *how* to read, as well as the related issue of *what* to read. The term 'desultory' was a favourite way to distinguish between the wasteful frivolity of unguided reading and the 'discipline and concentrated individual effort' engendered by the union's corrective, directional approach.[8] Useful and educative reading was key, generating commentary within and around the union over the benefits – or otherwise – of fiction, and especially what we would now call genre fiction (including romances and novels of crime and detection), which echoed a broader conversation being carried on throughout British and colonial societies. In a rare reference to Australian literature, the Hobart *Mercury* reported Bishop Montgomery's claim that he had read *The Mystery of a Hansom Cab* and *Three Men in a Boat*, 'both of which he had enjoyed, but he did not think his education had gained anything from them'.[9] The three touted benefits of the AHRU were summarised in 1892 in a report from the Victorian section which, unsurprisingly, given the economic depression which had gripped the colony, also argued for the economy of union membership:

> Guidance in the choice of reading, help, and a sense of brotherhood – these are the three great advantages that the Union holds out to its members. They are surely cheaply purchased at half-a-crown.[10]

The founders and early advocates of the Australasian union were well aware of the sometimes fraught interplay between the global and the local in their nascent organisation. The entanglement of identities that comprised the colonial subject is made clear when we consider that colonial readers saw themselves as co-inheritors of that 'vast [literary] treasure-house which belonged to the British people'[11] and also as distinctively Australian consumers of print located within numerous local networks of connection and identification. At the first assembly of the New South Wales section, Professor Francis Anderson negotiated the British and colonial fields of influence by claiming that they 'were trying to build up on Australian soil what might be called a new institution, but they were not innovators'. On the question of why they should not simply join the English union, 'he thought it would be a mistake to join themselves as a branch to any other society'. He continued, 'They were Australians, and there were desires and needs of readers in Australia which could not be altogether met by the English union'.[12]

The Australian context had also asserted itself at the union's foundational moment of Bishop Montgomery's Hobart address. In the practical matter of the selection of books to be studied, the English lists could act as a guide, but the antipodean reading environment demanded, he suggested, a degree of local specificity: it would not be advisable to adopt such lists 'as given', because it was 'clear that in many cases works suitable for this hemisphere, especially in certain departments of science, will need to be added'.[13] In the *West Austra-*

---

8 The Hon. T.J. Byrnes on the Queensland section, in *A.H.R.* 1.8 (1892), p. 219.
9 *Mercury*, 16 March 1892, p. 3.
10 *A.H.R.* 1.8 (1892), p. 218.
11 *Advertiser* (Adelaide), 25 April 1893, p. 6.
12 *Sydney Morning Herald*, 24 April 1893, p. 6.
13 *A.H.R.* 1.1 (1892), p. 8.

*lian*'s account of the Australasian union's origins, the section's discussion of the need or otherwise to establish an independent organisation was summarised thus: 'We are too far from the old home. Text books, especially in science, suitable there, would be unsuitable here, and we are strong enough to be out of leading strings'.[14] Six years later, facing financial difficulty and inevitable decline, the union continued to appeal to and draw upon the idea of the Australian reader as a specific type, operating within a particular market. 'The average Australian reader', one writer suggested, 'is omnivorous with an appetite satiated by the feast of literature which reaches these shores in the shape of the cheap "Colonial Editions"'. He (and 'he' is used here, despite the fact that women clearly outnumbered men in the union) 'has no reviews, at least none written *by* Australians *for* Australians, and more often than not he wastes his time in reading works which repay nothing for the energy spent on them.'[15]

The AHRU imagined and represented these Australian readers in place, and that place was often the bush. In step with Professor Edward Morris, who told the *Argus* in March 1892, 'I think that guidance in the choice of books is specially wanted in a land where people live, as in the Australian bush, far apart from each other',[16] Bishop Montgomery had argued in his Hobart address that the conditions in the bush required a tailor-made response: 'In my travels through secluded places', he claimed, 'I have often been touched by the anxiety expressed, both by men and women, to be aided in gaining information'. 'Bush people' were remote from 'educated people' in the cities, and were also deficient in leisure, but still they desired self-improvement through engagement with the printed word – 'it would be a grand achievement if this Association could devise a way by which its influence could be felt in the quiet back blocks in our Colonies'. He characterised his role, in the 'well organised hunt' to which he likened the pursuit of knowledge, as that of 'third whip … despatched to perform the hardest work in brambly and boggy places'. I would suggest that this image was intended to evoke for colonial readers the inhospitable parts of the Australian landscape, crying out to be more fully civilised by the English – and, in this case, also *by* English.[17]

The union was thus particularly interested in bringing literature to remote settlements and farms. Queensland stations were identified in one article as deficient in literary ardour:

> one reason for that state of things being that the farm libraries were of exceedingly scanty proportions. The formation of branches of the Home Reading Union would assist the farming population to gain a knowledge of the glorious English literature.[18]

Here the bounty of English literature is at variance with the scantiness of the literary offerings in Queensland, just as the perceived bareness of the Australian landscape was often contrasted with the verdure of England.

---

14  *West Australian*, 18 April 1892, p. 8.

15  Editorial, *Year Book of the Australasian Home Reading Union* (Sydney: The 'Christian World' Printing and Publishing House, 1898), p. 4.

16  Reprinted in the *Morning Bulletin* (Rockhampton), 31 March 1892, p. 3.

17  A.H.R. 1.1 (1892), pp. 6, 8.

18  A.H.R. 1.8 (1892), p. 219.

While this persistent reference to rural and remote reading conditions reflected colonial settlement patterns, it also betrays the undue cultural weight that has been accorded to the isolated rural experience in Australia. The colonial Australian reader was most likely to be an urban or suburban creature, by virtue of the fact that Australia had (and has) a highly urbanised population. As John Arnold has noted, in the light of the *Bulletin* and its urban readership, '[t]he power of the myth of the bush over a heavily suburbanised society has been one of the enduring paradoxes of Australian cultural history'.[19] While the distance between colonial readers and the heart of Empire was one issue, the geography of the country and patterns of settlement within Australia were equally troubling. If the colonial metropole suffered from a lack of literary guidance through the mass of imported books, how much more in danger was the reader 'in places away from the great centres of population where social and intellectual intercourse is either difficult or impossible, and it is to the dwellers in these more especially that the union extends its helping hand'.[20]

The landscape elements of that first address by Bishop Montgomery – the *West Australian*'s report had him journeying 'through the garden of Australasia'[21] – point to the manner in which the union's activities were represented, both in their journal and the wider press, in terms of Australian place. This connection between interior, intellectual landscapes associated with individual reading, and outside, actual spaces, allowed the rural Australian landscape to be re-imagined and re-written as a site of literary experience, consumption and the struggle for settlement. A union report from Tasmania, for example, made clear the implications of place for the Tasmanian union's reading activities: the Secretary's 'authentic information must be withheld until a break in the severity of a Tasmanian winter, accentuated as the severity is in the country districts by Tasmanian roads, permits the freer interchange of social intercourse'.[22] More positively, an account of a 'Literary Excursion', organised by the recently affiliated AHRU in Brisbane, showed that Australian vistas were suitable environments for literary musing. Along the river, where 'the horizon line was broken by clusters of bamboos and here and there a giant gum cut out against the clear blue', the members enjoyed a 'long programme', including papers on Thackeray, Lacordaire, the comic operas of W.S. Gilbert, and quotations from Tennyson's *The Princess*.[23] The reading figures in the Brisbane River landscape reconciled the union's activities with Australian place, despite the cultural preoccupations that meant that stretches of antipodean land were more likely to be imagined as playing or hunting fields. This confirms Martyn Lyons' observation that reading out of doors was not an uncommon or aberrant practice: from the pictorial and textual evidence, '[f]ar from being deterred by the climate [or, I would add, landscape], Australian readers took advantage of it'.[24]

While the physical conditions of the colonies were a preoccupation for the AHRU, the cultural context was also the subject of commentary. The discourse surrounding the

---

19  John Arnold, 'Newspapers and Daily Reading', in Lyons and Arnold, p. 264.
20  Editorial, *Year Book of the Australasian Home Reading Union*, p. 4.
21  *West Australian*, 18 April 1892, p. 8.
22  *A.H.R.* 1.4 (1892), p. 92.
23  *Brisbane Courier*, 23 October 1893, p. 6.
24  Lyons, 'Reading Practices in Australia', p. 345.

union betrayed and drew upon numerous cultural anxieties that were attached to colonial Australian readers and their literary scenes. Their very status as readers was represented as imperilled by the Australian love of sport and, echoing the pervasive anxieties that haunted post-goldrush Victoria, the relentless pursuit of material wealth.[25] At the same time, it was also feared that there was too much reading. General misgivings about mass literacy and the pernicious effects of popular fiction, especially amongst vulnerable subjects such as females and the working classes, anxieties which were pervasive throughout British culture in the late Victorian era, took on distinctively colonial overtones in Australia.[26] The Governor of South Australia, Lord Kintore, left his audience in no doubt that the literary crisis was as immediate in his colony as it was in England:

> in these days however, when the press teems, when of the making of books there is no end, in an age which is described as an age of reading, we have to confess that, while much is read, seldom or never has reading been to less profit. It is so at home, it is so here.

At the same meeting, the Rev. J. Day Thompson commented on the possibility that, in such a newspaper-loving colony, 'there was a danger of confining their reading to papers only'. Here, too, '[t]he course of literature suggested by the union would broaden their minds and teach them that there was more in those great questions than casual reading led them to imagine'.[27]

The AHRU's role in mitigating the damaging effects of Australian reading habits and tastes was emphasised in an article in the *Launceston Examiner*, which declared that 'some such society [as the AHRU] is necessary in Australia, where literature is too often subordinated to other pursuits'. The colonial people, it conceded,

> are essentially a reading community, but unfortunately in nine cases out of ten the reading is useless, desultory, and sometimes pernicious, because it is not properly directed, and many of the beauties of modern literature are after all but imperfectly understood by the student, however anxious he may be to profit by pursuing them, because he has not acquired a knowledge of the literature which is the key to it.[28]

The next day an article reported Archdeacon Francis Hales' reference to the enthusiasm in the colony for reading, 'shown by the enormous number of books that issue from the press, and the large number of purchasers'. However, many of these readers 'read a large quantity of trash, and the consequence was that the information they gained was far less than it should be'. Mr G.W. Waterhouse, citing borrowing records from the Launceston Mechanics' Institute, 'thought that novel reading was becoming rather an evil, inasmuch as

---

25 *Advertiser*, 25 April 1893, p. 6; 16 May 1894, p. 4. See also Susan K. Martin and Kylie Mirmohamadi, *Sensational Melbourne: Reading, Sensation Fiction and* Lady Audley's Secret *in the Victorian Metropolis* (North Melbourne: Australian Scholarly Publishing, 2011).

26 See Martin and Mirmohamadi, especially chapter 5.

27 *Advertiser*, 25 April 1893, p. 6.

28 *Launceston Examiner*, 22 March 1892, p. 2.

it induced desultory reading, the pith of the novelist's story being scanned while the best thoughts and ideas were skipped as dry'.[29] This use of statistics from the library in their city, past which many of the newspaper's readers must have strolled regularly, located literary anxiety in the centre of Launceston. Tasmanian cities were crying out, it was suggested, for the beneficial effects of the systematic reading encouraged by the AHRU.

The Australian context had implications for the union beyond the experience and representation of colonial landscapes. The specificity of colonial Australian reading subjectivity was noted in relation to a number of texts on the union lists. R.H. Roe suggested in the *Australian Home Reader* that being Australian would engender a specific response in the reading of Greek history. He argued that there are 'features … in Greek history to recommend it to Australian readers'. These included the fact that the Greeks 'were the first colonising power that history tells of', and, furthermore, 'rightly or wrongly they adhered to the principle of absolute independence on the part of the colony, whose members on leaving the parent State abandoned all claims to their original citizenship'. The Australian obsession with sport was one of the 'points in which Australians can warmly sympathise with the feelings of the old Greeks'. He identified further parallels that might suggest themselves to an Australian readership:

> our enjoyment of open-air life, in our athletic tastes, in our child-like enjoyment of our many public holidays, in our unrest in all matters of practice and theory in politics and religion, and yet again in the undernote of sadness and despondency, that runs through our highest thought.

Modestly he made the disclaimer that '[i]n many ways Australians are very Greek in temperament, though not perhaps so far in mental excellencies', attributing the Greek imaginative superiority to the fact that '[t]he brow of the world has become wrinkled with age and care, and we have grown grey and serious with the accumulated thought-treasures of the centuries'. The message of these observations was that Australian readers would approach Greek history in a specific and location-determined way. '[I]n all these points the characteristics of the old Greek life are being reproduced amongst us', Roe declared, 'and to us therefore the lessons of Greek history should be especially attractive and of especial value'.[30] The community of colonial readers, he intimates, could encounter themselves in the pages of Greek history if they read consciously as Australians, and were guided by a sufficiently perspicacious expert.

American history contained the same possibility of identification for Australian readers. Less flamboyantly, but no less revealingly, D.S. Robertson, writing in the *Australasian Home Reader* on the subject of the American Revolution, confidently claimed that '[n]othing in English history will better repay the careful attention of Australian readers than the War of American Independence, the great event of that period of the eighteenth century which is included in the history course of the Australasian Home Reading Union'. However, instead of counselling revolution, he intimated that Australian readers would more peacefully bring their emergent national experience to bear on their reading, as:

---

29  *Launceston Examiner*, 23 March 1892, p. 3.

30  *A.H.R.* 1.1 (1892), pp. 26–27.

> One hundred and fifteen years ago the states which were about to form a federal republic stood in much the same position as is occupied by the Australian colonies today. They had similar political constitutions, the same heterogeneous mixture of races, the same general absence of old world distinctions and traditions.[31]

As this suggests, the overwhelming political context that shaped the formation, function and representation of the AHRU was that of the federation of the Australian colonies. The reading communities that the union created, united and guided consciously anticipated the coming 'imagined community' of the federated nation.[32] Not surprisingly, then, the language of Federation seeped into the Australian literary discourse of this late colonial era. Maybanke Wolstenholme, the prominent colonial feminist and stalwart of the New South Wales section, as well as Honorary Secretary of the AHRU, could have been referring to national politics when she reported to the Australasian Association for the Advancement of Science in 1893 that, while the issue of class difference remained unresolved, the union had 'solved the difficulties of a federation of the colonies, for we have a system of government that makes each Section autonomous, and yet unites the whole under a central Council'.[33] Her husband, Professor Anderson, speaking to the New South Wales section in the same year, claimed that the union was 'in effect' federated; the next speaker went so far as to assert that the movement 'was helping to bring about gradually the natural federation of Australia'.[34] The union was characterised as 'a literary federation … an organisation extending over all the colonies except [in 1894] Western Australia'; it had, claimed the Chairman of the South Australian section, 'solved the question of federation from a literary standpoint'.[35] Nothing denoted the unifying theme of this imagined republic of letters so clearly as the claim that it bound 'the scattered members together in a federation of literary sympathy'.[36] Even after the Executive Committee of the AHRU had voted for its own dissolution, after the secession of a number of sections, the union's journal bitterly editorialised that the 'facts', as set forth in the General Secretary's report on the committee's deliberations in 1897, 'scarcely, we submit, show sufficient cause for the abandonment of the only movement in Australasia which tended towards a literary federation'.[37]

Martyn Lyons has provided historians of the book in Australia with an image of Australian readers looking 'both inward at themselves and outward at the world'.[38] If the AHRU had federation in their inward looking sights, their longer vision took in Australia's place in the ever-expanding British Empire of words. The union, like the rest of literary Australia, was clearly aware of the place and role of the colonies in the global marketplace of publishing. The Tasmanian bookseller T.L. Hood, for example, advertised that 'he

---

31   *A.H.R.* 1.1 (1892), p. 18.

32   Benedict Anderson, *Imagined Communities: Reflections on the Origin and Spread of Nationalism*, rev. edn (London and New York: Verso, 2006 [1983]).

33   M.S. Wolstenholme, 'The Progress of the A.H.R.U.', *A.H.R.* 2.8 (1893), p. 196.

34   *Sydney Morning Herald*, 24 April 1893, p. 6.

35   *Advertiser*, 16 May 1894, p. 4; *South Australian Register*, 16 May 1894, p. 3.

36   *West Australian*, 18 April 1892, p. 8.

37   *Year Book of the Australasian Home Reading Union*, p. 3.

38   Lyons, 'Reading Practices in Australia', p. 335.

is prepared to supply any book required by the members of the Australian [sic] Home Reading Union at London publishing prices, and should the book required not be in stock, to procure it without any advance in the price charged'.[39] The union commented proudly on its own small stream within the flood of books and print leaving British cities and arriving in southern ones: 'The influence of the Union made itself so much felt', reported the *Australasian Home Reader*, 'that after it had been in operation for a few weeks the leading booksellers in Melbourne found it necessary to order from England a large number of fresh copies of the prescribed books in order to meet the demand'.[40]

Less tangibly, the language and logic of empire and imperialism found its way into the AHRU literature. Nineteenth-century depictions of readers and reading in Australia were always produced within the wider collective context of the British Empire and the European presence in colonised lands. The racial and social theories that propped up and rationalised the colonisation of Australia were brought to bear on literature in a union article on 'Modernity in Fiction' in 1898. In discussing the writers of the day, the author explained that 'their novels are novels of incident only, in the field with the more advanced works of Meredith, Hardy, and James, just as the Australian aborigines live in the same century as the Anglo-Saxon race'. They are, the article continues, 'not anachronisms, they are merely the plainer fare provided for less cultured readers'.[41]

Like Bishop Montgomery's wandering and nomadic work in 'brambly and boggy places', the broader project of imperialism was to bring literacy, as the harbinger and symbol of 'civilisation', into what were seen as wild antipodean places and societies.[42] The enduring – if, by this time, fading – self-image of Europeans as bearers, promulgators and protectors of culture in the wilderness is echoed in the characterisation of the beleaguered remnant of the union, living its own desert experience in 1898:

> No man, no woman, can be so self-centred, so self-contained, as to derive no benefit whatever from the comradeship which in so many ways is the greatest of all – the comradeship of letters. For the more strongly cementing of this comradeship, for its extension, nay, for its very existence, we of the tents of Kedar have but one thing to look up to – the Union.[43]

While the 'savages' surrounding the tents were clearly uncultured colonials, including now those who had deserted the literary community of the union, this was still an imperially charged reference that would perhaps only resonate so within the anxious cultural context of a colony.

Book ended (appropriately enough) by two nation-defining events in Australian history and mythology, Federation and World War I, the Australasian Home Reading Union

---

39   *Mercury*, 23 May 1893, p. 2.

40   A.H.R. 1.1 (1892), p. 27.

41   *Year Book of the Australasian Home Reading Union*, p. 22.

42   In reality, as Penny van Toorn has shown, from the earliest point of contact, Aboriginal people have made their own, often resistant, incursions into and uses of reading and writing. See Penny van Toorn, *Writing Never Arrives Naked: Early Aboriginal Cultures of Writing in Australia* (Canberra: Aboriginal Studies Press, 2006).

43   *Year Book of the Australasian Home Reading Union*, pp. 4, 21.

offered the possibility that the new nation of Australia could be comprised of a network of reading communities as well as states. For their brief moment, readers in the union, were, like Benedict Anderson's newspaper readers,[44] united and defined by their shared consumption in an imagined community of print.

---

44  Anderson, p. 35.

# 3

## COMMUNITIES OF READERS: AUSTRALIAN READING HISTORY AND LIBRARY LOAN RECORDS

*Julieanne Lamond*

Recent accounts of Australian literary studies that have privileged book history, or empirical or digital approaches to the discipline, imply a shift of emphasis away from the text itself towards its reception.[1] Usually implicit in such accounts is the idea that the reader is a valid focus for scholarly attention in thinking about national literature. That is, that in thinking about 'Australian literature' we are applying the national descriptor not just to the books we study, but to their readers. We are thinking, in William St Clair's terms, of 'the reading nation' rather than the nation's writers.[2] What might it mean to think of Australia as a nation of readers, or of readerships as forms of local or national community in Australia?

*A National Audience for Australian Culture?*

One starting point might be to look at how, and under what circumstances, readerships and audiences have been considered in national terms in relation to Australian cultural productions. When I first started thinking about Australian readerships and audiences as a form of national community, I was thinking about Steele Rudd (A.H. Davis). This was because Steele Rudd's stories and their adaptations into theatre and film constituted a perfect example of a readership and then audience that were appealed to explicitly and successfully in national terms. The marketing and reception of these texts from 1899 through to the middle of the twentieth century helped build a public language about an Australian readership and audience as a distinct entity. The popularity of Rudd's stories and their adaptations was asserted as evidence for their value and as a key trope in marketing further volumes and adaptations. Reviews, articles and advertisements referred continually to an Australian audience and in doing so were instrumental in creating it. By 1908, the *Sydney Morning Herald* could assume 'Mr Davis' methods are well known to Australian readers'.[3] Ken G. Hall, defending his 1940 film *Dad Rudd, M.P.* against charges of misrepresenting rural Australia, asserted the existence and validity of the audience for Rudd family narratives: an audience ('Australian entertainment-seekers') defined explicitly in relation to

---

[1] See, for example, Katherine Bode and Robert Dixon, eds, *Resourceful Reading: The New Empiricism, eResearch and Australian Literary Culture* (Sydney: Sydney University Press, 2009).

[2] William St Clair, *The Reading Nation in the Romantic Period* (Cambridge: Cambridge University Press, 2004).

[3] *Sydney Morning Herald*, 18 April 1908, p. 4.

their enjoyment of Australian books, plays and films, and to their recognition of particular Australian characters and narratives.[4]

Steele Rudd is an excellent example of how a popular national readership can be invoked in relation to Australian books, and particularly in relation to nationalist tropes. Another example might be the way in which the *Bulletin* generated a broadly national readership defined in such terms.[5] Here is the Australian reader as invoked in 1915 by a man who could certainly claim a working knowledge of what Australian readers wanted to read, A.C. Rowlandson of the NSW Bookstall Company:

> You see most of our people have never seen England or America; most of them will never see any country but Australia. Education helps them to comprehend and be interested in other countries; but they're always most interested in their own. That's natural, isn't it: you can't expect Bill or Mary in the backblocks to really thrill about daisies in English meadows, or train-robbing in the Wild West. Tell them about the Big Flood or the Old Man Drought, and they sit down and take notice – they've been there.[6]

Rowlandson's 'people' were an emerging popular audience for light fiction, particularly Australian fiction, as travellers on Australia's trains in the first thirty years of the twentieth century. The Bookstall Company was to sell more than five million paperbacks in Australia over this period.[7]

It is possible to draw conclusions, based on such examples, about the role of a national literature in creating readerships defined explicitly in national terms, and that can be considered as a form of nascent national polity: a community united by their recognition of cultural commonplaces, as I have argued elsewhere.[8] However, these examples do not tell the whole story, for the very simple reason that, as Elizabeth Webby in her study of reading societies, and other Australian book historians have told us, Australians in the nineteenth century and ever since primarily read and watched culture from elsewhere.[9] Askew and Hubber suggest in relation to the late nineteenth century:

> Complaints by literary nationalists that there was little demand for the productions of local writers tend to confirm rather than deny the existence of a mass reading public in Australia. It was not that Australians did not read, it was that they did not read local books and journals.[10]

---

4  Julieanne Lamond, '*Dad Rudd, M.P.* and the Making of a National Audience', *Studies in Australasian Cinema* 1.1 (2007): 91–105 (102).

5  See Sylvia Lawson, *The Archibald Paradox: A Strange Case of Authorship* (Melbourne: Allen Lane, 1983).

6  *Bookfellow*, 15 January 1915, p. 21, quoted in Carol Mills, *The New South Wales Bookstall Company as a Publisher: With Notes on its Artists and Authors and a Bibliography of its Publications* (Canberra: Mulini Press, 1991), p. 10.

7  Mills, p. 18.

8  Lamond, '*Dad Rudd, M.P.*', and 'The Ghost of Dad Rudd, On the Stump', *JASAL* 6.1 (2007): 19–32.

9  Elizabeth Webby, 'Not Reading the Nation: Australian Readers of the 1890s', *Australian Literary Studies* 22.3 (2006): 308–13.

10  Marc Askew and Brian Hubber, 'The Colonial Reader Observed: Reading in its Cultural Context', in

If this was the case in the latter part of the nineteenth century, had this changed by the first part of the twentieth? Or is there is a limit to how far Rowlandson's 'people' can be taken to represent Australian readers as a whole?

Scholars in Australian literary studies have begun to suggest that if we are to say anything meaningful about Australian readerships in the past, constituted in national or even local terms, we need to take into consideration all of the non-Australian books people were reading. When Paul Eggert argued in 2008 that some of the longstanding questions in Australian literary history could not be answered without reference to detailed book history research into the reception and circulation of key Australian texts,[11] Robert Dixon responded by suggesting that looking at the reception of Australian books was not enough:

> Eggert has asked: what *Australian* books were people reading? He has not asked: what *books* were people reading? To do so would mean understanding the relation between Australian and non-Australian books, and the practices by which they were connected in 'the reading nation'.[12]

This argument can be situated within the context of more general calls for an opening-up of Australian literary studies to consider how our literary culture fits within broader cultural and intellectual shifts taking place across the nineteenth and twentieth centuries.[13] A focus on readerships necessitates this, as Tim Dolin's work has demonstrated.[14] This focus on 'literature in Australia' rather than 'Australian literature' is necessary not only to understanding the role reading played in the lives and cultures of Australians; it is also necessary, more specifically, to understanding Rowlandson's readers and what they read, too.

Understanding how books from elsewhere were read in Australia is important to understanding the position of Australian literary culture within international literary culture, but also more parochially in order to understand how the work of Australian writers was received and understood. How might Australian books have been read in the context not just of canonical British or American works but also the books described by Franco Moretti as dwelling in 'the cellars of culture'; those thousands of works that are not typically studied but nonetheless formed part of the literary and everyday culture of their time?[15]

There is a significant difference between Rowlandson's readers and Webby's literary society members. This is between the readership of 'light' and 'serious' fiction and poetry,

---

D.H. Borchardt and W. Kirsop, eds, *The Book in Australia: Essays towards a Cultural and Social History* (Melbourne: Australian Reference Publications in association with the Centre for Bibliographical and Textual Studies, Monash University, 1988), p. 115.

11  Paul Eggert, 'Australian Classics and the Price of Books: The Puzzle of the 1890s', *JASAL* (2008 *Special Issue: The Colonial Present*): 130–57.

12  Robert Dixon, 'Australian Literature and the New Empiricism: A Response to Paul Eggert, "Australian Classics and the Price of Books"', *JASAL* (2008 *Special Issue: The Colonial Present*): 158–162 (161).

13  Robert Dixon, 'Australian Literature: International Contexts', *Southerly* 67.1–2 (2007): 15–27.

14  Tim Dolin, 'The Secret Reading Life of Us', in Brian Matthews, ed., *Readers, Writers, Publishers* (Canberra: Australian Academy of the Humanities, 2004), pp. 115–34.

15  Cited in Marc Parry, 'The Humanities Go Google', *Chronicle of Higher Education*, 28 May 2010, available at chronicle.com/article/The-Humanities-Go-Google/65713/ [accessed 2 July 2011].

or between popular and literary works. Such a distinction is anything but straightforward at the turn of the century – and yet more complicated by the emergence of a 'middlebrow' reading culture from the 1920s[16] – but was clearly apparent in late nineteenth century commentary on what Australians were reading. Francis Adams, for example, observed in 1890 that:

> This is not a literary community. We are certainly voracious readers of novels, but a habit of novel reading scarcely implies the possession of literary taste any more than does the habit of newspaper reading.[17]

Such concern about what kinds of books Australians were reading can be seen throughout the history of discussions about the development and stocking of libraries in Australia. Detailed studies of Australian reading habits could provide a way of understanding the relationship between Australian books, canonical works from elsewhere, and their 'cellared' cousins.

Australian books have long formed a small part of the reading lives of Australians: they are read and written within the context of international shifts in literary taste, genre and fashion. Australian novelists position themselves in overseas as well as local markets; they are informed and buffeted by these broader cultural movements. Positioning Australians' reading in this broader context is particularly important in understanding Australian literary culture around the turn of the twentieth century, when not only, as Webby has suggested, did books from overseas seem to make up the majority of Australians' reading matter, but also many Australian writers published their work overseas, and so needed to consider how their works would fit within global literary markets. Australian literature in this period should be considered as a 'world literature', in Damrosch's sense.[18] How, then, might we go about understanding what Australians read, as individuals and – a more difficult task – as a community?

*The History of Reading: Beyond the Lone Reader*

Unlike critical approaches that assume a universalised reader, or consider how a reader is implied or conscripted by a literary text,[19] the history of reading has tended to emphasise the act of reading as taking place in specific geographical, temporal and social contexts. Guglielmo Cavallo and Roger Chartier, in their study of the history of reading, argue,

> We ... have to accept the notion that reading is a practice that is always realised in specific acts, places and habits ... we must identify the specific distinctive traits of communities of readers, reading traditions and ways of reading.[20]

---

16  David Carter, 'The Mystery of the Missing Middlebrow, or, The C(o)urse of Good Taste', in Judith Ryan and Chris Wallace-Crabbe, eds, *Imagining Australia: Literature and Culture in the New World* (Cambridge, Massachusetts: Harvard University, Committee on Australian Studies, 2004), pp. 173–201.

17  *Centennial Magazine* 2.4 (1890), p. 302, cited in Askew and Hubber, p. 115.

18  David Damrosch, *What is World Literature?* (Princeton: Princeton University Press, 2003).

19  See, for example, Garrett Stewart, *Dear Reader: The Conscripted Audience in Nineteenth-Century British Fiction* (Johns Hopkins University Press, 1996).

20  Guglielmo Cavallo and Roger Chartier, eds, *A History of Reading in the West* (Amherst: University of

There is a potential tension here between what Margaret Beetham describes as 'the historical specificity of the reader as a complex subject',[21] and the generalisations involved in understanding 'communities of readers, reading traditions and ways of reading'. Following Chartier, print culture and library historian Christine Pawley reminds us that even though the image of the lone reader continues to hold fast in the popular and scholarly imagination, reading is a social act. In light of this, she suggests, we need to think not just about who read what but where, and in what company: we need to try to reconstruct not just instances but communities of reading. This raises two questions: how do we imagine readers in collective terms, and 'how do we make the essential link between these groups of non-elite readers and their real texts?'[22]

The first of Pawley's questions is theoretical, the second methodological. The first, most pertinent to this book, is what it might mean to talk about readers in a collective sense: what is a community of readers? One available framework relates to questions of how people read, such as Stanley Fish's idea of the interpretive community.[23] However contentious this concept might be, it reminds us that an interest in commonalities between readers underlies our interest in shared reading habits. This need not be as specific as Fish's 'interpretive strategies' (the nature of their response to certain books), but could include the relationship of these reading acts to their circumstances, or even people's motivation in choosing those books in the first place. That is, if we take 'Australian readers' as our object of interest, we must presume there is something notable to be said about these readers as a group: that what they read, or perhaps the circumstances of their reading, is distinctive in some way. To put it more simply: the study of 'Australian readers' or 'reading in Australia' depends on the assumption that these readerships tell us something about our cultural history or our place in the world, and that these readers, or certain groups of readers, had something in common beyond the fact of their residence in the same country.

We might consider a community of readers to constitute a kind of imagined community, enabled (as in Benedict Anderson's sense of the term) by print culture and consisting of a community of shared interest in and experience of reading particular groups of books, but not necessarily constituted by personal relationships.[24] Thinking about readerships within the frame of a national community, might we not also consider communities of taste or interest within a particular geographical and historical context who might not self-identify as such? That is, readers who are unselfconsciously similar in terms of what they have read, and when and where they have read it? This kind of community of readers might tell us something about the culture of a time and place. But how would we study it?

---

Massachusetts Press, 1999), p. 2.

21  Margaret Beetham, 'In Search of the Historical Reader', cited in Stephen Colclough, 'Readers: Books and Biography', in Simon Eliot and Jonathan Rose, eds, *A Companion to the History of the Book* (Chichester: John Wiley, 2009), p. 54.

22  Christine Pawley, 'Seeking "Significance": Actual Readers, Specific Reading Communities', *Book History* 5 (2002): 143–60 (145).

23  Stanley Fish, *Is There a Text in This Class? The Authority of Interpretive Communities* (Cambridge, Mass.: Harvard University Press, 1980).

24  Benedict Anderson, *Imagined Communities: Reflections on the Origin and Spread of Nationalism*, rev. edn (London and New York: Verso, 2006 [1983]).

In the methodological question she poses above, Pawley is specific about 'non-elite' readers needing to be imagined collectively because the evidence available in terms of detailed accounts of individual reading practices – letters, diaries, commonplace books – is almost entirely from readers who were either famous or wealthy enough for their records to have been kept or published. Historians of reading have long asserted the difficulty of studying 'ordinary readers' as opposed to 'professional intellectuals'.[25] This might change into the future, as collaborative projects such as the Reading Experience Database (RED) (which has now expanded to collect data from Australia, among other countries) provide a forum for collecting individual reading experiences from a potentially broad range of people. Individual accounts of reading are important to any attempt to understand not just what but how people read: that necessarily limited endeavour of understanding the meanings people have made of what they read or the interpretive strategies they use to do so. Such individual accounts, however, are of limited use when seeking to generalise about reading communities or patterns of readership. As Michael Suarez suggests:

> It may well be impossible to write a representative history of reading based on the experiences of individuals because the overwhelming majority of reading events are ephemeral and those that are recorded are necessarily atypical. How can we develop historically sound approaches to scrutinizing reading practices when most direct evidence of actual reading is merely anecdotal?[26]

The methodological difficulty here centres on the fact that much book history data – for example, publication and sales figures, bookseller and library catalogues – tell us little about the people who actually bought or read or borrowed the books, leading historians of reading to rely on the anecdotal and perhaps atypical evidence left behind by individual readers. Suarez might be right about the possibility of using the material text itself, alongside what is used to market and review it, to tell us about its intended readership; that is, to ally the history of reading and reception more closely to the study of the material book.[27] This can be useful inasmuch as it tells us about the general reading culture of a point in time, as attempts to position a text in relation to a readership can generally be assumed to be based on that readership's past responses to similar texts. This is partly the approach I have used to consider how the trope of an Australian readership has been invoked in the marketing and reception of Steele Rudd's work. However, such approaches lead us back into the realm of the implied or imagined reader and away from the historically specific reader and what he or she read.

*Library Records and Reading History*

There is one field of evidence for reading history that enables us to study the reading choices of large numbers of individual readers that was not considered by Suarez: library

---

25  Jonathan Rose, *The Intellectual Life of the British Working Classes* (New Haven and London: Yale University Press, 2001), p. 1. See also Pawley, 'Seeking "Significance"', and Lydia Wevers, *Reading on the Farm: Victorian Fiction and the Colonial World* (Wellington: Victoria University Press, 2010).

26  Michael Felix Suarez, 'Historiographical Problems and Possibilities in Book History and National Histories of the Book', *Studies in Bibliography* 56 (2003-04): 140-70 (161).

27  Suarez, pp. 162-63.

circulation records. Loan or circulation records provide a unique opportunity to study the social and cultural history of reading in particular local and historical contexts. They provide an insight into collective reading practices that can nonetheless be examined at an individual level, enabling a researcher to look at the relationship between individual acts and broader patterns of borrowing.

Library data is invaluable for studying communities of readers: first and foremost, because libraries are social institutions whose primary rationale is reading;[28] and, secondly, because the library is a physical space, grounded in a particular location and utilised by people living near it. In this sense libraries represent reading communities defined by physical proximity and social relationships – local readerships, readers united by friendship, working relationships, school cohorts – so library loan records enable us to examine the reading patterns of particular local communities at a particular time.

Whether we consider library records to be a historically sound form of evidence for reading history depends on how representative and/or diverse we consider library users to be. This in turn depends on the period and place being studied. In Australia, from the middle of the nineteenth century, (mostly) low-fee subscription libraries such as literary, mechanics' or arts institutes were widespread and used by people from a range of social backgrounds. They were often supported by government and thus mandated to open their reading rooms for free.[29]

The usefulness of library records as evidence for reading history also depends on our judgement of the relationship between borrowing a library book and reading it. There is not necessarily a direct relationship between borrowing and reading; we all know from experience that we sometimes borrow books we do not read, and it has been common for one library patron to borrow books for others in their family.[30] Nonetheless, there is evidence that many library patrons actually read what they borrow.[31] As well as this, borrowing indicates at least an intention to read a book, or an interest in that book at that particular place and time. In his study of library loan records in antebellum New York, Ronald Zboray suggests that library records provide evidence of broader patterns of cultural meaning and use related to reading, regardless of how direct the relationship between borrowing and reading is:

> a library charge even for another person or for a group reading demonstrates participation to at least some degree in an interpretive community. One does not have to read a book to share something of its meaning – nor should one overprivilege the solitary reader. More than reflecting individual patterns, library

---

28 Christine Pawley, 'Retrieving Readers: Library Experiences', *Library Quarterly* 76.4 (2006): 379–87 (383).

29 Peter Biskup, *Libraries in Australia* (Wagga Wagga: Centre for Information Studies, Charles Sturt University, 1995), p. 4.

30 See, for example, evidence from the Gympie Mechanics' Institute in Annette Bremer and Martyn Lyons, 'Mechanics' Institute Libraries – The Readers Demand Fiction', in Martyn Lyons and John Arnold, eds, *A History of the Book in Australia 1891–1945: A National Culture in a Colonised Market* (St Lucia: University of Queensland Press, 2001), p. 221.

31 See, for example, Emily B. Todd, 'Antebellum Libraries in Richmond and New Orleans and the Search for the Practices and Preferences of "Real" Readers', *American Studies*, 42.3 (2001): 195–209.

charge records tell of the state of knowledge in the culture as expressed amid the little community of patrons.[32]

Despite the obvious usefulness of library loans data, libraries have been an underutilised resource for historians of reading – as Christine Pawley suggested in the introduction to a special issue of *Library Quarterly* in 2006.[33] Emily Todd observes that 'library history has tended to focus on institutional histories of various libraries, not on the agency of those people who have used libraries'.[34] Priya Joshi, writing in 2002, describes the location of circulation records from public libraries as 'every book historian's dream', but adds that, to the best of her knowledge, 'these data have proven extremely elusive'.[35] The data may have remained elusive simply because in many cases library records have not survived. Where circulation records have survived, the creation of searchable databases of such records is time-consuming and the kind of project unlikely to be supported by grant-funding bodies. Where detailed databases do exist, researchers may be uncertain about how to approach such masses of data in a way that is useful for literary or book history.[36]

The studies that have been undertaken on libraries and their loan records indicate the scope and potential of this kind of data for illuminating the history of reading and, more broadly, the role of print in the history of national and international culture. Zboray, for example, uses reading patterns revealed by library loan records to challenge key cultural commonplaces and critical assumptions about American culture in the antebellum period, particularly in relation to gender. He finds little difference in borrowing patterns between women and men – women borrowed just as many titles on science, philosophy, and so on as did their male counterparts – posing a challenge to the perceived wisdom about the emergence of a 'women's sphere' in America in this period. For the same period, the reading patterns identified by Emily Todd in antebellum libraries in Richmond and New Orleans complicate 'the thesis that by the nineteenth century people always read "extensively," covering a wide range of books and authors'.[37] Her findings are echoed by Pawley in her study of library records from later in the nineteenth century. Both find that although borrowers read extensively (borrowing a wide range of books) they also showed evidence of intensive reading practices, borrowing the same books and authors repeatedly, as well as returning to them periodically over the life of the library records.[38] Pawley uses library records as part of a broader investigation of the 'social meanings of print' in a particular town in late nineteenth-century Iowa. In *Reading on the Farm*, Lydia Wevers works with a

---

32  Ronald J. Zboray, 'Reading Patterns in Antebellum America: Evidence in the Charge Records of the New York Society Library', *Libraries & Culture*, 26.2 (1991): 301–33 (305).

33  Pawley, 'Retrieving Readers'.

34  Todd, p. 196.

35  Priya Joshi, *In Another Country: Colonialism, Culture, and the English Novel in India* (New York: Columbia University Press, 2002), p. 50, cited in Dolin, 'The Secret Reading Life of Us', p. 117.

36  See Julieanne Lamond and Mark Reid, 'Squinting at a Sea of Dots: Visualising Australian Readerships Using Statistical Machine Learning', in Bode and Dixon, pp. 223–39.

37  Todd, p. 199.

38  Christine Pawley, *Reading on the Middle Border: The Culture of Print in Late-Nineteenth-Century Osage, Iowa* (Amhurst: University of Massachusetts Press, 2001), p. 96.

different body of evidence – the material books themselves of the Brancepeth farm library – to write a detailed social history which is also an examination of the relationship between reading, class, gender and subjectivity in colonial New Zealand in the Victorian period. These studies point to what reading history can do in terms of rethinking the role of print in constituting a national or local culture.

*Reading History and Library Records in Australia: What We Have and How We Might Use It*

Writing in 1988, Askew and Hubbers describe the study of reading as 'a neglected aspect of social and cultural history in Australia'.[39] Since then, we have seen important work on the history of the book and of reading by Katherine Bode, Patrick Buckridge, David Carter, Paul Eggert, Wallace Kirsop, Elizabeth Webby and others. The 2006 special issue of *Australian Literary Studies* focusing on reading indicates the interest in this area. The essays forming this special issue represent the various modes of reading history being undertaken in Australia at the moment: an interest in the reception of literature – not necessarily Australian – in Australia in the nineteenth century (Dolin, Webby, Wevers), and in the ways in which the act of reading has been framed or mediated for Australian readers in the twentieth (Bode, Buckridge, Carter).[40]

The potential of library records as a source for reading history in Australia is also beginning to be realised by both book and library historians. Buckridge, for example, has looked at the material evidence of a Tasmanian family library over time.[41] Library historians and archivists are looking at the history and records of individual institutions: Andrew Sergeant on the Braidwood Literary Institute,[42] and Peter Thompson on the Sandhurst Mechanics' Institute and Free Library in Bendigo.[43]

Australia can also claim one of the most comprehensive online sources of library circulation records in the world: the *Australian Common Reader*.[44] This database, established by Tim Dolin, is unique in providing open online access to detailed circulation records of multiple libraries, including some demographic information about individual borrowers. It collates loan records and demographic data about borrowers – such as gender and occupation – from seven Australian libraries from 1861 to 1912. This database provides unprecedented potential to study the history of reading in Australia across this period, and to consider how patterns of reading differed between women and men, different classes, and different geographical and social contexts. This could provide the basis for analysing

---

39   Askew and Hubbers, p. 111.

40   *Australian Literary Studies* 22.3 (2006).

41   Patrick Buckridge, 'Generations of Books: A Tasmanian Family Library, 1816–1994', *Library Quarterly* 76.4 (2006): 388–402.

42   Andrew Sergeant, 'To Elevate the Tone of Moral and Intellectual Attainment: The Braidwood Literary Institute and its Subscribers, 1858–1862', National Library of Australia Staff Paper, 2009.

43   Peter Thompson, '"Does It Matter If the Users are Actually Dead?": A Database to Reconnect with the Borrowers and Collection of a Hundred Year Old Library', paper presented to the 2006 VALA Conference, available at www.valaconf.org.au/vala2006/papers2006/38_Thompson_Final.pdf [accessed 16 August 2011].

44   *Australian Common Reader*, available at www.australiancommonreader.com.

how these factors (gender, class, location) have affected the reception and production of literature in Australia. The only comparable database I have encountered is *What Middletown Read*,[45] a recently established database collating loan records from 1891 to 1902 for a single library in Muncie, Indiana – a town that is widely seen to be a barometer of social trends in America.[46]

Dolin's initial work on the *Australian Common Reader* indicates its potential for illuminating how literature from 'elsewhere' was read in the specific contexts of colonial Australia.[47] He focuses on the reading of Dickens' *Great Expectations* in one of the libraries in the database, using the other texts read in common with its readers to perform a 'locally situated re-reading' of Dickens' novel.[48] This is groundbreaking work but there is much more that this database can tell us, particularly about communities of readers in Australia in this period. There is a great deal of information in this database – some 2500 readers, 7000 texts and 100 000 individual loans. How, then, might we begin locating, describing, and understanding the acts of reading that it can reveal, along with the relationships between them?

*Researching Communities of Borrowers: One Example*

In using library loan databases, Pawley, Zboray and Dolin all find ways of limiting the data to usable chunks: Pawley through focusing on particular cohorts; Zboray by sampling the data (using every tenth borrower); and Dolin by focusing on the particular libraries in overview, or by the readership of particular texts (and what else their readers have read). In using such databases to research communities of readers, I wanted to look at the data in the *Australian Common Reader* as a whole to think about how reading communities might be defined in and by the data itself – communities defined by what they read. Identifying such patterns required the use of methodologies that fall under the disciplinary umbrella of 'digital humanities.'

In this case, I collaborated with a colleague, Mark Reid, who works in a field of computer science called statistical machine learning, which involves making meaning out of very large sets of data, using statistical algorithms to summarise, model or predict from the data.[49] Two techniques we used in approaching the *Australian Common Reader* were defining similarity and creating visualisations of the data. We created graphic representations of the library loans data according to the degree of similarity between books in terms of their readers, and readers in terms of the books they have borrowed. Figure 1 is an example of such a visualisation. Each of the borrowers in one of the libraries in the database, the Lambton Mechanics' and Miners' Institute, is represented as a circle, arranged so that those which share the highest proportion of books borrowed in common are closest together. Two

---

45 *What Middletown Read*, available at www.bsu.edu/libraries/wmr/.

46 See Robert S. Lynd and Helen Merrell Lynd, *Middletown: A Study in Contemporary Culture* (New York: Harcourt, Brace, 1930); *Middletown in Transition: A Study in Cultural Conflicts* (New York: Harcourt, Brace, 1937).

47 Dolin, 'The Secret Reading Life of Us', and 'First Steps toward a History of the Mid-Victorian Novel in Colonial Australia', *Australian Literary Studies* 22.3 (2006): 273-93.

48 Dolin, 'First Steps', p. 275.

49 Lamond and Reid.

circles (readers) in close proximity indicates a high likelihood of having borrowed similar books. The size of the circles relates to the number of books the reader has borrowed, and the colour of the circle indicates the gender of that reader. Focusing on a single reader reveals the most commonly borrowed texts he or she shared with the other readers.

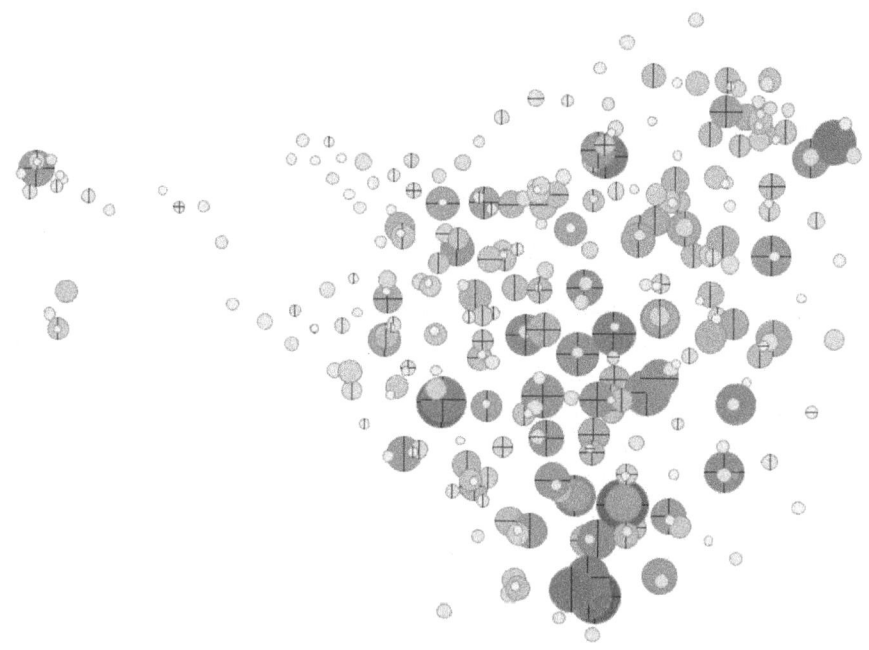

Figure 1. Viewing borrowers from Lambton Miners' and Mechanics' Institute.

This visual exploration of the data in relation to reading similarity provides a way to look at reading communities determined by the act of reading, first, and then to look beyond that to the kind of demographic detail Pawley considers. It enables us to find communities of readers who share not just one but a collection of texts in common, and then to look at the community – and the texts – in closer detail to think about the circumstances of these acts of reading.

It is here that we can start using these libraries to ask some questions that are quite specific to Australian literary history. For instance, how was the readership of Australian books affected by shifting tastes and patterns amongst Australian readers? More specific still, what can patterns of readership tell us about some hanging questions in Australian literary history, such as what became of the colonial romance?

To provide a brief example of the kind of directions in which such research could lead us, I would like to return to the writer I mentioned at the outset of this chapter: Steele Rudd. In what are now contested accounts of Australian literature at the turn of the twentieth century, Rudd might be seen to represent the kind of authentic, uniquely Australian realist writer who superseded the 'Anglo-Australian' women romance writers in the national tradition. A brief experiment with the library data reminds us that such 'realist' and 'romance' writers were actually contemporaneous, part of the same literary culture, and read by the same people.

I have marked each of the readers in the Lambton library who read the work of Rudd with a vertical line, and each of those who read Rosa Praed (an 'Anglo-Australian' romance writer) with a horizontal one. Figure 1 reveals that although there are some clusters of Rudd readers and some of Praed readers, they are not discrete readerships. This is strongly indicated by the number of readers who have read both Praed and Rudd (marked with a cross), and also these readers' proximity to one another in the visualisation. This suggests that these library patrons were reading similar books across the whole library collection, and that there were not separate sets of 'realism' and 'romance' readers – at least not across the life of this data. Closer examination reveals that many of these readers were borrowing Praed and Rudd contemporaneously; and, with a few exceptions, they were not reading Praed's Australian-set novels but those set in England, suggesting that it is not necessarily the 'Australianness' of these authors that might mark a common taste or preference amongst their readers.

The other authors the Praed and Rudd readers were most likely to have borrowed in common are E. Phillips Oppenheim, Joseph Hocking, Katherine Thurston, Annie Swan and Marie Corelli. Some of these (Oppenheim and Corelli) are unsurprising as they were bestselling writers from the period, but Hocking, Thurston and Swan (writers of adventure and domestic romances) might be said to dwell in Moretti's cultural cellars. How might we rethink both Rudd and Praed in terms of their being read as part of this, much more eclectic and not at all nationalist, literary culture?

This cursory example suggests just one way in which we might be able to use the data in the *Australian Common Reader* to re-evaluate some common assumptions about Australian literary culture in this period by testing them against what actual readers were doing. Buried in this database are social histories to be written: of individual libraries and their readers, of local reading communities, of women readers. The *Australian Common Reader* might also enable us to locate specific and distinctive patterns of readership amongst local readerships across time: to build the most detailed picture yet of how and what Australians read in this period, and the forms that their reading communities may have taken.

# 4

## Pacifying Brisbane: *The Muses' Magazine* and the 1920s

*Patrick Buckridge*

Brisbane in the 1920s certainly had its tense moments, but what has struck me most forcibly in browsing the local newspapers from the period is how successfully political and social conflicts were absorbed into the peaceful, civil and law-abiding fabric of Brisbane life. World-altering events like the Russian Revolution, the Armistice and the Treaty of Versailles, the Irish Troubles, and the rise of Mussolini were reported and discussed, in the press and elsewhere, but matters seldom went further than that despite the real potential – given the presence of significant Russian, German, Irish and Italian minorities in the city's population – for 'imported' tensions. Even the momentous political developments in Brisbane in the early 1920s, when the state government's efforts to secure foreign loans were sabotaged by an opposition-funded delegation to London, and the Premier (E.G. Theodore) forced the parliamentary Upper House to terminate its own existence, failed to polarise or fracture the community to any significant degree.[1]

In my view the civility and stability that seem to have characterised Brisbane society in the 1920s should not to be regarded (as it tends to be) as a passive state of resistance to change. It should be seen, rather, as a positive achievement in its own right, the active creation of a liberal polity that managed to balance a high level of inter-class cohesion and social harmony with a significant degree of ethnic and religious diversity. Things could certainly have been otherwise. Small as it was by comparison with Sydney and Melbourne – Brisbane's population grew from 200 000 to 300 000 in the course of the decade[2] – the city could easily have been the scene of political conflict, industrial confrontation, and inter-ethnic violence. During and immediately after the war, it was, but after that, such events stopped happening. Why?

I believe several factors – economic, political and cultural – underpinned this achievement. They included a buoyant state economy, a strong and (at least in the first half of the decade) moderately progressive Labor government, two culturally enlightened, politically compliant and popular State Governors (Sir Matthew Nathan and Sir John

---

1 Accounts of this period in Queensland history can be found in Ross Fitzgerald, *From 1915 to the Early 1980s: A History of Queensland* (St Lucia: University of Queensland Press, 1984), pp. 14–41; and Raymond Evans, *A History of Queensland* (Melbourne: Cambridge University Press, 2007), pp. 159ff. Despite their own differences of approach and emphasis, neither Fitzgerald nor Evans accords the same social, political and cultural distinctiveness to the 1920s as the present chapter proposes.

2 *ABC of Queensland and Australian Statistics 1927* (Brisbane: Registrar-General, Queensland, 1927), p. 96; *ABC of Queensland and Australian Statistics 1934* (Brisbane: Registrar-General, Queensland, 1934), p. 144.

Goodwin), a Catholic Archbishop (James Duhig) without much interest in parliamentary politics (or Irish politics), and a proliferating network of cultural and ethnic organisations. The last factor is the one I want to focus on in this chapter.

It is a surprising fact that the following organisations were all established in Brisbane during (or just before) the 1920s:

- The Lyceum Club (1919)
- The Queensland Authors and Artists Association (1921)
- The Dickens Fellowship (1921)
- The Brisbane Shakespeare Society (early 1920s)
- The Brisbane Repertory Theatre (1925)
- L'Alliance Française (Brisbane chapter, 1926)
- La Società Dante (Brisbane chapter, 1926)[3]
- El Centro Español de Queensland (1926)
- Kolonia Polska w Brisbane (Polish Club) (1927)
- The House of Israel (1927)
- The Hellenic Club of Brisbane (1927)
- Der Brisbane Goethe Bund (1927)
- Brisbana Esperanto-Societo (1927).[4]

Looking at that list we might be forgiven for thinking that not much in the way of culture can have been going on in Brisbane before World War I. This would not be quite true. As Leanne Day has shown, several literary, artistic and debating societies flourished from the 1880s and into the next century, including the Johnsonian Club, the Brisbane Literary Circle, and a handful of smaller literary, dramatic and debating societies.[5] But although a few of these early formations – the Johnsonian, the Irish Club and the Burns Club – survived well into the next century (the Queensland Irish Association is still going strong), most had disappeared by 1914. In that sense Brisbane really does seem to have had a quite sudden cultural awakening in the 1920s, one that by the middle of the decade had acquired a distinctly cosmopolitan complexion.

---

3  Not to be confused with the Dante Alighieri Society, the international organisation founded in Rome in 1889. An official branch of the DAS was set up in Sydney in 1925, but not in Brisbane until 1937. Based on the information contained in several issues of *The Muses' Magazine*, it seems clear that the 'Dante Society' that was formed in 1926 (with Archbishop Duhig as Patron, H.G. Tommerup as President, and J.J. Stable as Vice-President) was quite separate from the later DAS branch. I do not know if it still existed in 1937.

4  The list is compiled from several sources, including H.A. Tardent, 'Linguistic Study in Brisbane', *The Muses' Magazine* 11 (September 1928), p. 1, and Maximilien Brändle, ed., *Multicultural Queensland: 100 Years, 100 Communities – A Century of Contributions* (Brisbane: Multicultural Affairs Queensland, Department of the Premier and Cabinet, 2001), *passim*.

5  Leanne M. Day, 'Civilising the City: Literary Societies and Clubs in Brisbane during the 1880s and 1890s', PhD thesis (Griffith University, 2005), *passim*.

If cultural history, cultural studies and common sense have taught us anything in recent decades, it is that such processes do not happen spontaneously, whatever biological and horticultural metaphors may be used to describe and animate them, especially when they happen as fast as that. This was a piece of deliberate cultural work. Who was responsible for it? Why did they do it? How did they do it?

The first question is answerable, but complicated. The key figure in the first half of the decade was undoubtedly Joseph Jeremiah Stable. Stable was the first Professor of English at the University of Queensland, appointed to that post in 1922, having been lecturer in English, French and German for the previous ten years. More to the present purpose, he enlisted as an artillery officer in 1916, and was seconded shortly after (aged thirty-three) to the post of Chief Queensland Military Censor. In that capacity he played a controversial role in the escalating conflict between the federal and state governments over the issue of conscription: in November 1917, acting under instructions from the Prime Minister Billy Hughes, he entered the government printing office with an armed escort and confiscated copies of Hansard No. 37, the issue which contained the text of an anti-conscription speech in the Legislative Assembly by the Premier T.J. Ryan which he (Stable) had earlier censored as tending to promote civil disorder. Several violent clashes had already occurred in Brisbane between trade unionists and returned soldiers, and this episode came perilously close, as Raymond Evans has shown, to precipitating armed conflict between the state police and the army. A year or so later, Stable was again involved in the series of violent anti-Bolshevik demonstrations – the so-called Red Flag riots – which culminated in March 1919 in an attack on the Russian Hall in South Brisbane by several thousand ex-servicemen. The returned soldiers were repelled by armed mounted police and the melee ended with over a hundred men wounded by bayonets and three police horses shot.[6]

The point of this narrative is to show that Stable had seen the ugly reality of prolonged civil disorder from the inside. The left historian Raymond Evans' accounts of the anti-conscription and anti-Bolshevik riots make exciting reading; Stable is on the 'wrong' side in both conflicts, and Evans judges him accordingly. But in some respects, the judgment seems less than fair. Stable almost certainly favoured conscription and disliked Bolshevism, but there is documentary evidence – Evans cites it himself[7] – that he also deplored the reckless recourse to violence on both sides, and was unhappy at having to be involved in the Printing Office raid. As he wrote in his Censor's report a year later, in the lead-up to the Red Flag riots, 'Every second man in the street will prophesy trouble ... some talk as if

---

6  Raymond Evans, 'Conscription Riot', 'Government Printing Office, 1917', 'Red Flag Riots, 1919', in Raymond Evans and Carole Ferrier, with Jeff Rickertt, eds, *Radical Brisbane: An Unruly History* (Melbourne: Vulgar Press, 2004), pp. 156–74. See also Raymond Evans, *The Red Flag Riots: A Study of Intolerance* (St Lucia: University of Queensland Press, 1988), *passim*.

7  See, for example, Stable's urgent cable to Prime Minister Hughes on the eve of the Printing Office raid: 'Is there any way of preventing this other than by armed force?' In response, Hughes arrived in Brisbane the next day and personally directed the first of the raids by the army (Evans, *Radical Brisbane*, p. 164). There seems no doubt that Hughes, unlike Stable, was eager for violence: three days later, he responded to eggs being thrown at him during a speech in Warwick by leaping into the crowd 'reaching inside his overcoat for a revolver – fortunately left behind in another coat in the railway carriage – astonishing those watching with his "wildly infuriated manner"' (Evans, p.162).

revolution is a certainty.'⁸ It is clear that his overwhelming motive, in both conflicts, was a strong sense of civic duty, as well as a genuine desire to prevent violence if at all possible.

Seen in this perspective, the crusading zeal with which Stable masterminded the establishment of the Queensland Authors and Artists Association (QAAA) in 1921 assumes a particular significance. In the late 1940s, wags like John Blight, Val Vallis and Judith Wright might – and did – mock the stodgy old Queensland 'Horses and Arses',⁹ but in the early 1920s setting it up was a serious and ambitious attempt to co-ordinate, aggregate and magnify the power of culture to inspire, unify and – dare one say it? – *stabilise* a community which, for the last two or three years had begun to look very much as if it might be spiralling towards anarchy. What was innovative about the QAAA was precisely its breadth, the fact that unlike most such organisations it actively encouraged practitioners and consumers of all the art forms to join: painters, sculptors, architects and musicians were as welcome to the association as writers and readers, and the monthly programs of lectures and performances reflect this spread of interests.

Stable's conception of culture was generally Arnoldian, but particularly so in his view of it as a panacea for a society racked by mutual suspicions and warring factions. He certainly saw culture, in Matthew Arnold's phrase, as 'the great help out of our present difficulties'.¹⁰ He might even, I think, have agreed with Arnold that it 'seeks to do away with classes; to make the best that has been thought and known in the world current everywhere; to make all men live in an atmosphere of sweetness and light'.¹¹ To the extent, however, that the QAAA was by definition and constitution primarily interested in fostering creative practice across the arts, there were limits to how far it could realise the broader critical and intellectual functions of the Arnoldian ideal. Other, narrower organisations were able to contribute in that way, and as long as they had the ghost of an interest in literature or the arts – the Dickens Fellowship and the Brisbane Shakespeare Society, for example – Stable would be there as an office-holder or advisor. He also wrote many of the literary leaders – essentially mini-lectures in literary history – that were run every Saturday by the *Brisbane Courier*, and encouraged members of his staff to do the same. And he agitated publicly for improvements to the Public Library and the Queensland Art Gallery, both of which he considered a disgrace and an embarrassment to Queensland.¹²

What Stable achieved by the middle of the decade, through his own writing, organisational energy, and professional networking, was impressive – but while they may have been more wide-ranging, more integrated, and more urgent, his projects were not strikingly different from the cultural improvement programs promoted by Reginald Heber

---

8 Evans, p. 83.

9 Patrick Buckridge, 'Roles for Writers: Brisbane and Literature, 1859–1975', in Patrick Buckridge and Belinda McKay, eds, *By the Book: A Literary History of Queensland* (St Lucia: University of Queensland Press, 2007), p. 61.

10 Matthew Arnold in J. Dover Wilson, ed., *Culture and Anarchy*, (Cambridge: Cambridge University Press, 1960), p. 6.

11 Arnold, p. 70.

12 J.C. Mahoney, 'Stable, Jeremiah Joseph (1883–1953)', *Australian Dictionary of Biography*, vol. 12 (Carlton: Melbourne University Press, 1990), p. 42; 'Queensland Authors' and Artists' Association,' *The Muses' Magazine* 11 (September, 1928), p. 19.

Roe, the headmaster of Brisbane Grammar, in the 1890s, which blended an explicitly Arnoldian cultural idealism with the varied formats of the American Chautauquas.[13]

But at this stage – 1925 – two new players entered upon the scene, who would give the project of 'pacifying Brisbane' a new lease of life, making it livelier, more varied and more popular in its appeal than hitherto. The first was Henri Alexis Tardent (1853–1929), a Swiss-born polymath, educated in Russia, by occupation a horticulturist and former journalist, but also a linguist, scientist, art critic, philosopher and social visionary.[14] He was also the somewhat better-known 'Inky' Stephensen's maternal grandfather.[15]

Tardent had emigrated with his family to Queensland in 1887, and he lived and worked in various parts of the state, from Atherton to Toowoomba, ending up in Wynnum on the outskirts of Brisbane by the early 1920s. 'Wherever he lived', Maurice French observes, 'he helped to establish societies with musical, literary, scientific or agricultural interests'.[16] Part of that entrepreneurial streak was his ability to cultivate close relations with political and cultural elites: he was on familiar terms with Sir Samuel Griffith, with the former Prime Minister Andrew Fisher, and, importantly, with Sir Matthew Nathan, the State Governor from 1920 to 1925, who was an active supporter of many of Tardent's initiatives.

One of Tardent's abiding enthusiasms – hardly surprisingly, given his own background – was the promotion of European languages and cultures in Queensland, which he realised through his leading or enabling roles in the formation of most of the ethnic cultural organisations listed earlier – French, German, Italian, Greek, Polish, Spanish and Jewish – all of which sprang into being in 1926–27. Another enthusiasm was the future of Queensland's home-grown literary, artistic and musical culture, a subject on which he was irrepressibly bullish, and on which he dilated in his own books on individual Queensland painters and poets, and in his work, with Stable and the QAAA, on the annual Authors' Week programs in Brisbane. His love of horticulture provided him with a large inventory of optimistic metaphors for the variegated outgrowths of culture he saw all around him in the rich soil and temperate climate of sunny Queensland. But Tardent had a particular love of music; and this is where the third key figure enters the picture.

Luis Amadeo Parés (1893–1948), the son of a Catalonian father and an Australian mother, grew up in Mareeba, left school after eighth grade and started taking classes from the local violin teacher at the age of sixteen. A year later, he moved to Bowen to stay with his uncle Amadee, 'a Belgian musician of great ability' who refined his technique by 'overwhelming him with satire' at every opportunity, starting with his 'treacherous vibrato': 'That horrible gna-an-see-orr with which you begin each bow stroke begets notes shaped like giant tadpoles and about as attractive'.[17] Partly in retreat from such stern medicine, Luis and a friend set off through the mining towns and pastoral districts of northern,

---

13  E. Clarke, 'Roe, Reginald Heber (1850–1926)', *Australian Dictionary of Biography*, vol. 11 (Carlton: Melbourne University Press, 1988), pp. 437–39; Day, 'Civilising the City', pp. 26–69.

14  M. French, 'Tardent, Henry Alexis (1853–1929)', *Australian Dictionary of Biography*, vol. 12, pp. 167–68.

15  Craig Munro, *Inky Stephenson: Wild Man of Letters* (St Lucia: University of Queensland Press, 1992), pp. 4–5.

16  French, 'Tardent', p. 168.

17  Luis Amadeo Parés, *I Fiddled the Years Away* (Brisbane: s.n., 1943), p. 34.

central and western Queensland, alternately labouring and performing music, in cinemas, theatres, town halls, schools of arts and hotels, often with travelling vaudeville troupes such as the Forti Vaudeville Company and the Luzbel Brothers. Life on the road took its toll: after five years he had a nervous breakdown, and in 1919 married Sarah Lynch, began a family, and eventually kept a promise he had made to himself years before by moving to Sydney in 1921 to study privately with Cyril Monk, the eminent Australian violinist at the Sydney Conservatorium.[18]

He returned to Queensland, and after a short and miserable stay in Bundaberg and Maryborough, decided his destiny lay in Brisbane; so on 31 May 1923, he arrived with his wife and two young children at Brunswick Station 'with funds enough to provide a flat and food for a week', and proceeded to look for work. At one of his first engagements, a concert at the Manly and Wynnum Choral Society, he met Henri Tardent. And as he put it in his chaotic, often hilarious memoir of 1943, *I Fiddled the Years Away*, Tardent 'attracted me as a magnet draws steel ... a man of Pythagorean wisdom ... another Abou Ben Adhem, who backed his love for his fellow man by a life of service and self-abnegation'. He became 'a dynamic force at my back', encouraging 'the idea of creating a local habitation for music, art and letters in the city ... thus was established the Hall of the Muses'.[19]

It is not quite clear from Parés' account just whose idea the Hall of the Muses was. It was certainly Tardent's type of project, but Parés was himself extremely well read, and possessed of a lively intellect and wide cultural interests: his dozens of letters to the *Brisbane Courier* over three years (1923–26) provide ample evidence of this, ranging as they do (with considerable eloquence and sophistication) from the history of violin technique to the relations between art and commerce, beauty and truth, ideals and realisation, the nature of contentment, the evolutionary functions of the nervous system, and many other matters.[20] He would certainly have been an equal partner in the enterprise with Tardent, and in any case, with his flair for publicity, the ideal front-man.

The Hall of the Muses was established in late 1925, first in Little Roma Street, and later in slightly larger premises at 323 George Street in the centre of the city. It consisted of 'a miniature concert hall, a few studies, an office, an attic, passage way and staircases, all heaped up in each others' way'.[21] Here Parés conducted his violin lessons, provided meeting rooms for several clubs and societies, and a refuge for a varied collection of impoverished European bohemians and wanderers, mostly musical: the cleaner, Victor Scalabrini, occasional singer in Parés' operatic concerts on 4QG, a radio show stationed in Brisbane; Professor Vladimir Elin, from Petrograd by way of Siam and the Philippines, a fine baritone who used the hall to conduct voice coaching classes, and 'to conceal his mistresses from a wronged and irate Siamese spouse'; another Russian singer, Madame Kassovskaia, who claimed to have fought at the head of Kornilov's White Army as the 'Russian Joan of Arc', and who strode the streets of Brisbane in white Cossack boots and a flowery exotic robe; a Hungarian doctor, a Swedish nobleman, a French count (Comte

---

18  Parés, p. 61.

19  Parés, p. 79.

20  *Brisbane Courier*, 15 November 1923, p. 13; 6 November 1924, p. 12; 22 May 1924, p. 16; 4 July 1925, p. 12; 10 July 1924, p. 12; 19 June 1924, p. 13.

21  Parés, p. 106.

Gontran de Tournouer), and a brilliant young Swiss philosopher and painter whom Parés employed as an amanuensis in return for board at his home in Manly.[22] During this period the hall also served, extraordinarily, as the Queensland Bolivian Consulate, Parés having accepted the temporary post of Acting Consul for the Republic of Bolivia in October 1927, on the Comte De Tournouer's recommendation. During the year and a half of his tenure, several consular receptions were hosted there, but only one Bolivian subject was assisted, an Irishman named Murphy.[23]

The premises were also capacious enough to mount regular cultural events of a less fantastic kind – concerts, exhibitions, readings, and even plays – and to do it comfortably enough to accommodate the Governor or Lieutenant-Governor and his party, who attended several such events, including the inaugural one. Here Parés describes some of the activities on that occasion:

> An Evening with the Muses in the presence of Vice-Royalty, at which nine talented ladies represented the Parnassian sisters, made an auspicious opening to the rooms. Later, in an effort to unite the cultivated people of the various races residing in Brisbane, I arranged an evening at which polished addresses were delivered in thirteen respective languages and afterwards redelivered in English. Here too, as time went on, art displays were held, recitals were given, and Spanish, French, Italian and German literary clubs were domiciled.[24]

The yoking together of classical iconography, 'cultivation', and polyglot ethnic diversity – naive as it sounds in Parés' account – hints at a complex cultural strategy for neutralising the threat of social conflict inherent in ethnic difference by 'performing' it in exclusively cultural and linguistic forms. These differences are implicitly paralleled, and further distanced and harmonised by the unity-in-multiplicity of the Nine Muses. It is a novel, if somewhat erudite-seeming, strategy, but it has a certain logic and coherence and it does represent an important extension and enrichment of the Anglocentric pacification project Stable had initiated a few years earlier.

If the establishment of the Hall of the Muses was essentially a collaboration between Tardent and Parés, the next stage in the process was all Parés' work. Every few months since early 1925, he had been presenting musical concerts and soirées in venues in and around Brisbane, including the Elite Theatre in Toowong, the Theatre Royal in the city, the Sandgate and Ipswich town halls, and several others. These events featured soloists, both instrumental and vocal, some verse recitations, and orchestral pieces by Parés' own violin students, performing in groups of seventy or more. The audiences sometimes included governors, state politicians, mayors, judges, and senior academics such as Professor Stable and Dr F.W. Robinson of the English Department, many of them present, no doubt, with the active encouragement of the well-connected Tardent, who – with his wife and daughter – was a regular attendee and occasional performer.[25] In September 1927, after

---

22  Parés, p. 110.
23  Parés, pp. 83–86. See also *Brisbane Courier*, 13 March 1929, p. 16.
24  Parés, p. 80.
25  Reports on some of these events can be found in the *Brisbane Courier*, 7 February 1925, p. 5; 2 May

seven months of intensive recruitment, arrangement and rehearsal, Parés mounted and conducted a remarkable concert in the then Exhibition Hall (now the Old Museum) – a very large space, as it needed to be to accommodate the 1300 violinists, most of them schoolchildren, who performed, on three successive nights, a short program comprising an original composition by Parés (a lullaby, arranged in two parts), followed by the march from Wagner's *Tannhäuser*.[26] Against many expectations, the '1000 Violins Ensemble' as it was called was a resounding success. It received enthusiastic reviews in all three Brisbane dailies and the *Queenslander*, and admiring notices in music journals in Britain, France and the United States; some overseas reviewers had even been able to listen in to a short-wave broadcast of the concert by 4QG. Parés himself was in ecstasies at what he later described as 'the vast, ocean-like waves of music that swelled and sped away like swishing water'.[27]

But for others, the most sublime aspect of what the Brisbane *Daily Mail* called 'one of the most outstanding events in the history of music in Brisbane' was its demonstration of the sheer power, not just of the instrumental effect but of the Maestro himself. The Brisbane *Telegraph* put it quite baldly: 'Mr Parés has to his credit the remarkable performance of having controlled approximately 1000 violinists.'[28] But a Mr E.A. Francis ('Fanuel') may have captured his Promethean magnificence more justly in the following verses. (Parés certainly thought so, and quoted them in his memoir):

> A thousand notes that spread a cadence sweet,
> A thousand echoes tremble to the skies,
> A thousand souls awake to art and greet
> The God within their eyes.
>
> And on the stage a towering rugged shade –
> With dream-filled eyes and eager nervous beat,
> The Maestro guides the rhythm he has made
> To God's divine retreat.[29]

The excitement and interest the event generated made Parés something of a celebrity in Brisbane for a time, not just because of its spectacular scale and originality, but also because in the six months leading up to the event he offered free violin tuition to as many beginners as were prepared to commit themselves to a regimen of training for the great ensemble.[30] The gesture won him great kudos, and was remembered in his obituary twenty-one years

---

1925, p. 17; 6 May 1925, p. 12; 19 September 1925, p. 11.

26  The score of the lullaby, *La Cuna* [The Cradle Song], composed by L.A. Parés, with words by C.A. Neville, can be viewed online in the State Library of Queensland collection.

27  Parés, p. 93.

28  Both comments are quoted in the first issue of *The Muses' Magazine* 1 (November 1927), p. 32.

29  Parés, p. 95. The poem was also published in *The Muses' Magazine* 4 (February 1928), p. 16.

30  It was not totally original. A similar attempt had been made in England in 1911, resulting in a performance by over 1000 schoolchildren at the Crystal Palace, London. (On that occasion, however, as the *Courier* pointed out, the children were all 'pupils of teachers who were paid for their services', which served to highlight Parés' generosity and vision: *Brisbane Courier*, 5 March 1927, p. 26.)

later.[31] Parés himself saw the success of the concert as a vindication of the 'super-optimism' that was the keynote of his personality. But it was also a financial bonanza: most of the 6000 tickets printed were sold and this, with the commission he received from the Queen Street music retailer W.H. Palings & Co. on the sale of four hundred new violins, brought his gross income for the year to £1600.[32] Much of this was ploughed into various projects associated with the Hall of the Muses, and in particular a new publication, *The Muses' Magazine*, which made its first appearance in November 1927, just three months after the 'Grand Concert'.

*The Muses' Magazine* described itself, on the masthead, as 'A monthly review of the musical, artistic, literary, and intellectual life of Queensland', and Parés' opening editorial presented it as a stimulus to the innate creativity, intellectuality and talent of Queenslanders:

> The most casual observer could not fail to notice that there is a rejoicing awakening in the intellectual, musical and artistic life of Queensland. Although materialistic pursuits are predominant in our hustling modern civilization, there is nevertheless in our midst a very fair proportion of intellectual workers, who keep proudly flying the flag of idealism. Talent abounds in our people, although up to now it has received but scanty recognition and encouragement. It truly seems as if our sunny skies and pellucid atmosphere were, like those of ancient Greece, favourable to the production of talent. To the solid qualities inherited from our vigorous ancestral stock, we add something new: the cheerfulness, the *joie de vivre*, so characteristic of the nations living in sunny lands.

The cheery opening note of Queensland exceptionalism modulates seamlessly into a celebration of national scientific and technological modernity, an insistence on 'our' world-historical entitlements ('As a young nation we claim access to all the civilizations and literatures that have preceded us ... '), and a proper reverence for the institution that secured that access and disseminated its fruits:

> Our young University is a fecund nursery of energetic and learned professors, who are not only able exponents of the sciences which they are teaching, but take also a very active part in the intellectual life of the community.

But the magazine's central claim – like that of the Hall of the Muses which gave birth to it – was that it gave a voice to Brisbane's contemporary cultural diversity, a claim that was borne out in the list of contributors to this and subsequent issues, but also in the list of affiliated organisations on the front cover, to which the editor drew special attention:

> A glance on the cover of this Magazine will disclose the fact that among all the Australian cities Brisbane has the largest number of societies devoted to the study of foreign languages and literatures.[33]

---

31 *Brisbane Courier*, 4 May 1948, p. 4.
32 Parés, p. 90.
33 *The Muses' Magazine* 1 (November 1927), n.p. [1].

The cover does not in fact exactly substantiate this slightly surprising claim (though it may be true), but among the affiliates it does list six organisations of that kind (French, German, Greek, Italian, Spanish and Jewish), and these were later joined by the Polish and Esperanto societies. The value placed upon the multicultural aspiration was the important thing, and it certainly radiated an attitude not just of tolerance, but of interest and enthusiasm, towards non Anglo-Celtic cultures and languages.

*The Muses' Magazine* ran for only fourteen monthly issues, from November 1927 to January 1929, but in its short life it exhibited several remarkable features. It was quite lavishly produced, with up to half a dozen colour reproductions of botanical paintings, by (the late) Ellis Rowan and by Phoebe Kirwan, among others. This partly reflected Tardent's interests (he had written a book on Rowan); but women were also strongly represented in their own right as authors, especially poets. Every issue contained poems and essays by the best-known Queensland poets of the day, most of whom were women – Mabel Forrest, Emily Bulcock, E.M. England, Annie Powis Dunn, Margaret Curran and Doris Waraker – and some original poems in untranslated Italian, German, Greek and French. About halfway through its run, the magazine opened a special poetry section called 'The Pages of Calliope and Erato' (the Muses of epic and lyric poetry), edited from Canberra by R.A. Broinowski, Usher of the Black Rod in the Australian Senate, which attracted nationwide and even some overseas contributions. In most issues there was also an original ode to one of the Muses (again helping to reinforce the magazine's founding trope) by the eminent translator of classical Chinese poetry, W.J.B. Fletcher, then British Consul at Hoihow (Haikou) in China. Like the women poets, he contributed essays as well, mainly on Chinese subjects.

Most of the content, in fact, consisted of essays – many of them quite scholarly, but appropriately pitched for a well-read general readership – on a range of topics, from the great European literatures (Russian, German, French, Italian – but also the less familiar: Finnish, Swedish, modern Greek, ancient Chinese); to art, architecture and society; to literature, philosophy and psychology; to recent, modern and ancient history; to science (particularly botany, meteorology and astronomy); and to much else. Inigo Jones, the long-range weather forecaster, appeared in more than half the issues. Like Henri Tardent, Jones was a polymath, and his essays dealt, engagingly enough, with rainbows, planets, and sunspots on the one hand, and Dickens, Shakespeare and Rosa Praed on the other.

All this is cheerfully presented in the name of cosmopolitan cultivation; but at several points the more sensitive motive of postwar pacification is also acknowledged, and the need to use universal culture to counteract the postwar residues of bitterness and suspicion. H.G. Tommerup, a lecturer in German at the university, in speaking of the role of 'foreign associations'[1] like the newly established Goethe Bund, expresses this awkwardly but revealingly:

> There is still a great deal of misunderstanding about them ['foreign associations'] in our midst, and consequently prejudice against them. Those at any rate which profess to be 'cultural' – i.e. absolutely nonpolitical – are really British, and not foreign. A foreign language is of course also spoken at their meetings: but so too is English: and if a foreign language is taught there, so is English also. Alien 'purpose' does not, strictly speaking, exist: alien thought is studied, and alien

sympathy is aroused, but only for the purpose of bringing a better understanding and a friendlier feeling.[34]

Even more noticeable than the multiculturalism of the magazine is its preoccupation with music. In one way, this is hardly surprising. Parés himself was first and foremost a practising musician, after all, and he ensured that the music scene in Brisbane was comprehensively covered. But the 'musicality' of the magazine is not just a matter of the many reviews of musical events in every issue. It also has to do with the large number of historical, analytical and speculative articles about music (by George Sampson, Parés himself, Jerome Bell, Stefan de Polotynski and several anonymous academics), the snappy paragraphs of interesting musical facts and thoughts (technical, historical and philosophical), the plethora of music retailing advertisements, and the reproduction of the *Queenslander*'s flashlight photograph of the '1000 Violins' concert on the back flyleaf of every issue. And it has to do with a certain 'musicalisation' of the discourse of the whole journal, such that even essays and stories about non-musical subjects somehow contrive to focus on their musical aspects, or to consider them from a quasi-musical point of view. Stable's first article in the first issue, 'Music in Poetry', and Mabel Forrest's prose piece 'Bush Music' in the first issue are straightforward examples,[35] but there are other, more oblique instances: Tardent on the contemporary use of English, for example, where the degradation of language is analysed in terms of the corruption of musical taste.[36] Short stories (by E.M. England and Annie Powis Dunn), travel pieces, botanical essays, art appreciations, historical narratives and poems mostly seem able to find musical angles, analogies or just metaphors with noticeable frequency. It is almost as if the contributors were responding to an expectation that they should all at least try, in whatever way they could, to 'aspire to the condition of music'.

What impulse lies behind this tendency to integrate the social and cultural diversity of Brisbane through the lens of music? When placed in the context of an ongoing project to pacify Brisbane, to acknowledge, celebrate, but above all harmonise the class and ethnic differences that had proved threatening to civil order less than ten years earlier, the rationale is obvious: as William Congreve put it, 'Music has charms to soothe the savage breast'.[37] Since ancient times philosophers have believed that music can work as an instrument for producing both individual and social harmony, and in 1926 Frank Howes, the regular music critic of the London *Times*, published a book that sought to ground that belief in a modern psychological analysis of emotional responses to music and of the nature of musical pleasure.[38] The later issues of the *The Muses' Magazine* are liberally sprinkled

---

34 H.G. Tommerup, 'In Aid of Culture,' *The Muses' Magazine* 1 (November 1927), p. 26.

35 *The Muses' Magazine* 1 (November 1927), pp. 3ff., 6ff.

36 *The Muses' Magazine* 2 (December 1927), p. 1.

37 The phrase (often misquoted with 'beast' instead of 'breast') comes from William Congreve's tragedy, *The Mourning Bride*, act I, scene 1.

38 Both Tardent and Parés evince a keen interest in the psychology of musical experience. In addition to the 'morceaux' from Frank Howes' book, there is a similar number of quotations on the same subject by the aesthetician Vernon Lee (Violet Paget). Lee's chief work on the psychology of music, however, first appeared in 1932, and the source for the many quotations from her work in 1928 is something of a mystery.

with disconnected 'morceaux' (so called) taken directly from Howes' book, *The Borderland of Music and Psychology* – clearly a recent enthusiasm of Parés – in which these matters are explored in a straightforward and engaging style.[39]

The following passage, which deals with the meaning of applause, is one of about half a dozen that appeared:

> The amount of applause after any number in a concert programme is determined not by the depth of feeling or the intensity of the pleasure experienced by the audience but by the homogeneity of the feeling, i.e. by the number of persons who experience a similar enthusiasm for the same piece of music. Hearty applause indicates that some considerable amount of group feeling has been generated, and must not be regarded as a sign of any profound stirring of emotion, still less of the delivery of a critical judgment on the listeners' part. The truth of this statement may be confirmed by a consideration of the kind of music which receives most applause.[40]

These and other passages from Howes' book focus on the group dimension of the musical experience, and when juxtaposed with other 'morceaux' drawn from contemporary studies of crowd behaviour, such as Gustave Bon's *The Crowd* (1922), evince a strong impulse on Parés' part to think through in quite sophisticated ways the relevance of music itself, and of musical models and analogies, to an understanding of social and political behaviour. Bon's discussion of charismatic 'hero effects' in crowd contexts includes observations such as:

> The crowd cannot get on without a hero in the sense of a representative man, and upon him, who is thus only a personification of itself, it pours out its veneration. And so when at a concert a popular contralto sings a song of the kind which is itself a crowd-phenomenon, she becomes the idol of the audience, the crowd-representative, upon whom all its thwarted self-esteem descends in the form of hero-worship.[41]

It is difficult not to suspect that such an analysis would have struck Parés as fairly directly applicable to his own recent performances as maestro of the thousand violins, except that, where Gustave Bon's language conveys a critical perspective on the phenomenon, Parés, at least by implication, seems to offer it rather as a benevolent emotional substitute for mass disorder and violence. The iconic significance of the photograph of the Grand Ensemble for the whole project of *The Muses' Magazine* thus becomes clearer, if also, in retrospect, a little worrying in its ideological tendency.

If, as that last sentence intends to hint, the social perspective of the magazine was informed, at least in its later issues, by a certain streak of 'proto-fascism', it would not be a surprising finding. The last few issues published several articles of a eugenicist tendency

---

39  Frank Howes, *The Borderland of Music and Psychology* (London: Kegan Paul & Co., 1926). For Howes' career see Diana McVeagh, 'Howes, Frank Stewart (1891–1974)', *Oxford Dictionary of National Biography* (Oxford: Oxford University Press, 2004).

40  *The Muses' Magazine* 12 (November–December 1928), n.p.

41  *The Muses' Magazine* 12 (November–December 1928), n.p.

(J.P. Lowson on the treatment of delinquency, for example),[42] and Mussolini is referred to several times in neutral or favourable terms.[43] It is clear, more broadly, that the regular authors constitute an elite of sorts – a cultural and intellectual elite rather than a social or political one, though inevitably there is some overlap: several of the senior academic contributors (Professors Stable, Michie and Cumbrae-Stewart, for example) turned up at Government House levees, as did some of the non-Anglo contributors (such as Christie Freeleagus and the Comte de Tournouer), since they held diplomatic posts of one kind or another. It is, in short, the kind of group – culturally diverse though it certainly was – to whom benevolent, but (in hindsight) identifiably proto-fascist solutions to the problem of social disorder came fairly naturally.

The whole enterprise came to an end rather abruptly. Parés asserts in his memoir that trumpeting the success of their first year in the first issue of their second brought his creditors down upon him, forcing him into bankruptcy.[44] That may be true – and the proceedings against him in the Bankruptcy Court seem to confirm it[45] – but an equally disabling event would probably have been Tardent's worsening health. He died in September 1929, and the 'Muses' phenomenon, both hall and magazine, seem to have died with him. Whether the 'super-optimism' of its mission would have survived the sharpened class conflicts of the Great Depression and the rise of Hitler is in any case doubtful.

---

42  *The Muses' Magazine* 2 Second Year (December 1928), p.17. The first eleven issues (November 1927 – September 1928) are designated 'First Year, No. 1–11' on the front covers. The twelfth issue appeared in November and is jointly designated as 'No. 12 – First Year & No. 1 – Second Year / October–November 1928'. The last two issues, which appeared in December and January, are designated 'No. 2 – Second Year / December, 1928' and 'No. 3 – Second Year / January, 1929'.

43  For example, H.G. Tommerup, 'In Aid of Culture', *The Muses' Magazine* 1 (November 1927), p. 26. It remains true, however, that the Brisbane Dante Society of the 1920s, of which Tommerup was President, was not engaged in cultural activities in support of the fascist regime, which the Sydney branch of the Dante Alighieri Society was, and which its Brisbane branch, under the Presidency of Sir Raphael Cilento, would later be (see note 3). Some pro-fascist political and cultural activity had gone on in Brisbane in the late 1920s, but it was under the auspices of the Italo-Australian Society formed in 1925 by Fr Ernesto Coppo. See Gianfranco Cresciani, *Fascism, Anti-Fascism and Italians in Australia 1922–1945* (Canberra: ANU Press, 1980), pp. 9–10. This organisation had no links with the Hall of the Muses or the magazine, but in its third issue the magazine did publish an article on Siena by the newly appointed Italian Vice-Consul to Brisbane, Count Gabrio di San Marzano: see *The Muses' Magazine* 3 (January 1928), pp. 16–17.

44  Parés, p. 96.

45  *Brisbane Courier*, 13 March 1929, p. 16.

# 5

## Books and Debate About the Australian Government's Policies Towards Asylum Seekers

*Jan Zwar*

Arguably the most divisive Australian policy debate in the 2000s has been about our country's treatment of asylum seekers, particularly those arriving at Australia's shores by boat. It became a political touchpoint when the MV *Tampa*, a Norwegian freighter, rescued 438 people – who were headed to claim asylum in Australia – from a sinking boat on 26 August 2001. The Australian Government's refusal to accept the asylum seekers onshore proved politically popular and the September 11 attacks on the World Trade Centre in New York further compounded the anti-Muslim sentiment – many asylum seekers in the 2000s were from Afghanistan, Iraq and Iran.

The debate over the treatment of asylum seekers was also notable for the intervention of authors and publishers, including the writers' organisation PEN:

> Among intellectual and artistic elites, condemnation of the government's policies and practices in relation to refugees has been almost unanimous, activism on behalf of asylum-seekers is wide-spread, and the output of literary, artistic, journalistic and academic works which engage with these issues, generally from a highly critical perspective, has grown to massive proportions.[1]

Despite this, accounts of asylum–seeker activism during this period do not emphasise the significance of books. For example, Anne Coombs, one of the founders of Rural Australians for Refugees (RAR), emphasised the centrality of email technology in mobilising Australians: 'RAR could never have grown into a movement as quickly or as geographically dispersed as it is without email.'[2] Coombes also recounted the valuable contributions of writers in local regional communities, not through writing books, but by writing letters to politicians, local councils and to regional newspapers, supporting the formation of local activist groups, and working on submissions for the release of detainees. Perhaps books were not mentioned because the focus of her article lay elsewhere, but she was not the only person to give an account of activism from which books were absent. In her book *Blind Conscience*, an account of asylum–seeker activism published in 2008, ABC TV *Lateline* journalist Margot O'Neill emphasised the impact of ABC *Four Corners* and *Lateline*

---

[1] Wenche Ommundsen, 'In the Wake of the Tampa: Multiculturalism, Cultural Citizenship and Australian Refugee Narratives', in C.I. Armstrong and Ø. Hestetun, eds, *Postcolonial Dislocations: Travel, History, and the Ironies of Narrative* (Oslo: Novus Press, 2006), pp. 23–24.

[2] Anne Coombes, 'Mobilising Rural Australia', *Griffith Review* 3 (2004): 123–35.

episodes, *Daily Telegraph* and other newspaper feature articles, radio talkback, protests by activists, and the work of small-l liberal parliamentarians. The body of her text does not consider the impact of books but, importantly, in her book's acknowledgements, she pays tribute to 'other authors who blazed the trail and whose material and insights were fundamental, like Peter Mares in *Borderline*, and David Marr and Marian Wilkinson in their brilliant *Dark Victory*'.[3]

Clearly, radio, television, newspapers, email, the internet, writers' festivals, public meetings, and grassroots activism all played significant roles. This chapter does not seek to engage in a debate about the relative importance of respective players. Rather, it considers further the empirical traces left by books that were written and published about this debate, focusing mostly on the years 2003 to 2008 – and at times more broadly – to examine the role of the books in creating a public sphere for community debate about these issues.

In this research, empirical records in the media, academia, and Federal Parliament were examined for traces of books in narrative nonfiction genres – such as biography, autobiography, essay, memoir, and extended journalism – intended to contribute to the public debate. There are both strengths and weaknesses in this approach. The obvious strength is that rather than asserting that books played a role in public debates and drawing upon anecdotal evidence to justify this, empirical mapping locates data to support this assertion, and even identifies patterns from which inferences can be drawn. The most obvious weakness is that books play into public consciousness in many intangible ways: through conversations about them, or their symbolic use as an authoritative source, or through individual reader experiences that are not recorded. Therefore, this is not a holistic portrait but rather an investigation into one aspect of books as a 'republic of letters' in recent political history.

Nielsen BookScan top 5000 nonfiction sales data for the period 2003–2008 were examined to identify books that directly addressed the debate. Established in Australia in 2001, some publishers have observed that, in its early years of operation, Nielsen BookScan sales data under-represented sales of books that were more likely to be sold in independent and other specialised bookstores, particularly the types of books addressing serious public issues. The figures in this chapter should therefore be regarded as conservative. Twenty-one titles were found, of which three were reprints (sometimes updated) of existing works.[4]

---

3  Margot O'Neill, *Blind Conscience* (Sydney: UNSW Press, 2008), p. vii.

4  Cola Bilkuei, *Cola's Journey: From Sudanese Child Soldier to Australian Refugee* (Sydney: Macmillan, 2008); Linda Briskman, Christopher R. Goddard and Susie Latham, *Human Rights Overboard: Seeking Asylum in Australia* (Carlton North: Scribe Publishing, 2008); Margot O'Neill, *Blind Conscience* (Sydney: UNSW Press, 2008); Anne Tiernan, *Power without Responsibility: Ministerial Staffers in Australian Governments from Whitlam to Howard* (Sydney: UNSW Press, 2007); Mahboba Rawi with Vanessa Mickan-Gramazio, *Mahboba's Promise: How One Woman Made a World of Difference* (Sydney: Bantam Books, 2005); Julianne Schultz, ed., 'People Like Us', *Griffith Review* 8 (Meadowbrook: Griffith University, 2005); Tony Kevin, *A Certain Maritime Incident: The Sinking of* Siev X (Carlton North: Scribe Publications, 2004); Sandra Lee, *Guzin Najim's the Promise: An Iraqi Mother's Desperate Flight to Freedom* (Sydney: Bantam Books, 2004); Heather Millar, Eva Sallis and Sonja Dechian, *Dark Dreams: Australian Refugee Stories* (Kent Town: Wakefield Press, 2004); Klaus Neumann, *Refuge Australia: Australia's Humanitarian Record* (Sydney: UNSW Press, 2004); Peter Singer and Tom Gregg, *How Ethical Is Australia? An Examination of Australia's Record as a Global Citizen* (Melbourne: The Australian Collaboration in conjunction with Black Inc., 2004); Meaghan Amor and Janet Austin, eds, *From*

Some titles sold very well. *Borderline*, by Peter Mares, was first published in 2001 before the *Tampa* stand-off and was reprinted three times in 2001–2002, selling approximately 8000 copies in total, a bestseller for a work of serious Australian nonfiction.[5] *Dark Victory* by David Marr and Marian Wilkinson sold over 25 000 copies; and *Guzin Najim's the Promise* by Sandra Lee over 10 000. 'Sending Them Home', part of the *Quarterly Essay* series published by Black Inc., sold over 5000 copies in 2004 in addition to its subscriber base: another bestseller for works of this type.[6] Finally, *A Certain Maritime Incident* by Tony Kevin, released in 2004, sold out its initial print run of 4000 in one year.[7] Therefore, a number of policy-oriented books generated particularly strong sales from 2002–2004.

Another significant reading pattern was the popularity of life narratives of Arab and Muslim women, which were known as 'lifting the veil' in the publishing industry. Over 750 000 copies of these types of books were sold, worth over $20 million,[8] from 2003–2008. Although these types of books are deserving of a study on their own,[9] for the purposes of this chapter examining debate about Australia's asylum-seeker policies, three which are by or about Australian women are included here: *Guzin Najim's the Promise: An Iraqi Mother's Desperate Flight to Freedom* by Sandra Lee (2004), an updated edition of *Caravanserai* by Hanifa Deen (2003) eight years after its original publication, and *Mahboba's Promise: How One Woman Made a World of Difference* by Mahboba Rawi (2005). Other titles in this sub-genre proved to be fraudulent (*Forbidden Love: A Harrowing True Story of Love and Revenge in Jordan* by Norma Khouri, and *Burned Alive* by Souad[10]), but no such scandal

---

*Nothing to Zero: Letters from Refugees in Australia's Detention Centres* (Melbourne: Lonely Planet, 2003); Frank Brennan, *Tampering with Asylum: A Universal Humanitarian Problem* (St Lucia: University of Queensland Press, 2003); Hanifa Deen, *Caravanserai*, rev. edn (Fremantle: Fremantle Arts Centre Press, 2003 [1995]); Robert Manne and David Corlett, 'Sending Them Home: Refugees and the New Politics of Indifference', *Quarterly Essay* 13 (Melbourne: Black Inc., 2003); David Marr and Marian Wilkinson, *Dark Victory* (Sydney: Allen & Unwin, 2003); Sandy Thorne, *Beyond the Razor Wire: Is Australia, Where Everything's Free: The True Story of a Detention Officer's Experiences at Woomera and Curtin Illegal Immigrant Camps and at a Queensland Maximum Security Prison* (Lightning Ridge: S. Thorne, 2003); Heather Tyler, *Asylum: Voices Behind the Razor Wire* (South Melbourne: Lothian, 2003); Peter Mares, *Borderline: Australia's Response to Refugees and Asylum Seekers in the Wake of the* Tampa (Sydney: UNSW Press, 2001). There were two editions of *Dark Victory* and *Guzin's Promise* in this period. (*Borderline* is counted as one title because one edition appeared in the 2003–2008 dataset.)

5 One edition of *Borderline* is counted as part of the 2003–2008 total of books.

6 Mungo MacCallum's *Quarterly Essay*, 'Girt by Sea: Australia, the Refugees and the Politics of Fear' was published in 2002, for which sales figures are not available; however, it was reprinted as part of a collection of four *Quarterly Essays* in 2006 and sold an additional several thousand copies.

7 Tony Kevin, 'Asking Awkward Questions: The Uncomfortable Terrain of Moral Dissent', talk delivered at the National Library of Australia, 11 May 2008, Canberra ACT Refugee Action Committee, available at www.refugeeaction.org/tony_kevin.html [accessed 30 November 2011].

8 Australian dollars adjusted for inflation to 2009 values.

9 See Gillian Whitlock's *Soft Weapons: Autobiography in Transit* (Chicago: University of Chicago Press, 2007).

10 Norma Khouri, *Forbidden Love: A Harrowing True Story of Love and Revenge in Jordan* (Milsons Point: Bantam Books, 2003); Souad, *Burned Alive: A Victim of the Law of Men* (North Sydney, Bantam Books, 2005). For information about this latter, less well-known hoax see www.smh.com.au/news/Books/Historian-challenges-Palestinian-bestseller/2005/04/12/1113251628102.html.

was associated with these titles and Mahboba Rawi was made a member of the Order of Australia in 2010 for her humanitarian work, which was described in her book.[11]

Overall, though, most of the books identified sold 3000 copies or less, and in many cases fewer than 1000 copies, according to the Nielsen BookScan data.[12] However, closer analysis reveals a variety of ways in which they contributed to public discourse.

*The Media*

For the empirical searches in this and the following sections, a list was compiled comprising the relevant Nielsen BookScan top 5000 nonfiction titles 2003–2008, some key books published in 2002, and a small number of other significant books. Unfortunately, the data recording mentions of case-study books on talkback radio and television were not available from a public or commercial data agency. Therefore, after considering several sources of media mentions,[13] the decision was made to use Factiva to trace newspaper mentions. The following books appeared in the Factiva listings more than ten times, with *Dark Victory* recording 127 mentions. The results were as follows:

Table 1. Newspaper mentions of texts relating to asylum seekers, as tracked on Factiva.

| Title | Author/Editor | Factiva mentions 1 Jan 2002 – 11 Oct 2010 |
|---|---|---|
| *Dark Victory* (2003 & 2004 editions) | David Marr & Marian Wilkinson | 127 |
| *A Certain Maritime Incident* (2004) | Tony Kevin | ? |
| *Guzin Najim's the Promise* (2005) | Sandra Lee | 32 |
| *Following Them Home: The Fate of the Returned Asylum Seekers* (2005) | David Corlett | 31 |
| *Borderline: Australia's Response to Refugees and Asylum Seekers in the Wake of the Tampa* (2001 & 2002) | Peter Mares | 29 |

---

11 *Mahboba's Promise: An Australian Aid Organisation*, available at www.mahbobaspromise.org/home/ [accessed 30 November 2011].

12 These should be treated as conservative figures, given that this was early in the establishment of Nielsen BookScan. Thank you to the Nielsen BookScan for the opportunity to undertake this research.

13 The Thorpe Bowker Media Mx database was trialled but rejected because it dates from 2005. Media Monitors advised that their records do not extend back to 2002 on such a specific, non-contracted subject. Note that checks were made of each Factiva mention and in some cases searches using different words were conducted (e.g., searches for *Dark Victory* included 'Marr' and 'refugees'). It was not possible to combine the results, so in some cases the Factiva chart summaries of year-by-year mentions are lower than this manually compiled list.

| Title | Author/Editor | Factiva mentions 1 Jan 2002 – 11 Oct 2010 |
| --- | --- | --- |
| *Tampering with Asylum: A Universal Humanitarian Problem* (2003) | Frank Brennan | 28 |
| *Blind Conscience* (2008) | Margot O'Neill | 24 |
| *Don't Tell the Prime Minister* (2002) | Patrick Weller | 24 |
| *The Bitter Shore* (2008) | Jacquie Everitt | 22 |
| *From Nothing to Zero: Stories from Australia's Detention Centres* (2003) | Meaghan Amor & Janet Austin, eds | 21 |
| *Another Country: Southerly Special Edition* (2004) | Rosie Scott & Tom Keneally, guest eds | 20 |
| *Dark Dreams: Australian Refugee Stories* (2004) | Sonja Dechian, Heather Millar & Eva Sallis, eds | 16 |
| *Human Rights Overboard: Seeking Asylum in Australia* (2008) | Linda Briskman, Susie Latham & Chris Goddard | 14 |
| *Acting from the Heart: Australian Advocates for Asylum Seekers Tell Their Stories* (2007) | Sarah Mares & Louise Newman | 14 |
| *Watching Brief: Reflections on Human Rights, Law and Justice* (2008) | Julian Burnside | 13 |
| *Time for Change: Australia in the twenty-first Century* (2006) | Tim Wright | 13 |
| 'Sending Them Home', *Quarterly Essay* (2003) | Robert Manne & David Corlett | 12 |
| *Beyond the Razor Wire: – is Australia, Where Everything's Free* (2003) | Sandy Thorne | 11 |

In addition, although it was not possible to track media mentions of *A Certain Maritime Incident* because of the Senate Select Committee investigation of the same name, David Marr advised, 'My impression is that Tony Kevin's book, when it appeared in 2004, was the subject of at least as much media attention as ours'.[14] Another seven books received up to ten mentions.[15]

The majority of the media mentions occurred around the time of each book's publication. The pattern for *Dark Victory* is typical, and the following graph clearly illustrates this. This

---

14 David Marr, personal communication, 30 June 2011.

15 In addition, Hanifa Deen received over forty mentions in the Factiva database. Many of these were in relation to her book *The Jihad Seminar*, which was released in 2008 and is not in the dataset used in this research. The revised edition of her *Caravanserai*, received fewer than ten mentions.

pattern was also similar for other books, although the total number of mentions was both lower and more sporadic in the years after publication.

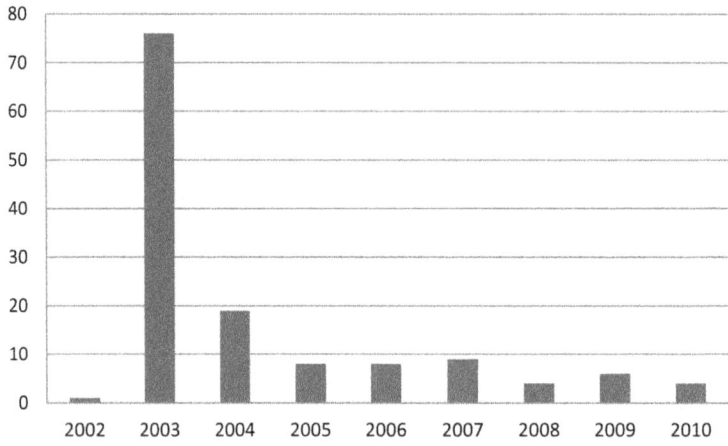

Figure 1. Newspaper mentions of *Dark Victory* 2002–2010, recorded in Factiva.

Newspaper coverage made the ideas and arguments in *Dark Victory* available to vastly more numerous readerships and, although they peaked at the time of the book's launch, they demonstrate considerable longevity. (There is also evidence of pre-publicity associated with the book in late 2001.)

Each newspaper mention corresponded to an individual edition with a circulation in the tens or hundreds of thousands. In this research, a conservative approach was taken which used average circulation figures for the period, although circulation numbers are sometimes multiplied in audited readership figures, when auditors confirm the assumption that several people may read a single newspaper. Of course, most people do not read every page of a newspaper and some people who buy a newspaper don't have time to read it at all. In a simple exercise, the Factiva newspaper mentions of *Dark Victory* were set out below in relation to the circulation figures of the following newspapers, averaged over 2003–2008.[16]

---

16  Monday to Saturday circulation figures were used for daily newspapers such as the *Australian*, the *Sydney Morning Herald*, the *Canberra Times*, the *Age*, the *Townsville Bulletin* and the *Courier Mail*. Saturday circulation figures are usually substantially higher, so this raised the average; however, it was reasonable to assume that some of the coverage occurred in Saturday newspapers. My thanks to Victor Isaacs who provided me with the newspaper circulation figures for the period of this study. With John Russell and Rod Kirkpatrick, Isaacs is the joint editor of *Australian Newspaper History: A Bibliography* (Middle Park: Australian Newspaper History Group, 2009) and one of Australia's foremost newspaper historians.

Table 2. Newspaper mentions of *Dark Victory* and circulation figures.

| Newspaper | Average circulation 2003–2008 | Factiva mentions | Total (circulation x mentions) |
|---|---:|---:|---:|
| The Australian | 161 000 | 19 | 3 059 000 |
| Canberra Times | 41 000 | 18 | 738 000 |
| The Age | 216 000 | 15 | 3 240 000 |
| Sydney Morning Herald | 240 000 | 12 | 2 880 000 |
| Townsville Bulletin | 29 000 | 7 | 203 000 |
| The Courier Mail | 234 000 | 6 | 1 404 000 |
| Sun Herald (Syd) | 513 000 | 6 | 3 078 000 |
| Sunday Age (Melb) | 208 000 | 5 | 1 040 000 |
| Total newspaper circulation | 1 642 000 | 88 | 15 642 000 |

The media provided a powerful platform for disseminating the book's ideas to hundreds of thousands of people beyond those who bought it. Although they may never have picked up a copy, people had repeated opportunities to become familiar with the title of the book, the names of the authors and their arguments.

Of course, most books do not receive newspaper reviews or other forms of media coverage. Many independent publishers lament the difficulty of obtaining reviews for their titles. The spectrum in this debate ranged from books that sold poorly and received little or no newspaper coverage to books that attracted extensive newspaper coverage.

Next we turn to a book that sold modestly according to the Nielsen BookScan data in this period – as did most of the books relating to this debate – but which also attracted newspaper coverage. *Borderline: Australia's Response to Refugees and Asylum Seekers in the Wake of the* Tampa, by Peter Mares,[17] was recorded with sales of 702 in 2003–2008, but this figure records the book sales at the end of its sales life. By 2003, sales were tapering off but the book was still generating newspaper coverage.

---

17  Peter Mares, *Borderline: Australia's Response to Refugees and Asylum Seekers in the Wake of the* Tampa, 2nd edn (Sydney: UNSW Press, 2002).

Table 3. Newspaper mentions of *Borderline* and circulation figures.

| Newspaper | Average circulation 2003–2008 | Factiva mentions | Total (circulation x mentions) |
|---|---|---|---|
| The Age | 216 000 | 5 | 1 080 000 |
| Sydney Morning Herald | 240 000 | 5 | 1 200 000 |
| The Australian | 161 000 | 2 | 322 000 |
| Canberra Times | 41 000 | 2 | 82 000 |
| Northcote Leader | n/a | 2 | – |
| Herald-Sun (Melb) | 537 000 | 2 | 1 074 000 |
| The West-Australian | 23 000 | 1 | 23 000 |
| Townsville Bulletin | 29 000 | 1 | 29 000 |
| Sunday Age (Melb) | 208 000 | 1 | 28 000 |
| Preston Leader | n/a | 1 | – |
| Total newspaper circulation | 1 455 000 | 22 | 4 018 000 |

Although this book sold fewer than 1000 copies in 2003–2008, it received over four million mentions in individual newspapers during this period. Of course many mentions would have passed unnoticed by many readers, but this is a powerful example of the way in which a modestly selling book during this period can play into a larger public sphere through the media.

In this debate, books and the media (represented by newspapers) complemented each other. The launch of books or public events connected with their authors provided occasions for filling newspaper columns through news reporting, author interviews and book reviews. Marr emphasised the importance of book reviews: 'Reviews reach an audience of millions, an audience that's unlikely to learn anything more about a book than the thumbnail portrait in a review.'[18] Newspapers vastly increased the platform from which authors and publishers could disseminate the titles' ideas.[19]

---

18  Marr, personal communication, 30 June 2011.

19  There is an ongoing debate about whether the serialisation of books in newspapers and magazines cannibalises book sales. This research does not engage with the debate but it is noted here.

## Academic Citations

Not unexpectedly, a different pattern occurs when examining the time frame of academic citations.[20] Rather than peaking early and dropping away, as with media mentions, the citations build over a number of years, in this case five years, before dropping away, with 272 in total. This pattern could also be observed in other cited books. Academic references to the books occured over a number of years but, in some cases after citations had dropped off, a new spike occurred.

Clearly, a longer time frame and a different cycle – with a longer-lasting build, peak and decline – is evident. Academic citations by their nature also reach different types of audiences. To access the online journals, readers must usually have a profession that includes access to such databases, or else take the trouble to locate them using a public library. Such journals are arguably likely to have a greater proportion of international readers. Notably, it is difficult to reach conclusions about the circulation of the journals because many online readers and researchers download individual articles without reading or scanning an entire issue. The patterns, however, reflect the traditional model of academic research which involves building on previous contributions to knowledge and acknowledging relevant works in a literature review or through citations. In summary, we can conclude the key features are:

- longer time frames lasting for years before mentions of a book title generally peaks
- a longer lasting peak and a slower decline in mentions
- a more specialised professional readership: these articles are not easily available to the general public
- the likelihood of significant numbers of international readers
- a lower chance of the articles being randomly encountered and read than in newspapers.

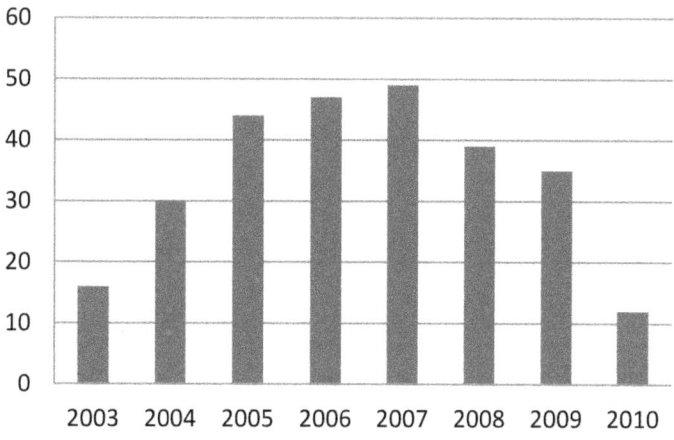

Figure 2. Academic citations of *Dark Victory*.

---

20  Each book's citations were searched using Google Scholar. A list of academic citations was prepared by copying each full citation into a spreadsheet, and checking through the online listings for duplications.

*Parliament*

Another way to consider whether the case-study books played into the political debate is to examine parliamentary records. Australia's policies were determined at the national level of government, therefore research was conducted using the Hansard records of the Australian Federal Parliament. After consulting with the librarian at the Australian Parliamentary Library, searches were conducted on the ParlInfo website.[21]

The results clearly indicated empirical mentions of eighteen case-study books directly within the parliamentary sphere, including:

- parliamentary debate or in a question in parliament
- Parliamentary Committee reports
- submissions to Parliamentary Committees from refugee activist groups and private citizens
- book launches in Canberra, notably the launch of *Dark Victory* at the Canberra Press Gallery
- the one-off use by PEN of an anthology of writing by detainees to lobby politicians directly.

One powerful record of books playing a role in public debate is through mentions on the floor of parliament. There were twenty-six mentions of case-study books in parliamentary debates or in question time. Of these, nineteen related to *Dark Victory*, two related to *Refuge Australia*, and one each to *Guzin Najim's the Promise*, *Another Country*, *A Certain Maritime Incident*, *The Bitter Shore* and *Human Rights Overboard*.

Table 4. Books mentioned in parliamentary debate or questions in parliament.

| Title & Year Publication | 2003 | 2004 | 2005 | 2006 | 2007 | 2008 | 2009 | 2010 |
|---|---|---|---|---|---|---|---|---|
| Dark Victory (2003) | 12 | 4 | 2 | 1 | | | | |
| Guzin Najim's the Promise (2003) | 1 | | | | | | | |
| Another Country (2004) | | | 1 | | | | | |
| Refuge Australia (2004) | | | | 2 | | | | |
| A Certain Maritime Incident (2004) | | | | | | | 1 | |

---

21 *Parliament of Australia: ParlInfo Search*, parlinfo.aph.gov.au/parlInfo/search/search.w3p;adv=yes.

| Title & Year Publication | 2003 | 2004 | 2005 | 2006 | 2007 | 2008 | 2009 | 2010 |
|---|---|---|---|---|---|---|---|---|
| *The Bitter Shore* (2008) | | | | | | | | 1 |
| *Human Rights Overboard* (2008) | | | | | | 1 | | |
| Total mentions | 13 | 4 | 3 | 3 | 0 | 1 | 1 | 1 |

Several politicians in fact urged that particular books be read by Australians. *Dark Victory* was recommended by the ALP's Anthony Albanese (18/8/2003, 10/11/2005 and 28/2/06) and Robert McClelland (8/10/03), as well as the Australian Democrats' Andrew Bartlett (25/3/04 and 5/10/05). Bartlett also recommended *Refuge Australia* (8/2/2006 and 2/3/2006). Members of Government, on the other hand, were clearly less likely to endorse these works. Here, for instance, is the Liberal Party's Peter Dutton in 2003:

> The very clear message from my electorate, not just prior to the election but since that time, is that they wholeheartedly endorse and support the government in relation to this policy position. There are other people in the Australian community who are completely out of touch on this issue. David Marr is one of those. I understand that in his latest publication of propaganda, *Dark Victory*, he makes some mention of the government's position in relation to this policy during the course of the 2001 election campaign. He is completely devoid of any real understanding of the facts in relation to this matter.[22]

How can we summarise this activity? Firstly, most of the mentions were by critics of the Australian Government's policies (twenty-one mentions); two mentions were to dispute the books and to defend the government's policies; and there were two others that were tangential.[23] It seems clear from the number of mentions and the impassioned nature of the mentions that the arguments within *Dark Victory* achieved a high level of awareness within the political sphere. Likewise, without knowing the extent to which they were actually read, it seems feasible that the other books also acted as symbolic rallying points. Politicians who referred to a case-study book on the floor of parliament were as follows. ALP: Kim Wilkie, Jacinta Collins, Duncan Kerr (three mentions), Anthony Albanese (four mentions), Rob McClelland, Kevin Rudd, Mike Kelly, Anna Burke and John Faulkner (three mentions);

---

22 Migration Legislation Amendment (Further Border Protection Measures) Bill 2002 [No. 2] – Second Reading – House of Reps Hansard, 13 May 2003 [accessed from ParlInfo 30 November 2011].

23 The two other references were by Senator Ruth Mackay, ALP, in Senate Estimates hearings. She questioned the Director of ABC TV, Sandra Levy, about a *Media Watch* episode in which the *Dark Victory* author David Marr joked about 'albrechting', a reference to a member of the ABC Board, Janet Albrechtsen. (The Hansard record also includes brief references to the book.) Senate Estimates: Environment, Communications, Information Technology and the Arts Legislation Committee: Communications, Information Technology and the Arts Portfolio: Australian Broadcasting Corporation, 25 May 2004 [accessed from ParlInfo 30 November 2011].

Australian Democrats: Andrew Bartlett (four mentions); Liberal Party: Alan Ferguson and Peter Dutton (one mention each); and Australian Greens: Sarah Hanson-Young (one mention).

Table 5. Number of mentions of case-study books in parliamentary debate or questions (minus two Senate Estimates Committee tangential references) by political party.

| Party | ALP | Democrats | Liberal | Greens |
|---|---|---|---|---|
| Mentions | 16 | 4 | 2 | 1 |

Although genuine concern was expressed about the treatment of asylum seekers in the opposition parties and in some sectors of the governing party, *Dark Victory* in particular was also used for political point-scoring in parliamentary debates by the ALP to criticise the general trustworthiness of the Howard government. One Greens politician, however, used the publication of *Human Rights Overboard* as an occasion to call (unsuccessfully) for a royal commission.[24] The evidence clearly points to books playing a direct role in parliamentary debate, notably *Dark Victory*, but also a number of other books on a less visible scale.

Because the Howard government did not have majority control of the Senate, ALP, Democrats and Greens Senators were able to form a majority to support several inquiries, including an Inquiry into Immigration Detention in Australia by the Joint Standing Committee on Migration, and an Inquiry into the Administration and Operation of the *Migration Act 1958*. In all, twelve inquiries, out of a large number of submissions, received one or two that either quoted or cited case-study books in the context of expressing concern about the conditions for asylum seekers, and to request improvements (records are publicly available through ParlInfo).

The evidence clearly demonstrates that opponents of the government's policies used case-study books as part of a broader range of material, including government and NGO reports and legal precedents, to support their arguments through submissions to parliamentary inquiries and committee hearings. References to such books were made in submissions to twelve parliamentary inquiries, in three parliamentary reports (usually listed in the appendices or lists of submissions), and there were two recorded mentions in Parliamentary Committee discussion. Other references were made in Senate Occasional Lectures and NGO reports.

In addition to these findings, some of the most powerful examples of books in public debate may be intangible and difficult to trace empirically. For example, in 2008 Dr Susan

---

24 This was Senator Sarah Hanson-Young: 'My question is to the Minister for Immigration and Citizenship, Senator Evans. In light of the publication of a new book, *Human Rights Overboard*, detailing the horrific stories of children in detention and the ongoing long-term psychological effects that this has had on children and their families, as reported in the *Australian* [newspaper] on Monday, will the minister confirm that the government will look into establishing a royal commission looking into the effects that Australia's immigration policy has had on refugees?' Questions Without Notice – Immigration Detention – Senate Hansard, 3 September 2008 [accessed from ParlInfo 30 November 2011].

Harris-Rimmer, while giving evidence in relation to the Standing Committee on Legal and Constitutional Affairs inquiry into whistleblowing protections within the Australian Government public sector, recalled the launch of *Dark Victory* five years earlier:

> I remember being at a Press Club launch of the David Marr–Marian Wilkinson book *Dark Victory*, where he [Marr] was yelling at the audience of public servants and press: 'Leak! Leak early! Leak often!' All the media people were going 'Yeah!' and all the public servants were just going 'No, no, no.' It was terrible. You could see the struggles and the tensions in the room about that particular issue.[25]

Therefore it was not just through reading books but by attending associated events or hearing anecdotal accounts of such events that the presence of books such as *Dark Victory* was felt in political debates.

A number of Australian writers who were members of PEN became involved in lobbying politicians to change the treatment of asylum seekers. In 2004 two writers, Rosie Scott and Tom Keneally, edited a special issue of the literary journal *Southerly – Another Country: Southerly Special Edition* 64.1 (2004). Importantly, this title does not appear in the Nielsen BookScan top 5000 nonfiction sales because – outside of normal copies – a limited edition of 100 was printed. These were used to raise funds and were also personally presented by PEN members to politicians with requests that the cases of individual detainees whose writing was included in the journal be investigated fairly. Typical of a broader range of related events was the Canberra PEN lecture that Keneally gave on 15 November 2004 titled, 'Hysteria, Tolerance, Race and Writing'. Nick Jose, the President of Sydney PEN at the time, later recalled: 'around that time some of the people [involved in *Another Country*] gave performances, gave readings of their work, published their work elsewhere and a kind of sub-genre developed of refugee memoir, particularly from the Middle East.'[26] *Another Country* was also noted on the floor of parliament by Anna Burke (ALP), Member for Chisholm, Victoria:

> A collection of poems by asylum seekers was recently published by PEN. It gives an insight into another world, another country – one of greater uncertainty, without hope, without dreams or trees and where children are placed behind barbed wire.[27]

Jose noted that mainstream Australian writers such as Eva Sallis (now Eva Hornung), Linda Jaivin and Tom Keneally turned their attention to Australian refugee stories, expanding the interest of publishers and audiences in these themes. Sydney PEN set up a sub-committee called Writers in Detention, a new category which required approval from International

---

25 Standing Committee on Legal and Constitutional Affairs: Whistleblowing protections within the Australian Government public sector: House of Representatives Committee Hansard, 16 October 2008 [accessed from ParlInfo 30 November 2011].

26 Jan Zwar, interview with Nick Jose, 15 July 2009.

27 Migration Amendment (Detention Arrangements) Bill 2005 – Second Reading – House of Representatives Hansard, 22 June 2005 [accessed from ParlInfo 30 November 2011].

PEN.[28] The International PEN Congress passed a resolution condemning Australia's asylum-seeker policies.

The role of *Another Country* and of Sydney PEN in this debate can be considered through a number of prisms. First, Sydney PEN members proved themselves to be articulate and astute lobbyists in communicating their messages. Already possessed of personal connections with elite circles, they expanded them and pressed their messages strongly, to the extent of co-opting Nobel Prize winners to their cause who endorsed the international resolution. Second, individual writers such as Tom Keneally possessed some of the cache of celebrity, and were able to draw public audiences in person and through the media. Politicians presumably attempted to manage relations with the Sydney PEN executive diplomatically, even if they were resistant to PEN's message and unwilling to change government policies. Finally, however, it is worth noting the symbolic power in operation in this milieu. Sydney PEN executives and publishers used the gravitas associated with books and serious writers to lend weight to their lobbying.

*Conclusion*

The asylum–seeker debate inspired many books about the issue, some of which became bestsellers and others which sold in the low thousands, or hundreds, of copies. Elizabeth Weiss, the Trade Marketing Director for Allen & Unwin, observed:

> It seems to me as a (very interested) observer that having a recently published book means that a commentator has more credibility and more leverage in getting their message across. With mixed success of course: a few books seem to set the tone for a debate and others fall by the wayside or only have a modest impact upon publication, despite best efforts.[29]

This spectrum appears to have occured across the books discussed in this chapter, although David Marr stressed that 'the public impact of quite small sales of a book can be high'.[30] As such, empirical investigation uncovered the surprising extent to which a range of these books were recorded in media mentions, in academic citations, and in parliamentary records. The books were also part of a broader, ongoing set of works that represented longer-term reflections about the law and ethics, the media and race relations, nationalism, and globalisation, in which this debate could be framed. Further, chapters from books such as *Borderline* are still used in university courses, in this case a decade after its initial publication. A permanent memorial to the 353 people who drowned on their way to seek asylum when the *SIEV X* sank in October 2001 – the subject of *A Certain Maritime Incident* – has been erected in Canberra.[31] Another important aspect which is not captured fully in this research is the way in which books provided a platform for the authors to participate in public events. Yet for all the professional publicity campaign around the launch of

---

28  For further information about the sub-committee's activities see pen.org.au/static/files/assets/9f8f4f71/SYDNEY_PEN_WRITERS_IN_DETENTION_COMMITTEE.pdf.

29  Elizabeth Weiss, personal communication, 14 June 2011.

30  Marr, personal communication, 30 June 2011.

31  Kevin, 'Asking Awkward Questions'.

*Dark Victory*, Marr has reflected, 'that the book sold so well was due to that impossible to measure phenomenon, word of mouth.'[32]

The ways in which we can characterise the effects of this activity are less clear. Although opinion polls and interpretations of them vary,[33] Robert Manne has observed in public forums, newspaper columns and journal contributions that, despite the commitment of writers and intellectuals:

> Every recent opinion poll makes it clear that hostility to unauthorised asylum seekers represents the opinion not of a small racist minority but of the overwhelming majority of the Australian mainstream. Neither 'education' nor 'leadership' seem likely in the near future to make Australians open their hearts to asylum seekers or to challenge the mood of the conservative populist political culture that crystalised at the time of *Tampa*.[34]

The effects on the lives of people seeking asylum come before any consideration of the impact of Australia's writers and publishers but that research does not fall within the scope of this chapter. If individual lives were saved or made more bearable through the efforts of committed writers and activists, we cannot undertake counter-factual analysis; that is, examine what would have happened without these interventions. Ultimately, the books were not successful in contributing to a broad change of public opinion – although we do not know their effects on individual readers. It could be suggested that the books and the debate surrounding them contributed to a political climate in which the newly elected Rudd government introduced some more humane policies, but these changes were short-lived and electorally unpopular.

There is, however, a range of ways in which this publishing activity had significant value. First, authors, publishers and books were actively part of the democratic process in the 2000s. The book was not 'dead' in this period, and readers engaged with issues by buying books, by reading about them in the media, and by directing the attention of Australian politicians to them. As the parliamentary records show, they were particularly successful in this regard. Further, the arguments contained within had a lifespan of years in academic citations: a less visible part of the fabric of public debate, and some of this work is still being studied by university students. Also, importantly, they served as resources for journalists such as Margot O'Neill and contributed to a body of work available for future historians and interested citizens.

In 2009 Nick Jose reflected on PEN's activism:

> One role for writers in society is to have that seismic sense of what are the big issues, and where the society might split or where it might need to be pushed

---

32 Marr, personal communication, 29 June 2011.

33 See, for example, William Maley, 'Fear, Asylum, and Hansonism in Australian Politics', *Dialogue* 29.2 (2010): 10–19; Andrew Markus, 'Public Opinion Divided on Population, Immigration and Asylum', *Policy* 26.3 (2010): 7–13; Janet Phillips and Harriet Spinks, 'Boat Arrivals in Australia Since 1976', Background Note, Parliamentary Library (Canberra: Parliament of Australia, 2011), available at www.aph.gov.au/library/pubs/bn/sp/BoatArrivals.htm.

34 Robert Manne, 'Comment: Asylum Seekers', *The Monthly* 60 (2010), p. 14.

forward in some way. This is a very difficult issue for Australia. It's an ongoing and difficult issue, a defining issue for the country … The most mature way to deal with it is not to turn it into a wedge issue but to try and keep a capacity to make policy as calmly and effectively as it can be done. Maybe there's a sense that we've been through the fire, we went through a very difficult period on this and we've come out of it and there's a greater appreciation of how delicately it needs to be handled.

I think it was important for writers in Australia and the publishing industry, the literary community to repoliticise, which they did around this issue. It was a re-energising of Australian writing which included the emergence of strong essayistic polemical writing in a way that hadn't been there before, and I think it restated the international context for Australian writers and Australian intellectual life.[35]

Counting empirical mentions does not capture the dynamics of ways in which books contribute to contemporary public debate. Yet it is undeniable that books played an important role in contemporary Australian public life and the processes by which that occurred, and which still occur, form a potentially rich area for future investigation.

---

35  Jose, personal communication, 15 July 2009.

# Part 2

# Republics of Letters: Local, National and International Literary Communities

# 6

## Scenes of Reading: Is Australian Literature a World Literature?

*Robert Dixon*

Recently influential accounts of world literature define it either as a discipline concerned with the 'effective life' of a text 'whenever, and wherever, it is actively present within a literary system beyond that of its original culture';[1] as a field of cultural production competitively divided into national and international literary space;[2] or as a field of practice, 'a mode of circulation and of reading'.[3] As both Jonathan Arac and David Damrosch have remarked, these various definitions present a range of methodological challenges to the study of national literatures that are as yet unresolved, especially the relationship between close and distant reading, and the relative value of specialist versus general knowledge as we move from national to transnational and comparative reading practices.[4]

Can Australian literature today be considered a world literature in any of these terms or does it remain a relatively minor national literature embedded uncertainly in world literary space? In relation to the first of these definitions, it increasingly enjoys an effective life beyond its point of origin. New works by contemporary Australian writers are translated rapidly into other languages, win international literary awards, and increasingly attract the expert attention of non-Australian critics. Yet the extent to which Australian literature has an effective life beyond Australia through its critical reception remains limited. The MLA bibliography indicates that the bulk of critical work on most Australian writers is still being done by Australian critics and published in Australian journals, and it is a singular fact that no Australian writers or texts appear as examples of world literature in any of the currently influential accounts, including those by Pascale Casanova, David Damrosch, Wai Chee Dimock and Franco Moretti.[5] I do not propose, however, to take up these questions of reception here. In this chapter, I'll pursue, instead, what seems to be the important question arising from that other sense of world literature as a mode of reading: what are the methodological implications of applying transnational reading practices to Australian literature?

---

1 David Damrosch, *What is World Literature?* (Princeton: Princeton University Press, 2003), p. 4.
2 Pascale Casanova, trans. M.B. DeBevoise, *The World Republic of Letters* (Cambridge, Mass. & London: Harvard University Press, 2004 [1999]).
3 Damrosch, *What is World Literature?*, p. 5.
4 Jonathan Arac, 'Anglo-Globalism?', *New Left Review* 16 (July–August 2002): 35–45.
5 Franco Moretti, 'Conjectures on World Literature', *New Left Review* 1 (2000): 55–67.

Let me begin by saying that at the very moment it appears to be on the verge of unprecedented internationalisation, as an academic discipline Australian literature remains overwhelmingly a national literature. Here is an example. On 30 July 2009, the *Macquarie PEN Anthology of Australian Literature* was launched by the Governor-General of Australia at Admiralty House in Sydney. In his introduction, the General Editor, Nicholas Jose, imagines himself looking down on his homeland from the window of an aeroplane:

> Looking from my window seat as the plane crosses Australia … I reflect on the intimate relationship between this extreme, subtle land and the human experiences it has shaped and been shaped by … Australian writing, then, is inseparable from the environment and circumstances of its origins … That's what we explore and honour in this new anthology.[6]

This aero-visual conceit is an example of what Homi K. Bhabha calls 'the recurrent metaphor of landscape as the inscape of national identity'.[7] It offers a synoptic view of Australian literature as an expression of the nation that is in turn symbolised by the land, connecting literature, land and nation in an expressive totality. As British critic Graham Huggan remarks, 'Australian literary criticism continues to be hindered by its reliance on national(ist) tropes'.[8] As he looks down on Australia from his window seat, Jose's meditation plays out what Paul Giles describes as the 'isomorphic fallacy' endemic in mid-twentieth-century area studies, both American and Australian. The area studies model, Giles argues, has involved

> the attempt to encompass a particular bounded territory – characteristically, a nation, but also smaller variants of national space, such as a region or a city – and through this enabling circumscription to treat that space allegorically, as emblematic of a particular kind of identity.[9]

For a different understanding of area studies, we might turn to Benedict Anderson's book, *The Spectre of Comparisons* (1998), in which he reflects on the comparative methodology of Southeast Asian studies. Anderson recalls how, in 1963, after an extended period of fieldwork in Indonesia, he experienced 'a kind of vertigo' caused by seeing European history for the first time from an Indonesian perspective: it was as if 'I had been invited to see my Europe … through an inverted telescope'.[10] Anderson had no name for this experience until many years later when he read Jose Rizal's novel, *Noli Me Tangere* (1887):

---

6  Nicholas Jose, 'General Introduction', in Nicholas Jose et al., eds, *Macquarie Pen Anthology of Australian Literature* (Sydney: Allen & Unwin, 2009), pp. 1–2.

7  Homi K. Bhabha, *The Location of Culture* (London: Routledge, 1994), p. 143.

8  Graham Huggan, *Australian Literature: Postcolonialism, Racism, Transnationalism* (Oxford: Oxford University Press, 2002), p. vii.

9  Paul Giles, *Virtual Americas: Transnational Fictions and the Transatlantic Imaginary* (Durham: Duke University Press, 2002), pp. 6–7.

10  Benedict Anderson, *The Spectre of Comparisons: Nationalism, Southeast Asia, and the World* (London: Verso, 1998), p. 2.

> There is a dizzying moment early in the narrative when the young mestizo hero, recently returned to colonial Manila ... from a long sojourn in Europe, looks out of his carriage window at the municipal botanical gardens, and finds that he too is, so to speak, at the end of an inverted telescope. These gardens are shadowed automatically ... and inescapably by images of their sister gardens in Europe. He can no longer matter-of-factly experience them, but sees them simultaneously close up and from far away. The novelist arrestingly names the agent of this incurable doubled vision ... the spectre of comparisons.[11]

Jose's view of Australia from his aeroplane window is the singular vision of cultural nationalism, which sees land, literature and nation as expressive of a distinctive, organic identity. Rizal's gaze from the carriage window is one of those moments when the scales of nationalism fall from the eyes, when what was thought to be nationally distinctive is seen to be part of a universal series. This is the 'incurable doubled vision' of the comparatist. It understands that national identity is relational, that it can no longer be regarded 'matter-of-factly', and that its claims on the individual subject are relative and provisional. What interests me here is the recursive nature of the inverted telescope. Rizal does not suggest that the colonial gardens are necessarily diminished by the European comparison – nor, for that matter, that they are aggrandised by it. What he notices is the doubling itself, the fact that he now sees his own nation 'simultaneously close up and from far away'. Anderson offers this as an explanation of comparatism as a methodology. His own experience is that seeing 'my Europe' through the wrong end of the telescope 'had made it forever impossible to take Europe for granted'.[12] In a word, Europe has been provincialised.

It is something like this doubled vision, the defamiliarising effect of seeing a national literature 'simultaneously close up and from far away', that we are beginning to see now in some of the best new work in transnational literary studies. And, significantly, much of this work is taking place inside the specialisation of national literatures, albeit transformed by approaches derived from world literature. A good example is the work of Paul Giles, a British-born American literature specialist, now Challis Professor of English at the University of Sydney. In *Virtual Americas* (2002), Giles starts with the premise that 'national histories ... cannot be written simply from the inside', and goes on to examine a series of refractions between British and American literature in what he calls the 'transatlantic imaginary'.[13] The reason for introducing transnational perspectives into the study of national literatures is not to transcend national cultures, which retain a spectral or residual presence, but to provoke discussion on 'the meaning of the "national" today'. As a 'formal method of inquiry', Giles argues, 'transnationalism works to reveal the circumference of national formations and thus to empty out their peremptory claims to legitimacy'. Again,

> Transnationalism ... positions itself at a point of intersection ... where the coercive aspects of imagined communities are turned back on themselves, reversed or

---

11 Quoted in Anderson, *The Spectre of Comparisons*, p. 2.
12 Anderson, p. 20.
13 Giles, *Virtual Americas*, pp. 2, 5.

> mirrored, so that their covert presuppositions and ideological inflections become apparent.¹⁴

These are useful reflections on a transnational methodology. Without seeking to detach a national literature entirely from its origin, it is nonetheless bi- or even multi-laterally comparative, placing works of national literature in a field of inquiry generated by two or more perspectives at once. Following Damrosch, Giles describes this method of reading as 'elliptical', a way of interrupting the inward-looking definitions of area studies and repositioning the national literature 'not as a mode of autonomy but as a mode of alterity'.¹⁵

As a way of exemplifying this idea of doubled vision, I want now to offer brief readings of two Australian novels. Without attempting to detach them from their national context, I want to interrupt the 'inward-looking' perspective of Australian literary studies, seeing them at once from close up and from far away: that is, in relation to both a nationalist tradition and to world literary space. The first is Joseph Furphy's *Such is Life* (1903), which is normally regarded as a canonical text of Australian literary nationalism; the second is Henry Handel Richardson's *Maurice Guest* (1908), which has often been excluded from the nationalist canon as a cosmopolitan or European novel written by an expatriate.

I've chosen these two texts because of the role they play in one of the classic works of Australian cultural–nationalist historiography, Miles Franklin's *Laughter Not for a Cage* (1956). As Casanova argues, once the nation was seen as 'the natural and unsurpassable horizon of literature, national literary histories were composed and taught in such a way that they became closed in upon themselves'.¹⁶ In other words, national literary traditions are defined both by acts of inclusion and acts of exclusion. Furphy and Richardson play just this role in Franklin's history of the Australian novel. She begins by making a rigorous distinction between what Casanova, with her typical hard binaries, would call 'national' and 'international' writers; between those who are 'rooted in their native soil', who write from 'authentic' national experience, and those 'expatriate-minded' writers who have lost touch with their native culture and fallen victim to international fashions. Franklin illustrates this distinction by comparing two near-contemporaries, the expatriate American novelist Henry James, and the Australian novelist Joseph Furphy. Both were born into newly formed English-speaking communities; both experienced the sense of dislocation from the richer culture of the old world. James responded by cultivating 'cosmopolitanism', Furphy by grounding himself more deeply in his native culture. In Franklin's view, James doomed himself to a 'double exile'. Having 'turned his back' on America, he remained 'haunted by his desertion'. A creature of European 'drawing rooms' and 'cosmopolitan Bohemian haunts', he became 'a literary master' at the cost of being 'a man astray'. Furphy neither sought nor gained recognition overseas. 'Rooted to his native soil', he is 'in every sense antipodean', 'a founding father of the Australian novel'.¹⁷

---

14  Giles, p. 17.

15  Giles, p. 261.

16  Casanova, *The World Republic of Letters*, p. 105.

17  Miles Franklin, *Laughter Not for a Cage: Notes on Australian Writing, with Biographical Emphasis on the Struggles, Function and Achievements of the Novel in Three Half-Centuries* (Sydney: Angus & Robertson, 1956), pp. 125–28.

Franklin's contrast between James and Furphy is the benchmark for her dismissive accounts of other expatriate or internationally minded Australians, including Richardson and Christina Stead, as writers who also 'turned their backs' on their national culture while never quite becoming British or European or American. *Maurice Guest* only received good reviews, she argues, because of Richardson's modish 'absorption of the Continental approach to her theme', while Stead's characters are 'touched with the brush of the coteries of the Latin Quarter, or Greenwich Village, or Bloomsbury'.[18] These unbalanced assessments reflect Franklin's own rejection of modernism, which led her to adopt a defensive provincialism that was enshrined in the terms of Australia's most famous literary award, the Miles Franklin Literary Award, which is given annually to the most outstanding novel dealing with 'Australian life in any of its phases'.

As *Laughter Not for a Cage* demonstrates, expatriatism has not been a neutral concept in Australian literary history but is an artifact of cultural nationalism. To be sure, there are often compelling reasons – political, pedagogical and even moral – to appropriate a select group of writers above others as articulating a national consciousness. Yet this also means that at certain moments in its history the institution of Australian literary criticism has been blind to the internationalism of Australian writers and writing. How, then, might we read Australian works differently, though without detaching them entirely from their point of origin? How might we develop a reading practice that would see key works of Australian literature 'simultaneously close up and from far away'?

## Joseph Furphy: A 'National' Author

Australian literary history reads Furphy as an epitome of the 'national' writer. *Such is Life* was written at Shepparton in rural Victoria during the 1880s and published in 1903, two years after the Federation of the Commonwealth of Australia in 1901. The leading nationalist critic of the day, A.G. Stephens, hailed it as an 'Australian classic, or semi-classic, since it embalms accurate representations of our character and customs, life and scenery'; here, he believed, was 'a national Australian book, a Bush book that would be relished 100 years hence'.[19]

Yet there is much that is ambivalent about Furphy's attitude to the nation and literary nationalism. As Julian Croft observes, *Such is Life* is an elusive object that 'cannot be pinned down to one meaning' because it 'endlessly retreats before you like a mirage'.[20] This is partly attributable to the nature of its construction, particularly those tissues of citation, those routes of connectivity that Dimock has in mind when she describes the way a national text connects itself with transnational space and deep time.[21] Drawing on his wide reading in the classics, as well as modern British and European literature, Furphy set out 'to establish an encyclopaedic context' for his record of life in the Riverina in the 1880s. To achieve this,

---

18  Franklin, *Laughter Not for a Cage*, pp. 147, 179.

19  Quoted in Julian Croft, *The Life and Opinions of Tom Collins: A Study of the Works of Joseph Furphy* (St Lucia: University of Queensland Press, 1991), pp. 48, 54.

20  Croft, *The Life and Opinions of Tom Collins*, p. 3.

21  Wai Chee Dimock, *Through Other Continents: American Literature Across Deep Time* (Princeton: Princeton University Press, 2006), p. 3.

he created 'a fictional device' that would allow both the real and the 'epic' or the 'mythic' to register within a single text.²² *Such is Life* is therefore a doubled text comprising two distinctive lenses that offer incommensurable perspectives on the same material. In one part we have a realistic account of life in the Riverina between September 1883 and March 1884, comprising the diaries of the narrator, Tom Collins; in the other, a cluster of stories in the register of high romance written by Joseph Furphy.

Furphy builds the literary dimension of his work through a pattern of allusions to the texts he deemed to be among the masterworks of world literature: Dante's *Inferno*, Spencer's *Faerie Queen*, Goethe's *Faust*, Ovid's *Metamorphoses*, the King James Bible and the works of Shakespeare. But his attitude to these texts is itself ambivalent. On the one hand, it reflects the structural anxiety of being a writer in a new-world culture, the sense of belatedness and the problem of origins. Croft argues that

> Despite his vigorous renunciation of English publication for *Such is Life* … deep within him was the desire to be judged against the civilised standard of the 'home' cultures, and not to create a form of art which would make its own terms and therefore be found wanting.²³

On the other hand, it is often difficult to distinguish in Furphy's literary allusions between homage and parody. In the recursive structure of his doubled text, the authority of these masterworks works is undermined by the problems of everyday life in a country settled by immigrants. So too are the claims of nationalism in a nation that is still in the process of formation, both as an imagined community and a legislative reality.

This suggests that, like Herman Melville in America in the 1850s, Furphy was writing at a point of cross-cultural exchange and that his citational practice enacts the problem of literary origins in new-world literatures. In *Virtual Americas*, Giles describes a very different Melville from that of the American renaissance critics of the mid twentieth century. Instead of seeing him as a national writer, he argues that 'Melville's fiction negotiates intertextually with … English literature', 'refracting the complications of the international scene'.²⁴ Through parody and other forms of intertextual negotiation, Melville aestheticises the problem of origins in a settler society, acknowledging its belatedness, and enacting the 'circuit' of 'tradition and originality'.²⁵ In *Redburn* (1849), *Mardi* (1849), *Moby Dick* (1851) and *Pierre* (1852), 'nationalist teleologies and traditions become problematised by theoretical confrontation between different cultures'.²⁶ In a similar way, *Such is Life* hollows out both nationalist teleologies and the authority of canonical texts through their cross-cultural exchange at the site of his hybrid literary practice. The 'cultural nationalist core' that generations of critics claimed to find in *Such is Life* does not exist.²⁷ But at the same time, the authority of its 'encyclopedic' or 'epic' frame is eviscerated by the specificity of local knowledge that is neither imperial nor national.

---

22  Croft, p. 9.
23  Croft, p. 17.
24  Giles, p. 54.
25  Giles, p. 62.
26  Giles, p. 56.
27  Croft, p. 19.

This collision between transational space and deep time, and the local and contingent, can be seen in the famous episode of Tom Collins' crossing of the Murray River. The threads of connection to world literature are particularly dense at this point, including explicit references to the *Iliad*, the *Aeneid*, the *Metamorphoses*, the *Inferno*, *Paradise Lost* and *Gilgamesh*, especially the epic convention of the hero's visit to the underworld. As Croft puts it,

> In Canto III of the *Inferno*, Dante and Virgil reach the River Acheron and are ferried across by Charon into the first circles of Hell. In Chapter Three of *Such is Life*, Tom crosses the Murray and unknowingly ends up in Victoria.[28]

Tom descends temporarily into the hell of poverty when he strips to cross the Murray but loses his bearings and his clothes, and swims south into the colony of Victoria instead of north into New South Wales. He asks the reader, 'Wouldn't you be very likely to take the sunset on your left, and swim for the north bank … ? That is what I did. It never occurred to my mind that Victoria could be on the north side of New South Wales'.[29]

This is a lesson in misreading. Furphy is challenging the reader to decide which is more difficult: following the threads of his erudition around the masterworks of world literature or being able to tell north from south at sunset in the bush. Is this a sincere attempt to write a vernacular epic or the assertion of a stubborn provincialism in which grand literary allusions are brought undone by the twists and turns of a river in the Australian bush? And there is more. The Murray River is also the official boundary between the colonies of Victoria and New South Wales, which Tom finds literally unreadable, perhaps in demonstration of the fact that Australia, in 1883, does not yet exist. As Andrew McCann observes, in pre-Federation literature, the nation functions as an *absence*.[30] The broad comedy of this episode leaves Tom lost and naked in the bush; it leaves the reader stranded between the grandeur of epic and the bathos of parody. Like Tom, the reader is unable to navigate safely either by following the threads of allusion into the inter-text of the European classics, or into the literal but equally unreadable state boundaries. Land, text and nation refuse to align themselves into the isomorphic fallacy of literary nationalism.

For all its citation of the masterworks of world literature, Furphy's novel is therefore a complex refracting device, testing the value of imported and canonical knowledge against what he calls 'local reference'.[31] But that same local reference also refuses the authority of the nation as an imagined community, whose governing image is the mirage. Generations of readers who hailed *Such is Life* as an epitome of the national literature have failed to see that it is an elaborate cross-cultural device designed to show that all such categories are contingent and unstable. As Croft warns, 'Beware … of the mirage. To speculate on why there are inconsistencies in *Such is Life* is to start looking into a mirror arcade of recessive mirrors'.[32]

---

28  Croft, p. 148.

29  Joseph Furphy, in Frances Devlin Glass et al., eds, *Such is Life* by Joseph Furphy (Braddon, ACT: Halstead Press, 1999 [1903]), p. 100.

30  Andrew McCann, *Marcus Clarke's Bohemia: Literature and Modernity in Colonial Melbourne* (Carlton: Melbourne University Publishing, 2004), p. 7.

31  Furphy, *Such is Life*, p. 53.

32  Croft, p. 80.

## Henry Handel Richardson: An 'International' Writer

Unlike Furphy, who spent his entire life in country Victoria, Henry Handel Richardson left Australia in 1888 to study music at the Leipzig Conservatorium. She there met her future husband, the British-born German scholar John George Robertson. After their marriage in 1895, they lived in Munich and Strassburg, where *Maurice Guest* was begun, and then in England from 1903 until her death in 1945. Through her wide reading in contemporary European literature and philosophy, and her study of modern languages, especially French, German and Danish, Richardson transformed herself into a European intellectual. In the introduction to their edition of *Maurice Guest*, Clive Probyn and Bruce Steele describe her practising the piano 'with a play of Ibsen or a novel by Tolstoy propped open on the music rack', and much of what she read was in German translation.[33] No wonder that her new year's resolution in 1900 was to read more in English.

The most detailed analysis of Richardson's sources in *Maurice Guest* is her husband's article, 'The Art of Henry Handel Richardson', published in 1948. Robertson speaks of *Maurice Guest* as a 'mosaic of influences', discounting its autobiographical references in favour of what he calls its 'literary provenance' in continental Europe, especially in German and Scandinavian literatures, and as 'the last link in the chain [of naturalism] which practically began with Madame Bovary in 1856'.[34] Robertson's term 'provenance' is an interesting one, and as a comparative literature scholar himself he has a clear sense of Richardson as what Casanova would call an 'international' writer, one who has escaped from the literary province by adopting the techniques of the modern European novel. Most Richardson scholars have continued to read *Maurice Guest* in this way, concerned to further illuminate its European provenance, especially for Australian readers. While not detaching *Maurice Guest* from that European provenance, I want now to double this vision of the novel by asking what is its colonial provenance – or better, what is its provincial provenance?

I want to argue that the marks of its provincial origins are everywhere apparent, and that it displays and explores what might be called, following the logic of Casanova's account of world literary space, a provincial anxiety. *Maurice Guest* may be set in Leipzig, but it is not about Europeans, who largely flicker in and out of its settings and events like extras in a film. There are exceptions, such as Heinz Krafft and Eugene Schilsky, but even Schilsky, Richardson's main portrait of the European artist, is off-stage for much of the action and only returns at the end after Maurice's suicide. Its core cast of characters are 'guests' in Europe, like Maurice himself, visitors from a range of provincial and new-world locations who are drawn to Leipzig because it is the Greenwich Meridian of world musical culture. Louise Dufrayer, loosely based on the Italian actress Eleanora Duse, is from Queensland. The Cayhill's are from the United States, reminding us of Henry James' conviction that art requires a deep soil, and of the cultural 'destitution' of America. While 'foreigners' are not excluded from the Cayhill's circle, their German friends find that they are required to speak

---

33 Clive Probyn and Bruce Steele, Introduction, in Probyn and Steele, eds, *Maurice Guest* by Henry Handel Richardson (St Lucia: University of Queensland Press [Academy Editions of Australian Literature], 1998 [1908]), p. l.

34 Quoted in Probyn and Steele, Introduction, p. li.

English.[35] Maurice himself is from a 'cheerless middle-class home' in the north of England with a 'provincial population'.[36] The novel's point of view is not from within the richness of Leipzig's native musical tradition, but at various points within this cast of provincial and largely mediocre people who have come to Leipzig for a limited time to study at its world-famous institutions and who will return to the provinces as teachers rather than as performers and artists. This point of view is immediately apparent in the contrast between Maurice's naively romantic response to Leipzig – 'he looked about, eager to discover beauty in the strip of landscape that stretched before him' – and the more prosaic quality of the local people: 'he was sensible ... of the spiritual *Gemutlicheit*, the absence of any pomp or pride in their romantic past'.[37] Madeline Wade, another American, attempts to rescue Maurice from his infatuation with Louise by proposing that they become music teachers together in small-town America. But Maurice is incapable of recognising and accepting his own mediocrity as a musician, and his romantic idealism and bourgeois morality are, as Krafft realises, the very things that distinguish him from true artists like Schilsky. Maurice encounters this difference early in the novel when he audits his first recital and sees that his provincial training has not prepared him for competitive performance on the European stage: 'he had never heard playing like this, and he leaned forward in his seat, and gazed full at the player, in open admiration'.[38] A generation of Australian feminist critics have rightly argued that Richardson questions the late nineteenth-century cult of the male artist, but it is not just gender that determines whether or not her characters will have access to creative agency: there is also the matter of their culture of origin.

In *Maurice Guest*, the focus on provinciality is sustained to the very end, when Maurice's suicide so shockingly extinguishes the consciousness with which the reader has been engaged for some seven hundred pages. The description is forensic: 'Then, as suddenly as the flame of a candle is puffed out by the wind, his life went from him'.[39] In the final moments, Schilsky and his entourage sweep in to fill the space occupied so inadequately by Maurice. After a triumphant performance at the Leipzig Gewandhaus, Schilsky leaves the stage door and is whisked away in his carriage:

> The driver gathered up the reins, cracked his whip, and the big-bodied droschke went swerving round the corner, clattering gutturally on the cobbled stone pavement.
>
> The group of loiterers round the door dispersed.[40]

In this cinematic moment, Schilsky, the European-trained musical genius, literally exits the stage, leaving in his wake the next generation of foreign students. The reader's point of view is aligned with these 'loiterers'.

---

35 Richardson, *Maurice Guest*, p. 87.
36 Richardson, pp. 22–5.
37 Richardson, pp. 11–12.
38 Richardson, p. 35.
39 Richardson, p. 725.
40 Richardson, p. 727.

*Maurice Guest* therefore has a divided provenance that includes not just the European novel that Robertson could see so clearly but also the mark of what Casanova calls the literary suburb. It may well be a European novel, but it is Europe seen through the wrong end of the telescope, as the final, receding, tracking shot suggests. To think otherwise would be to share Maurice Guest's own romantic delusions of being at the centre of modern time and space, which are subject to merciless irony in the opening pages:

> What a single-minded devotion to art, he promised himself his should be! … he vowed that to himself this day, when he stood for the first time on historic ground, where the famous musicians of the past had found inspiration for their immortal works … he saw himself already of these masters' craft, their art his … becoming one of themselves.[41]

The dominant mode of Richardson's anti-romantic irony, we might say, is one of provincialisation.

## Sublimation/De-sublimation

I want now to draw some general conclusions about applying transnational reading practices to what is still effectively a national literature like Australia's. To do this, I want to reflect on the important work of Wai Chee Dimock, an American literature specialist engaged in a sustained attempt to disentangle the originary connection between literary studies and the nation. In *Through Other Continents* (2006) Dimock dismantles the isomorphic fallacy that is foundational to national literatures. 'Nationhood', she argues, 'is endlessly reproduced in a seamless correspondence between the temporal and spatial boundaries of the nation and the boundaries of all other expressive domains', including the literary.[42] Dimock goes on to develop both a theory of the text and a phenomenology of reading, which she calls 'proximate' reading, in which citations within the apparently bounded, national text are traced like threads into transnational space and what she calls 'deep time':

> 'American' literature is quite often a shorthand, a simplified name for a much more complex tangle of relations. Rather than being a discrete entity, it is better seen as a crisscrossing set of pathways, open-ended and ever multiplying, weaving in and out of other geographies, other languages and cultures. These are input channels, kinship networks, routes of transit, and forms of attachment – connective tissues binding America to the rest of the world.[43]

This formulation is intended to produce the kind of doubled reading that I have modelled in my own readings of *Such is Life* and *Maurice Guest*. The effect is to relativise the national text by placing it in a series of ever-expanding horizons of interpretation, allowing it to be seen, in Benedict Anderson's phrase, 'simultaneously close up and from far away'.

In her earlier article, 'Literature for the Planet', Dimock approaches this work of 'messing up territorial sovereignty' by invoking Einstein's concept of the 'relativity of

---

41  Richardson, p. 12.
42  Dimock, *Through Other Continents*, p. 3.
43  Dimock, *Through Other Continents*, p. 3.

simultaneity': that is, that different 'frames of reference' produce different 'operational effects'.[44] In literary terms, we might say that the relevant 'frames' that produce such relativising effects on the phenomenology of reading are the local, the sub- or pre-national, the national, the transnational and the global. I understand Dimock's argument to be that for this relativising to occur, two or more frames of reference need to be put in relation to each other, not that they can be transcended entirely. Reading beyond the nation is not an experience of timelessness and placelessness, but of the 'adjacency' and 'proximity' of two or more coordinates. And yet there is a tendency in Dimock's work, and in the work of other advocates of world literature, to imply in some of their more extreme formulations that world literature is a practice of reading that transcends such frames of reference altogether. This is often accompanied by a loss of the material dimension of literature, often in specifically national fields of cultural production, that has been built up so strongly, for example, by the methodologies associated with the history of the book and publishing studies. I was struck by the fact that in *Death of a Discipline* (2003), Gayatri Spivak's own reflections on the future of comparative methodologies, she mis-reads Dimock's article in just this way. Spivak summarises Dimock's argument as being 'that a classic of European literature may become timeless because people all over the world may feel moved by it at other times'. This, says Spivak, is 'a good argument for the ahistoricity of literature'.[45]

The tendency in Dimock's model is to place national and world literatures in a relation that I would call one of sublimation. This is perhaps betrayed in the title of one of her earlier papers, 'Scales of Aggregation: Prenational, Subnational, Transnational'.[46] Although she insists on a model of the text and a phenomenology of reading that are based on a 'double threading' that runs in both directions – we might say, all the way up and all the way down – in practice there is a preference for the higher term: the transnational above the local, 'deep time' and the *longue durée* above 'local irregularities', 'scale enlargement' rather than scale reduction, extension rather than contraction of the frame of reference. What would American literature look like, she asks, 'restored to a *longue durée*, a scale enlargement along the temporal axis that also enlarges its spatial compass?'[47] At such moments, Dimock seems to exceed her brief, calling for a 'globalizing readership' that not only 'relativises' the nation but appears to transcend it altogether; she slips from denying the nation 'absolute' jurisdiction to its having no jurisdiction at all, replacing it with the idea of a 'global civil society' and 'the entire planet as a unit of analysis'.[48]

The sublimity of Dimock's figurative language may well be a consequence of her viewing the world literary system and other national literatures from the perspective of the United States rather than a less commanding point of vantage like Australia. I am reminded here of Jonathan Arac's warning in 'Anglo-Globalism?' that distant reading threatens to place the national literature specialist in a subservient relation to the generalist or comparatist.

---

44  Wai Chee Dimock, 'Literature for the Planet', *PMLA* 116.1 (2001): 173–88 (174).

45  Gayatri Chakravorty Spivak, *Death of a Discipline* (New York: Columbia University Press, 2003), p. 114.

46  Wai Chee Dimock, 'Scale of Aggregation: Prenational, Subnational, Transnational', *American Literary History* 18.2 (2006): 119–228.

47  Dimock, *Through Other Continents*, p. 4.

48  Dimock, 'Literature for the Planet', p. 175.

Arac is critical of what he calls the 'utopian dimension' of Moretti's recently founded Centre for the Study of the Novel at Stanford.[49] And as Ken Gelder suggests, Dimock's plea for a global civil society has 'a benign cosmopolitanising imperative' that I hear echoed today in much writing about world literature.[50] This suggests that as world literature matures as a discipline, it must resist the tendency to abstraction and thematic homogenisation that marked postcolonial studies at a similar point in its history in the early 1990s.

My instinct, then, is to endorse Dimock's argument against the limits of nationalist reading practices. But I am wary of the more extreme locutions in her argument, which I think she shares with other advocates of world literature, which imply the transcendence of all categories of determination beneath that of a global or planetary system, ending in what Spivak misreads as an argument for the ahistoricity of literature. As *Such is Life* and *Maurice Guest* remind us, the double threading runs deep in both directions, both all the way up to world literary space and all the way down to local epistemologies, often invisible to comparatists like Robertson, that are sub- or pre-national. What I find valuable in Dimock's work is not the implicit argument for deterritorialising our reading practices, but her embrace of the relativity of simultaneity, in which two or more frames of reference produce a range of operational effects. None of these frames has 'absolute jurisdiction' yet all retain some force, including the spectral presence of the nation.

In the introduction to *Shades of the Planet* (2007), Dimock draws on Douglas Hofstadter's set theory to suggest that these frames of analysis are not hierarchical but recursive. In set theory, recursive series display the phenomenon of 'nesting', which means that individual elements can be recombined in varying sequences of priority. Hofstadter calls this a *heterarchy*.[51] The local, the pre-national, the national and the transnational are just such a recursive series that relativise each other's authority: each point is 'a kind of switch mechanism in the reversible hierarchy between the local and the global'.[52] When reading practices work to nest the local within the transnational, to interrogate the jurisdiction of nation from the wider perspectives of deep time and transnational space, we might say that they have a tendency to *sublimation*: in Webster's suggestive definition, this is 'to direct the energy of (an impulse) from its primitive aim to one that is culturally or ethically higher'. When they work to reverse this apparent hierarchy and counter the tendency to a benign or utopian cosmopolitanism, we might say that they are moments of desublimation or, as I prefer, following Dipesh Chakrabarty, moments of *provincialisation*.[53] If I began by accepting the need to fold back the demands of cultural nationalism, I end, as an Australian critic of what remains a national literature, with a commitment to the relativising force of provincial epistemologies. This is the paradox that Amitav Gosh observes in his prize-winning essay, 'The March of the Novel through History':

---

49  Arac, pp. 44–45.

50  Ken Gelder, 'Proximate Reading: Australian Literature in Transnational Reading Frameworks', *JASAL* (2010 *Special Issue: Common Readers*): 4.

51  Quoted in Wai Chee Dimock, Introduction, in Wai Chee Dimock and Lawrence Buell, eds, *Shades of the Planet: American Literature as World Literature* (Princeton: Princeton University Press, 2007), p. 4.

52  Dimock, Introduction, *Shades of the Planet*, p. 12.

53  Dipesh Chakrabarty, *Provincialising Europe: Postcolonial Thought and Historical Difference* (Princeton: Princeton University Press, 2000).

It is the very vastness and cosmopolitanism of the fictional bookcase that requires novelists to locate themselves in relation to it; that demands of their work that it carry marks to establish their location.

This then is the peculiar paradox of the novel: those of us who love novels often read them because of the eloquence with which they communicate a 'sense of place'. Yet the truth is that it is the very loss of a lived sense of place that makes their fictional representation possible.[54]

---

54  Amitav Ghosh, 'The March of the Novel through History: The Testimony of My Grandfather's Bookcase', *Kenyon Review* 20.2 (1998): 23–24.

# 7

## Modernising Anglocentrism: *Desiderata* and Literary Time

*David Carter*

The appealing notion of a 'republic of letters' has been in wide circulation since the English-language publication of Pascale Casanova's *The World Republic of Letters* in 2004. Even before Casanova's book, the phrase had been applied to situations as diverse as eighteenth-century America, English working-class writing, and postwar American literary opinion.[1] Breaking loose from its origins in the European Enlightenment – the republic of letters addressed by Fanny Burney, for example, in her 1778 Preface to *Evelina* – the term has been taken up in many different accounts of writing, publishing or reading communities, past and present. Its seemingly irresistible attraction is part of a renewed attention in literary scholarship over the last decade or so to cultural institutions and the function of intermediaries within those institutions – the roles editors, agents, critics, schoolteachers, booksellers, bureaucrats, entrepreneurs and enthusiasts play in producing literature and literary value. This focus is shared across a range of work in book history, cultural history and the sociology of culture, work often drawing on Bourdieu's foundational accounts of the 'field of cultural production' and the associated concepts of habitus and cultural capital: Casanova's book or James English's study of cultural prizes, *The Economy of Prestige*, are strong examples.[2]

As English's title indicates, what these studies tend to have in common is the understanding of culture as a field, structure or economy whose dynamic is generated and maintained by unequal relations of power and prestige (of prestige as power). While the focus on literary communities gives us purchase on various aspects of literature's sociability, 'community' itself seems to represent these relations of power in a weak form at best. It is important, in other words, not to lose sight of the political dimensions – the power and violence in play in the game of culture – which perhaps drew Casanova to the notion of a *republic* of letters in the first place. For a republic is an essentially political institution or set of institutions, designed precisely to regulate the distribution of power and representation. Casanova's republic is by no means a benign or supportive structure wherein all citizens are

---

1 Pascale Casanova, trans. M.B. DeBevoise, *The World Republic of Letters* (Cambridge, Mass., and London: Harvard University Press, 2004 [1999]); James Morton Smith, ed., *The Republic of Letters: The Correspondence between Thomas Jefferson and James Madison, 1776-1826* (New York: Norton, 1995); Ken Worpole and Dave Morley, eds, *The Republic of Letters: Working Class Writing and Local Publishing* (London: Comedia, 1982); Grant Webster, *The Republic of Letters: A History of Postwar American Literary Opinion* (Balimore: Johns Hopkins University Press, 1979).

2 James F. English, *The Economy of Prestige: Prizes, Awards, and the Circulation of Cultural Value* (Cambridge, Mass.: Harvard University Press, 2005).

equal, but 'a world of rivalry, struggle, and inequality,' where 'rival languages compete for dominance' and where 'revolutions are always at once literary and political'.

> This world republic of letters has its own mode of operation: its own economy, which produces hierarchies and various forms of violence ... Its history is one of incessant struggle and competition over the very nature of literature itself – an endless succession of literary manifestos, movements, assaults, and revolutions.[3]

Interestingly, the term 'republic' disappears from Casanova's restatement of her argument in 'Literature as a World', published in *New Left Review* the year after the book's appearance in English. Perhaps the shift of metaphor was due to the hint of gallocentrism in the term, a charge to which her model as a whole was susceptible.[4] But although articulated in the later essay through the more neutral notion of a literature *world*, none of the original emphasis on inequality or violence disappears.

I want to invoke both the weak and strong versions of the republic of letters in order to examine one small example of the creation of a community built around shared notions of books and reading, but one which can also be understood through the dynamics of the unequal distribution of cultural resources across local and international borders. Notions of symbolic violence would seem to be a long way from the world of a rather genteel magazine promoting good books and good book-talk. My example is the little-known magazine *Desiderata*, produced from a bookshop in Adelaide for a decade from 1929.[5] And yet, however small its own immediate world, the magazine occupied (in the active sense of that word – it had to occupy) a specific position within the literary world system. It had to make space for itself, work out its relationships to the more powerful cultural centres to which it was inevitably in a dependent and subordinate relation; and work out its relationships, too, to an emerging national literature. Casanova's arguments about the double position of individual writers, especially those in cultures 'less well-endowed' with literary resources, can be extended to apply to other cultural agents and other forms of expression such as literary magazines, all necessarily involved, in Bourdieu's terms, in position-taking:

> Each writer enters into international competition armed (or unarmed) with his entire literary 'past': by virtue solely of his membership in a linguistic area and a national grouping, he embodies and reactivates a whole literary history, carrying this 'literary time' with him without even being fully conscious of it.
>
> ... [U]nderstanding the way in which writers invent their own freedom – which is to say perpetuate, or alter, or reject, or add to, or deny, or forget, or betray their national (and linguistic) heritage – makes it possible to chart the course of their work and discover its very purpose ... In other words, the writer stands in a particular relation to world literary space by virtue of the place occupied in it

---

3 Casanova, *The World Republic of Letters*, pp. 4, 11–12.

4 Casanova, 'Literature as a World', *New Left Review* 31 (2005): 71–90. For a critical reading of the original book see Christopher Prendergast, 'Negotiating World Literature', *New Left Review* 6 (2001): 100–21 (especially 106–08).

5 *Desiderata: A Guide to Good Books* appeared quarterly between August 1929 and August 1939.

by the national space into which he has been born. But his position also depends on the way in which he deals with this unavoidable inheritance ... He may reject his national heritage ... he may acknowledge his patrimony while trying at the same time to transform it ... or he may affirm the difference and importance of a national literature ... [I]n trying to characterize a writer's work, one must situate it with respect to two things: the place occupied by his native literary space within world literature and his own position within this space.[6]

A literary magazine established in Adelaide between the wars was of course in a doubly disadvantaged position, not only 'inheriting' the national literature's marginal place within the world literary system but also being subordinate within national literary space to the more powerful cultural centres of Sydney and Melbourne. To what degree we can even speak of a national literature at this point remains unclear, just as it was unclear to *Desiderata*'s writers and editors. Nonetheless, they inherited a complex past, a 'whole literary history,' at once British, imperial and national, and this meant inhabiting a complex present. How, then, did the magazine 'invent its own freedom'? How did it position itself in 'literary time'? To what extent did it reject, acknowledge, transform or affirm its unavoidable inheritance?

*Desiderata* was edited by John Preece, co-manager with his brother Edgar of Preece's Bookshop in Adelaide's King William Street. The bookshop had been founded in 1907 by their father, F.W. Preece, who died in 1928 just before the magazine was launched. According to Geoffrey Dutton, the bookshop, which also ran a circulating library, was 'a centre of literary and artistic culture in Adelaide'.[7] John Preece already had contact beyond Adelaide, in particular with the Lindsays; from 1934 to 1940 he also ran a branch of the bookshop in Sydney.

Figure 1. John Preece thought of the idea of holding Artists' Week in Adelaide in 1924. 'Artists' Week in Adelaide July 29th–August 2nd', *Home* (September) 1924: 20.

---

6   Casanova, *The World Republic of Letters*, pp. 40–41.

7   Geoffrey Dutton, *Snow on the Saltbush: The Australian Literary Experience* (Ringwood: Penguin, 1984), p. 194. Historical details in this paragraph are from Chapter 11.

A woodcut by Lionel Lindsay, a white cockatoo devouring a book, featured on the front cover of the magazine's first issue; inside, Norman Lindsay reviewed M. Barnard Eldershaw's *A House is Built*; and Jack Lindsay was an agent of the Preece's in London. The bookshop had a gallery space upstairs, and in 1924 it had held an exhibition including three of Norman Lindsay's etchings after the local Society of Arts had banned them from its Artists' Week show. Preece's own tastes nonetheless appear to have been closer to Lionel's conservatism than Norman's vitalism; there is nothing of the destructive energy of Norman's polemics. And yet, like both Lindsays, in fact despite their sometimes strident anti-modernism, *Desiderata* was intensely interested in the state of contemporary – that is, modern – arts and letters.

The magazine's first act of positioning was to define itself as contemporary, concerned above all with 'current literature'. Its opening editorial begins:

> The paucity of good Australian journals devoting much space to current literature has made us feel that this publication might be acceptable to many who not only seek guidance concerning good and important books, but like to read further criticisms and to glean bibliographical notes of interest.

These modest goals can be fairly aligned with those of 'middlebrow' culture understood in its historically specific form; that is, as indicating a distinct constellation of cultural values and attitudes that emerged in Anglophone literary cultures in the 1920s and 1930s.[8] Although the term has been used to cover a very wide range of literary modes, critical viewpoints, and class aspirations, the dynamic that drove the development of middlebrow 'book talk' from the mid-twenties to the mid-thirties was that of modernity, modernity under pressure from modernism. The historical middlebrow depended not merely upon the existence of a hierarchy of cultural values scaled between high and low but on the distinctive segmentation of cultures produced in the decades around the First World War by the emergence of avant-garde or high modernist movements, on one side, and the rapid expansion, then consolidation, of modern forms of 'mass' commercial culture on the other. Although often charged with conservatism or mere complacency, the middlebrow describes a conflicted space, a culture in transition, divided and pressed into new shapes by the tensions of these divergent modernising forces. This conflicted present was also experienced as the absence of serious criticism or intelligent book talk for 'discriminating readers'. Hence *Desiderata*, its title invoking things desired, things lacking in the present: a criticism at once 'impartial and outspoken' and a contemporary literature adequate to the moment.[9]

The middlebrow in this register took culture seriously; it was committed, like *Desiderata*, to the 'good and important books' among current literature, although it might also distinguish its tastes from those it considered 'highbrow' or 'ultra-modernist'. Thus the editorial celebrating the magazine's fifth year announced: 'If the esoteric have found *Desid-*

---

8 David Carter, 'The Mystery of the Missing Middlebrow', in Judith Ryan and Chris Wallace-Crabbe, eds, *Imagining Australia: Literature and Culture in the New New World* (Cambridge, Mass.: Harvard University Press, 2004), pp. 173–202.

9 Quotation from a review of *Essays on the Cultural Appreciation of Modern English Literature and Drama* by Francis Jackson and Philip Alcock in *Desiderata* 10 (November 1931).

*erata* of no help, many less exacting have come to value it'.[10] In a period of rapid expansion, when more books were being published than ever before – more *new* books and especially new novels – the need for 'guidance' was expressed repeatedly by readers, professional and amateur alike. *Desiderata* thus saw itself in the words of its subtitle as 'A Guide to Good Books', and it promised that the books chosen for discussion and advertised in its pages would be 'books of merit', chosen with 'thought and discrimination'.[11] Nor was it just a matter of the sheer abundance of new books. The need for guidance and discrimination was felt with some urgency by readers for whom the present moment seemed caught between the pressures of unprecedented artistic innovation on the one hand and accelerated production and commercialisation on the other; or, in slightly different terms, between the narrowing of literature pursued by modernism and its profligate broadening in the marketplace. The literary present was experienced as a time of surfeit *and* lack – when 'too many good books lay unnoticed on the shelves … hidden by the heavy stocks of best sellers, lost and made inconspicuous by the flaring covers of the latest out'; when 'the word masterpiece had come to mean about as much as "topping" [and] was misapplied to anything ranging from a cocktail to a negroid dance'; when, at the same time, 'the qualities which make for permanence have been lacking'; and when the 'majority of modern novels' were marked by 'bitter disillusionment and contempt for everything', by 'verbal dialectics [and] vibrational reproductions of life,' or by the fashion for sex problems and 'scientific exposition of the species'.[12] In short, when settled ideas about literature, poetry or the novel were being unsettled in every dimension.

Consciously or unconsciously, then, for *Desiderata*'s editor and contributing authors the acts of writing and reading meant assuming a position, first in relation to their complex literary inheritance and second in relation to modernity and the literary present. This recalls Casanova's second principle in the organisation of the world literary system, its temporal dimension organised around what she calls the Greenwich Meridian of literature: aesthetic modernity. 'What is considered modern [let us say in Paris or London] will be declared to be the "present" … Texts granted modern status create the chronology of literary history'.[13] The function of modernity as a measure of cultural momentousness is governed by its very instability: its susceptibility to fashion, to the processes of 'more or less rapid obsolescence', to permanent struggle and the 'constant classification and de-classification of works' through such temporal metaphors as '"passé" or "outmoded", archaic or innovative, anachronistic or imbued with "the spirit of the times"'.[14] While anything but revolutionary in its aims, *Desiderata* constantly sought to know what the present looked like, to assess the 'spirit of the times', and, increasingly, to judge just where Australian literature might sit on the scale of modernity.

---

10  Editorial, *Desiderata* 17 (August 1933), p. 3.

11  Editorial, *Desiderata* 1 (August 1929), p. 3.

12  Quotations in this sentence in order from *Desiderata* 1 (August 1929), review of *The Temple on the Hill* by Elsa de Szasz, p. 20; 10 (November 1931), review of *Maid in Waiting* by John Galsworthy, pp. 21–22; 12 (May 1932), review of *The Fountain* by Charles Morgan, p. 13; 3 (February 1930), review of *A High Wind in Jamaica* by Richard Hughes, pp. 27–28; 9 (August 1931), Editorial, p. 5 (quoting Galsworthy). Tenses have been silently altered in the first two quotations.

13  Casanova, 'Literature as a World', p. 75.

14  Casanova, 'Literature as a World', p. 76.

At the same time – and this is part of what makes it interesting as a case study – the magazine was scarcely nationalist in its aims and imaginings, although it was always well-disposed towards new developments in Australian writing. We might distinguish four possible modes of relating Australian literary space to world literary space in this inter-war period, although these are not exhaustive. They do not, for example, account well for Norman Lindsay and *Vision* or the avant-garde movements of the early thirties. But if we imagine a scale extending from nationalism to 'Anglocentrism' (for want of a better word) then we might distinguish provincial and modernising forms of cultural adherence at each end. There was a *provincial nationalism* that sought to quarantine Australian literature from the modern, which also meant from foreign influence. It is present just once in *Desiderata*, in the first issue, in a brief bit of bluster from Randolph Bedford about the future of Australian literature (he was much more confident about its past):

> The new Australian 'novels' are without blood or movement; because it has become fashionable to imitate the anaemia of novels done in England. Whereas the earlier Australians wrote of men and women they had known, these pallid prattlers do not write of even men and women they have met in books …
>
> It is a bad thing for the future of Australian literature when you find the writers of a new strong country accepting as models those dull people – the Compton Mackenzies and Walpoles and Galsworthys – even duller and more foolish in this new country than in the weaker and more sophisticated conditions of the old.[15]

There are aspects of this judgement that Vance and Nettie Palmer, say, might well have supported, but I want to take them as representing, by contrast, a *modernising nationalism*, one that was also internationalist in its sympathies. Although they inherited the organic metaphors of nineteenth-century nationalism, their project was defined by a distinctively modern sense of social crisis, heightened in a colonial society but shared across the industrialised, capitalist world. Its meaning lay not in the celebration of pastoral or 'digger' tradition but in the problem of modern democracy. Looking to the Irish revival or modern Scandinavian literatures, for example, they grasped nationalism (in this period at least) as a democratic movement occurring more or less contemporaneously in different parts of the world, as minor nations achieved distinctive forms of self-expression through their emerging literatures. Nettie Palmer's criticism, in Robert Dixon's words, created

> an impression that the national literature exists in the same time and space as international writing, and that it can and should be judged from that broad perspective. The effect is generous, inclusive and dialectical: it is, in a word, 'cosmopolitan'.[16]

---

15  Randolph Bedford, 'The Future of Australian Literature', *Desiderata* 1 (August 1929), p. 8. An essay in *Desiderata* 2 (November 1929), pp. 4–9, by W.H. Ifould, which asked 'Has Henry Lawson's Verse Any Permanent Value?', produced a storm of correspondence in the following number from well-known authors and critics including John Le Gay Brereton, R.H. Croll, Zora Cross, Percival Serle, Fred Broomfield and E.J. Brady.

16  Robert Dixon, 'Home or Away: The Trope of Place in Australian Literary Criticism and Literary History', *Westerly* 54 (2009): 12–17 (14).

While seeking a useable past, these nationalist critics and intellectuals were not reactively anti-modern.

At the other end of the scale, a *provincial Anglocentrism* might be identified with those who found cultural value simply in the English tradition or in Englishness *per se*, a position familiar enough in local cultural history and predictably anti-modernist. Much less familiar is what I want to call a *modernising Anglocentrism*, and this is where I locate *Desiderata*, alongside its contemporaries *All About Books* and *Art in Australia*.[17] John Preece's British patriotism was evident in his black-bordered editorial in the February 1936 edition on the death of King George V, 'the best-beloved man in all his dominions'. But as Casanova reminds us, literary space is not the same as political space. Although *Desiderata* happily assumed the glories of the English literary heritage, its focus, as I have suggested, was almost wholly on the present. Rather than complacency, then, in the magazine's attachment to British books there was a quietly radical act of the imagination: that is, in imagining that Adelaide was contemporaneous with London, that Australian readers were modern readers, and that the challenges and confusions of modern literature were as pressing for them as for their contemporaries in the great cultural centres abroad. This was the nature of the magazine's community, its small republic of discriminating or responsive readers, likely to be keenly interested in the latest London fiction and new Australian books side by side.

In November 1929 Preece announced that the magazine would feature a regular London Letter from novelist, publisher and patron of modernist art, Michael Sadleir, 'setting forth the latest movements in literature'. Sadly, it never eventuated. What we find in the pages of *Desiderata* nonetheless is a magazine thoroughly attuned to the London book world and therefore utterly contemporary (and this is a 'book world' perspective rather than an academic one, its contemporaneity a function of its engagement in the marketplace). Through London, the magazine's Australian readers might also inhabit a broader international literary world, American and European, and Australian literature, as it came increasingly to the magazine's attention, was conceived in this same relationship, as part of the same world of contemporary books. M. Barnard Eldershaw, Ion L. Idriess, G.B. Lancaster, and Frank Dalby Davison, all noticed in *Desiderata*, were assumed to be part of the same contemporary book culture as 'the Compton Mackenzies and Walpoles and Galsworthys' (whom the magazine in general rather liked). Although in some ways it looked through the other end of the cultural telescope – or chronotope perhaps – *Desiderata* arrived at something very like what Dixon finds in Palmer: it creates the impression that the national literature exists in the same cosmopolitan space and time as international writing; but also, reversing the terms, that contemporary English literature exists in the same time and space as Australian writing and reading. The British connection in this instance was a means of connecting to the modern, to the literary Greenwich Meridian, rather than a thwarting, constraining force.

---

17  David Carter, '"Some Means of Learning of the Best New Books": *All About Books* and the Modern Reader', *Australian Literary Studies* 22.3 (2006): 329–41. *All About Books* also emerged from a bookselling milieu. *Art in Australia* emerged from the commercial as well as the fine arts community. See Nancy Underhill, *Making Australian Art 1916–49: Sydney Ure Smith, Patron and Publisher* (South Melbourne: Oxford University Press, 1991).

In May 1932, to take one example, the editor drew attention to Harold Nicolson's recent pamphlet derived from a series of BBC talks on 'The New Spirit in Literature'. He insists that Nicolson's criticism

> *should* come before our notice because of its 'main purpose to examine the changes in literary taste and intention,' because of its attempt to point out the desirability of a more sincere effort on our part to understand those changes, and because of its controversial nature [my emphasis].

But Preece was also careful to underscore local knowledge of the moderns:

> In Australia we have not been altogether neglectful of these new spirits. Among those specially cited by Mr Nicolson are Mrs Virginia Woolf, Aldous Huxley, T.S. Eliot, David Garnett, Lytton Strachey, Sacheverell Sitwell, Stella Benson, and James Joyce. All of these are known if not familiar to the Australian reading public – even James Joyce, to those who have been so fortunate as to escape the too wary eye of the censor; they are known by their more notable works, though we may have been impatient with some of their efforts that frankly have proved to be beyond our understanding.[18]

As the last phrase suggests, the new spirit in literature could be accepted only so far. If a book requires an explanatory key for the reader to understand it, Preece wondered, 'even when we are in the desired receptive mood', wherein lies its value? Does the interest of the new works lie more in their 'decadence' than their 'literary merit'? And was Nicolson's argument itself just 'another instance of a coterie determined to thrust itself upon a deluded and exotic public'?

Nonetheless the magazine's credentials in the field of modern literature are impressive. In the first issue – alongside Randolph Bedford and Norman Lindsay – it featured an article by Sylvia Townsend Warner on T.F. Powys; a positive review of Eugene O'Neill's *Strange Interlude* ('His work is torrential, prodigal, reckless, full of colour, passion, and movement … And with the restless violence … goes a delight in experiment'); and another, by Preece, of Virginia Woolf's *Orlando*: 'if Mrs Woolf's exquisite prose is read in the right spirit, as we read and re-read we will recognise her genius and the definite place which she has established for herself in the literature of the age'. An excerpt from Woolf's 'Beau Brummell' later appeared in the magazine's third number, which sold out because of her presence in it; *A Room of One's Own* was reviewed positively in May 1930; and *The Common Reader* was reviewed, again positively, in February 1933.[19] Still in the first issue, *All Quiet on the Western Front* was proclaimed the greatest of all the Great War books that had recently appeared, while Katharine Susannah Prichard's *Coonardoo* was welcomed with curious praise: 'The fact that [her] prose is not sophisticated gives her book extraordinary strength'. Subsequent

---

18 'Editorial: The New Spirit in Literature', *Desiderata* 12 (May 1932), p. 3.

19 Woolf responded to the editors, probably on being sent an early number: 'I have read the copy of *Desiderata* with pleasure. I think that it is admirably got up, and has so much of interest in it that it should certainly help people to know what books are the best at the moment'. Printed with other comments on a subscription flyer (Fryer Library, University of Queensland).

issues included positive appreciations of American 'exquisite' Joseph Hergesheimer, Richard Aldington's *Death of a Hero*, J.B. Priestley's *The Good Companions*, Nobel Prize winner Sigrid Undset ('one of the greatest modern novelists'), Ernest Hemingway's *Fiesta* (a 'brilliant modern novel'), Robert Graves' *Goodbye to All That*, and a wide range of authors including Norman Douglas, Thornton Wilder, Charles Morgan, Arnold Bennett, Francis Brett Young, Storm Jameson, D.H. Lawrence, Robert Bridges, Henry Handel Richardson, Sinclair Lewis, Rosamund Lehmann, Aldous Huxley ('every phrase and idea is sharp as the dissecting knife of a scientist, and tissue by tissue the poems are unfolded'), and the modern poets – Baudelaire, Mallarmé, Eliot, Pound, Lawrence and Herbert Read – and this just in its first five years. In 1932, Preece's bookshop published a pamphlet on *The Waste Land*, a poem Preece himself declared 'undoubtedly the most important of our generation'.[20]

This list of contemporary authors is certainly mixed, but the mixture accurately represents both the magazine's own tastes and its sense of the present in literary time. Clearly it includes some who failed to become 'modern classics' and others, like Bennett and Priestley, against whom inter-war modernism was at times explicitly defined. Indeed, while the magazine was often appreciative of the new spirit in literature, its most expansive or assured critical praise was reserved for figures like Bennett and Galsworthy – the Edwardians, in Virginia Woolf's terms, rather than the Georgians – and middlebrow contemporaries such as Priestley, Brett Young, E.V. Lucas, or Hugh Walpole. An article from November 1934, for example, lists some of the very few 'great' novels of recent years and does so in characteristically middlebrow terms:

> the few novels that have had the power of taking us out of ourselves, that we have talked of with pleasure to our friends, read with delight, and finished with regret: *Precious Bane*, *The Good Companions*, *The Fountain*, *Kristin Lavransdatter*, *Imperial Palace*, *The Lonely Plough*, *Maid in Waiting*, *Rogue Herries*.[21]

Almost all are now forgotten; and yet it would be anachronistic to see such preferences as merely residual, reactionary or provincial. What we need is an act of historical imagination, to enter into the mind of a cultured, 'discriminating' reader in the early 1930s, confronted with a very wide array of modern literature in a time *before* the verdict of history had been announced, before the processes of canon formation had established the narrow trajectory of the 'modern tradition' which is now part of our own second nature. For the great modernists came to the bulk of their contemporaries as just a few among the many, a minor note in a crowded literary marketplace (even if they made the most noise). In fact there was a surprising degree of consensus, one largely shared by *Desiderata*, that Woolf, Huxley, Lawrence, Joyce and Eliot were the major modernists, whatever one ultimately thought of them. But we can get from the magazine's own pages a more accurate sense of 'how it struck a contemporary', of how the works that now stand clear in the modernist

---

20  C.R. Jury, *T.S. Eliot's 'The Waste Land': Some Annotations* (Adelaide: F.W. Preece, 1932). Noted in *Desiderata* 14 (November 1932), p. 20. Jury would later become Professor of English Literature at Adelaide University. Dutton, *Snow on the Saltbush*, p. 190. The article on poetry is James M. Hannah, 'The Modern Poet', *Desiderata* 16 (May 1933), pp. 7–9.

21  The authors are, in order, Mary Webb, J.B. Priestley, Charles Morgan, Sigrid Undset, Arnold Bennett, Constance Holme, John Galsworthy and Hugh Walpole.

canon arrived to contemporary readers. In a review of the year's fiction for 1931, Woolf's *The Waves* appears as a novel 'deserving of mention', but it does so alongside works by Galsworthy, Walpole, Brett Young, Clemence Dane, Esther Meynell, Stella Benson, Vita Sackville-West, Philip Gibbs, Edna Ferber, E.M. Delafield, Richard Aldington, G.B. Stern, Vicki Baum, and Margaret Kennedy.[22] *This* was what 'modern literature' looked like in February 1932.

As Christopher Baldick puts it, writing of England in the twenties and thirties, although modernism 'now dominates our map of the literary scene in these decades, [it] was in its own time a minority current'.[23] This correction is perhaps even more necessary in the Australian context, where a narrow focus on modernism tends to produce a deficit model of Australian cultural development, all lack and lag, as if its destiny lay simply in 'catching up'. But if Australia's modernity was provincial, *Desiderata* suggests that it was no more so than Edinburgh's, Birmingham's or Baltimore's, say, or for that matter most of London's. The magazine's modernity is present not just in its close attention to 'the modern movement' but even more so in the way that its surveys of current literature are driven by the sense of being in a critical moment of transition across a generational divide – something it shares, of course, with Virginia Woolf. Thus, in one version of the divide:

> The old traditional world of literature has broken down. Some there are still holding the outer defences, but they are few. Men and women alike have been pursuing a policy of realism in art that long ago broke down all romantic conceptions of life and made the factual the goal.[24]

If the new spirit in literature could be accepted only up to a point, *Desiderata* expressed little nostalgia for the past. The Victorian period, for all its great achievements, was now irrevocably on the other side of history, and on the other side of modernism. But strangely, at least to our way of understanding the history of twentieth century art, it could appear as if modernism itself had come and gone, or at least that it had left the future open. 'After' modernism, the effect of Priestley's *The Good Companions*, for example, could be seen to be like the 'clear and bracing atmosphere' after a storm breaks, 'clearing English fiction after the period of novels, good and bad, of psychological analyses, of sociological problems, and of entanglements and "soul scratchings" '.[25] The period of radical experimentation, of the new *isms* and *ologies*, had made its mark, breaking with the decadence of late-Victorianism: 'the twentieth century [had] seen great advances in the technique of the novel'.[26] But what came next? What came *after* modernism? And what of permanent value remained?

If Lawrence, Joyce, Huxley and Woolf were widely acknowledged as significant authors, their status as models for the future was much less certain. Despite the technical advances and the new good books, the present seemed diminished. On the positive side, 'modern

---

22 'Editorial: English Fiction in 1932', *Desiderata* 11 (February 1932), pp. 5–7.

23 Christopher Baldick, *The Oxford English Literary History. Volume 10: The Modern Movement (1910–1940)* (Oxford: Oxford University Press, 2004), p. 3.

24 I.M. Foster, 'Poets and Prophets', *Desiderata* 28 (May 1936), p. 10.

25 Review of *Angel Pavement* by J.B. Priestley, *Desiderata* 6 (November 1930), p. 12.

26 'The Natural Background in Fiction', *Desiderata* 10 (November 1931), p. 6.

fiction [had] become the most flexible and mobile instrument ever used in literature ... the vehicle for much of the best thinking of our time'; but on the other, 'novelists can still write cleverly about nothing, and are still capable of experimenting in narrative and character, but they cannot write about something definite and carry conviction'.[27] A 1935 review of Frank Swinnerton's *The Georgian Literary Scene* allowed the reviewer, possibly Preece himself, to articulate what was a common position in the magazine, suspended between old and new. The brilliant stars of the previous generation – C.E. Montague, George Moore, Joseph Conrad, Arnold Bennett, and John Galsworthy – had passed on, and so 'once again we look about for new giants, and with the increasing pessimism of this age find it hard to discover writers today who can satisfy our standard'.[28] And yet the reviewer resists Swinnerton's own antipathy towards the moderns, his impatient dismissal of the 'post-Freudians, post-war pessimists, and later visionaries delving into obscurities'. Compared to Swinnerton, he ventures, 'we have become more tolerant and more experimental', even if, with rapid and constant change, criticism had yet to find a true perspective:

> New discoveries are being heaped upon us, whether they are in science or in the detailed analyses of inhibitions and the at present fashionable abnormalities of mankind. Presumably there are fashions in science, apparently there are fashions in vice, certainly there are fashions in literature. These 'new' things are thrust before our notice. Today a fashion reigns supreme: tomorrow will find it swept into oblivion. The sound writers of a very few years back are resting in a sort of literary purgatory. There is a haze about them. They are beyond the mark of today's critics whose shafts are aimed at easier victims. They are waiting to go to their rightful niches.
>
> ... Not all who are modern are pretentious, and all who are old-fashioned are not what one of Huxley's characters calls 'rather second-rate'.[29]

It is difficult to think our way back into this period's experience of the contemporary moment, to think through our sense of modernism's inevitable triumph and its narrow account of what was worthwhile in contemporary culture. Perhaps Preece's own tastes remained stranded somewhere on the cusp between 'Edwardian' and 'Georgian', although he opened the pages of the magazine to more modernist sympathies. The point is that one did not need to be a closed-mind conservative to be unconvinced about modernism's staying power or to imagine that the future lay in continuity rather than endless disruption.[30]

Given its orientation towards London, it would be easy to interpret *Desiderata* as yet more evidence of Australia's dominated position within world literary space, and more specifically, in this instance, within British imperial space. Certainly, Preece and his contributors were conscious of the lack of local literary 'assets', in Casanova's term:

---

27 Review of *Time's Door* by Esther Meynell, *Desiderata* 24 (May 1935), p. 9; Editorial, *Desiderata* 23 (February 1935), p. 3.
28 'The Georgian Literary Scene', *Desiderata* 25 (August 1935), p. 10.
29 'The Georgian Literary Scene', p. 12.
30 See Baldick, *The Modern Movement*, pp. 1–35 and *passim*.

> Anchored, as we are, far from the hub of things, true standards of comparison have been largely lost to sight ... In our own literature we are weak and floundering, and therefore in need of the sound critic. Australia has had few writers possessed of a sound critical faculty.

Ironically perhaps, given his own calls for more serious Australian criticism, Vance Palmer's *The Passage* provided the case study.

> In certain descriptive paragraphs the author shows to what heights he is capable of rising ... then we put down the book, and wonder why Mr Palmer is not more self-critical ... It appears to be an outstanding example of what we want in our fiction and of how easily without self-criticism our writers leave us lamenting.[31]

And yet the strongest impression the magazine creates is not of its dependence upon or subservience to British culture but of its contemporaneity – with 'the English scene', with 'modern literature', and with the London book world. This was how it imagined its community, its 'republic' of readers, but it was also how it 'invented its own freedom', its own claim on the present – not by asserting difference but by rejecting belatedness, by claiming a space within modernity where, we might say, its own middlebrow 'modernism' could be articulated, assessed, and updated.

This contemporaneity is also what enables the magazine's growing interest in modern Australian literature, prompted by the relatively sudden appearance of new and important Australian books from the early 1930s onwards. It reviewed Australian literature from the start, supplemented by occasional essays; by February 1932 it had a regular section entitled 'The Australian Contribution'; and it later introduced a special section for Australian publications in its lists of new and forthcoming books. It had serious, intelligent critics in D.P. (Paul) McGuire, an innovative poet, successful crime novelist, and later Australia's Ambassador to Italy; and I.M. Foster, 'a woman who deserves to be remembered,' as Dutton comments, 'as she wrote enlightened reviews, especially of Australian books, in Adelaide for more than thirty years'.[32] With new novels from M. Barnard Eldershaw, Henry Handel Richardson, 'Martin Mills' (Martin Boyd), Frank Dalby Davison, Velia Ercole, 'Brent of Bin Bin' (Miles Franklin), and Ion L. Idriess there was a growing sense that Australian literature was breaking away 'from the old atmosphere of eucalyptus and billy-tea' and beginning to *be* (there was scarcely any sense that a national tradition existed).[33] The choice of novels to be highlighted, in August 1934, is revealing:

> In the steady flow of books by Australian authors, whether published here or overseas, it is interesting to observe how Australian literature is growing up. Where hitherto knowledge, sophistication, breadth of mind, cosmopolitan thought, and ability to write appeared only at infrequent intervals, tended and

---

31 'Eulogy or Criticism?' *Desiderata* 7 (February 1931), p. 8. It later praised the way the new magazine *Manuscripts* addressed 'thoughtful readers desirous of expressing their comments in intelligent groups': *Desiderata* 11 (February 1932), p. 22.

32 Dutton, *Snow on the Saltbush*, p. 186.

33 Review of *Only the Morning* by John Dalley, *Desiderata* 8 (May 1931), p. 16.

> sheltered like some hothouse plant, there is now found hardy growth in the open air.
>
> A few years ago no Australian publisher would have looked at *Prelude to Christopher*, Eleanor Dark's powerful and terribly moving story, and more than likely Brian Penton's *Landtakers* would have gone a-begging. That Miss Stead's *Salzburg Tales* and Philip Lindsay's *London Bridge is Falling* have been printed overseas is due entirely to the fact that the authors live abroad …
>
> We are building up on literary tradition, and 'literary tradition is alive only so long as there is a tradition of taste, kept alive by the educated (who are not identified with any social class)' – and taste is the faculty of discernment.[34]

Australia was even, at last, 'evolving a "popular" novel to add to the world's literature', alongside the '"thrillers" from England and the "wild west" stories from America'.[35] In its final years the magazine began to notice the new poets, reviewing Douglas Stewart and R.D. Fitzgerald among others, and in 1938 the publishing branch of the business released Rex Ingamells' *Conditional Culture* and the *Jindyworobak Anthology*. Over 1939 and 1940 it published the Jindyworobak magazine *Venture*, reminding us again that the Jindys' own attempt to leap backwards over the colonial inheritance, into an 'Aboriginal' connection to the environment, was also a step forwards into modernity, into the problem of inventing a language adequate to the present.

As suggested earlier, Australian literature was read in its international as much as its national context, to be assessed 'as thought and word worthy to be placed beside the best that is offered on the world's market'. This is the move Foster made in locating *The Fortunes of Richard Mahony*:

> With this one book Australian fiction has been placed in line, not with the romantic convention of great English fiction, but with the modern European conception of the novel as a form of art … Mrs Richardson therefore may be considered to be, from one point of view, on the side of the experimenters in fiction.

As to readers' tastes, while the launch of P.R. Stephensen's *Australian Mercury* was welcomed by Preece, he felt the need to qualify Stephensen's nationalism:

> Indisputably, but a small percentage of our people is interested in Australian literature only; and though it is easy to accuse them of lack of patriotism, the great majority of them have many ties in other lands. Moreover, if better material be obtainable from other sources, some hardihood would be needed to condemn our own people's preference for it.

Preece also offers an unexpected, concrete reason why Australians might have felt at one with the London book world: the fact that 'Booksellers [in Australia] are so far from the

---

34  Editorial, *Desiderata* 21 (August 1934), p. 3. The internal quotation is from F.R. Leavis and Denys Thompson's very current *Culture and Environment*, first published in 1933.

35  'A Group of Australian Stories', *Desiderata* 13 (August 1932), p. 20.

source of supply that they are forced to carry large and representative stocks of English books undreamed of by a London bookseller.'[36]

*Desiderata* deserves to be better known, not only for the quality of its best criticism, but because of the way it shows, first, that cultural nationalism was not the only alternative to the colonial condition and, second, that British cultural domination was not simply domination but involved a complex network of attachments and transfers of value that could be worked in both directions. It reminds us again of the essential role of cultural intermediaries in the 'republic of letters' and the exchanges across public sphere and marketplace through which a book culture is formed. And it adds a further chapter to the study of Australian modernities. On the surface it is not a good fit for Casanova's typology of responses to minority status in the power struggles of the republic of letters, in part because its sense of any national literary heritage is so fragmentary: it can scarcely reject or affirm. And yet the magazine's invention of its own contemporaneity with London – its refusal to turn distance into belatedness – does support, even as it complicates, her argument for the significance of both spatial and temporal dimensions in the literary world system.

The magazine lasted just long enough – before being suspended due to the war – to welcome Patrick White's first novel, *Happy Valley*, which it reviewed twice. The first brief notice finds a 'tragic, significant novel … a really compelling narrative'. In the second, longer review, Seaforth Mackenzie finds the novel only good rather than great, but praises its method and uncompromising nature. He likens it to Faulkner rather than Joyce, and concludes rather mischievously: 'It is the first time such a work has been written by an Australian about Australia – but I do not think that should matter, either!'[37] Of course it does matter – and of course it does not matter, either.

---

36 Quotations in this paragraph from Editorial, *Desiderata* 14 (November 1932), p. 3; I.M. Foster, 'The Art of Henry Handel Richardson', 7 (February 1931), p. 10; Editorial, 25 (August 1935), p. 3; 'Eulogy or Criticism?', 7 (February 1931), p. 8.

37 Seaforth Mackenzie, 'Happy or Unhappy', review of *Happy Valley* by Patrick White, *Desiderata* 40 (May 1939), pp. 19–20. Earlier notice, 39 (February 1939), p. 15.

# 8

## Jindy Modernist: The Jindyworobaks as Avant-Garde

*Peter Kirkpatrick*

> [Y]ou have done what some of us ought to have attempted much earlier; you've brought people together, sifted them, held to a literary credo and be-damned.
>
> Nettie Palmer to Rex Ingamells, April 1941[1]

In his 2008 book *Networked Language*, Philip Mead compares the fortunes of Ern Malley with those of the Jindyworobak movement by means of a striking metaphor:

> unlike the dwindling fate of that other cultural movement of the 1940s, Jindyworobak, what survives of the Malley affair is a resilient disposition towards polar positions about avant-garde poetic practice, a kind of cultural herpes that once it's been caught can't be eradicated, and that leads to a series of secondary infections.[2]

I take issue with Mead's description of the Jindyworobaks as having experienced a 'dwindling fate'. Like the recurring 'disposition' produced by Malley, in many ways Jindyworobakism also became viral, re-emerging at those times when white Australian artists have attempted to represent forms of Aboriginal experience. The herpes metaphor is particularly appropriate, since Jindyworobak is manifestly a condition that affects the skin: a kind of high cultural blackface, or a case of 'white Aborigines', to borrow Ian McLean's term.[3] Notable literary examples might include Patrick White's *Riders in the Chariot* (1961), Thomas Keneally's *The Chant of Jimmy Blacksmith* (1972), and certain poems by Les Murray and Billy Mashall-Stoneking. Among the painters, as well as Margaret Preston's many experiments in a quasi-Indigenous style, Arthur Boyd's 'Bride' series from the 1950s also qualifies. So too do such musical works as John Antill's ballet *Corroboree* (1950), and possibly Ross Edwards' fourth symphony, *Star Chant* (2001), in which the chorus sing Indigenous names of the southern stars alongside their Western and Arabic equivalents.

---

1 Quoted in Rex Ingamells, 'Introduction', *Jindyworobak Review 1938–1948* (Melbourne: Jindyworobak, 1948), p. 26.

2 Philip Mead, *Networked Language: Culture & History in Australian Poetry* (North Melbourne: Australian Scholarly Publishing, 2008), p. 149.

3 Ian McLean, *White Aborigines: Identity Politics in Australian Art* (Cambridge: Cambridge University Press, 1998).

For Mead, the kafuffle over Ern Malley expressed a deep-seated fear of 'the (threatening) ambiguity and unlawfulness of poetic language' within official Australian culture, one that culminated in an attempt literally to police the meaning of Malley's poems through the justice system.[4] When cross-examined by the South Australian prosecutor, however, *The Darkening Ecliptic* could reveal no clear field of reference beyond a vague 'indecency' that circulated around its own ambiguities, as if it were a series of *multiple* entendres – as in Detective Vogelsang's confession regarding the poem 'Egyptian Register' that 'I don't know what "incestuous" means ... I think there is a suggestion of indecency about it'.[5]

The language of the Jindyworobaks has also been accused of inappropriate behaviour. In 1941 A.D. Hope objected to a poem by the movement's founder, in which he compared the flight of a bird to the movement of a spear: 'Mr Rex Ingamells, may, for all I know, write with [his] spears and throwing sticks beside [him], but I should like to know for how many other Australians a spear is a natural simile for a parakeet, or taken from "the very world around"'.[6] Such faux-Aboriginal gestures are now likely to convict the Jindies more on ethical rather than aesthetic grounds: those of cultural appropriation. Certainly they seem guilty of what Renato Rosaldo has called 'imperialist nostalgia': 'a particular kind of nostalgia, often found under imperialism, where people mourn the passing of what they themselves have transformed'.[7]

This chapter considers the rise of the Jindyworobaks as a literary community, from a tiny Adelaide club into a national movement. It also examines Rex Ingamells' focal role in this process, seeking to reframe the Aboriginalism of his program from the limiting context of a parochial nationalism into that of modernist primitivism. In the terms suggested by Pascale Casanova, then, for all their vehement 'centrifugal' assertion of national space, as de facto modernists the Jindyworobaks were nonetheless caught up in 'the centripetal forces that strengthen the autonomous and unifying pole of world literary space'.[8] The first part of this chapter reviews the Jindyworobak movement as a national literary community; the second, its meaning in terms of the modernist avant-garde.

The prolific author of 'at least forty-four volumes of poetry and literary comment ... between 1938 and 1953',[9] Rex Ingamells (1913–1955) has claims to being the most energetic mover and shaker that Australian poetry has ever seen. Yet when, as a twenty-five-year-old,

---

4  Mead, p. 145.

5  Quoted in Michael Heyward, *The Ern Malley Affair* (St Lucia: University of Queensland Press, 1993), p. 191. See also Mead, p. 122. Heyward's book contains the now standard account of the Malley trial.

6  A.D. Hope, 'Cultural Corroboree', *Southerly* 2.3 (1941): 28–31 (29). The poem in question is 'Garrakeen'.

7  Renato Rosaldo, *Culture and Truth: The Remaking of Social Analysis* (Boston: Beacon Press, 1989), p. 69. The relevance of this notion to the Jindyworobaks is suggested by Graham Huggan in *Australian Literature: Postcolonialism, Racism and Transnationalism* (Oxford: Oxford University Press, 2007), p. 106.

8  Pascale Casanova, trans. M.B. DeBevoise, *The World Republic of Letters* (Cambridge, Mass., and London: Harvard University Press, 2004 [1999]), p. 109.

9  John Dally, 'Ingamells, Reginald Charles (Rex) (1913–1955)', *Australian Dictionary of Biography*, vol. 14, available at adb.anu.edu.au/biography/ingamells-reginald-charles-rex-10588/text18809 [accessed 8 July 2011].

he launched the first *Jindyworobak Anthology* in 1938 he could only appeal for contributions 'through academic channels', confessing, 'I know few Australian poets personally' – a statement that might serve to underline Humphrey McQueen's description of him as 'a primitive', for whom '[a]lmost everything about Australian literature came as a great surprise'.[10] Yet within a couple of years the Jindyworobak movement was a force in the land, with many passionate adherents – and not a few vehement opponents – right across the continent. By the time he edited the retrospective *Jindyworobak Review* in 1948, Ingamells could truly say that he knew a great many Australian poets personally.

Ingamells recalled that the germ of the movement was him, Flexmore Hudson, and another South Australian friend, the now forgotten poet Ian Tilbrook, along with a precocious Max Harris, 'then in his final year at school'. 'I would have leapt at any opportunity to link up with a constituted body of writers', Ingamells wrote, 'but there was none'. His ignorance of the Fellowship of Australian Writers, founded in 1928, he put down to its then 'circumscribed activities' and to 'the dinner-party and salon-like corners in which Australian literary activity variously flourished and wilted in those days'.[11] If he saw his own movement as distinct from such lame dilettantism, in that remark there is also, perhaps, the resentment of an angry young Adelaide poet at the cultural hegemony of the eastern cities.

At heart, Jindyworobak was a South Australian revolution and, though it had national ambitions, its core poets – Ingamells, Hudson and, slightly later, Ian Mudie – were all South Australians. Those national ambitions posed a direct challenge to the *Bulletin*, especially, which remained the major literary journal, and which refused to review Jindyworobak publications for several years after Ingamells had a very public scrap with the Red Page editor, Douglas Stewart, in 1941. Often prickly – occasionally with good reason – Ingamells also quarrelled with R.G. Howarth, who edited *Southerly*, and had a distrustful relationship with the otherwise sympathetic Clem Christesen at *Meanjin*.[12]

The Jindyworobaks are the only serious literary movement in Australia to have begun life as a so-called club. While there have been numerous literary and bohemian clubs in this country, their roles have been either social, an excuse to network and carouse – like the Yorick Club in nineteenth-century Melbourne, or *I Felici, Letterati, Conoscenti e Lunatici* in Sydney during the 1920s and 1930s[13] – or else educational – like Brisbane's Hall of the Muses (see Patrick Buckridge's chapter in this volume). The Jindyworobak Club was founded with

---

10  Humphrey McQueen, *The Black Swan of Trespass: The Emergence of Modernist Painting in Australia to 1944* (Sydney: Alternative Publishing, 1979), p. 124.

11  Ingamells, Introduction, *Jindyworobak Review*, pp. 14, 12.

12  See John Dally, 'The Jindyworobak Movement 1935–1945', PhD thesis (Flinders University, 1978), chapter 7 'Jindyworobak Literary Battles 1940–43'. Dally shows that, though Howarth went on to edit the 1949 *Jindyworobak Anthology*, Ingamells felt that his literary values were ultimately British rather than Australian, and that he failed truly to understand Jindyworobak principles (pp. 192–93). Correspondence in the Ingamells Papers in the State Library of Victoria indicates that Ingamells' relationship with Christesen was more complex, as their positions vis-a-vis nationalism were intially closer, as Dally also observes. Dally notes that, 'as late as 1952, Ingamells harboured a strong resentment towards *Meanjin* and Christesen' (p. 230).

13  See Peter Kirkpatrick, *The Sea Coast of Bohemia: Literary Life in Sydney's Roaring Twenties*, 2nd edn (Curtin University of Technology: API Network, 2007 [1992]), pp. 38–39, 111ff.

a clear artistic agenda, as spelt out in Ingamells' manifesto, *Conditional Culture* (1938), and demonstrated in the first *Jindyworobak Anthology*. By contrast, the Bread and Cheese Club, formed at the same time in Melbourne with the general aim of fostering Australian art and literature, had no immediate program as to how to go about this beyond, it would seem, 'luminous conversation and good fellowship'.[14] Anyone joining the Jindyworobaks looking for a rollicking time would have been sorely disappointed. What they offered, right from the very start, however, was a plan, a mission. And, as the son of a Methodist minister, Ingamells was fired with missionary zeal in its execution.

The basis of this was a concern for what he called 'environmental values', a phrase that implies both the nationalistic basis of his project and the Aboriginalism of its execution. The key passage in *Conditional Culture* is as follows:

> The Jindyworobaks, I say, are those individuals who are endeavouring to free Australian art from whatever alien influences trammel it, that is, to bring it into proper contact with its material. They are the few who seriously realise that an Australian culture depends on the fulfilment and sublimation of certain definite conditions, namely:
>
> 1 A clear recognition of environmental values.
>
> 2 The debunking of much nonsense.
>
> 3 An understanding of Australia's history and traditions, primaeval, colonial and modern.[15]

Ingamells regarded his first 'condition' as the most important. 'The debunking of much nonsense' refers to an ongoing critique of 'imported' – that is, British – literary language and imagery inappropriate to the Australian environment. The third condition follows from the preceding two, especially the inclusion of 'primaeval' traditions. Later in *Conditional Culture*, Ingamells wrote, 'to ensure imaginative truth our writers and painters must become hard working students of Aboriginal culture, something initially far-removed from the engaging and controlling factors of modern European life'.[16]

In 1938, then, Aboriginalism figures as just one element of a much broader program, but potentially a defining one. After all, Ingamells' choice of name – 'Jindyworobak' meaning 'to annex, to join'[17] – implies a fundamental engagement with Indigenous culture. The problem, of course, is that *annexing* and *joining* are two very different actions. What

---

14 Harry Malloch, *A Brief History of the Bread and Cheese Club Melbourne* (Melbourne: The Club, 1940), p. [1]; also P.I. O'Leary, *The Bread and Cheese Club: Founded to Serve Literature, Luminous Conversation and Good Fellowship* (Melbourne: Hawthorne Press, 1938).

15 Ingamells, *Conditional Culture*, in John Barnes, ed., *The Writer in Australia: A Collection of Literary Documents* (Melbourne: Oxford University Press, 1969), p. 249. A version of *Conditional Culture* was first delivered as an address, 'On Environmental Values', to the English Association, Adelaide, in early 1937, and published as 'Concerning Environmental Values' in the only issue of the first series of Ingamells' journal *Venture*.

16 Ingamells, *Conditional Culture*, p. 264.

17 Ingamells, *Conditional Culture*, p. 249. He took the word from the glossary to James Devaney's collection of Aboriginal legendary tales, *The Vanished Tribes* (Sydney: Cornstalk, 1929), p. 240.

happened was much more a process of annexation, of appropriating Aboriginality, rather than 'joining' with it in a co-operative cross-cultural spirit; though even 'joining' might suggest 'assimilation': a deeply fraught term these days. Les Murray, who is sympathetic to the Jindyworobaks' aims, prefers the word 'convergence', claiming that '[t]he Jindies represent a creolising impulse in our culture'.[18]

At the time Ingamells founded the club, he was working in a range of lowly part-time educational jobs.[19] He had completed a BA at the University of Adelaide in 1934, majoring in history, and then over 1935–36 took some further history subjects, apparently with the view to undertaking an Honours program. But by March 1936 he was accepted as an MA student – only to have his thesis rejected by the History Department later that year because 'his subject had not been approved'.[20] Ingamells' topic was 'Australian History as a Background to Australian Literature', and John Dally speculates that *Conditional Culture* may have been lifted from it.[21]

It seems, then, that Ingamells had been planning an academic career, intending to use it as an institutional base from which to promote his ideas. It is possibly for this reason that the idea of a club was so appealing. In areas such as politics and the theatre, university clubs often form a bridge between the amateur and professional worlds. Also, as noted earlier, it is painfully apparent that Ingamells did not have a wide circle of literary friends with whom he could launch his movement. Even among those who would become key Jindyworobak poets, Ingamells had an uneasy relationship with Flexmore Hudson, whom he had known at university, and was yet to meet Ian Mudie, soon to be his greatest supporter.[22] Whatever the case, with a membership fee of 2/6d, in twelve months the Jindyworobak Club had expanded to 150 members,[23] and by 1940 to 500, evidently the maximum extent of its growth.[24]

Ingamells was nothing if not ambitious. When he reissued his journal, *Venture* (1939–1940), he announced the aim of 'provid[ing] an annual scholarship to enable some young Australian writer … to spend six or eight weeks in the outback country'. The Broken Hill Jindyworobak sub-branch was even planning its very own calendar.[25] Small wonder that A.D. Hope famously mocked the Jindies as 'the Boy Scout School of Poetry'.[26] With the

---

18  Les Murray, 'The Human-Hair Thread', *Persistence in Folly* (London: Angus & Robertson, 1984), p. 29.

19  Dally, 'Ingamells'.

20  Quoted in Dally, 'The Jindyworobak Movement', p. 60.

21  Dally, 'The Jindyworobak Movement', p. 61.

22  Mudie's first correspondence with Ingamells seems to be a note dated 5 July 1940: Rex Ingamells Papers, State Library of Victoria, MS6244, 4/114.

23  Ingamells, Editor's Note, *Venture* 2.2 (1940): 1.

24  Ingamells, Introduction, *Jindyworobak Review*, pp. 14–15. In 'The Jindyworobak Movement' Dally seriously questions this figure (p. 103).

25  Ingamells, Editorial,*Venture* 1.1 (1939): 3–5 (3, 5). An earlier *Venture*, subtitled *An Australian Literary Quarterly*, appeared in 1937, but lasted only one issue. The later *Venture* was subtitled *Jindyworobak Quarterly Pamphlet*.

26  Hope, p. 28

beginning of the Second World War, though, these more extraneous projects quickly fell away, along with *Venture* itself, which had justified the membership fee.

By the time he edited the *Jindyworobak Review* in 1948, Scout Leader Ingamells could write that, 'The Club idea … became nebulous, and of secondary importance to the loose association of writers in the yearly *Anthology*'.[27] For his part, Hudson thought that Ingamells always imagined 'less a club of writers than of readers'[28] who would support their work. John Dally thinks his motives were more complex:

> He envisaged a fellowship of writers (and commentators perhaps) who would contribute poems to the *Anthology* and poems and articles to *Venture*. As editor of both publications, he would ensure that most of the contributions enhanced the Jindyworobak ideal while recognising that, at least for a while, he could not afford to be totally prescriptive. This grouping of poets would ensure that Jindyworobak became a literary force simply by being a recognisable landmark in the amorphous and featureless landscape of Australian literature. He envisaged also that this dynamic superstructure would be supported by a large number of relatively passive helots who would be members of the Club, pay dues, subscribe to *Venture* and the *Anthologies* but not necessarily *contribute* to them.[29]

Focus on the *Anthology*, which ran from 1938 to 1953, meant that the Jindyworobaks became less a corporeal than an imagined community.[30] As there was no other such annual Australia-wide collection of verse, the *Anthology* proved a significant innovation – so significant that Angus & Robertson copied it in 1941. Ingamells' falling out with Douglas Stewart occurred when he discovered that the seemingly unsympathetic Stewart was to edit their new *Australian Poetry* anthology, which offered direct competition with his own.

Though Ingamells was prepared to deputise his editorial role, he retained ideological authority. During their editorships in 1943 and 1944 respectively, both Flexmore Hudson and William Hart-Smith suffered his displeasure at their selections, Hart-Smith being informed that 'I am telling you, in as reasonable and logical a way as I am capable of, that I'm disappointed at your *grasp* of Jindyworobak in the present anthology'.[31] For the editor's benefit, Ingamells spelt out what the proper criteria should be, and reproduced them in that year's *Anthology*:

> 1 *Positive Jindyworobak verse*, in which Australian environmental values are faithfully observed.
>
> 2 *Neutral verse*, in which environmental values are no issue.
>
> 3 *Un-Jindyworobak verse*, in which environmental values of other countries are represented.

---

27  Ingamells, Introduction, *Jindyworobak Review*, p. 15.
28  Dally, 'The Jindyworobak Movement', p. 95.
29  Dally, 'The Jindyworobak Movement', p. 100.
30  See Benedict Anderson, *Imagined Communities: Reflections on the Origin and Spread of Nationalism*, rev. edn (London and New York: Verso, 2006 [1983]).
31  Ingamells to William Hart-Smith, 28 October 1944, Ingamells Papers 2/281.

>   4 *Anti-Jindyworobak verse*, flouting Australian environmental values.
>
>   Of these divisions, only the last is inimical to the spirit of Jindyworobak.[32]

For his part, Hart-Smith confessed to Ingamells that he had never actually paid his 2/6d membership dues.[33]

Ingamells really did think that poetry could change the world – or at least the way in which white Australians engaged with their country. His insistence on 'environmental values' was intended as a serious attack on mainstream British-Australian aesthetic values, and the presumed autonomy of art in general and poetry in particular. So, in his jibe at 'the dinner-party and salon-like corners' of the Australian literary establishment of the 1930s, is there a underlying note of *épater les bourgeois*? Humphrey McQueen correctly observes that 'Ingamells was concerned more with culture in the broad, anthropological sense of how people live … much more than with those things normally associated with culture in its narrow sense of the arts'.[34] In an age when the word 'environmental' lacked its present conflation with 'ecological', it is Australian 'culture' in this wider sense that is linked to the demand for 'environmental values'.[35] To that extent, then, the Jindies' program affirms one of Peter Bürger's criteria for an avant-garde; namely, the political re-engagement of art with everyday life, or 'the attempt to organize a new life praxis from a basis in art'.[36] Because of this, the Jindies were often accused of writing propaganda and 'bad' poetry. Take, for instance, Ingamells' 'The Gangrened People' (1941):

>   We who are called Australians have no country;
>   no country holds us native heart and soul:
>   our boast that Federation made a nation;
>   our boast that Anzac proved it with our blood
>   are tragic fictions. Our standards are fictitious:
>   we dwell in the limbo of a harsh deception,
>   a criminal betrayal, guaranteeing
>   the selfish satisfaction of the cunning
>   exploiting us for money, money, money,
>   spreading the itch to purchase every day,
>   filling our hearts with fatal loyalties
>   to notions not our own, nor suited to us.[37]

Beyond their sometimes wavering adherence to Ingamells' poetic principles, however, most of the Jindies remained politically inert. The notable exception was Ian Mudie, whom

---

32  Ingamells, Note, in William Hart Smith, ed., *Jindyworobak Anthology, 1944*, (Melbourne: Georgian House, 1944), verso of title-page.

33  William Hart-Smith to Ingamells, 19 August 1943, Ingamells Papers 2/208.

34  McQueen, p. 128.

35  The *OED*'s first citation of 'environmental' in its secondary meaning, 'Of or relating to the natural environment', is from an academic journal in 1935.

36  Peter Bürger, trans. Michael Shaw, *Theory of the Avant-Garde* (Minneapolis: University of Minnesota Press, 1984), p. 49.

37  Ingamells, 'The Gangrened People', in *Rex Ingamells: Selected Poems* (Melbourne: Georgian House, 1944), p. 32.

Ingamells finally met in 1940. The hectoring nationalism of Mudie's verse found an early home in P.R. Stephensen's quasi-fascist journal the *Publicist* – Stephensen's biographer, Craig Munro, going so far as to describe Mudie as 'the *Publicist*'s captive poet'.[38] Ingamells' *Conditional Culture* had been much influenced by Stephensen's essay *The Foundations of Culture in Australia*, which he read in 1935,[39] but it would be Mudie who brought the two men into contact with each other in 1941. Dally sees the influence of both Mudie and Stephensen on 'The Gangrened People', and in particular Stephensen's pamphlet, *Fifty Points for Australia: A Forecast of the New Order* (1941).[40]

Stephensen went on to found the Australia First Movement in October 1941; Ingamells joined it in December, Dally noting that his 'sense of timing was deplorable'.[41] For, owing to unfounded fears that the movement was a hotbed of collaborators, on 10 March 1942 Stephensen and other Sydney members of Australia-First were arrested and interned; in Stephensen's case, for the duration of the war. Ingamells and Mudie had their houses searched and were interrogated by the South Australian police, and were lucky that it ended for them there.[42] Subsequently, Ingamells made no secret of his Australia-First links, but downplayed the depth of his initial commitment to Stephensen's 'Tribe'.[43] Nationalism induces emotive rather than rational affiliations, particularly during wartime, and no doubt with hindsight Ingamells grew to realise where he and Stephensen differed, he being neither anti-Semitic nor particularly right-wing. Writing to the newspaper magnate Sir Keith Murdoch in September 1943 to seek some 'practical support for Jindyworobak', he stated that '[m]y position with regard to A.F. is that I applaud a great deal of it, but am in strong opposition to some of it'.[44]

As Dally suggests, it seems likely that the Australia-First connection did the Jindyworobaks no favours, and may have turned many in the broader literary community against them. Rather than strengthening their oppositional status, though, they instead became viewed as misguided, even deluded. Dally argues that, 'some sort of literary "set" was taken against the hapless Jindyworobaks and that it became rapidly fashionable to deride them'.[45] Because the trend was not to take them wholly seriously, they never generated a sufficiently strong 'polar position' (to use Mead's term) against their practice; and therefore they never became an effective avant-garde. Hope's 1941 review in *Southerly*, cited above, marked one turning point, but another had been Ingamells' spat with Douglas Stewart and the *Bulletin* earlier the same year.

---

38  Craig Munro, *Wild Man of Letters: The Story of P.R. Stephensen* (Carlton: Melbourne University Press), p. 200.

39  Ingamells, Introduction, *Jindyworobak Review*, p. 10. He read the first instalment of the essay in the first and only issue of Stephensen's journal *Australian Mercury* (1935).

40  Dally, 'The Jindyworobak Movement', pp. 152–56; Munro, p. 209.

41  Dally, 'The Jindyworobak Movement', p. 158.

42  Munro, p. 224.

43  See Ingamells, 'Jindyworobak', in Gina Ballantyne, ed., *Jindyworobak Anthology 1945*, (Adelaide: F.W. Preece, 1945), p. 65; also Introduction, *Jindyworobak Review*, p. 19.

44  Ingamells to Sir Keith Murdoch, 28 September 1943, Ingamells Papers 4/227.

45  Dally, 'The Jindyworobak Movement', p. 236.

Another was the defection of Max Harris during 1940 to found *Angry Penguins*. This was despite the fact that Harris' first book of verse, *The Gift of Blood* (1940), had recently been published under the Jindyworobak imprimatur. He was an early enthusiast for the club, but by the second issue of *Venture* in 1939 found he had to reinvent Jindyworobakism to take account of his own burgeoning surrealism. His confused essay, 'An Approach to Australian Poetry', reads the movement in terms of a modern *Weltanschauung* for which the primordial uncanniness of the bush stands as a kind of objective correlative: 'for above all Australian environment is not in itself romantic, nor require [sic] romantic interpretation'. And so, 'through their intense concentration on Australia [the Jindyworobaks] have arrived at a poetry which unknowingly parallels in approach the poetry of the new world-attitude. For this reason I support them unreservedly'.[46] In other words, their obsession with an estranging landscape was turning the Jindies into modernists in spite of themselves.

Did Harris get something of his polemical manner from Ingamells? He joined the Jindyworobaks because it was the only radical literary scene in town, but found that his own radicalism quickly outstripped it. In *Meanjin* in 1943, Harris berated his former fellow Jindies for their 'Aboriginalising' of English, and insisted – *pace* 'environmental values' – that a poet's 'fundamental environment is himself'.[47] Still, his initial attraction to the group is worth stressing, especially since it has been overlooked by critics.

Mead's account of the aesthetic divisions over the Malley hoax – 'artistic experiment and international perspectives versus the backward-looking preservation of traditional, often nationalistically oriented, artistic practices' – implicitly relegates the Jindyworobaks to the camp of those who opposed *Angry Penguins* and all it stood for. But it is by no means clear how Ingamells and Mudie, to pick the two most 'nationalistically oriented' Jindies, might line up with what he also describes as 'nascent Australian neo-classicism',[48] a prime exemplar of which was that old enemy of the Boy Scout School, A.D. Hope. In contrast, Humphrey McQueen argues that Ingamells, at least, 'did not close his mind to the rest of the world', and lists some of his reading over 1939–40 that included essays by Herbert Read, poetry by Louis MacNiece, and 'an explanation of Surrealism by Hugh Sykes Davies'. Politically, too, McQueen sees 'causal links between the European crisis and Jindyworobak' (although he wrongly assumes Ingamells was a communist).[49]

Before reflecting on the Jindyworobak project within an international context, however, it is worth quoting from Harris' fond reminiscence of the club in the *Jindyworobak Review*, not least for what it affirms about the role Ingamells played as a force for literary change. He saw the Jindies and the *Angry Penguins*, not as bitter anatagonists, but rather as Blakean 'contraries without which there is no progression'; and he was very positive about the varied literary community they formed:

---

46   Max Harris, 'An Approach to Australian Poetry', *Venture* 1.2 (1939): 14.

47   Harris, 'Dance Little Wombat', *Meanjin* 2.2 (1943): 33–35 (35).

48   Mead, p. 149.

49   McQueen, pp. 128–29. Davies' 'explanation' is presumably 'Surrealism in This Time and Place' from Read's edited collection *Surrealism*, produced in conjunction with the 1936 International Surrealist Exhibition in London.

> To achieve intellectual stimulus it is necessary for writers to be gregarious, even if gregariousness can only be expressed in 'little' magazines. The early days of Jindyworobak were to me, a process of establishing contact, contacts with poetic outlooks ranging from [Paul] Grano and [James] Devaney in Brisbane to the Bread and Cheesers in Melbourne. This interchange of viewpoints, to which Ingamells' controversial theory gave rise, caused a feeling of coherence between various individuals, and a feeling that literary thought was moving ahead in an exciting way.[50]

In *The World Republic of Letters*, Pascale Casanova links literary nationalism with the codification of local languages, arguing that, for all their regional particularities, nationalist struggles within what she calls 'dominated' literary spaces share 'an almost universal and transhistorical order of development'.[51] During Federation, the argument for a local vernacular realism had been successfully carried by the *Bulletin*, but by the 1930s the literary possibilities of demotic Australian English were substantially exhausted, as were poetic forms, such as the ballad, used to express it. Hence Ingamells' desire to shift his focus from the gangrened people of a still colonial society towards their own, distinctly Australian 'environmental values'. Herein lies the specific attraction of Aboriginal culture as a fully 'indigenising' resource. But in the primitivist desire to go back to the future in this way, Ingamells also made common cause with a powerful modernising movement within the world republic of letters itself: the European avant-garde.

At this point an example is helpful. 'Kuark's Mockery' (1938) by Ingamells belongs to the early 'high Jindyworobak' phase, and there are only a handful of poems in this radical, macaronic style, but it highlights a central problem of trying to 'Aboriginalise' Australian poetry. I have included relevant 'translations' from the accompanying glossary:

> Where jindyneelingo gwingy [gaunt tall] gums
> lift pinaroo [old man] knees and twisted thumbs,
> Kuark [kookaburra] calls in dherang [valley] dark,
> with bararang [ghost] men there to hark:
> 'Uh! bararang men look about,
> but all their cooking fires are out.
> Goomblegubbon [scrub turkey] in the scrub
> does not fear the boondee club.
> Billaburra [platypus] at erragodin [waterhole]
> need not haste from plunging in …
> Bimbaroora [behold] – while I mock –
> crumbled gunyah [native hut] and totem-rock!'[52]

When glossed, 'Kuark's Mockery' represents the kookaburra's laugh as the natural world's derisive elegy for the destruction of Aboriginal society, which remains a ghostly presence

---

50   Max Harris, 'The Importance of Disagreeing', *Jindyworobak Review*, p. 74.
51   Casanova, p. 179.
52   Ingamells, 'Kuark's Mockery', *Sun-Freedom* (Adelaide: F.W. Preece, 1938), p. 19; 'Glossary', p. 48.

nonetheless, embodied in the 'jindyneelingo gwingy gums' which frame the scene like tribal elders. The Jindyworobaks were fond of what Bob Hodge and Vijay Mishra have termed 'premature elegies' like this, and their memorialisations of the so-called forgotten people[53] constitute the repeated, melancholy return of an Aboriginal repressed that would subsequently take as its philosophical focus the notion of Alcheringa, 'the Dreamtime'.

Despite – or perhaps because – of its risible potential, 'Kuark's Mockery' might almost be a piece of Dada. In 1917 on stage at Zurich's Cabaret Voltaire, Tristan Tzara had chanted his own French versions of Carl Strehlow's German translations of traditional Arrernte songs of the snake and the cockatoo:

> 'ici pointes de branches
> certainement'
> ici des grains mêlés à la balle
> certainement
> sur la place creusée les poser
> des amas des amas y poser
> beaucoup d'amas poser
> des amas des amas poser
> de grands amas poser
> profonds amas poser
> de grands amas poser[54]

Tzara was following in the footsteps of his fellow avant-gardists Richard Huelsenbeck and Hugo Ball, who had earlier performed so-called Negro Poems there: experiments in a wild made-up language, for the incantation of which Ball dressed in a special 'magic bishop' outfit. Then there's the sound poetry of Hanover-based Kurt Schwitters, best represented by his *Ursonate* or 'primaeval sonata' (1922–32):

> Fümms bö wö tää zää Uu, pögiff, kwii Ee.
> Dedesnn nn rrrrr, Ii Ee, mpiff tillff toooo, tillll, Jüü-Kaa?
> Rinnzekete bee bee nnz krr müüüü, ziiuu ennze ziiuu rinnzkrrmüüüü,
> Rakete bee bee.[55]

Tim Armstrong has suggested that '[m]odernist primitivism can be considered under three headings: vitalism; magic thinking; and abstraction.'[56] To varying extents, it is possible to read both 'Kuark's Mockery' and Schwitters' *Ursonate* under all three of these categories.

---

53 Bob Hodge and Vijay Mishra, *Dark Side of the Dream: Australian Literature and the Postcolonial Mind* (North Sydney: Allen & Unwin, 1990), p. 42. *Forgotten People* was Ingamells' second collection of verse, published in 1936. It includes a suite of sonnets with the same title on the theme of Aboriginal dispossession.

54 Tristan Tzara, trans. 'Chanson du Cacadou', in Ann Stephen, Andrew McNamara and Philip Goad, eds, *Modernism & Australia: Documents on Art, Design and Architecture 1917–1967* (Carlton: Miegunyah, 2006), p. 34.

55 Kurt Schwitters, *Ursonate*, UbuWeb: *Ursonate de Kurt Schwitters*, available at www.ubu.com/historical/schwitters/ursonate.html [accessed 16 August 2011].

56 Tim Armstrong, *Modernism: A Cultural History* (Cambridge: Polity, 2005), p. 140.

Formal and phonetic abstraction is clearly more conspicuous in Dada sound poems, but it is present in Ingamells' estranging deployment of Indigenous words, which evoke a haunted landscape through an uncanny, 'ghostly' language. Evidently these are 'magic' words, like those of the shamanistic anti- or, rather, *pre*-languages declaimed in Dada poetry. There's a sense, too, in which Ingamells is also employing an atavistic pre-language, since he lifted his Aboriginal words from the glossary at the back of James Devaney's literary refashioning of Indigenous myths, *The Vanished Tribes* (1929). Closely linked to this kind of uncanny 'magic thinking' is vitalism; in psychoanalytic terms, the desire to return to pre-Oedipal origins, to retreat from the Western symbolic to an Indigenous imaginary. 'Kuark's Mockery' and the *Ursonate* are both provocations, but each, in its different way, addresses a more authentic mode of being to be found in the 'savage' Other. In Ingamells' words, 'The Stone Age man in us has watched his fire/die as the cruel heaven of desire'.[57]

Along with this romantic nostalgia was the growing recognition – from Durkheim, from Freud – that there were fundamental social and psychic affinities between tribal and modern cultures. Thus in 1919 T.S. Eliot could write, in part influenced by Baldwin Spencer and F.J. Gillen's ethnographic studies of Central Australia, that:

> as it is certain that some study of primitive man furthers our understanding of civilised man, so it is certain that primitive art and poetry can help our understanding of civilised art and poetry. Primitive art and poetry can even, through the studies and experiments of the artist or poet, revivify the contemporary activities. The maxim, 'Return to the sources', is a good one.[58]

Anthropology therefore provides a compelling context for modernist primitivism, and for the Jindyworobaks' version of it. It was from *The Arunta* (1927), to take a notable instance, that Ian Mudie introduced the word 'Alcheringa' into the movement's philosophy.[59] Later, in the *Jindyworobak Review*, Ingamells also highlighted the significance of Spencer and Gillen, along with that of A.P. Elkin and T.G.H. Strehlow. Indeed, he closely identified the Jindys' literary 'campaign' with anthropological discoveries:

> [The continent's] uniqueness is properly explained only by understanding of Australia's primeval story, as revealed by scientists. There are many aspects to this story, and we are interested in all of them; but our interest, like that of the scientists, is necessarily a twentieth century interest.[60]

---

57 Ingamells, 'The Gangrened People', p. 31.

58 T.S. Eliot, 'Warpaint and Feathers', 1919, quoted in Ronald Bush, 'The Presence of the Past', in Elazar Barkan and Ronald Bush, eds, *Prehistories of the Future: The Primitivist Project and the Culture of Modernism* (Stanford: Stanford University Press, 1995), p. 35. On Eliot, ethnography, and Spencer and Gillen see also Caroline Patey, 'T.S. Eliot and the Text of Anthropology', in Giovanni Cianci and Jason Harding, eds, *T.S. Eliot and the Concept of Tradition* (Cambridge: Cambridge University Press, 2007).

59 '[I]t was I.M. who awakened me to the significance of the Alcheringa as being a symbol, and not only a subject, within Australian Literature': Ingamells, in 'Jindyworobak', *Jindyworobak Anthology 1945*, p. 65.

60 Ingamells, Introduction, *Jindyworobak Review*, pp. 19, 25. Ingamells asserts there that at Hermannsberg in 1930–31 Strehlow 'told me what the Alchera was, and first drew my attention to native legends, those of the Aranda [sic] that he had translated' (p. 11). In 'The Jindyworobak Movement',

Even so, Elazar Barkin and Ronald Bush have observed that, 'try as it might, [ethnographic discourse] never succeeded in being the culture's prime access to the primitive'.[61] They point to the effects of the long history of Western imperialism by the late nineteenth century, and to the increasing trade in artifacts, souvenir pictures and photographs, as well as new technologies such as film in bringing the primitive Other back 'home', so to speak. For it is also the case that by the 1930s the Aboriginal frontier had already begun to figure more prominently in white Australian consciousness. Aborigines began to appear in documentaries and in films, like Charles Chauvel's *Heritage* (1935) and *Uncivilised* (1936) – the latter about another kind of white Aborigine, a 'wild white man' à la Tarzan called 'Mara'.[62] Katharine Susannah Prichard's novel *Coonardoo* (1929) should be mentioned in this context, along with the vastly more popular works of Ion Idriess, such as *Man Tracks* (1935) and *Nemarluk, King of the Wilds* (1941).

That Jindy poetry was so fixated upon Central Australia might be put down to the fact that, in W.H. Auden's phrase, 'The desert sighs in the bed' more insistently in Adelaide than in the more well-watered east. Nevertheless, with the opening of the Trans-Australian Railway in 1917, a royal road to the continent's 'Stone Age' interior opened up, and a desert tourist industry slowly evolved, marketed through the Australian National Travel Association's journal *Walkabout* (1934–74). Ingamells' first serious poems, published as *Gumtops* (1935), were in fact written in response to a holiday in Central Australia in 1930–31, where he claimed to have met T.G.H. Strehlow at Hermannsberg.[63]

By this time, too, what Ian McLean has called 'desert pastoralism' featured in the work of highly popular South Australian artist Hans Heysen, to be followed in the next two decades by such major modernists as Russell Drysdale and Sidney Nolan. Significantly, the Indigenous watercolourist Albert Namatjira held his first exhibition in Melbourne in 1938 – the same year the Jindyworobak Club was formed. By the 1950s, reproductions of Namatjira's outback landscapes would appear on biscuit tins, and in suburban loungerooms and dentists' surgeries, alongside mass-produced copies of Heysen's heroic gumtrees. In no time at all almost every home could boast a mulga-wood ashtray or an *hors-d'oeuvres* platter with a faux-Indigenous design. By the 1980s, when Ted Bullpitt of TV's *Kingswood*

---

Dally discusses Strehlow's early influence at length (pp. 47–53), but in a later essay, 'The Quest for the Jindyworobaks', he is 'very clear' that the concept of Alcheringa came from Mudie and not Strehlow: *Meanjin* 39.3 (1980): 404.

61  Elazar Barkan and Ronald Bush, Introduction, *Prehistories of the Future*, p. 7.

62  Paul Byrne, Curator's Notes, '*Uncivilised* 1936', *Australian Screen*, available at aso.gov.au/titles/features/uncivilised/notes/ [accessed 16 August 2011].

63  Ingamells, Introduction, *Jindyworobak Review*, p. 11. Doubt is cast on this meeting by Strehlow, who Dally interviewed in 1972. Strehlow said that he was not at Hermannsberg when Ingamells was supposedly there, and in fact first met him in 1934 ('The Jindyworobak Movement', pp. 47–49). Whatever the case, Ingamells was keen to get Strehlow's opinion of his poetry, and of the authenticity of his outback depictions. Strehlow responded warmly to the manuscript of *Gumtops*; his biographer, Barry Hill, describing its arrival as a 'godsend to Strehlow, alone in the Centre': *Broken Song: T.G.H. Strehlow and Aboriginal Possession* (Milsons Point: Random House, 2003), p. 391.

*Country* was so protective of 'Neville', his concrete Aboriginal garden statue,[64] such objects – and such attitudes – had long become a joke. As McLean writes:

> The precepts of modernist primitivism had so penetrated the fabric of Australia by the 1950s that its influence was evident across a wide range of competing art practices, from kitsch to high art, from pastoralism to modernism. By this time the significance of Aboriginal culture to Australian identity was incontestable.[65]

I began by invoking Philip Mead's 'viral' metaphor to describe the recurrence of Jindyworobak symptoms in Australian culture; and symptomatic they are, I think. The virus itself is more deep-rooted, the product of a disposition towards primitivism within rapidly industrialising Western societies as part of their collective membership of the modern world – including its republic of letters. At the level of high culture the Jindies can thus be read within that transnational modernist context, and not exclusively through the nationalism of their stated program. In any case, that nationalism has itself been mistaken for a simple thing, a form of kitsch pastoralism, instead of a considered, if nonetheless troubled – and still troubling – affirmation of the incontestable significance of Aboriginal culture to modern Australian life.

---

64  The name was evidently a joking reference to Senator Neville Bonner (1922–99), the first Aboriginal person to sit in federal parliament.

65  McLean, p. 96.

# 9

## BOBBIN UP IN THE LESELAND: AUSTRALIAN LITERATURE IN THE GERMAN DEMOCRATIC REPUBLIC

*Nicole Moore and Christina Spittel*

The Australian writer Dorothy Hewett's first novel, and her only socialist one, *Bobbin Up*, was published in 1959 by the Australasian Book Society (ABS) in Melbourne. The ABS was a small, cooperative publishing society, strongly supported when not controlled by the Communist Party of Australia, which released literary novels, short story collections and other books of note from 1952 until the early 1980s. In its most productive period, members could expect up to four titles a year. The ABS was paralleled by the Realist Writers Groups, which in turn were relatively small but certainly productive (especially in their early years) state-based writers' groups affiliated with the Communist Party of Australia and the trade union movement.[1] As Hewett herself described them, while a prominent member of the Perth RWG:

> the groups acted as a yeast within the Communist Party and trade unions to establish the role, importance and need for the writer as a part of the forces for social change. By their work they helped establish the bona fides of the writer at a time of extremely backward narrow views on the value of creative literature in the Australian left.[2]

The Australasian Book Society released 3000 copies of *Bobbin Up* and these sold out in eight weeks.[3] The novel was not republished in Australia until 1999, however. Vulgar Press then marketed its anniversary edition as a homecoming: 'a classic of industrial fiction is coming home'.[4] It was indeed a return, from overseas, where Hewett's book had had a long career after falling out of print in Australia. It appeared in editions in the Netherlands (1962) and the UK (1985), but it was in Eastern Europe that the novel received its most

---

[1] See Allen Gardiner's account of the formation of the ABS and its connections with the Realist Writers Groups: Allen Gardiner, 'Frank Hardy and Communist Cultural Institutions', in Paul Adams and Christopher Lee, eds, *Frank Hardy and the Literature of Commitment* (Carlton: Vulgar Press, 2003), pp. 35–52 (42–44).

[2] Dorothy Hewett, 'The Times They Are a'Changin'', in Fiona Morrison, ed., *Selected Prose of Dorothy Hewett* (Perth: University of Western Australia Press, 2011), pp. 152–57 (154). First published in *Hecate* 21.2 (1995): 133–36.

[3] Dorothy Hewett, 'Introduction to the 1985 Virago Edition', in Ian Syson, ed., *Bobbin Up* by Dorothy Hewett (Melbourne: Vulgar Press, 1999 [1959]), pp. x–xviii (xviii).

[4] H. Gustav Klaus, in *Bobbin Up*, back cover.

substantial print runs, media attention and plaudits. *Bobbin Up*'s career in Eastern Europe began in the German Democratic Republic, with an English-language edition, published in 1961. It was then translated and published in Hungarian, in July 1962, as *Pörög az orsó* (*The Spinning Reel/Spindle*), with a print run of 25 000; in Russian, in November 1962 (a letter from one of Hewett's Moscow correspondents declared it 'quite successful'); in Romanian in the same year, with 10 000 copies (for which she received fifty pounds sterling paid on release); and then in German, in a run of 3000 in 1965.[5] This second East German edition was released by Volk und Welt, the German Democratic Republic's largest publishing house for international writing, established in 1947. The German translation was by the highly experienced Ernst Alder, who had spent some time in Australia, and it was released as *Die Mädchen von Sydney* (*The Girls from Sydney*) in the middle of 1965. A second German print run of 5000 was sold outright to a Leipzig book club in 1966, and a Bulgarian edition of 10 000 copies was also released.

About a group of women workers at a textile factory in Sydney, the interwoven narratives of which end in a sit-in strike, Hewett's socialist realist novel was in many ways a predictable choice for the arbiters of publication in the socialist East, and thus its evident popularity seems easily explained. It is not greatly surprising that, halfway through 1960, Hewett had a contract with an East German publisher, negotiated by the ABS. But close examination of *Bobbin Up*'s publication history in the GDR, where its first European edition appeared, positions the novel as at once a usefully illuminating instance – paradigmatic in many ways of East German centralised publication control – and a richly textured exception. As noted, it was first published in the GDR in English (the language of the class enemy) by the specialist English-language publisher Seven Seas, from which more than ninety percent of the print run was destined for the English-speaking, non-communist world, including Australia.[6] It was also marketed as a women's novel – quite differently to Australia, where the reservations of the ABS and some communist readers about its 'sensual' approach and frank discussion of sexuality were made plain.[7] And despite meeting the prescriptive doxa required by the Ministry of Culture, its official reception was by no means formulaic or ideologically hollow. Assessors embraced it warmly, praising its psychological penetration and lively characters.

---

5 These figures are compiled from the contracts held in Hewett's papers, the records of Volk und Welt, and the GDR Ministry of Culture's permission to publish files. The figure of 3000 for the Volk und Welt print run is from Hewett's copy of her contract, held in her papers (National Library of Australia, MS6184, folders 3–4), but contrasts with the figure of 5000 recorded on the permission to publish form submitted by Volk und Welt to the GDR's Ministry of Culture (Bundesarchiv Berlin, DR1/4000/124). This may reflect the tendency of East German publishers to inflate print runs for the ministry, since it was these that determined their centralised funding, rather than actual sales. Siegfried Lokatis, 'Paradoxien der Zensur in der DDR', in Martin Sabrow, ed., *Der geteilte Himmel: Literatur und ihre Grenzen in der DDR* (Leipzig: Akademische Verlagsanstalt, 2004), pp. 75–99 (79–80).

6 Rebecca Jany, 'Rewriting as Cultural Politics: The Role and Function of the Publisher Seven Seas', MA thesis (Freie Universität Berlin, 2007), pp. 20–23.

7 Communist Paul Mortier's review in the *Realist Writer*, the newly established journal of the RWG, while celebrating 'the first woman revolutionary hero I know in Australian literature', disliked the novel's 'sensual rather than fully conscious picture of reality', and feared that sexual imagery would devalue it. Paul Mortier, 'Bobbin' Up', *Realist Writer* 1.2 (1960): 19–20. Cf. Nathan Hollier, 'The Critical Reception of *Bobbin Up*', in *Bobbin Up*, p. 227–33.

*Bobbin Up*'s distinct reception histories in Australia and the GDR work as revealingly transposed opposites, as is the case for many of the Australian books published in East Germany in the 1950s and 60s. Leftist or radical nationalist titles with limited reach in Menzies' Australia were given large print runs, substantial media attention, and explicit state sanction in the ideologically controlled distribution systems of the GDR. It was not unusual for East Germans to look beyond their own writers as they rebuilt their country and their literature, and Australian books figured among those of Shakespeare, Defoe, Hemingway and others, as well as the Soviets. From 1949, some of Australia's most important writers were published in East Germany. The war correspondence of venturesome expatriate journalist Wilfred Burchett was followed by Frank Hardy's politically controversial (and marketed as such) *Power without Glory* in 1952, and then by novels and short stories by Marcus Clarke, Katharine Susannah Prichard, Xavier Herbert, Dorothy Hewett, Walter Kaufmann, Thomas Keneally, Patrick White and many others. Stretching to 1990, when a translated collection of Judith Wright's poetry became the last Australian title released by an East German publisher – reviewed by the *Frankfurter Allgemeine Zeitung* as a contribution to reunification, speaking to Germans in East and West – the forty years of Australian titles published in the GDR form an alternative canon, a shadowy literary archive that rewrites Australia's postwar cultural history from behind the Iron Curtain. In 1965, one assessor of *Bobbin Up* rejoiced: 'we have another Australian before us at last'.[8] These contrasting national reception histories throw light onto the mid-century communist book trade as a transnational Cold War phenomenon with some profound cultural penetration from West to East and back again, even as the East German trade was among the most regulated and tightly controlled in the world.

Commended by the judges of the Mary Gilmore award in 1959 as the 'best' of the 'Labor-influenced' novels chronicling working-class lives in Australia, *Bobbin Up* is warm, lively, frank, and richly realist in its portrait of inner Sydney. It boasts an innovative structure that does without a nominal protagonist, following the interlinked lives of fifteen women in and outside the factory, and is remembered as a notable Australian advance on its genre within the international body of working-class fiction.[9] For Stephen Knight, in its 'structural daring', it combines a realisation of 'the environmental understructures of urban life' with the 'affective character of industrial life', demonstrating both 'sharp-edged politics' and 'humanly located' identification. 'Before Barthes, before Pynchon's practices', he wrote in 1993, 'Hewett structures antiauthoritarianism, collectivity and affective values into the very shape of her text'.[10]

Discussed at special meetings of Sydney Communist Party branches, and conceived and produced through the Realist Writers Groups, the novel is a distinct product of those

---

8   Undated reader's report, supplied by Volk und Welt to the East German Ministry of Culture in January 1965, in support of an application for permission to print, now held at the Bundesarchiv Berlin, DR1/4000/136-37 (136).

9   Cf. Carole Ferrier, 'These Girls are on the Right Track: Hardy, Devanny and Hewett', in *Frank Hardy and the Literature of Commitment*, pp. 71–87; Nicole Moore, 'Dorothy Hewett', in Nicholas Birns and Rebecca McNeer, eds, *A Companion to Australian Literature Since 1900* (Rochester, NY: Camden House, 2007), pp. 321–34.

10   Stephen Knight, '*Bobbin Up* and the Working-Class Novel', in Bruce Bennett, ed., *Dorothy Hewett: Selected Critical Essays* (Perth: Fremantle Arts Centre Press, 1985), pp. 70–88 (80, 81, 82).

at once highly institutionalised and in Australia profoundly marginal, dissident or even antagonistic reading formations. One contemporary reviewer's observation that it seemed written for communist rather than ordinary working-class Australian readers is salient, as Nathan Hollier notes.[11] Hewett reported that, as far as she knew, only one of the girls at the mill on which it was based read it.[12] In the middle of the novel, which is set in 1957, Hewett conjures the appearance of the Sputnik Soviet satellite in Sydney's sky as a literally global beacon for communist ideals, an inspiration to the Australian workers of the Jumbuk factory, far from the USSR. Sputnik declares: 'look what the workers' state can do'. As Hewett recalls in her preface for the 1999 edition, for communists it was 'sublime proof of socialism's success'.[13] It is also a neat figure for her book's networked Eastern Bloc reception, connecting the communist world, but blinkingly far from Australia, and (for the southern hemisphere) functionally (that is, perhaps merely) ideal.

That *Bobbin Up*'s first publisher in Europe was the unusual East Berlin-based Seven Seas is an interesting fact in itself. Seven Seas was the creation of its chief editor Gertrude Gelbin, wife of high-profile East German writer Stefan Heym, who had achieved notable success as an anti-fascist writer in the US and remained a voice of committed critique for East Germans until the fall of the Berlin Wall in 1989. In 1953, immediately upon their arrival in the GDR, Gelbin was looking for a means to publish Heym's English-language work, as well as the work of the 'Hollywood ten' screenwriters blacklisted under McCarthy. She began this work with Panther Books, an imprint of private publishing house Paul List. In 1958, after some disagreement, the list was transferred to the state-owned Volk und Welt, East Germany's largest publishing house for international writing, which operated as Seven Seas Publishers until 1980.[14] With Gelbin at the helm until the mid 1960s ('she was the boss who determined our program'[15]), Seven Seas published a range of writers working in English. 'From the outset', Gelbin recalled in 1967, 'we published the classics and nonfiction such as autobiography, biography, history, and travel, in addition to modern fiction by authors who were currently in disfavour in their own societies'.[16] From 1960, Seven Seas also produced translations of East German works. 'Literature in English was hard to sell in the GDR', recalls one of Gelbin's early co-workers,[17] and, indeed, ninety percent of Seven Seas' books were earmarked for export, to both capitalist and socialist countries, including Britain, the US, India, Ghana and Australia. Seeking support from East German Minister of Culture, Erich Wendt, in 1961, Gelbin declared that by exporting both current GDR writing in English translation and 'progressive' English-language literature 'throughout the world in all countries, whether NATO, SEATO, or neutral', Seven Seas would counteract 'capitalist

---

11   Hollier, 'The Critical Reception of *Bobbin Up*', p. 230.
12   Hewett, Introduction, p. xv.
13   Dorothy Hewett, 'Afterthoughts on *Bobbin Up*', in *Bobbin Up*, pp. vii–ix (viii).
14   Jany, pp. 17–18.
15   Ursula Lutz, 'Werbung, Vertrieb und Export – Bücherklau zur Messe', in Siegfried Lokatis and Simone Barck, eds, *Fenster zur Welt: Eine Geschichte des DDR-Verlags Volk und Welt* (Berlin: Christoph Links, 2004), pp. 379–84 (379).
16   Gertrude Gelbin, 'Story of Seven Seas Books', *New World Review* 35.2 (1967): 38–42 (39).
17   Lutz, p. 379.

propaganda advanced through American and British paperbacks' and publicise the 'democratic nature' of the GDR.[18]

It may have been a not altogether positive review of Hewett's novel in the *Times Literary Supplement* in November 1959 that caught the attention of the English-speaking East Germans. Under the title 'Labour and Pains', *Bobbin Up* was grouped in a quite diverse clutch of books, including a children's book about Siamese cats, but also Earle Burney's *Down the Long Table*, a US novel featuring a leftist professor facing off the Un-American Activities Committee. While *Bobbin Up*'s experimental structure proved 'confusing' and wearisome to the reviewer, Hewett's book was still praised as 'vivacious' and 'memorable', and Hewett herself described as 'one of the new generation of novelists that is bringing vitality to the Australian literary scene'.[19]

By July 1960, Les Greenfield at the ABS had accepted an offer from Seven Seas on Hewett's behalf, and the Seven Seas paperback edition of *Bobbin Up* was released in February 1961, with a print run of 5000.[20] Gelbin appears to have purchased the European copyright, contracted from the ABS,[21] so that her edition then became the basis for the Eastern European translations, with Gelbin acting almost as an agent to Hewett, fielding publishers' inquiries and representing her interests. 'Please be sure it is worth your while financially to accept their terms', she wrote to Hewett about the prospective Bulgarian edition. 'Perhaps what the Soviet Union gave as terms might be a guide. I just don't want to see you sold down the river!'[22] A warm and highly personal correspondence between the two women stretches from 1961 to 1967, built on visits by Hewett to East Germany, and including the exchange of family photographs: Gertrude reports standing a photo of Dorothy and children on the dresser in her bedroom where she could see it from her bed.[23]

Before this germinal Seven Seas edition, however, came a rigorous process of examination. The procedures to which *Bobbin Up* was subject in the GDR demonstrate the workings of the nation's centralised cultural administration – its explicitly political aims and methods – in a regime of prepublication censorship that had absolute power of selection over which titles could and could not be released in the small nation. At the same time, we can map the process of *Bobbin Up*'s publication against shifting political positions for Hewett, as well as for the role and administration of cultural production in the GDR, as the cultural ideologies of socialism were brought into international public contest, particularly by writers, and then were strongly defended by the state.

The GDR saw itself as a literary society, a *Leseland* or 'reading nation'. The country boasted a dense web of bookshops and libraries, and, while it produced fewer titles per

---

18  Quoted in Jany, p. 17.

19  'Labour and Pains', *Times Literary Supplement*, 27 November 1959.

20  Jack Beasley to Hewett, 16 January 1962. See also Les Greenfield's telegraph to Hewett, dated 3 February 1961: 'Accepting Offer Sevenseas Edition Bobbinup Details Later Les'. Hewett Papers, National Library of Australia, MS6184, folders 3–4.

21  Gelbin to Bulgarian Copyright Agency, replying to enquiry about copyright in *Bobbin Up*, June 20 1966, Hewett Papers, folders 3–4.

22  Gelbin to Hewett, 20 June 1966, Hewett Papers, folders 3–4.

23  Gelbin to Hewett, 4 December 1965, Hewett Papers, folders 3–4.

year than its West German neighbour, these appeared in astronomical print runs.[24] An anthology of Australian short stories in German translation, for example, first published in 1976, sold 80 000 copies.[25] Its quick sale testifies to the population's hunger for books from the outside world. As former editor Gabriele Bock recalls, 'the mere first name of an author could signal that the purchase of a book might afford a journey in the mind, to a country where English was spoken'.[26]

Like those of other socialist states, authorities in East Germany necessarily conceived of books and their production as political phenomena. Ideological objectives, not market demands, determined literary production. Books were considered building blocks with which to construct a new, truly socialist German state. Indeed, the first publishing house founded in the Soviet-occupied zone was called 'Aufbau' Verlag (*aufbauen* – to build, to construct). By 1946, East Germany had its first censorship body, whose authority was extended so that by 1963, when the Central Administration for Publishing Houses and the Book Trade [Hauptverwaltung Verlage und Buchhandel] was founded, East Germany's entire literary system was firmly under state control.[27] Located within the Ministry of Culture, this regime ruled a stratified network of publishers with predetermined profiles and designated market shares. It approved annual plans that specified titles and print-runs, allocated paper and hard currency, and, most importantly, subjected each new title to a rigorous approval process. As did those of both the Australian and South African censors, although in unlike ways, in many respects the Ministry of Culture's endeavours delimited the nation's institutional or even practical construction of the literary as a category.[28]

Most books published in the GDR bear traces of this process. They come with prefaces and afterwords – travel permits to the *Leseland* – that position authors and their texts within the GDR's changing ideological climate. East German print permit files, now held in the Federal Archives in Berlin, reveal the complex negotiations behind the books' admission. These include ideological considerations, aesthetic and moral judgments (interestingly inflected both through and notionally outside ideology), economic imperatives (such as the cost of licensing fees), and concerns regarding the GDR's reputation abroad. Records contain application forms requesting details on titles, editions, authors, translators, printers,

---

24 Christoph Links, 'Leseland DDR: Bedingungen, Hintergründe, Veränderungen', in Thomas Großbölting, ed., *Friedensstaat, Leseland, Sportnation* (Berlin: Christoph Links Verlag, 2009), pp. 196–207 (196–97). See also Margit Resch: 'East Germany was a nation of avid readers. Book sales relative to the size of the population – around seventeen million – were the highest in the world'. Margit Resch, *Understanding Christa Wolf: Returning Home to a Foreign Land* (Columbia: University of South Carolina Press, 1997), p. 17.

25 Siegfried Lokatis with Simone Barck, *Zensurspiele: Heimliche Literaturgeschichten der DDR* (Halle: MDV, 2008), p. 21.

26 Gabriele Bock, 'Lesen in der eingeschlossenen Gesellschaft: Zur Veröffentlichungspolitik und Rezeption britischer Literatur in der DDR', in Barbara Korte, Sandra Schaur and Stefan Welz, eds, *Britische Literatur in der DDR* (Würzburg: Königshausen and Neumann), pp. 41–47 (44).

27 Lokatis, 'Paradoxien der Zensur in der DDR', pp. 76–77.

28 Peter McDonald, *The Literature Police: Apartheid Censorship and its Cultural Consequences* (Oxford: Oxford University Press, 2009); Marita Bullock and Nicole Moore, Introduction, *Banned in Australia: A Bibliography of Books Banned by Federal Censorship in Australia 1901–1975* (AustLit, 2008), available at www.austlit.edu.au/specialistDatasets/.

editors, and the amounts of paper and foreign currency required. Also preserved are the readers' reports: usually one from within the publishing house and one commissioned by the publisher. Censors could – and often did – request additional assessments. Thus, five reports were needed to publish an anthology of West German short stories in 1965, and even then permission depended on changes to the selection and the afterword.[29] East German readers had to wait for a change in government to see a second volume (in 1977), and until 1989 for a volume of Samuel Beckett's plays. In practice, censorship began at the publishers' desks: having successfully 'trained' their publishers, the censorship authority never rejected more than one to two per cent of the manuscripts submitted.[30]

*Bobbin Up*'s arrival in the *Leseland* was smooth, uncomplicated and unsensational. It took Seven Seas just under a fortnight and only one short report to be granted the permission to print its English language edition in late 1960. Volk und Welt's German language edition, *Die Mädchen von Sydney*, received its imprimatur in less than three weeks in early 1965.[31] For the latter edition, censors were provided two detailed assessments and requested a third, perhaps reflecting increasingly formal administration and the fact that this edition was destined for East German readers. On both occasions, assessors recognised the ideological aims of the novel, welcoming it without reservations as a 'Marxist analysis',[32] a 'valuable'[33] and 'very useful book for our readers who no longer know what unemployment and exploitation mean'.[34] Hewett's timing was perfect, in fact. *Bobbin Up* made its first appearance on the desk of the East German censors in the wake of the Bitterfeld Conference of April 1959, a defining event in East German literary history. In the small industrial town of Bitterfeld, the heart of East Germany's chemical industry, artists and writers had been asked to 'come to the factories, to the construction sites of socialism, and to celebrate the heroism of work in their novels, stories, plays and poems',[35] while, in turn, workers had been encouraged to 'seize the pen'.[36] Hewett's first assessor singled out her preoccupation with the world of work, commending the novel as:

---

29  Werner Liersch, 'Erkundungen der Erkundungen: Westdeutsche Literatur 1964', in *Fenster zur Welt, Eine Geschichte des DDR-Verlags Volk und Welt*, pp. 215–19.

30  Lokatis, 'Paradoxien der Zensur in der DDR', p. 81.

31  Permission to print Seven Seas' English edition was sought on 27 October 1960 and issued on 7 November. The application for the German translation was filed 9 January 1965 and granted 27 January.

32  Report for *Bobbin Up* supplied by Seven Seas, undated, Bundesarchiv Berlin, DR1/4000/142-43 (142). All translations of archival material by Christina Spittel.

33  Report for *Die Mädchen von Sydney* supplied by Volk und Welt, undated, Bundesarchiv Berlin, DR1/4000/132-35 (135).

34  External report for *Die Mädchen von Sydney*, 22 January 1964, Bundesarchiv Berlin, DR1/4000/128-31 (131).

35  The words are Otto Gotsche's, a close colleague of then head of state Walter Ulbricht. Quoted in Manfred Jäger, *Kultur und Politik in der DDR: 1945–1990* (Köln: Edition Deutschland Archiv, 1995), p. 87.

36  The conference's much-quoted motto was: 'Seize your pen, workmate, our national literature needs you'. Quoted in Jürgen Weber, *Germany, 1945–1990: A Parallel History* (Budapest: Central University Press, 2004), p. 71.

> a lively, stirring image of the human relationships of the working class in the family, at work and among neighbours ... The author has done a wonderful job in her presentation of the workers, in particular the female workers, with their pithy conversations and their realist notions of the day-to-day griefs of life, without pretending to stand above them.

This reader emphasised that Hewett's women 'basically never lose courage', and described how the novel's logical unfolding of events forces them to recognise reality and their true leader – Nell, the communist: 'The story approaches an exciting climax, when the women decide to go on strike together.'[37]

By 1965, however, when the novel was once again submitted for assessment, parts of the Bitterfeld Path had worn thin. East German writer Christa Wolf had published *Der Geteilte Himmel* (1963, *Divided Heaven*), a novel that drew on her own experience working in a factory in the industrial town of Halle. Frustrated with authorities' rejection of his ideas, Manfred, an ambitious young chemist, leaves for the West; his girlfriend, Rita, remains behind, unable to find her place in West Berlin. When the wall is built, Rita attempts suicide, and it is from her hospital bed that the novel's narrative is told. At a second Bitterfeld Conference, in April 1964, writers like Wolf insisted on the need for literature to be less dogmatic and more 'truthful', reflecting strong criticism of the formulae for socialist realism that had begun to be expressed from writers otherwise committed to the political aims of the GDR.

The 1965 print permit form for Hewett's novel contains a brief blurb that stresses its frank realism, by then a highly contested term, as well as its 'success with its audience in Australia':

> It is a women's novel that impresses with its knowledge of the milieu, and which tells with healthy Anglo-Saxon humour and realist openness of the joys and woes of Australian women and girls ... Realist diversity and colour make this novel a good piece of popular fiction with effective political accents.[38]

Assessors agreed that these were indeed the novel's main selling points. Volk und Welt's internal reader described the book as being 'one of the very few women's novels, in the best sense of the word', concluding:

> Woman as a member of society (and not just as mother, mistress, worker) is at its centre; and this complex rendering of woman makes the book valuable. It is conceivable that the publisher's advertising focuses especially on this point, to ensure the book a wide distribution.[39]

---

37  Report for *Bobbin Up*, supplied by Seven Seas, undated, Bundesarchiv Berlin, DR1/4000/142-43 (142).

38  Application form for *Die Mädchen von Sydney* supplied by Volk und Welt, undated, Bundesarchiv Berlin, DR1/4000/124 verso.

39  Report for *Die Mädchen von Sydney* supplied by Volk und Welt, undated, Bundesarchiv Berlin, DR1/4000/132-35 (135).

The publisher's second, external reader concurred, advising to 'publish this book as soon as possible.' While she detected traces of 'that biggest danger of all Australian literature – sentimentality', she also emphasised the book's political effectiveness, particularly for a female readership:

> What is most valuable about this book is that the reader, and especially the female reader, is forced – not through political declamation, but through the simple presentation of facts – to draw comparisons between our situation and that in a capitalist country.[40]

These reports together provide a mediated measure of the GDR's official reception of books like *Bobbin Up*, evidencing the weave of literary critical approaches, affective reading, material pragmatism and political idealism that constituted the assessment/censorship process. At the same time, they show that even for communist books the process was not automatic. These assessors were also real readers, engaged by Hewett's work, which was written 'without any intellectual snobbery, but with the mastery of a clever woman',[41] on various levels. The 1960 reader for the Seven Seas edition declared:

> The meeting of the party group, at which the bulletin was being discussed, is easily one of the most humane, humorous and realist descriptions of such a meeting that I have read in a long time.[42]

In September 1965, Walter Czollek, the director of Volk und Welt, mailed to Hewett a letter from one of her East German readers. He sent both an 'almost literal translation' in English as well as the original German letter, 'because we think that you will be glad to hear words of praise from your readers'. Lieselotte Assmann from Berlin-Weissensee wrote in terms that resonate with those of the book's assessors, evidencing convergence between the aims of the Ministry of Culture and the response of conscientious, identifying readers, especially women, as predicted:

> Your work has made a deep and lasting impression on me. You can be proud of your gift of finding such warm-hearted words for the fate of your brave women. Sydney is far away, but there is no distance between human beings who are feeling the same. If women from all over the world feel like you, there will be more love and less tears in the future.
>
> Your girls – Shirley, Lil, Dawnie, Nell, Patty, and the others – are drawn from life and urge us to support them in their struggle. And that we will do! There are many Nells in my country, but Maisies, too, who want to live a selfish life.
>
> Sometimes [sic] I also was somewhat like Maisie and thought that the others could do their part, but your book has taught me that human values can only develop in and for a human community. If I had your talent I could express my

---

40 Bundesarchiv Berlin, DR1/4000/136-7.
41 Bundesarchiv Berlin, DR1/4000/136.
42 Bundesarchiv Berlin, DR1/4000/142-43 (143).

feelings in a better way, but I ask you to take my simple words as a sign of my high esteem for you.

I thank you once more for the hours I could spend in reading your book and for the deep feelings it gave me. I shall not cease fighting for more joy in the life of the Sydney girls in my way. The sun shall shine for everybody! Men often think that their strength governs the world, but I feel it is the love of women which preserves it. We give life and want to guard it, and that is the greatest power.[43]

As a rare document evidencing *Bobbin Up*'s East German reading reception, Assmann's letter illuminates the humanist and universalist models through which its transnational literary meaning circulated, even (or perhaps especially) when mediated through international socialism and Eastern European postwar feminism. It allows rich comparisons with *Bobbin Up*'s Australian popularity, where such frames had much less authority and were perhaps in contest with the appeal of its vernacular localism.

On the one hand, the publication of Australian socialist realism in the Eastern Bloc provides direct literary instancing of the communist vision of internationalist solidarity, in a mid-century, pro-Soviet convergence that countered Cold War divisions. The leftist books of Western writers provided fortifying versions of socialist commitment within capitalism, deployed in East Germany by publishers and the Ministry of Culture to hearten and confirm the sometimes fragile status quo. 'In the eyes of many of our readers', wrote one Ministry of Culture assessor of *Bobbin Up* in 1964, 'Australia, too, belongs to that unreachable paradise of cars and fridges; and it won't do them any harm to find out what it is really like there.'[44] On the other hand, as this report suggests, the books carried with them an intriguing and powerful thread of local realism that proved at once alien and exotic, opaque and appealing. The Seven Seas edition of *Bobbin Up* included a two-page glossary of Australian words, possibly supplied by Hewett herself. This revealing list is one oblique trace of such a reading, presenting a catalogue of the book's attractive unknowns. It marks the book as coming from a different world, and foremostly a capitalist world: think of the pop songs that punctuate Hewett's text or the glaring ads for Pepsi Cola. Glossary entries also include Australian commodities ('Weeties packet'), as well as the everyday world of working-class Australian speech ('mozzies', 'pommy', 'cozzie').[45] The title of the East German translation also marks the appeal of this difference, '*von Sydney*', while entries like 'A.W.U. organizers' in the English Seven Seas glossary explain Australian labour institutions to GDR readers.

According to Hewett's contract, Volk und Welt published 3000 copies of *Bobbin Up* in its first print run, for which Hewett was assigned seven percent of the royalties from the price of the 'unbound copies', calculated at 5.40 Ostmark or East German Marks each. If

---

43  Lieselotte Assmann to Volk und Welt, 8 September 1965, enclosed in Czollek to Hewett, 24 September 1965, Hewett Papers, folders 3–4.

44  Reader's report on *Bobbin Up*, supplied by Volk und Welt to Ministry of Culture, Bundesarchiv Berlin, DR1/4000/136.

45  Peter Doyle suggests that the period's popular songs work as a 'virtual soundtrack' for the novel, cueing scene changes and narrative transitions: 'Writing Sound: Popular Music in Australian Fiction', *Altitude* 8 (2007), available at pandora.nla.gov.au/pan/13197/20070927-0014/www.api-network.com/altitude/articlef7c9.html?issue=8&nid=7&theme=Eight&inprogress [accessed 7 December 2011].

the edition sold out, minus press editions, her payments would have totalled no less than 1077.3 Ostmark. At the official GDR exchange rate, pegged 1:1 with the West's Deutsche Mark, this would have come to approximately US$270.00. The black market exchange rate returned from five to ten Ostmark to the DM, however, and exports generally made it 4:1. This rate for Hewett would have given her only US$67.00, when the average Australian annual wage for 1966 was about A$3000, so less than a fortnight's pay. In 1966, the second edition was sold outright to the Kleine Hausbibliothek book club in Leipzig at 6.15 Ostmark and Hewett's royalty reduced to five percent – 'but you needn't wait so long for the payment', noted Walter Czollek.[46]

Hewett visited the GDR in May 1965, attending the Weimar Writers' Congress of that year, just before Volk und Welt released *Die Mädchen von Sydney*.[47] The distance between Gelbin's edition of 1961 and this one was as long in Hewett's life, however, as was the distance between the two Bitterfeld conferences. Gelbin wrote to her in 1965, at the news that her poem 'Testament' had won first prize in a notable Soviet award: 'And there's that special feeling that such a gifted writer stands on our side of the fence'.[48] But tensions and fractures between Hewett's position and the Soviet line had already emerged. Her report on the Weimar Congress was published in three installments in the Australian communist *Tribune* through August and September 1965, the second of these beginning with praise for the speeches of German writer Anna Seghers, Russian Konstantin Fedin, and British (originally Australian) communist James Aldridge, drawing Australian readers into this richly internationalist socialist literary experience. Hewett described the Chilean poet Pablo Neruda reading a poem in lieu of a speech, which

> translated rather badly into English through my earphones. I took them off and listened to that great voice rolling and resounding like waves through the theatre. I never knew what Neruda's poem meant, but I will never forget it.

Her list of celebrated writers extended to also include:

> Tibor Dery who led the Petoefi Circle of Hungarian Writers through the streets of Budapest during the counter revolution, crying 'Speak the Truth'. Two years ago today he was released from jail, today his books are published in Hungary and in East German translations. He was the elected spokesman of the Hungarian writers at the Congress.
>
> 'I am against Fascism in whatever form it raises its head. I can only support a socialism based on freedom,' he said. 'A writer who does not write the truth is no writer. I wish you a peaceful mind and truthful friends.'
>
> There was silence for a moment. Then the whole Congress gave tribute to this grey headed, stooped, burning-eyed man.[49]

---

46   Czollek to Hewett, 17 October 1966, Hewett Papers, folders 3–4.
47   Akademie der Künste, Berlin, Volk und Welt Archiv, folder 1558.
48   Gelbin to Hewett, 2 November 1965, Hewett Papers, folders 3–4.
49   Hewett, report, *Tribune*, 1 September 1965.

As Susan Sheridan chronicles in *Nine Lives,* her group biography of women writers publishing mid century, Hewett's disillusionment with Soviet models and communism deepened markedly after this visit to the USSR and Eastern Europe in 1965.[50] *Bobbin Up* was published in Hungarian before it was released in German, as we have noted; a Bulgarian edition was mooted for 1966. The characteristic rhetorical flourish at the end of this passage, evoking Dery's aged passion as a vividly conflicted bodily state, marks it out from the rest of the piece: a sign perhaps of Hewett's own affective interest in the question of the writerly conscience. Hewett's doubled, distanced position in communist Eastern Europe, as at once speaker and audience, writer and reader, but also tourist, visitor, observer, alien, is evident in these passages.

In the same year, in an essay she did not publish, Hewett was condemning the 'inhibiting effect of the Communist writer's conscience … not his conscience about humanity in general but his conscience about his Party and the working class', declaring that 'we have to free *ourselves* to both think and feel deeply'.[51] By 1966 she was attacking the Realist Writers Groups as of appeal to nobody except 'an old-fashioned, hard-core left … and they are a dying race'. Her ideals were by then finding echoes in the newer forms of social dissent. 'Never has there been such a ferment of anti-establishment ideas fighting against a build-up of extreme reactionary ideology', she announced in a similarly unpublished essay named after Bob Dylan's 1964 anthem, 'The Times They Are a'Changin''. Hewett noted particularly the failure of the *Realist*, the new RWG magazine, 'to even comment, let alone take a stand on the Sinyavsky–Daniel affair'.[52] The trial and imprisonment of Russian writers Andrei Sinyavsky and Yuli Daniel in February 1966 for anti-Soviet satire now stands for many commentators as the initiating event in the development of modern Soviet dissidence, leading to the end of Russian communist rule. It is a key event to be articulated here, as Hewett does, under Dylan's exhortation to 'gather round people, wherever you roam', along with her report on Perth's anti-conscription demonstration in June 1966 which included 'public draft card burning'. 'Yet the outlook for left-wing writers has never been so good.' Particularly, 'No longer do left wing novelists have to depend on A.B.S. to publish their novels'.[53]

In a brief survey of the content of other literary magazines in the same essay, Hewett noted the publication of Stefan Heym's article 'The Boredom of Minsk' in *Meanjin* 25.2 (1966), an essay that had been 'attacked and refused publication in the GDR'.[54] Heym's article was the third in a series of anti-Stalinist pieces from him attacking the restrictions of socialist realism, which had had notable reception in the West, including in West Germany's *Die Zeit*,

---

50  Susan Sheridan, *Nine Lives: Postwar Women Writers Making Their Mark* (St Lucia: University of Queensland Press, 2011), p. 96.

51  Hewett, 'Eat Bread and Salt and Speak the Truth', in *Selected Prose of Dorothy Hewett*, pp. 147–51 (148–50).

52  Hewett, 'The Times', *Selected Prose*, p. 155. The RWG magazine the *Realist Writer* was renamed the *Realist* in 1964, while the *Realist Writer* emerged in a split from *Overland* in 1959 after its editor Stephen Murray-Smith declared that magazine's independence from the CPA. See Gardiner, 'Frank Hardy and Communist Cultural Institutions', p. 49.

53  Hewett, 'The Times', p. 156.

54  Hewett, 'The Times', p. 155.

and which had resulted in the banning of his works and restrictions on his activities in the GDR, from July 1964.[55] His language is strikingly similar to Hewett's and Deny's: 'Freedom is freedom and justice is justice and classes are classes, and between these three points of reference we must grope our way forwards'.[56] The shifts in her position were undergirded by those of her close associates internationally, and began to fracture the reading formations for *Bobbin Up* also, even as it was still finding new ones further into Eastern Europe. In June 1968 the new editor of Seven Seas, Kay Pankey, wrote asking Hewett's permission, after selling 8897 copies, to pulp the remainder of their *Bobbin Up* edition.[57] In August 1968, only two months after the Soviet invasion of Czechoslovakia, Hewett resigned her party membership in protest and her extended romance with communist Europe appeared over. The East Germans still looked to her, however, including her short story, 'The Strawberry Pickers', in an international anthology for the World Youth Festival in 1973, after its previous inclusion in a 1964 Seven Seas collection edited by Gelbin.[58]

Recounting the writing of *Bobbin Up* in a preface for its next edition by feminist publisher Virago in London in 1985, Hewett described the eight years preceding its first appearance in 1959 in lines that have been well quoted in debates about her changing political positions:

> For eight years I had scarcely written anything, except the odd piece of left-wing journalism. Silenced by political activism, the deep-seated anti-culturalism and socialist realist dogmas of the Australian Communist Party, plus the terrible struggle to survive, I found myself for the first time for years facing a typewriter with time to spare.[59]

In 1985 she described the result as a book which 'still mirrors a naïve political idealism that had little to do with reality', with 'reality' figuring in a quite different kind of way than in its GDR reception.[60] By 1999, in a new preface for the Vulgar Press edition, Hewett first recalled that when she left the party she felt 'something close to revulsion' for her book, but, reading it again forty years after its first release, 'I'm inclined to be less critical than I once was'.[61]

As in Hewett's biography, there are complex and multiple returns, reflections and refractions that can be traced in the publishing history of Australian literature in the GDR, which in turn illuminate the conflicted transnational dynamics of Cold War reading and publishing. Eastern Bloc editions of English-language works formed threads along which

---

55 Peter Hutchinson, *Stefan Heym: The Perpetual Dissident* (Cambridge: Cambridge University Press, 1992), p. 118.

56 Stefan Heym, 'The Boredom of Minsk', *Meanjin* 25.2 (1966): 196–99 (197).

57 Kay Pankey to Australasian Book Society, 28 June 1968, Hewett Papers, folders 3–4.

58 *Jugend der Welt: Erzählungen aus fünf Kontinenten* (Berlin/Weimar: Aufbau Verlag, 1973). Gertrude Gelbin, ed., *Australians Have a Word For It: Short Stories from Down Under* (Berlin: Seven Seas, 1964): 42–52.

59 Hewett, Introduction, p. x.

60 Hewett, Introduction, p. xvi.

61 Hewett, 'Afterthoughts', p. vii.

literary realisations of intensely localised expressive identity, as *Bobbin Up* so thoroughly is, travelled beyond themselves and their reading worlds. Socialist realism was their passport, as a determinedly international genre, but it did not necessarily function as a means of evacuating difference. In the communist world, Australian books encountered complexly modelled, materially determining, and politically affective rereading and remaking, and could even return to Australia, as did the Seven Seas *Bobbin Up*, bringing that rereading to commentate on their immediate origins.

# 10

## An American Introduction: Perfect Readers, Unread Books and Christina Stead's *The Man Who Loved Children*

*Fiona Morrison*

In 2010 Melbourne University Press (MUP) published a new edition of Christina Stead's *The Man Who Loved Children* (originally published in 1940) through their Miegunyah Press imprint under the banner of the Miegunyah Modern Library. This was the first of three fresh editions of Stead's mid-career novels that also included *For Love Alone* (1944) in 2010, and *Letty Fox: Her Luck* (1946) in 2011. Some of the necessary impetus for this publishing schedule was the considerable critical and commercial impact of an article written by Jonathan Franzen in the *New York Times* on 3 June 2010, called 'Rereading *The Man Who Loved Children*'. So important was Franzen's article, seen as a 'hymn', 'paean' or 'rave', that it became the introduction to the Miegunyah edition, a fact proudly displayed on the cover and supplemented by italicised quotation on the back.[1] Franzen is the latest of a substantial and fascinating list of American creative writers who have championed this particular novel of Christina Stead's since the mid 1950s, including most notably Robert Lowell, Elizabeth Hardwick and Randall Jarrell. This chapter attends in some detail to the introductions written by Jarrell (1965) and Franzen (2010) to *The Man Who Loved Children* in the context of the gendered rhetoric of unjust neglect, international literary canonicity and global authorship that accompanies Stead's reputation. The fact that Stead's most effective and vociferous champions in the international public sphere were and are creative writers, American, and men, is of central interest to this consideration of the ways in which Stead's claim to canonical status is always belatedly read through the critical fortunes of her 'masterpiece', as these fortunes are still a matter of literary critical contestation and reputational weight amongst writers. Nevertheless, the question of what is really valuable about the unjustly neglected and seemingly resistant *The Man Who Loved Children* is at the heart of both introductions. The comparison this entails gives us a sense of the historical nature of assessments of literary value in American letters, as well as different ways in which national and gender identity are weighed and considered in different periods of American literary history.

---

1 International sales at Picador received a boost from Franzen's positive piece and Picador was forced to the edge of another print run. The *Guardian* on 14 July 2010 reported that 'Jonathan Franzen's paean to Christina Stead's 1940 novel has prompted renewed interest in a neglected book', and that 'in 2010, Jonathan Franzen reignited interest in Christina Stead's "masterpiece" with a hymning appreciation' ('Jonathan Franzen Rave Revives Interest in Neglected Australian Writer').

With the exception of an introduction by Doris Lessing to the 1995 Everyman's Library edition of *The Man Who Loved Children*,[2] Jonathan Franzen's piece for the *New York Times* in June 2010 was the first introduction to replace Randall Jarrell's introduction, 'An Unread Book', written for the Holt, Rinehart & Winston reissue of Stead's novel in 1965. Jarrell, who had first written about Stead's novel in the *New York Times* in 1955, spent a good portion of 1964 producing his long and impassioned introduction, which was then used by English, American and Australian publishers who produced an edition of *The Man Who Loved Children* after 1965 – including Penguin, Macmillan, Secker & Warburg, Picador USA, and Angus & Robertson. Such is the symbiotic relationship between the novel and the belated introduction that revived its fortunes, that it can be found appended to the MUP edition as an *Afterword*. Jarrell's 'An Unread Book' is an introduction with the imprimatur of the author as having got something fundamentally right, and an introduction that, in turn, single-handedly recuperated Stead's career and saved her from yet further Cold War obscurity and poverty.

In 'Rereading *The Man Who Loved Children*' (used, without emendation, as the 2010 Introduction), Franzen acknowledges the shadow of 'Jarrell's long and dazzling introduction' but adds that 'one very good reason to read the novel is that you can then read Jarrell's introduction and be reminded of what outstanding literary criticism used to look like.'[3] His warm acknowledgement of Jarrell is typical of the overall register of positive sociality amongst fellow writers that characterises introductions written by one creative writer for another. It is also nostalgic in a way that is typical of the generally anti-academic creative writers and journalists in America at present, as we are reminded that Jarrell's personal and affective rhetoric is part of a lost mode of literary criticism. Franzen's position as a twenty-first century literary lion and defender of complexity in novels,[4] and Jarrell's reputation as the pre-eminent man of mid-century American letters and defender of highbrow taste, certainly makes them an interesting pair. Where Jarrell recovered Stead from critical darkness with the full force of his highbrow prestige, Franzen put her in front of book clubs in America, Australia and the United Kingdom with the full force of his global market profile and commercial selling power. Copies of *The Man Who Loved Children* sold very strongly on the strength of his piece in the *New York Times*. The whole-hearted endorsement of a writer associated with great American literary writing, and powerful enough to bypass the honour of being part of Oprah's Book Club and live to tell the tale (indeed, to thrive), had a very significant effect on readers and other publishers around the world.

Both Jarrell and Franzen present themselves as resistant and nonconformist readers. In their recuperation of *The Man Who Loved Children* they recognise it as a singularly great if

---

2 Doris Lessing, Introduction, *The Man Who Loved Children* by Christina Stead (London: David Campbell [Everyman's Library], 1995 [1940]), pp. ix–xxiii.

3 Jonathan Franzen, Introduction, *The Man Who Loved Children* by Christina Stead (Carlton: Miegunyah, 2010 [1940]), p. ix. Subsequent page references are given in-text.

4 For instance, 'I'm in a lifelong struggle to produce texts that have that kind of interior depth that is not immediately apparent, that repay some kind of careful analysis without losing people who just want to follow along on the surface': Jonathan Franzen, cited in Alison S. Cohn, 'With Critic, Franzen Criticizes Criticism', *The Harvard Crimson*, 29 April 2008, available at www.thecrimson.com/article/2008/4/29/with-critic-franzen-criticizes-criticism-the/ [accessed 10 January 2011].

also singularly difficult masterpiece of family life, unhappy childhood and domestic tragedy. This is the kind of rescue mission that only turns out to be commercially effective if undertaken by one author about another. As Louise Yelin points out in her excellent essay, 'Fifty Years of Reading: A Reception Study of *The Man Who Loved Children*', there is, of course, a rich history of the academic reception of Stead's work, one that demonstrates the complex contours of gender, genre, national identity, geography, literary history and literary theory that shape the Stead 'field'.[5] Yelin's essay delivers a detailed account of the importance of geographies of production and reception, and this uncovers quite neatly the dimension of the 'international' when dealing with Stead's oeuvre. Franzen and Jarrell note Stead's biographical details in passing, but neither focuses at any length on her Americanness or any other national identity. She is an original and, as Yelin suggests, seems to occupy the same sort of anomalous critical position as Emily Brontë, in that she is positioned as a kind of savage original.[6] *The Man Who Loved Children* was written in America, set in America and published in America, but based on an Australian childhood. Interestingly it has become a key novel in the world canon of unread twentieth-century masterpieces, but this claim materially emerges from American writers without any overt claims that it is an American book in some essential sense.

In 1992, the anthropologist James Clifford suggested as part of his early work on 'travelling theory' that much more attention ought to be paid to the role of the 'cosmopolitan intermediaries' in terms of their constitutive roles in Western access to and construction of non-Western ethnographic accounts.[7] If we regard Franzen and Jarrell as cosmopolitan intermediaries translating and ushering a peripheral Stead into American centres of literary value, then we can see that they play a central role in what Pascale Casanova suggests is a contemporary transnational literary field fully magnetised to vectors of value, dominance, circulation and reputation.[8] This field requires significant gatekeepers and assessors of literary value for the great epicentres of world literary value to function as sites of cultural and literary capital. In the case of Christina Stead and her intermediaries/champions/introducers, this was avowedly New York. This explains why the powerful claims about Stead's canonicity are from American authors: they are the ones speaking for New York as the centre of publishing power in the mid to late twentieth and early twenty-first century.

The imperial struggle between centre and periphery for literary power is not the only way to regard the literary politics of the American introductions to *The Man Who Loved Children*. Concerns about literary value and the effect of the mass market and mass media on American reading, writing and criticism surfaced in both 1965 and 2010, and Stead's uncompromisingly difficult and avowedly 'literary' style and subject are seen by both men as significant in cultural and literary markets dominated accordingly by the middlebrow, mediocre or mass-produced. The introductions also have curiously eighteenth-century

---

5 Louise Yelin, 'Fifty Years of Reading: A Reception Study of *The Man Who Loved Children*', *Contemporary Literature* 31.4 (1990): 472–98.

6 Yelin, p. 473.

7 James Clifford, 'Traveling Cultures', in Lawrence Grossberg, Cary Nelson and Paula Treichler, eds, *Cultural Studies* (London: Routledge, 1992), p. 100.

8 Pascale Casanova, trans. M.B. DeBevoise, *The World Republic of Letters* (Cambridge, Mass., and London: Harvard University Press, 2004 [1999]).

qualities. Although Casanova's account of literary politics is convincingly explanatory about the effects of these introductions, there is also a residual Enlightenment sociability evident in them. The introduction to a work of fiction by another writer is a privileged moment in the sociality of reading. It is a threshold moment: a courteous moment of mutual bowing and sizing up, a moment of deferral and also of instruction. It is usually an extremely positive literary critical moment – a deliberative undertaking, to assert that the work is worth reading – as well as a ceremonial one, with praise provided for the many virtues of the work. In the mid twentieth century, Jarrell's introductory essay addresses itself to a non-academic reader (it is not a critical edition, for example), but one clearly assumed to have highbrow interests and tastes. This was a kind of literary criticism that straddled the academic essay and journalistic review that many American intellectuals, particularly in New York, wrote at the time, and from which a number of them – such as Elizabeth Hardwick, among others – made a good living. Strong partiality was a given, strong arguments were often advanced in favour of the work, and the rhetorical context for these arguments was the overarching and very serious debates about canonicity and value in the American literary market.

'An Unread Book' runs to over thirty pages. This sustained rhetorical plea on behalf of the 'unread' and 'neglected' towed *The Man Who Loved Children* – and Stead's career – out of obscurity and attempted, but perhaps failed, to set it up in a rhetorical and cultural continuum reminiscent of American 'rediscoveries' of Herman Melville's *Moby Dick* and Theodore Dreiser's *An American Tragedy*. Even though it had a very significant impact on Stead's critical and commercial fortunes, it ultimately failed to solidify her place in the canon: any canon, even an Australian one. The difficulties with her categorical 'place' have always been, and still are, so persistent in public, commercial and academic spheres. The categorical problems with *The Man Who Loved Children* concern aesthetics, national identity, gender, geography and genre. The work has a truly worldly profile: a book by a peripatetic Australian about her Australian childhood, in great part, the action of which was 'transferred', at the behest of her newly expansionist publisher, Simon & Schuster, to America.[9] In the first year of the Second World War (in which they were soon to be involved), it was read by American critics as an American novel, criticised by some of them for being insufficiently or poorly American, and mainly ignored by Australian critics. Most of the reviewers in 1940 acknowledged the anomalousness and force of *The Man Who Loved Children*, and the difficulty and unevenness of the 'transfer' of autobiographical action from an Australian childhood to America in the 1930s. Depoliticised (with the exception of Isidor Schneider's positive and robustly left-wing review for the *New Masses* in 1940), unclassifiable and running out of publishers, Stead eventually ran into the further inhospitalities of the Cold War in America, Europe and England.

The 1965 introduction was provided by a prestigious American man of letters who read it as a European, mainly Russian, book. He came to write this introduction through the agency of Stanley Burnshaw, a friend of Stead from the 1930s. Burnshaw was the architect

---

9  Letter from Christina Stead to Robie Macauley, editor of the *Kenyon Review*, 20 Sept 1965, in Robert L. Ross, 'Christina Stead's Encounter with "The True Reader": The Origin and Outgrowth of Randall Jarrell's Introduction to *The Man Who Loved Children*', *Library Chronicle of the University of Texas at Austin* 42–43 (1988): 160–79 (179).

of the reissue, working tirelessly on Holt Rinehart & Winston from the late 1950s to get *The Man Who Loved Children* back into print. Robert Ross tells us that in 1959 Burnshaw was energetically working on Robert Frost for support for the reissue in these terms: 'It's a rare novel – we can *rescue* the book and *resuscitate* a truly remarkable writer'.[10] Holt, Rinehart & Winston finally agreed to the reissue in 1965 and it was time to find a champion. Both Randall Jarrell and Elizabeth Hardwick had written about Stead in 1955, and the terms were already those of 'genius', 'absolute originality' and 'unjust neglect'. Hardwick's 1955 essay 'The Neglected Novels of Christina Stead' refers to the neglected masterpiece as a 'Vermeer in the hayloft' which has a loyal band of friends in New York (including Lowell, Bishop, Blanche Knopf and Lillian Hellmann).[11] In a review column for the *New York Times* in the same year, Jarrell's distinctive critical voice and enthusiasm are strongly evident: 'Readers, real readers, are always telling other readers what to read … I've been getting people to read it [*The Man Who Loved Children*] for ten years, with the most dazzling results'.[12] Burnshaw picked Jarrell, the self-professed 'real reader' to write the introduction.

Jarrell's position as a prestigious highbrow critic and well-known poet made him a key member of the middle generation – a key group of American mid-century writers including Plath, Berryman, Lowell, Roethke and Sexton – whose work was generally characterised by melancholy, trauma and confession. Jarrell's early work, though, was as a critic, and his critical voice was famously idiosyncratic and colloquial, almost speakerly. Where his early criticism could be ferocious, his later criticism was full of the stylistic and rhetorical marks of a man trying to make his judgments and evaluations more personal and more present to other readers. His introduction starts with a poetic image of a lonely man on a bench, but his rhetorical use of pronouns and his dedication to anecdote and highly rhythmic sentences indicate this desire for presence: 'you end here; beyond this single separate being you cannot go'.[13] The organic and unseparated bodies of childhood, the 'earlier plural being' that was falsely 'separated off', is the centre of a powerful nostalgia for Jarrell (5). For him the enduring power of Stead's book is the sustained and enviable recreation of the whole world of childhood that is both implausible and extreme, and therefore real and true. For Jarrell, the very particularity that distinguishes this book (of family, of speech, of characters) is the same thing that makes it powerfully universal and appealing. It is striking that, almost fifty years later, these notions of the real and modes of realism, questions of truth and the universal, also appear in Jonathan Franzen's introduction.

Jarrell's focus on childhood is unsurprising given the enduring themes of his own poetry and prose, and he writes most movingly on it. He claims that there are evocations of a child's experience so powerful it is as if 'you are touching childhood itself' (26). He talks in exalted terms about the private realm of the family that Stead so relentlessly and powerfully conveyed:

---

10 Stanley Burnshaw, *Robert Frost Himself* (New York: George Braziller, 1968), pp. 178–79.

11 Elizabeth Hardwick, 'The Neglected Novels of Christina Stead', *A View of My Own: Essays in Literature and Society* (New York: Farrar, Strauss & Cudahy, 1962), p. 42.

12 Randall Jarrell, 'Speaking of Books', *New York Times* 24 July 1955: BR 2.

13 Randall Jarrell, 'An Unread Book', *The Man Who Loved Children* by Christina Stead (Penguin: London, 1970 [1940]), p. 5. Subsequent page references are given in-text.

> Warm, dark, second womb, the bosom of the family, everything is carried far past plausibility: a family's private life is as immoderate and insensate, compared to its public life, as our thoughts are, compared to our speech. (O secret, satisfactory, shameless things! Things that, this side of Judgement Day, no stranger will ever discover.) (6)

The dark bosom, the immoderate, the insensate, the private, the 'secret, satisfactory and shameless' – these are all elements of the novel that lead Jarrell inexorably to the body of the mother. Henny Pollit is the collecting point for Jarrell's appreciation of organic, unseparated, messy and engulfing life. For him, she is a towering dark figure, extraordinary in her difference, her tirades and her excess. He reaches for the language of archetype as he tries to manage the impressive combination of gender and semiosis in *The Man Who Loved Children*: 'there is something grand and final, indifferent to our pity, about Henny: one of the immortal beings in whom the tragedy of existence is embodied, she looks unseeingly past her mortal readers' (11); she is 'never more herself than when she destroys herself' (32). Jarrell's attempt to get to grips with Henny at the outset is rhetorically quite strange, but also extremely heartening – as though, for him, it is the tragic feminine that drives the power of the novel.

The excessive body of the book, its excessive, indecorous and unshapely truthfulness, and the excessive figure of its central adult female character, are all collocated in the early stages of Jarrell's introduction, articulated under the sign of nostalgia about the lost world of childhood and the acutely remembered private sphere. The status of the realism of the work is associated with a prodigious power of memory, and he exclaims over Stead's enviable, almost ethnographic, capacity to remember – trying to get at what Angela Carter so succinctly claimed in 1982, that she was a naturalist by training with the inclinations of a modernist/expressionist.[14] The ability to convey life – direct, immediate and incredible – this was the heart of Stead's genius and her strange realism, and it was founded in her capacity to remember and record. This recording has the effect on readers of a kind of de-repression. For Jarrell, Stead could combine extremity and 'immediately plausible naturalism' (6), and in this way was 'able to imagine with complete realism the structures, textures and atmosphere of one family's spoken and unspoken life' (23).

If Henny makes the reader frightened, then Sam makes him really anxious: 'As he reads about Henny the reader feels, in awe, how terrible it must be to be Henny; as he reads about Sam he blurts "Oh, please don't let me be like Sam!"' (12). Jarrell returns to his theme: 'He (Sam) is so idealistically hypocritically, transcendentally masculine that a male reader worries "Ought I to be a man?"' (14). Jarrell's reading of Sam is echoed by Franzen's and both note the laughter, fun, energy, comedy, the Balzacian repellence and the pity of the portrait of the 'man who loved children'. Jarrell suggests that, 'We can bear to read about Sam, a finally exasperating man, only because he is absolutely funny and absolutely true … entirely real … Anglo-Saxon buffoon, hypocrite' (13). These terms of the comic, the real and the true are reiterated and recast a number of times: 'Sam is one of those providential, larger than life size creations like Falstaff, whom we wonder and laugh at and can't get enough of' (21). In fact, Jarrell seems relatively comfortable with the bitter pessimism and

---

14  Angela Carter, 'Unhappy Families', *London Review of Books* 4.17 (16 September 1982): 11–13.

raging excesses of Henny as the dark star and witch-mother, and he is relatively composed and generous in his handling of Louie as the portrait of an artist as an unruly young girl ('truthful, real, a force of nature'), and his work on her texts is very sustained and compelling. The assessment of Sam, however, remains repetitive and experimental, and there are moments of rhetorical defeat and redundancy:

> about him there is the grandeur of completeness: beyond Sam we cannot go. Christina Stead's understanding of him is without hatred; her descriptions of his vilest actions never forget how much fun it is to be Sam. (15)

In the last section of his introduction Jarrell devotes some time to acknowledging the imperfections of Stead's novel, but he ultimately marries her novelistic strengths to her weaknesses. Where there is 'a kind of natural excess and lack of discrimination' or 'an occasional awkwardness or disparity is the result of her having created from an Australian memory an American reality' (33); this is also the price of absolute originality and sheer linguistic texture. Jarrell finally and resoundingly sees Stead as being as 'plainly good' as Tolstoy, Dostoyevsky, Proust and Melville for her representation of the universal experience in the particular family (37). The obviousness of her merit, and her appearance in this international list, is an outright assertion that she is canonical in international terms, and that realism and linguistic texture are central to the case of belated recognition.

In the context of his circuitous handling of Stead's realism, Jarrell cites Aristotle: 'Aristotle speaks of the pleasure of recognition; you read *The Man Who Loved Children* with an almost ecstatic pleasure of recognition. You get used to saying "Yes, that's the way it is" ... but can never get used to saying "I didn't know *anybody* knew that"' (21). Recognition, sympathy, sensitivity, openness, engagement, sincerity – a capacity to see and value the category of life in all its organic shapes – these were New Critical and later Leavisite criteria for the reading of prose, although Jarrell (taught as an undergraduate by John Crowe Ransom, Allen Tate and Robert Penn Warren) determinedly resisted the high seriousness of the New Critical project. These kinds of terms were applied to D.H. Lawrence and they are applied here with the same apolitical force.

These terms of ecstasy and recognition are curiously, and somewhat uncharacteristically, echoed in Stead's response to Jarrell's introduction. The galleys of Jarrell's introduction were sent by Burnshaw to Stead, who was very nervous about reading them. Stead wrote to Burnshaw upon receipt in December 1964:

> With this I had the feeling one has about someone who truly loves you – 'How can it be? How can he love me? How puzzling!' It's not quite the same ... but I have the same feeling almost – the perfect reader, the real reader. Who does one write for? Oneself – and the true reader.[15]

Here, the notion of a perfect, real and true reader is allied unapologetically to true love, understood here as love despite the revelations of flaws and weakness. This is unaccountable and yet extremely powerful for Stead. In a letter to Burnshaw in early 1965, she tried to explain further:

---

15 Stead to Burnshaw, 7 December 1964, in R.G. Geering, ed., *A Web of Friendship: Selected Letters 1928–1973* by Christina Stead (Sydney: Angus and Robertson, 1992), p. 220.

His wonderful sympathy ... I have such a curious feeling, as if he has written me the one letter of a lifetime, as if one was born to get a letter and I have got it. And then he understands me so well. It's not exactly difficult, it's delicate. You can't say thank you so much for wrapping me in rose and gold – as it were.[16]

The terms of Stead's response are powerful indeed – with the true reader, the real reader (sensitive, attentive, forgiving, kind), the author achieves the genuine and true transaction: love, recognition and a kind of sublime understanding ('delicate', 'rose and gold'). Not surprisingly, this kind of imprimatur from the author about the true reading of her 'unread book' meant that Jarrell became the enduring 'real reader' and champion of the unread and the unreadable (because only able to be experienced) novel.

As Jonathan Franzen suggests, however, the contemporary market is less and less likely to take the time to read and appreciate the kind of literary criticism Jarrell's represents – a sustained meditation on difficulty and the value of a certain kind of original realism which he sees allied to art, life and truth. Franzen's own work on Stead is characterised by a kind of upbeat, vigorous and engaging wittiness. He is also determined to speak to a general reader and deliver some kind of evaluation of greatness, although his article is so much shorter than Jarrell's introduction (seven pages rather than thirty-four). In Franzen's essay, the prevailing rhetoric of good reading and canonicity driving the mid-century literary champion has transformed into the rhetorical terms of the 'death of the novel' debates familiar in the last fifteen years, and related citation of the post-print crisis in a time-poor late capitalist world where things are meant to be fast and easy. He starts with an engaging erotesis: a series of negative assertions that we mentally negate as he proposes them. And how rhetorically engaging they are: don't read this book; novels are out; it's not about anything important, just a singular family; it's not really about enjoyment; there are aspects of psychological violence that you laugh at and abuse that is potentially comic, all of which has the qualities of a bad dream. The inevitable refutation of these reasons not to read is coming, of course, but first there is Franzen's primary focus on Sam Pollit.

According to Franzen, it is through the agency of Stead's extraordinary powers of realism and specificity we have this portrait of narcissistic Sam, but we are thankfully spared 'a grim, abstract, feminist parable' (xiii) because he is funny; Sam is awful but 'there is not a more hilarious narcissist of all literature' (x). Franzen argues Jarrell's line about Sam that, 'though monstrous, he isn't a monster' (x). He goes on to argue that 'it's Stead's genius to make palpable on page after page the childlike need and weakness at the core of his overbearing masculinity, and to make the reader pity him and like him and, therefore, find him funny' (x). In direct contrast to Jarrell in 1965, Franzen identifies the overly caricatured Henny as the central weakness of the work, and dismisses her in short order. For Franzen, the novel circles around Sam and his relationship with his children, rather than Jarrell's reading of a twin gravitational field of enormously powerful and dominating parents that must be negotiated at all costs.

Franzen's reading of the political dimension of Sam indicates some of the contemporary critical, academic and biographical traction on *The Man Who Loved Children*. He

---

16   Stead to Burnshaw, 23 February 1965, *A Web of Friendship*, p. 227.

acknowledges the material conditions of expatriate production and reception of the novel in terms of 'the fine accident of being forced to set the novel in America', wherein

> Stead was also able to map his (Sam's) imperialism and his innocent faith in his own good intentions directly onto those of the city he works in. He is literally the Great White Father, he is literally Uncle Sam. (x)

However, Franzen turns from this promising reading of politics and gender to the rhetoric of archetypes when dealing with Louie, whom he sees as 'the one, endearing, miraculous, indelible archetype' – the miraculous piece of characterisation – and applauds her triumph over her father (xi). Franzen's attention to Louie is particularly striking, but he concludes his piece with an autobiographically based argument that makes a parallel between Sam Pollitt/David Stead and Louie Pollitt/Christina Stead. Franzen argues that Christina Stead the daughter is configured to her father/Sam as a son, with a son's hatred, ambition and rivalry. Louie is really a boy, too. It looks for a moment as though Franzen might offer a commentary on fathers and daughters, but he is really most interested in fathers and sons, as his own fiction suggests. Despite the half century separating the two American introductions, Franzen's account of the work indicates a net decline in the possibilities of a nuanced reading of gender as part of an introduction to *The Man Who Loved Children* for the general reader.

Franzen's language of archetypes (familiar from Northrop Frye) is matched by a now-familiar rhetoric of truth (familiar from Leavis and others) at the end of his article. Franzen claims – and here is the refutation that makes it really clear why you would bother with *The Man Who Loved Children* – that this is a true novel that conveys the *real* texture of inner life: 'only novels can do this and that, by extension, is why they are important. This was family life. And telling the story of this inner life is what novels, and only novels, are for' (xiii). This claim as to what novels might truly be for is the central argumentative move in Franzen's introduction to *The Man Who Loved Children*, and it is reminiscent of his more general commentary on the state of American writing since 2001. Franzen, in the final analysis, is interested in Stead as a certain kind of realist writer, and his reading of her pulls together several different traditions of literary criticism, but makes a final stand on her capacity to convey something about real life. The act of recuperating the neglected masterpiece (the 'Vermeer in the hayloft') is about the importance of what only great literary novels can do, and it has nothing to do with emails, web speed, pleasure or ease. It has to do with the kind of worldly, textured, detailed and tragic-comic portraits of family life which, if his own novels are anything to go by, clearly warrant the long and difficult realist novel.

Franzen's vigourous actions as an intermediary on Stead's behalf are based on the sense of recognition and truth he experiences in reading her. He is quoted on the cover of the Picador USA edition of *The Man Who Loved Children* (which carries the Jarrell introduction but is newly identified as a 'contemporary classic') in July 2001. Franzen's own novel, *The Corrections*, appeared in September 2001. His *New York Times* article on Stead appeared in June 2010, and his next novel, *Freedom*, was published August 2010. In 2010, Amazon, the online book retailer, recommended that you buy *The Man Who Loved Children* and *Freedom* together. The pattern in which Franzen's comments on Stead precede the imminent arrival of his next book plainly and instrumentally aligns his fictional project with Stead's, and suggests that he sees himself as her heir as well as champion in the global literary marketplace. The literary and cultural capital of recuperating an unjustly neglected masterpiece is a very great prize in American letters, and although Franzen's article has had a very appreciable impact on the sales of *The Man Who Loved Children*, it remains to be seen whether this latest deployment of Stead's novel will somehow give it the kind of standing required to enter the even larger world literature canon, or whether, as Simon During argues in his essay 'World Literature, Stalinism, and the Nation', intractable issues to do with gender, politics, classification and uncompromising realism will continue to prevent Stead's work from gaining the kind of worldly traction it might otherwise possess.[17] This may require further introduction in America and elsewhere.

---

17 Simon During, 'World Literature, Stalinism and the Nation: Christina Stead as Lost Object', in *Exit Capitalism: Literary Culture, Theory and Post-Secular Modernity* (Routledge: New York, 2010).

# 11

## Connectivity, Community and the Question of Literary Universality: Reading Kim Scott's Chronotope and John Kinsella's Commedia

*Philip Mead*

The human world is busy social networking at the speed of blur: on Facebook, MySpace, Twitter, LinkedIn, Second Life, email lists – via blogging, tweeting, avatars, ping-chatting, and text messaging. These digitised modes of communication and site-interaction include increasing millions around the globe. Facebook alone now has more than 900 million active users, more than 10.5 million of them 'in Australia'.[1] Humanity's professionals may connect to these globalised networks in various ways, if only for non-professional uses (checking out walls, chest-bumping, throwing a sheep). But social sites are also adapting specifically to the practices of academic work: conferences and symposia can be followed on official conference blogs or socially on Twitter; papers can be skyped in; sites like Academia.edu are netspaces that allow those who sign up to 'share and follow research' (academia.edu/). Even if, as literary studies educationalists, we are not involved in social sites as such, we are likely to have some professional investment in web-uses such as discussion groups, listservs, digitisation projects, born-digital e-journals, databases, archives and open source software that have been developed by writers, e-researchers, and readers interested in the 'literary' applications of IT and the net. Younger critics in the field, like Kate Fagan, have an ethnographic-user's interest in the ways in which online environments and new media, in particular, are shaping literary production and literary community.[2] Other critics and historians of culture follow the social networking of reading collectives, including professional critical ones, from the point of view of the ecology of reading experience and the history of print culture, either as advocates of resourceful reading, as critics of the informating of literature and the death of the book, or, as in my case, as intermediaries in search of a multidimensional matrix of reading, history and locale.

Whatever our involvements in social sites and/or professional net-based resources, whatever our commitments to or ambivalence about the legacy of Gutenberg technologies,

---

[1] Available at newsroom.fb.com/content/default.aspx?NewsAreaId=22; www.socialbakers.com/facebook-statistics/australia [accessed 11 May 2012].

[2] Kate Fagan, '"Scan My Glowing Interior/and Write Down What You See There": A Few Questions About Online Environments and Australian Poetry Communities', unpublished paper, Association for the Study of Australian Literature conference, Common Readers and Cultural Critics, Australian National University, 8–12 July 2009.

we move between these technological and discursive spheres, as private individuals, as friends, as colleagues, as associates, as members of fluxual communities, and even perhaps as individuals with some adherence to a typified ideal called 'the public'. And these movements are all in real, virtual and historical time. Our social collectivity (or community), as a professionalised, discipline-based fraction, is multi-dimensional, multi-layered, and plurally connected to other professional institutions and groups. Our individual selves, in unstable and complex ontologies and performances, both constitute and are constituted by this social collectivity and its subgroupings (like the quiet little poetry and poetics neighbourhood) – from outside, on the margins, and from within, all at different times, and with a whole range of affective positions, public and private. There's no doubt that future disciplinary and institutional histories of literary education will have to find new ways of narrating this radical change in how communities of readers, teachers and researchers are constituted.

There are unavoidable questions and anxieties about the foundational elements of personhood, community and sociability that arise from this potentiality of movement between cyber and other social spaces. There is a lot of noise out there about the effects of web-based applications on the self and society. The social networking I just mentioned is a product of the digital revolution, which is not a simple rearrangement of the technological apparatus of the external world, but an evolution with fundamental effects, including constitutive ones, on practices and styles of the self, definitions of knowledge, interpersonal relationships and political structures, local, national and global. Because of its narrative generativeness and its index of interiority, literature represents a privileged understanding of media and technological change. We have learnt from the thematics of technology in Anglo-European modernism, for example – Benjamin on photography, Proust on the telephone, Thomas Mann in the x-ray surgery, Stein at the movies – to recognise how the technologically evolved environment of postmodernity is also hard-wired into literary works, either as part of their representation of individual subjects and social relations, or in re-mediated genres and linguistic modes.

One question, though, is what kind of critico-discursive resources do we currently have to think about literature in relation to the self and collectivities of selves? I mean from inside the (intermediated) critical traditions, rather than as differentiated cultural artefacts (high/ serious, middlebrow, popular) that provide occasions for cultural analysis of expressive forms. Because of their more or less essential and historically marked structures of feeling, are novels and poems only readable in the context of legacy media, in relation to historical modes of historicism rather than a Web 2.0 world of 'posthuman' subjectivity?[3] This question tends to arise most urgently when we're thinking about pedagogy and the role of literary texts in what is often a diversified and culturally de-exceptionalised setting. It's easy enough to say that a novel, play or poem is simply one in a range of cultural expressions that doesn't have to be read on a historicist screen of some kind, but this empties out the expressive forms of the past in favour of an amnesiac present, shifting the focus on historical markers to modes of technology: 'let's turn this poem into a tag cloud'. That's probably fun, but it

---

3  Alan Liu, *Local Transcendence: Essays on Postmodern Historicism and the Database* (Chicago and London: Chicago University Press, 2008), p. 5.

means we have to rethink how we understand the interoperability of reading (as teachers and critics) and the positionalities afforded by historicisms.

Two recent critiques of the cultural outworkings of the digital revolution that might be relevant here are Meaghan Morris' *Australian Humanities Review* article, 'Grizzling about Facebook' (November 2009), and Zadie Smith's *New York Review of Books* review of David Fincher's 2010 film *The Social Network* (and Jaron Lanier's *You Are Not a Gadget: A Manifesto*). Smith starts from the apparent accelerated precession of generations: she is only nine years older than Mark Zuckerberg and shared an institutional and educational background with him at Harvard. Coming out of *The Social Network*, though, she feels that her 'idea of personhood is nostalgic, irrational, inaccurate'. She feels like a 1.0 person in a Web 2.0 world. David Fincher's film represents the social and economic milieu out of which Facebook was invented as compellingly 'hyperreal' and at the same time under-representative of reality (like all information; even, especially, personal data), notwithstanding its core value of connectivity. Smith is struck by Zuckerberg's strangely affectless mantra about the Facebook application, that it allows people to 'connect'. Smith writes from the position of someone who went through an obsessive Facebook phase, but who ultimately kicked the habit. So her critique is not the kind of commentariat-led panic about the 'perils and inanities of Facebook' that Meaghan Morris begins by citing. Nevertheless, for Smith, Facebook creates

> something like a Noosphere, an internet with one mind, a uniform environment in which it genuinely doesn't matter who you are, as long as you make 'choices' (which means, finally, purchases). If the aim is to be liked by more and more people, whatever is unusual about a person gets flattened out – one nation under a 'format'.

Connectivity is rapidly evolving in a posthuman world, replacing community as the structuring practice of societies and nations, turning simulacra of private selves into mediatised social entities.

Morris' spirited defence of Facebook also begins with a recognition of the generational aspects of technological uptake with social sites: grizzling is done by grizzled types, or oldies, Net 1.0 types. Morris is well aware of the economy of the digital divide and of the

> serious legal, ethical and political issues ... arising from or being intensified by the 'Facebook' phenomenon ... free speech and its limits, censorship, the right to privacy, the negotiation of social protocols for a transnational economy that thrives on difference as well as inequality, the foundations of community, the power of corporations in our personal lives, and the technological transformation of work.

By contrast with Smith, Morris is overwhelmingly in favour of, even utopian at moments about, the 'new era of global-popular participation on-line' represented by social sites. For Morris, Facebook

> has increased my affective quality of life, and not only because it offers a break from academic service work. The collective stream of posts brings me word of

> books, articles, music, films, video clips and news that I would otherwise never discover.

She also identifies the potential of social sites like Facebook for internet political activism; global disaster relief, for example, is a page on Facebook. What drives Morris' enthusiasm is the realisation that the social media exemplify the theoretical insight that 'everyday life [including work] is not a human universal' and so can evolve and be shaped.[4] Smith also realises that the 'idea of personhood is certainly changing' but, by contrast with Morris, is worried about her agreement with Zuckerberg that 'selves evolve'.[5]

These two small windows on contemporary cultural phenomena are worth thinking about in relation to contexts of literature, community and reading. They point to aspects of everyday life in the present, including movies and academic work, by a writer and a critic, responding to changes in the forms of sociability. By analogy, what is the historical moment from which we understand the literary versions of human collectivity? Insofar as we can grasp the history of the present this seems like a remarkably complex and engaging moment to be thinking about the forms that literary sociability, or changing personhood, are or have taken. The Smith's and Morris' essays are not isolated instances; they exist within a broad set of debates, in popular and intellectual registers, about how personhood, community and collectivity are experienced and understood. And they are driven by a strong historical 'concern [going back at least a century] about the future of sociability' in consumption-driven societies, a future that seems finally to have arrived.[6] Generational tensions and disjuncts, in particular, are at the core of these contentions, as are economic and cultural politics in the form of the film industry, finance and business, online purchasing, and media consumption. In relation to net-effects on everyday life and theoretical thinking, I am particularly interested in how critical reading works across space and time, and how it is shaped by contemporary discursive frames like world literature, the transnational imagination, distant reading, network interoperability, and critical regionalism, and what kinds of connections (to use Zuckerberg's word) these theoretically generated and institutional critical projects might have to web-based self and sociability, and to new medial ecologies. If literary studies is about how meanings are created, about the rhetorical and material textuality of those meanings, and what their connectivity to the spheres of social life might be, then the kind of individuals and collectivities (readers and critics) we are will depend on the nature of our intervening roles at every point of these multidimensional and complexly structured intersections.

*Literary Connectivity*

It might be useful to use an historical bookmark (as with a web-browser). Going back more than a decade to 1999, when Leigh Dale was taking over as the new editor of *Australian Literary Studies* she drew attention to a shift in the discipline of Australian literary studies and

---

4 Meaghan Morris, 'Grizzling about Facebook', *Australian Humanities Review* 47 (2009), available at www.australianhumanitiesreview.org/archive/Issue-November-2009/morris.html.

5 Zadie Smith, 'Generation Why?', *New York Review of Books*, 25 November 2010, available at www.nybooks.com/articles/archives/2010/nov/25/generation-why/?pagination=false.

6 Morris.

presented two essays, one by Gillian Whitlock, one by David Carter, about new directions. Dale identified the lack of 'a new narrative that ... is appropriate to the dramatically changed cultural, political and intellectual conditions in which writers, critics and teachers of Australian literature now work'.[7] In her editorial the words 'international' and 'overseas' occur numerous times, as markers of a break with an older idea of 'the nation apart', but words like transnational, global, translation, cosmopolitan, planetary, world, universal, translocal, transcultural, subnational, distant reading, translingual, hemispherical, intercrossings, mobility studies, and diaspora, do not. As Dale recognises, there was a shift taking place and it could not be fully named or recounted at that point. In the intervening decade or so, though, the critical vocabulary and theoretical discourse of a newly 'worlded' literary studies has emerged from various quarters and spread across literary studies in Australia, as we now say.[8] This chain of thinking outside the mononationalist descends to the present from postcolonial and diasporic paradigms – Azade Seyhan's *Writing Outside the Nation* (2000), for example – and via David Damrosch's numerous writings about world literature.[9] It also includes studies of specific relevance to the development of an Australian-inflected globalised literary studies, like Christopher Prendergast's *Debating World Literature* (2004) and John Pizer's *The Idea of World Literature* (2006), as well as work by Robert Dixon ('Boundary Work', 2004; 'An Agenda for Our Own Literature', 2007; 'Australian Literature – International Contexts', 2007), Russell West-Pavlov (*Transcultural Graffiti*, 2005), Graham Huggan (*Australian Literature*, 2005; 'Globaloney and the Australian Writer', 2009), Nicholas Birns and Rebecca McNeer (*A Companion to Australian Literature Since 1900*, 2007), Helen Gilbert and Jacqueline Lo (*Performance and Cosmopolitics*, 2007), Mads Rosendahl Thomsen (*Mapping World Literature*, 2008), Ken Gelder ('English, Autonomy, and the Republic of Letters', 2009), Simon During (*Exit Capitalism*, 2009), and Ann Vickery and Margaret Henderson (*ALS: Manifesting Literary Feminisms*, 2009).[10] This loose constella-

---

7  Leigh Dale, 'New Directions: Introduction to Australian Literary Culture and Australian Literary Criticism', *Australian Literary Studies* 19.2 (1999): 131–35 (134).

8  See, for example, Ankhi Mukherjee, 'What is a Classic? International Literary Criticism and the Classic Question', *PMLA* 125.4 (2010): 1026–42 (1037); and Bill Ashcroft, 'Australian Transnation', *Southerly* 71.1 (2011 *Modern Mobilities: Australian-Transnational Writing*): 18–40.

9  It is relevant here to note that David Damrosch's *What is World Literature?* (Princeton: Princeton University Press, 2003) consists of readings of works that, with the possible exception of *The Epic of Gilgamesh*, are highly unlikely to appear on the shelves of a world literature section of any large bookshop: Sixteenth-century Spanish-Mexican missionary poetry; the Zairean/Congolese novelist Mbwil a M. Ngal's novel *Giambatista Viko: ou, Le Viol du discours africain* (1975), still untranslated into English; marginalia verse on Egyptian papyri; Mechthild von Magdeburg's mystical verse; Kafka; P.G. Wodehouse; Rigoberta Menchú's life writing; Milorad Pavic's *Dictionary of the Khazars* (1988). The only overlap with Casanova, although it is a substantial one, is Kafka: both critics chart in detail, in their different ways, the shift from a universal, denationalised modernist Kafka (of previous decades) to an ethnic, Yiddish, German-dialect speaking Czech, theorist of minor literature.

10  Full bibliographical details are as follows. Robert Dixon, 'Boundary Work: Australian Literary Studies in the Field of Knowledge Production', *JASAL* 3 (2004): 27–43; 'An Agenda for Our Own Literature', *Australian*, 28 March, 2007, available at www.theaustralian.com.au/higher-education/an-agenda-for-our-own-literature/story-e6frgcjx-1111113234442; 'Australian Literature – International Contexts', *Southerly* 67.1–2 (2007): 15–27. Russell West-Pavlov, *Transcultural Graffiti: Diasporic Writing and the Teaching of Literary Studies* (Amsterdam and New York: Rodopi, 2005). Graham Huggan,

tion of readings and arguments in theory about variously globalised literary systems has enabled transnationally and transhistorically framed accounts of authorship, expatriation, reputation, mobility, text reception, institutions, pedagogy, the dynamics of transhistorical canonisation, the politics of metropole and periphery, and the role of fractions of literary sociability (like communities, small groups and coteries).

Part of the reason for going back to 1999 is that that was also the year that Pascale Casanova's *La République Mondiale des Lettres* was published, although it did not appear in English until 2004. For a country like white Australia, with foundationally nineteenth-century and repeatedly assertive institutions of national literature, Casanova's critique is particularly relevant, even while it ignores the southern hemisphere. Casanova's study begins with the observation that literatures and literary histories were appropriated by political nations in the nineteenth century.[11] 'We do not always realize it, [but] our literary unconscious is largely national' (xii), Casanova asserts, and the predominant organisation of literary studies 'along national lines' makes us blind to transnational phenomena like world literary space, or what she calls the world republic of letters as a distinctive and separate cultural sphere (xi). The nationalisation of literature, or the assertion of self-invested, soil-based national languages and literatures, is one of Casanova's primary targets, hence her critique of the Herder effect, and the exceptional role of Goethe in the inception of a cosmopolitan recognition of how writers 'detach themselves from historical and literary forces' (xiii). For this reason she sees the post-Second World War period of global decolonisation as homologous to the 'national and literary upheavals of nineteenth-century Europe', in their claims to autonomy and legitimacy in the nation and national language and literature (79–80).

Casanova wants readers and critics to live in the literature world, a virtual republic or ideal community of writing and reading, that is 'relatively independent of the everyday world and its political divisions' (xii). At the same time she is well aware that literary capital is inherently national, often and mainly because of language (34). Thus she postulates a kind of paradoxical structuring of the cultural field:

> On the one hand, there is a progressive enlargement of literary space that accompanies the spread of national independence in the various parts of the

---

*Australian Literature: Postcolonialism, Racism, Transnationalism* (Oxford: Oxford University Press, 2007); 'Globaloney and the Australian Writer', *JASAL* (2009 *Special Issue: Australian Literature in a Global World*): 1–17. Nicholas Birns and Rebecca McNeer, eds, *A Companion to Australian Literature Since 1900* (Rochester, NY, and Woodbridge, UK: Camden House, 2007). Helen Gilbert and Jacqueline Lo, *Performance and Cosmopolitics: Cross-Cultural Transactions in Australasia* (Basingstoke: Palgrave Macmillan, 2007). Mads Rosendahl Thomsen, *Mapping World Literature: International Canonization and Transnational Literatures* (London and New York: Continuum, 2008). Ken Gelder, 'English, Autonomy, and the Republic of Letters', *Australian Humanities Review* 47 (2009), available at www.australianhumanitiesreview.org/archive/Issue-November-2009/gelder.html. Simon During, *Exit Capitalism: Literary Culture, Theory, and Post-Secular Modernity* (London and New York: Routledge, 2009). Ann Vickery and Margaret Henderson, eds, *Australian Literary Studies: Manifesting Australian Literary Feminisms*, 24.3–4 (2009).

11   Pascale Casanova, trans. M.B. DeBevoise, *The World Republic of Letters* (Cambridge, Mass., and London: Harvard University Press, 2004 [1999]), p. xi. All subsequent references are given in-text.

world. And, on the other, there is a tendency toward autonomy, which is to say literary emancipation in the face of political (and national) claims to authority

– although this autonomy remains abstract (39). As Goethe intuited in the late 1820s, world literary space is both international and competitively generated; it is enabled more than anything by historical depth of literary heritage, which allows 'cultures to escape the hold of national politics' (39).

Casanova's book has been influential but critique has quickly identified its blind spots: it is seriously Eurocentric, even Paris-centric – at least until its final pages – and the abstracted literary state she describes, even at its most extensive, is geographically limited to the northern hemisphere. The world republic of letters has no antipodes, or at least only an implied one.[12] Casanova makes two brief mentions of Australia, and not in relation to any body of literature, small, minor or otherwise, but in relation to the imperium of the English language centred on London. She makes no mention of any Australian writer. Casanova's account, also problematically, is unapologetically social-Darwinist in its assumptions about the evolution of world literary space: 'the literary world needs to be seen', she argues, 'as the product of antagonistic forces rather than as the result of a linear and gradually increasing tendency to autonomy' (109). This reminds us of Andrew Ross' *The Chicago Gangster Theory of Life*, a critique of the way science makes its way into the broader culture, usually badly or inaccurately. Ross' title refers to Richard Dawkins' metaphor to describe the 'selfish gene', an instance of the way in which ideas about nature invariably have their origin in ideas about society.[13] For Casanova, ideas about literature clearly have their origin in ideas about European political history, a history characterised by national conflicts and evolutionary historicism. As Simon During points out, it is also a dichotomised world: 'literature is either linked to autonomy or not; it is either modern or anachronistic, either consecrated or unconsecrated, either national or international, even if over time the status of particular works may change'.[14] Notably, also, Casanova's argument for a determinate and ubiquitous world system of literature nowhere acknowledges the digital revolution; in fact her republic of letters emerges alongside a world system of social connectivity that it never recognises.

Perhaps one of the most useful aspects of Casanova's study is its insistence on and analysis of the importance of translation (although this also comes with an under-recognition of the centrality of 'Überseztungen' to Goethe's idea of Weltliteratur).[15] The powerfully value-adding process of translation – and that means much more than simply converting a literary work from one language to another – is usually one in which the 'consecrating' nation reduces foreign works of literature to its own categories of value and

---

12 David Damrosch remarks that her book might be more accurately titled *The Parisian Republic of Letters*; 'an unsatisfactory account of world literature in general', he says, 'it is actually a good account of the operation of world literature within the modern French context' (p. 27).

13 Andrew Ross, *The Chicago Gangster Theory of Life: Nature's Debt to Society* (London: Verso, 1994), p. 15.

14 During, *Exit Capitalism*, p. 62.

15 John Pizer, *The Idea of World Literature: History and Pedagogical Practice* (Baton Rouge: Louisiana State University Press, 2006), p. 8.

perception, which it mistakes for universal norms (154). Universality is not something that small literatures or hinterlands and margins can bestow: only the cultural capitals can do that. And only the capitals think – blindly, as Casanova recognises – that they know what universality is. Political power structures tend to correlate with literary and cultural ones (81). Hence the virtual absence of the southern hemisphere in the world republic of letters. As noted, Casanova is also surprisingly unaware of new media, the web, and their obvious and significant structuring effects on the contemporary net-based republic of letters – very different from the republic she imagines – although she is aware that the old struggle between imperial centres like Paris, London and New York has morphed into a de-metropolitanised rivalry between the 'commercial pole' of literary publishing and distribution, and the autonomous pole of literary universalism (169). This is why internationalisation is a positive term in Casanova's thinking, as opposed to globalisation, a negative term. More seriously, I think, as critics interested in transnational literary criticism (like Ankhi Mukherjee) have noticed, there is a problem with the exclusion of literary criticism in Casanova's republic, or rather her repeated derogation of the metropolitan critic in favour of a transcendent, innocent and abstract reader. There is no sense in Casanova that a peripheral or localised critical position is possible, within the field, or on the globe.

*Distant Readings*

At almost the same moment as the interventions of Casanova and Dale I'm pointing to, Franco Moretti's influential article 'Conjectures on World Literature' (2000) was published in the *New Left Review*,[16] and it remains in some ways the most interesting and powerful version of his position. It is not relevant to take up space here with a genealogical sketch of the spread of Moretti's developing theory and methodology. But given the range of quasi-sociological research in literary studies that distant reading has fostered, it is worth recalling the original provocation (and the good humour, I guess) of his method. From the beginning, as Daniel Shore argues, Moretti emphasised the sociological provenance of what was an oppositional project, the understanding of literary meanings from outside the varieties of literary humanism, and in terms of a world system:

> In order to understand literature as a world system we must abandon traditional close reading as a 'theological exercise,' concerned only with the very solemn treatment of very few texts taken very seriously.' [Moretti] proposes instead that we practice 'distant reading,' which would allow us 'to focus on units that are much smaller or much larger than the text: devices, themes, tropes – or genres and systems.' Systematic study of world literature must proceed '*without a single direct textual reading*,' jettisoning the rich experience of individual poems and novels to rely instead on 'poor' and 'abstract' concepts … The limiting factor for such a study is not distance (in which 'the text disappears') but quantity (in which texts are multiplied).[17]

---

16   Franco Moretti, 'Conjectures on World Literature', *New Left Review* 1 (January–February 2000): 54–68.

17   Daniel Shore, 'WWJD? The Genealogy of a Syntactic Form', *Critical Inquiry* 37 (2010): 1–25 (23–24).

Moretti was always a formalist and a comparatist:

> From the moment I started using external models for literary study – evolutionary theory, over twenty years ago – I realised that their great advantage lies precisely in the fact that they renew and galvanise formal analysis. At times the external model makes literary structures more perspicuous: it's the case of maps. At other times, it provides a conceptual architecture for the history of forms: evolutionary theory. And quantitative series, for their part, allow us to see new problems, whose solution is usually found at the level of formal choices (linguistic, rhetorical, or a mix thereof).[18]

The Resourceful Reading project and the papers from the conference focused on that project (2010) have filiations to Moretti's approach and are an important compilation of work in the application of information technologies, theories of reading from the 'outside', to broadly formalist literary analysis, book history, and archival research (in the Australian setting).[19] And like current thinking about the 'world system' of literature, the set of practices under the 'new empiricist' heading should interest us for any understanding of the granular social settings of reading, and also, perhaps, as a further instance of the 'nationalist cosmopolitan longings' of 'Auslit'.[20] This set of practices constelled around 'Moretti' is shadowed by a less marketable but nevertheless influential extension of literary deconstruction that reasserts the singularity of literary texts and their resistance to all programmatic projects of reading.[21]

## 'his province, his town, his countryside'[22]

So these complexly inter-related shifts in literary studies and cultural theory, with influential methodological outworkings – whatever else they might enable – carry implications for any reading practice that privileges the singular, the internal, the local, the iterative, the contingent, the contextual, the up-close. This essay is moving towards articulating a problematic about how these regimes of reading do or do not reciprocate with each other

---

18  Franco Moretti, 'Critical Response II: "Relatively Blunt"', *Critical Inquiry* 36.1 (2009): 172–74 (173–74).

19  Katherine Bode and Robert Dixon, eds, *Resourceful Reading: The New Empiricism, eResearch and Australian Literary Culture* (Sydney: Sydney University Press, 2010). A parallel development of 'distant reading' was Tony Bennett's 1990 study *Outside Literature*, which has its provenance in Macherey and Barthes, and whose version of revisioning the history of the institutions of literature, rather than works and authors, was entirely swamped by Moretti's version of the sociology of literary forms in *Signs Taken for Wonders* (London: Verso, 1983).

20  During, p. 84.

21  The MLA convention, held annually as a global, national and local event: the study of all literatures is becoming more transnational, while at another level the institutional categories remain firmly in place. 'Australian' is a small category under 'Other Literature in English', following British Literature, along with General, Canadian, Irish and Scottish. See Derek Attridge, *The Singularity of Literature* (London and New York: Routledge, 2004).

22  From Czeslaw Milosz, *Road-Side Dog* (1998), used by Pizer as an epigraph to the Introduction to his *The Idea of World Literature* (p. 1): 'A poet, thrown into the international bouillabaisse where, if anything can be distinguished at all, it is only lumps of overboiled fish and shrimp, suddenly discovers that he sits firmly in his province, his town, his countryside, and begins to bless it'.

and circulate together, and what kind of relations this calculus might have to localised critical reading and specific fictional and poetic texts. At one level, the problematic I offer is actually about methodology: that close reading is multidimensional and not necessarily delimited by exceptionalist assumptions about individual literary texts but comprises, rather, 'an assemblage of practices, themselves often positioned against one another in debates about method' and extendable, I think, into site-specific but globally informed readings and other developments in new contextualist and geopsychoanalytic methods.[23] In the back of my mind, though, is the sense that a problematic is not necessarily something with any single or sufficient answer. I'll come back to this after looking briefly at Kim Scott's *That Deadman Dance* (2011) and John Kinsella's *Divine Comedy* (2008). But I should say, since I have mentioned methodology, that not being able to offer fully extended readings of Scott's novel and Kinsella's poem is fortuitous in the Levinasian terms of how I understand reading (or re-reading) and criticism: as having 'no interest in distilling the content of a text into a "said"'.[24]

## Kim Scott's Chronotope

Kim Scott's novel *That Deadman Dance*, published towards the end of 2010 (Miles Franklin Literary Award 2011), 'is inspired by the history of early contact between Aboriginal people – the Noongar – and Europeans in the area of [Scott's] hometown of Albany, Western Australia, a region known by some historians as the "friendly frontier"'.[25] Like his previous novel *Benang* (and the co-written family/community history, *Kayang & Me*), the novel draws deeply on published histories as well as archival documents of the region. Its four sections cover the period 1826 to 1844, although it also refers to the earlier European maritime presence of 'horizon people': Vancouver (1791) and d'Entrecasteaux (1792). The title of the novel refers to an incident from Matthew Flinders' time at Princess Royal Harbour at the very end of 1801, where he had anchored before exploring the 'Unknown Coast' to the east. The day before Flinders left the harbour and King George Sound (30 December), he ordered the marines ashore from the *Investigator*, for the entertainment of 'Our friends the natives':

> The red coats and white-crossed belts were greatly admired, having some resemblance to their own manner of ornamenting themselves: and the drum, but particularly the fife, excited their astonishment, but when they saw these beautiful red-and-white men, with their bright muskets, drawn up in a line, they absolutely screamed with delight; nor were their wild gestures and vociferation to be silenced, but by commencing the exercise, to which they paid the most earnest and silent attention. Several of them moved their hands, involuntarily, according to the motions; and the old man placed himself at the end of the rank, with a short staff in his hand, which he shouldered, presented, grounded, as did the marines their muskets, without, I believe, knowing what he did.[26]

---

23 During, p. 85.
24 Robert Bernasconi and Simon Critchley, cited in Attridge, p. 141.
25 Kim Scott, 'Author's Note', *That Deadman Dance* (Sydney: Pan Macmillan Picador, 2010), p. 397.
26 Flinders' journal, 1803–1814, pp. 60–61, cited in Tim Flannery, ed., *Terra Australis: Matthew*

This moment, available in the textual trace of Flinders' journal, and later in Daisy Bates' writing, but also rereadable through the oral and performative traditions of Noongar artistic practices, provides the meditative germ of Scott's novel.[27] These historical traces, variously intertwined, allow Scott to imagine a past and a 'fictional geography', as a way of understanding the self and its genealogies (including collective ones).[28] *That Deadman Dance* has the generic appearance of a historical novel of frontier contact but it seriously resists appropriation to that nationalist form: primarily via its poetic narrative mode – intensely imagined moments rather than linear diegesis – and its thematics of a 'global' shore-based whaling industry. It belongs to a different cultural project, one that Spivak would recognise as the work of the singular imagination, building a chronotope of sub-national regionalism, unmooring the cultural nationalism that controls the 'historical novel' and that disguises the workings of the state.[29] It is a meditation on the past but not as an archaeological layer of a national present.

The novel is also a project that can only be fully grasped with some knowledge of Scott's work as a whole, including its authorial threads. In this connection, the 'struggle to articulate the significance and energy of a specific Indigenous heritage' has a relation to Scott's awareness of his own father's impoverished linguistic and narrative sense of his Aboriginality.[30] It is about retrieving and reviving language. As he writes in the 'Author's Note' to *That Deadman Dance*:

> rather than write an account of historical events or Noongar individuals with whom I was particularly intrigued, I wanted to build a story from their confidence, their inclusiveness and sense of play, and their readiness to appropriate new cultural forms – language and songs, guns and boats – as soon as they became available. Believing themselves manifestations of a spirit of place impossible to conquer, they appreciated reciprocity and the nuances of cross-cultural exchange.[31]

Not 'oppression culture', as he describes it in *Kayang & Me*, but 'high culture, creation stories, language and songs'.[32] In this sense, *That Deadman Dance* explores an idea of Aboriginal cosmopolitanism, openness to strangers, to the non-local and the value of mobility.[33]

---

*Flinders' Great Adventures in the Circumnavigation of Australia* (Melbourne: Text, 2000), p. 54. See also Anthony J. Brown, *Ill-Starred Captains: Flinders and Baudin* (Adelaide: Crawford House, 2000), p. 157.

27  As recounted by Kim Scott, at the end of nineteenth century Daisy Bates recorded a Noongar man doing the Flinders dance. See www.youtube.com/watch?v=xqY8v1l9Pls.

28  Scott, 'Author's Note', p. 399.

29  Gayatri Chakravorty Spivak, *Nationalism and the Imagination* (London, New York and Calcutta: Seagull, 2010), p. 50.

30  Kim Scott and Hazel Brown, *Kayang & Me* (Fremantle: Fremantle Arts Centre Press, 2005), p. 13.

31  Scott, 'Author's Note', p. 398.

32  Scott and Brown, *Kayang & Me*, p. 17. In that work Scott recounts, from a settler diary, a similarly fascinating moment of Indigenous cosmopolitanism in a visit by south-coast Noongars to the Swan River Colony and their attendance at a piano recital. See Scott and Brown, *Kayang & Me*, p. 35.

33  Zlatko Skrbis and Ian Woodward, 'The Ambivalence of Ordinary Cosmopolitanism: Investigating the Limits of Cosmopolitan Openness', *The Sociological Review* 55.4 (2007): 730–47 (730).

Significantly, then, the novel's 'Prologue' begins with a scene that dramatises Bobby Wabalanginy's playful adaptation of the European and American technology of writing:

> Kaya.
>
> Writing such a word, Bobby Wabalanginy couldn't help but smile. Nobody ever done write that before, he thought. Nobody ever write *hello* or *yes* that way!
>
> *Roze a wail ...*
>
> Bobby Wabalanginy wrote with damp chalk, brittle as weak bone. Bobby wrote on a thin piece of slate. Moving between languages, Bobby wrote on stone.[34]

Figure 1. Map on the inside front cover of *Kayang & Me*. Reproduced courtesy of Fremantle Arts Centre Press.

Bobby is trying out the potential of writing to represent Aboriginal language, '*Kaya*' (hello), and consciously or not, it is a word of welcome that he uses, translated into the encountered cultural technology of writing. But he is also aware of the cultural limitations of that technology of writing which has never been used to script a Noongar word or name. Bobby moves between languages, thinking about their material forms and the relations to meaning, a cosmopolitan skill not shared by the young white settler, Kongk Chaine, who joins him in the hut. This is a complexly figured scene in the diegesis of imagined frontier settlement, dramatising as it does an ephemeral moment in the meeting of an oral and a literate culture. This is the moment Scott chooses as the first in his series of meditations on moments of history, one in which the story is difficult to retrieve, or to recall, but that is nevertheless centred on the totemic and economic figure of the whale. While he can

---

34  Scott, *That Deadman Dance*, p. 1. All subsequent references are given in-text.

move between languages, Bobby cannot recall the full story he wants to write down. Following his opening sentence '*Boby Wablngn ... roze a wail*' (1), he 'couldn't even remember the proper song' (3), and so he erases the writing on the slate. Writing cannot help him retrieve the song of the whale in the Noongar oral tradition. Later, though, he uses writing to embody the story of the 'wailz' (5). This 'Prologue' then functions as a *mise-en-abyme* of the novel as a whole, drawing a moment from the temporal margins of (imagined) history into the centre and opening of the diegesis, narrating the centrality of language and writing technologies, as well as the social realities that frustrate the cosmopolitan impulse. Scott imagines the difficulties Bobby has in being able to tell his own stories, despite his cosmopolitan mentality. Their traces, though, survive to be retrieved and written by Kim Scott.

Scott's imagination also works with a kind of alternating documentary current, cross-checking 'oral [settler and Indigenous] history against the [often] scanty written records' (59), always resisting and probing the imperialisms embedded in the technologies and genres of writing – maritime and land explorers' journals, settler diaries and letters, 'anthropological' records, government reports and documents – for their bias and prejudice. While he generously acknowledges the archive of colonisation and its curators in the extra-diegetic (or is it?) 'Author's Note' to *That Deadman Dance*, Scott is not about to trust the archive, not even in its powerfully originary form of Flinders' journal. The novel is an explicit correction to Flinders' observation that the old man at the end of the column of marines in 1801 did not know what he was doing. *Benang*, also in its imaginative renegotiations and rememorisations of the record of government administration and pseudo-science of racism, is initiated by a kind of diagnostic response to what Scott identified as the symptomatic markers of white settler history: the 'FWMB' and the 'LFBA', the first white man born in such and such a place (the legitimacy of noble pioneering), and the last full blood Aboriginal (the sublimated memory of dispossession).[35] *Benang* is a fictional critique of such racist language and history (native welfare and Aboriginal protection were the euphemisms of governmentality) by way of exploring personal and collective identity. Relevant here is the scorching treatment of A.O. Neville's eugenics in Scott's 2001 Alfred Deakin Lecture. Neville's 1948 publication, *Australia's Coloured Minority*, was subtitled *Its Place in the Community*. Scott asks: 'What place is that, do you think?'[36] Neville's community is produced by eugenics, and Aboriginal people have only a disappearing place within it.

But Scott's project is not only one of critique: it is part of a broader commitment to Aboriginal land rights (with the South-West Land Council), to language and literacy education (with the Western Australian Education Department), to the mental health of Aboriginal people (his current professional context), and to cultural retrieval. In relation to this last point, he notes the importance to *That Deadman Dance* of the Wirlomin Noongar Language and Story Regeneration Project.[37] And for Scott, 'research' is not an invisible or unproblematic practice: it is political, community based and self-reflexive. Research into Noongar language and stories and their 'daily "narrative construction"' of history

---

35  Scott and Brown, pp. 27–28.

36  Scott, 'Australia's Continuing Neurosis: Identity, Race and History', ABC Alfred Deakin Lecture, broadcast 15 May, 2001, available at www.abc.net.au/rn/deakin/stories/s291485.htm.

37  Scott, 'Author's Note', p. 398.

and culture 'would be of limited value unless it can also contribute in some way to the wellbeing of the community descended from its first speakers, and – best of all – to keeping the language alive'.[38] All Scott's work – its literary imaginative core, as well as its other professional and cultural aspects – is an ongoing, fragmentary, individual, geographically specific and inter-personal project in articulating a self in relation to place and community, a project that deploys (just as it resists) the formal, narrative possibilities of the novel to articulate that project to history, but not to any incipient or hegemonic narrative of nation.

That is why Scott's novel does not begin with the great navigator Flinders and his prejudice about what the 'natives' may or may not have understood about the marines' performance. The cultural memory of the deadman dance, rather, belongs to Noongar oral and performative heritage and Bobby's creative curatorship of that heritage, rather than to the published annals of European maritime exploration or Daisy Bates' anthropological recording. It is also part of the reason the conclusion to the novel, which also feels like a beginning, has a carefully muted, tragic resonance. The moment of friendly and performative interaction between Flinders' crew and the Noongar people on the south coast of Western Australia in December 1801 bore within it the isotopes of different cultural possibilities: the mutually significant recognition of the role of performance, adornment and (male) warrior culture; an environmentally sustainable exchange of natural resources (*Investigator*'s wooding, watering and refitting); and the cosmopolitan practices of cross-cultural exchange. Even up until 1830, the military garrisons at Albany and at Cape Riche 'hadn't competed for resources; nor had [they] excluded Noongars from their own land, or insist[ed] they be enslaved'.[39] But the destructive potential is there as well; it is an armed military force that Flinders deploys. The marines appear only mechanically alive in their ritualised movements and identical markings. They are the dead men in the dance: drilled, uniformed, performing to orders.

By the time the *mulga*, Bobby Wabalanginy, re-enacts the dance of his Noongar ancestor in the final scene of the novel, the context has become a violent and menacing one. Bobby will only avoid prison by signing a document that falsifies the history of his disastrous and murderous return expedition from the east with the white settler Chaine, the ex-soldier Killam, and the two east-coast Aboriginees James and Jeffrey. Bobby, though, as a cosmopolitan, still believes in the importance of cultural performance, like dance, and that the land is his as a Noongar, inherited from his ancestors, and that it can be shared with the white settlers, that written documents are only one form of cultural power. 'Bobby Wabalanginy believed he'd won them over with his dance, his speech, and of course his usual trick of performance-and-costume stuff' (394–95). But it is now (in 1844) another world, full of anxiety and violence. His dance has no meaning for his white audience whatsoever. Outside he hears gunshots (395).

In Scott's chronotope of West Australian frontier contact – the 'intrinsic connectedness of temporal and spatial relationships' – he imagines the (ultimately unknowable) moments of history, not as constituting some kind of facsimile of the historical past, when Aboriginality was presumed to be authentic, but as a question: How are the potentialities

---

38  Scott, 'A Noongar Voice, an Anomalous History', *Westerly* 53 (2008): 93–106 (103–04).

39  Scott and Brown, p. 36.

of history present in that first contact?[40] Has the history of these moments actually been fulfilled or concluded? Can moments in history that appear to be concluded, past, in fact start up again? What possibilities for Noongar individuals and communities exist today in these narratives is a serious question for Scott. In thinking about such questions, Scott uses what Spivak calls the de-transcendentalising imagination, to narrate a sub-national history and place. The narrative that emerges from complex, situated community engagements also, whatever else it might do, provides a community resource.

## John Kinsella's Commedia

John Kinsella's *Divine Comedy: Journeys Through a Regional Geography*, published in 2008 simultaneously in Australia by UQP and in New York and London by W.W. Norton, is a 400-page poetic sequence. I can only offer a very preliminary reading here. The results of a decades-long interest in Dante, and a desire to 'write a work over a period of time about one small section of land', Kinsella's *Comedy* reterritorialises Dante's medieval Christian epic onto a five-and-a-half acre block of land on the outskirts of York, the oldest inland settlement in the West Australian wheatbelt.[41] It is a serial poem, with filiations to modernist works like Williams' *Paterson* and James Merrill's *The Changing Light at Sandover*, and to longer postmodern works like Armand Schwerner's *The Tablets*, and Susan Howe's *The Europe of Trusts*, with their thematics of cyclical human culture, angelology, ruin, and procedural composition. It is a powerful contribution to the wheatbelt imaginary. Kinsella's reterritorialisation of Dante's three canticles distracts, collapses and reformats the original schema in multiple ways: for example, it begins with Purgatory (Up Close), followed by Paradiso (Rupture), and ends with Inferno (Leisure Centre). The journeys through these imaginatively terraformed landscapes are through multiple entries and exits, and are repetitious, not unidirectional across souls always moving in circles, like Dante's. It is a regional geography, with doors into actual places but, like Dante's imaginary worlds, it is travelled through via language and mentalities. Kinsella frequently evokes the möbius strip in relation to the inseparability of his three realms/canticles/states of mind.

The Preface to Purgatory is one of multiple examples where Kinsella reimagines Dante's schema in an antipodean locale:

> York is a place of fault lines and earthquakes. The tremor/earthquake in Canto 20 of *Purgatorio* takes on a particular significance in my local version. As I wrote my version [over a period of three years], probably hundreds of tremors occurred, most undetectable by anything but machines, but still, the house we live in has been 'earthquake-proofed'. Earthquakes are taken seriously. Phenomena and phenomenology are major variables around 'our' place. The stars are bright, and astronomy and astrological matters are at the core of Dante's work. As they are of mine. The five acres and its extensions are a cosmology. Wind, rain, lightning (especially), tremors, and all other natural events fuse with the imagined, the constructed. The smaller the space examined – the bark of a tree, for example

---

40  Pizer, p. 36; Scott, 'Australia's Continuing Neurosis'.
41  John Kinsella, *Divine Comedy: Journeys Through a Regional Geography* (St Lucia: University of Queensland Press, 2008; New York: W.W. Norton, 2008), p. 3. All subsequent references are given in-text.

[a wasp's nest] – the more intense these associations and juxtapositions become. Dante's work is allegorical, and so is this version. (5)

Dante's *Purgatorio* begins on the antipodean beach that surrounds the mount of Purgatory, as he and Virgil emerge out of the back door of Hell. This is the first poem of Kinsella's Purgatory, titled 'Dream Canto: Egotistical Sublime':

> They dream ocean currents here: landlocked,
> low-rise valley, foot of purgatory
> tidal and exposed to the drag of planets.
>
> Farmers travel to Albany for holidays,
> and the Southern Ocean pounds and grinds
> continental granite, contorted vegetation
>
> low to fronts always crossing, brushing …
> a five-hour drive a stone's throw away,
> the white-sand beaches of Frenchman's Bay,
>
> white-pointers cruising deep waters
> malodorous with sea shanties. Sometimes,
> after retirement, it's the Greek Islands,
>
> or the Peloponnese or Sicily … and these coastlines
> also gnaw as pain and salvation, a nervous tic,
> yes, yes … our paddocks were salt-water and krill. (7)

Where Kinsella's Purgatory is a distraction on Dante's cosmology, his Paradiso is ruptured, 'charged with light and glued together by darkness' (161). This is a space travelled across sideways rather than upwards (163) as 'ultra real', full of birds and car accidents (162). This is also the part of the journey where he acknowledges that Paradise is land stolen from others, the Ballardong Noongar people. This Paradise is 'colonisation, it is theft, it is subjugation' (162) – perhaps like Dante's *Paradiso* it is undergirded by dogma (a concept Kinsella is unafraid of); it is also a canticle of 'environment and family' (163).

Inferno, the third of the geo-states, is spatially rearranged, with 'Other circles and layers and strips and echoes … in place of Dante's 'circles/pits/ditches/pouches' (265). 'Hell is an easy place to populate – mainly with oneself' (271). The York district's Mount Bakewell (Walwalinj), re-named by English surveyor Ensign Dale in 1830, is both a threatened earthly paradise and a kind of portal into another world. But Kinsella's Inferno is 'not the place of nuclear abomination, pesticides, land degradation and political horror in the same way that … *Purgatorio* is. It does have elements of them, of course, but the prime drift is psychological' (267). Inferno

> is the place where we are all complicit, where the cliché is paramount, rather than twists of words. They too have their place, as exclusion and rejection – 'othering' – and the sub-alternising – make for a concept of Babel in which none of us understands those outside our immediate circles. Inferno is internationally

regional: we're all there with the same possibility of trauma and wrongdoing. (267)

This is hardly bioregional communitarianism. Like Dante, Kinsella seems furiously to pursue his critique of government, settlement history and global mythography 'while travelling through heaven, hell, and purgatory'.[42] There are lots of other levels: astronomy, microscopically fine calibrations of place and flora names, animal life, local politics, national politics, regional environmental history, geology, bad land management, allegorisation of children's toys, etc. The 'journey' through this regional geography, deeply layered in Noongar, settlement and geological times, is at least as allegorical and fractally imagined as Dante's through his tri-world *Commedia*.

Kinsella describes his divine comedy as a provincial cosmology, stretching the spatial referents to the extreme (272). This is the rhetoric of the paradoxical and fissionable core of literary particularity and universality. It also clearly applies to Kinsella's understanding of Dante, not as the universal poet of historical transition between classical and Renaissance paradigms, but as a writer who imagined the eternal in the local, the cosmological in the provincial. In a chapter of *The World Republic of Letters* entitled 'The Revolutionaries', Casanova argues that great modernist writers like Joyce, Faulkner, Beckett, Reuben Dario, and Cortazar 'break away from the national and nationalist model of literature and, in inventing the conditions of their autonomy, achieve freedom. In other words, whereas the first national intellectuals refer to a political idea of literature in order to create a particular national identity, the newcomers refer to autonomous international literary laws in order to bring into existence, still on a national level, another type of literature and literary capital' (324–25). I am representing Casanova's argument somewhat sketchily – it is more nuanced in fact – but the point I want to draw alongside my own reading of Kinsella is that Casanova sees the 'paradigm surely of all these [modernist and postmodernist] reworkings as the use that the Irish (first Joyce, then Beckett and Heaney) made of Dante' (Joyce was '[n]icknamed "the Dante of Dublin"'). Each of these writers, she argues,

> Reappropriated the work of the Tuscan poet – noble before all others – as an instrument of struggle on behalf of cosmopolitan and antinationalist Irish poets. Through a sort of reactualization of the linguistic and literary project laid out in *De vulgari eloquentia* (On Vernacular Eloquence) – a project that only writers concretely and directly concerned with the status of a national language in relation to the literary language of their space could understand – Joyce and Beckett in turn recreated, recovered, and invoked Dante's subversive power ... Dante became at once a resource and a weapon in the struggle of the most international writers in the Irish space. (328–29)

Casanova goes on to detail the case of Beckett's defence of Joyce, using *On Vernacular Eloquence* in his 1929 essay (in fact his first publication), 'Dante ... Bruno. Vico ... Joyce', 'a defense of the linguistic – which is to say political – dimension to Joyce's enterprise' and his allegiance to Dante throughout his career (329). Of course *De vulgaria eloquentia* is not the

---

42 David Wallace, *Premodern Places: Calais to Surinam, Chaucer to Aphra Behn* (Oxford: Blackwell, 2004), p. 140.

*Commedia,* but my context here is the use that Casanova is putting Dante to in her reading of Joyce and Beckett, modernist heroes who resisted 'the narrow limits of national realism', thereby expanding world literary space (330). Casanova herself argues, and this is hardly acknowledged by her critics, that the

> international and historical model that has been proposed [in *The World Republic of Letters*], and quite particularly an appreciation of the historical link established since the 16th century between literature and the nation, can give the literary projects of writers on the periphery their justification and their aesthetic and political coherence. By drawing up a map of the literary world and highlighting the gap between great and small literary nations, one may hope to be delivered at last from the prejudices inculcated by literary critics in the center (354).

At the outset, I suggested that the pathologies of net-based sociability are part of our lifeworlds and impinge also on our professional practices. These ecstasies and anxieties are about the depth and connectivity of selves, which is to say, about what it is to be human in a posthuman world (that is, one where selves might evolve), connected to the political and historical specificities of time and place. Communities are dimensional in the way space is; they exist in time, in historical incarnations, but also in the existential constellations of individual consciousness. Multiple and virtual, they are always expanding and shifting. They can only be modelled rather than defined or definitively described; their embodiment in practices is interspersed with the social imaginary at every point. Neither Kim Scott nor John Kinsella is writing with the intention of revivifying some transhistorical humanism, neither withdraws into subjectivity in the face of a powerfully standardising globalism, both write out of a processual knowledge of a geography and its history, both are deeply committed to local-molecular inflections of language, neither has any discernible allegiance to any kind of overarching national question or narrative; their drive is into the detranscendent, the locally temporal.[43] They up-end mythic schema, antipodise them, they Indigenise narrative modes and styles, they reterritorialise literary forms, they are extreme in their particularism (but not regionalist), they bypass the question of identity, they defamiliarise the subtle politics of oppression.[44] Multiple temporalities course through their writings.[45] As a critic, like many I suspect, with little interest in the rhetoric and practice of pure, disinterested or historically privileged positionality within the field of reading, one of the attractions of these examples of fiction and poetry is the challenge their 'extreme particularism' offers to theory and modes of literary knowledge (354). As my merely introductory readings here seek to demonstrate, Scott's novel and Kinsella's poem are complex, contradictory representations of connectivity and cosmopolitanism that also happen to be West Australian, four-dimensional LandPrint models.

But it is worth noting the careful dissonance of Casanova's vocabulary. Her reading, in the end, is motivated by an inquiry into what she describes as 'the question of how

---

43 During, p. 59.

44 'Advance Australia Fair – that's that eugenics stuff all over again, isn't it?' See Scott, 'Australia's Continuing Neurosis'.

45 Wallace, p. 11.

literary universality is manufactured' (354). 'Universality' and 'manufactured': two terms with incommensurate denotations. With 'universality' she is thinking both of the evident escape of some (modern European) writers from the bonds of nation and language, and also of its circulation within non-professional, public discourses about literature, where, by various misprisions, 'universality' expresses an ultimate value. And that is a real-world effect. 'Manufactured', though, empties 'universality' of any trace of the transcendent and the transhistorical. What is left, then? Scott and Kinsella would no doubt qualify, in Casanova's terms, as peripheral literary figures, a long way from the Greenwich Meridian of the world republic of letters, perhaps even from the Eastern Standard Time (and Space) of a national literature. As such, communications about their works will be subject to uneven and unreliable connectivity, always threatening to drop out of the cellular networks of critical reading. But that is not the only point. Reformulating the world literary system as less orientalist or First-World-northern, moving to where there is more signal, is not the only use of disciplinary time and effort. To refine the problematic I outlined earlier: it is about how to represent the ways in which the individual reader – who is also multiple, in so far as she/he participates in plural real and virtual communities of reading – contributes to the hierarchies of literary value. Are we going to include specific fictions and poems like *That Deadman Dance* and *Divine Comedy: A Journey Through a Regional Geography* in 'our' inquiries about particularity and universality – which is also the question of singular literariness itself – or zoom out, as in Google maps, to the satellite view of place and history, of form and language? Where does our reading begin?

# Part 3

# Sociality, Gender and Genre

# 12

## The Great Parenting Tradition: Charting a History of Parenting-Book Writers and Readers in Colonial Australia

*Michelle De Stefani*

The nonfiction print-genre of the parenting book – or child-rearing guide – has a long and complex history. Despite its pervasiveness across generations, cultures and communities, the evolution of this genre and its introduction into Australian colonial society has hitherto evaded scholarly investigation. This is due, in part, to the ambiguity of these rich textual productions and the scant existence of archival material illuminating this earliest part of our nation's history. As cultural artefacts, parenting books provide a window through which social attitudes towards the family, motherhood, fatherhood and the child may be observed within their historical context. Yet equally so these books exist as 'texts' ripe for literary analysis. Examining not what, but how child-rearing concepts are communicated across time through the changing textual structure of the parenting book provides a unique entry point from which to begin reconstructing the history of this genre in Australia.

The production of parenting literature in Australia signalled a shift in both the conceptualisation of 'the Australian family' and the evolution of the Australian book trade. Parenting books are thus, by their very nature, deeply implicated by and in the communities that create them. This chapter will explore one of the earliest Australian-published parenting books, Hannah Villiers Boyd's *Letters on Education: Addressed to a Friend in the Bush of Australia* (1848), as an example of the sense of community parenting-book writers shared with their reading public in a defining period of colonial book trade history.[1] First, a brief historical sketch of book production in the first half of the nineteenth century will contextualise the appearance of the parenting book in colonial Australia. Following this, I will examine how the textual features and narrative form of *Letters on Education* construct the author and parent/reader as members within a collective community. Situating early colonial parenting books within their social context and alongside historical evidence of their production and reception provides a window through which to examine how the imagined and actual experience of community, the fact and the fiction, coexist in the conceptualisation of the parenting book as both literary text and material artefact.

---

1 Hannah Villiers Boyd, *Letters on Education: Addressed to a Friend in the Bush of Australia* (Sydney: W. and F. Ford, 1848). Subsequent page references are given in-text.

## Structure and Tradition

*Letters on Education* is a representative example of the emergent tradition of Australian parenting-book production. Australian publication before the 1890s is often characterised as a sporadic and individualistic endeavour, with domestic authors required either to fund the production of their own works or seek finance via reader subscription.[2] The most viable avenues for publication were therefore newspaper serialisation or publication in Britain for a predominately European readership.[3] Thus early Australian publications can be seen to coexist alongside a spate of foreign-authored imports offered to the general reading public. As Australia's white, migrant, rural gentry grew during the mid nineteenth century, advocating the values of 'mental and moral improvement', preoccupations with education and the domestic sphere of family life consequently increased, creating a new demand for utilitarian reading in order to 'foster a greater sense of social duty among colonists, promote virtue and sobriety, and particularly self-education through reading and study'.[4] Moreover, as evangelical Protestant philanthropy focused its interests on the moral instruction of the working-class poor and Indigenous communities, its participants were proactive in the importation of bibles and didactic religious tracts to further the promotion of Christian ideals. A significant importation of 'useful' nonfiction books was thus a distinctive feature of the colonial book trade, amongst which parenting books by British and American authors played a part. Preliminary research indicates that a steady flow of these publications were imported and offered for sale to the Australian public, often categorised as 'miscellaneous' books, from as early as the 1820s.[5]

Regardless of their alignment with wider social discourses including religion, medicine and education, we can begin a rearticulation of these nonfiction works as 'parenting books' – books pertaining to the rearing and education of children produced for a general parenting public – and thus begin to recognise them as existing within a print genre of its own delineation. This can be achieved by shifting the critical focus from one purely concerned with the content or subject matter of the parenting book, to a focus on formal features as generic markers. The historian's almost exclusive attention to the child-rearing content of parenting books as historical evidence of actual social practice has, according to scholar Jay Mechling, concealed their potential to serve as, more appropriately, 'evidence of the "manual-writing values" of the group of men and women who wrote the manuals'.[6] In the context of Australian literary studies, a focus on religious, educational and medical

---

2 Elizabeth Webby, 'The Beginnings of Literature in Colonial Australia', in Peter Pierce, ed., *The Cambridge History of Australian Literature*, (Cambridge: Cambridge University Press, 2009), p. 45.

3 Wallace Kirsop, *Books for Colonial Readers: The Nineteenth-Century Australian Experience* (Melbourne: Bibliographical Society of Australia and New Zealand, 1995), p .7.

4 Mark Askew and Brian Hubber, 'The Colonial Reader Observed: Reading in Its Cultural Context', in D.H. Borchardt and Wallace Kirsop, eds, *The Book in Australia: Essays Towards a Cultural and Social History* (Melbourne: Australian Reference Publications in association with the Centre for Bibliographical and Textual Studies, Monash University, 1988), p. 113.

5 This finding is the preliminary outcome of my ongoing investigation of New South Wales and Tasmanian newspaper advertisements for the years 1803–1850.

6 Jay Mechling, 'Advice to Historians on Advice to Mothers', *Journal of Social History* 9.1 (1975): 44–63 (55).

content has led to the separation of nonfiction works into subject-specific bibliographies, thus concealing amongst these compilations early examples of literature addressed to a parenting readership. Re-identifying 'parenting books' amongst works that have been categorised otherwise, allows one to trace the genre in Australia from its early colonial roots to its contemporary manifestations amongst the myriad of 'pop-psych' publications and more recent, online media forms. This rearticulation revises the notion that parenting books, in the form of popular medical works such as those by Dr Philip E. Muskett and Dr George Fullerton, did not find a ready market of production until the establishment of paediatrics as a scientific discipline in Australia.[7] As culturally catalytic periods for growing interests in child development in Australia, the public health and infant welfare movements at the turn of the century and the inter-war period in the twentieth century, have thus far been the more predominant historic periods for scholarly focus.[8]

Despite these social observations, the lack of medical works in the early colony reveals as much about the economic realities of the print industry as it does the intentions of colonists to produce works pertaining to child health. Medical professionals who were keen to publish works specifically adapted for the Australian public were met with a relatively disinclined, and limited, readership that could neither geographically procure, nor afford, works offered for sale.[9] The mere fact that parenting books published in Australia seemed to increase by the end of the nineteenth century does not, therefore, indicate a total lack of social interest in the production of such literature prior to this period.

Defining the parenting book according to its peculiar formalistic features, we find that the interests and concerns of early colonists, and thus the parenting books produced in Australia during the first half of the nineteenth century, do not fit within established conceptions of parenting books as, typically, medical advice manuals. Rather, it is the books aligning with domestic propriety, religion and education that highlight the sense of national identity colonists were forming within the wider parenting-book tradition. We find in these works a consciousness of this emergent tradition through their dichotomous juxtapositions between old and new: between the Old World concept of the motherland and the newfound community of Australia; between old modes of print production and distribution and the new incidence of domestic publication in the colony. By investigating the isolated and erratic incidences of domestic publication, and examining the content of these works, we can thus capture a defining national period of print production that saw a conscious use and development of the existing parenting book genre in an effort to reconfigure a 'new' nation within a longstanding literary tradition.

---

7  Lisa Featherstone, 'The Value of an Infant: The Rise of Paediatrics in Australia, 1880–1910', *Health & History* 10.1 (2008): 110–33.

8  Kerreen Reiger, 'Women's Labour Redefined: Child-Bearing and Rearing Advice in Australia, 1880–1930s', in Margaret Bevege, Margaret James and Carmel Shute, eds, *Worth Her Salt: Women at Work in Australia* (Sydney: Hale and Iremonger, 1982), pp. 72–83.

9  See, for example, the advertisement in the *Sydney Gazette*, 17 January 1837, for subscriptions in support of the publication of C. Smith M.D., *Treatise on the Diseases and Medical Treatment of Children and Females in New South Wales*.

## Internal and External Communities

Scholarly critique of parenting literature generally depends on its nature as nonfictional prose. Parenting books are thus conventionally viewed as historically bound objects of social commentary that somehow reflect the cultural realities of a given temporal moment. Accepting a parenting book as, rather, a cultural and, in some sense, a literary 'text' is a recognition of its constructedness both formally (as a work of literature) and physically (as a material product). A parenting book can also be considered ' "fictional" to the extent that its relation to the real behaviour of children or parents is inaccessible to the historian ... the manuals are a kind of linguistic behaviour addressed to adults by adults'.[10] The consequences of this appreciation are twofold: parenting books represent both a textually constructed community – generated by their internal narrative structure and formalistic features – and at the same time reference the external community of flesh-and-blood participants who partake in and contribute to the 'real' life cycle of the book – the producers, disseminators and readers of parenting books. It seems plausible, therefore, that theoretical approaches otherwise reserved for fictional texts could equally be applied to the nonfiction text of the parenting book. As George L. Dillon writes,

> As long as we assume experience is being presented 'for itself' – to be savoured by the reader – the way that experience is presented, the style, tone and voice in the passage, are proper foci for criticism.[11]

Employing the terminology of scholar David Herman, parenting books are a 'fuzzy' form of text-type that blur distinct boundaries between fact and fiction, narrative and non-narrative representation. The instruction or advice found in parenting books can thus be viewed as:

> necessarily embedded in stories, rather than as raw experiential inputs ... From this perspective, the chief analytical goal is not to disentangle descriptions from narratives (an impossible task), but instead to study narratives as both causes and symptoms of the webs of belief in which any (scientific or other) description of the world must be situated.[12]

Literary tools such as narratological theory can therefore shed new light on the nature of the parenting book as a specific text-type and account for both their internal and external constructions of 'community'. As a basic element of narrative, the 'narrative situation' or the 'context for telling' inherent within parenting books constitutes its 'internal community' – the 'multi-layered process of narrative communication' that establishes relations among parties on both the telling side (the actual authors, implied authors and narrators) and interpreting side (the actual readers, implied readers and narratees) of the storytelling

---

10   Mechling, 'Advice to Historians on Advice to Mothers', p. 56.

11   George L. Dillon, 'Fiction in Persuasion: Personal Experience as Evidence and as Art', in Chris Anderson, ed., *Literary Nonfiction: Theory, Criticism, Pedagogy*, (Carbondale and Edwardsville: Southern Illinois University Press, 1989), p. 197.

12   David Herman, *Basic Elements of Narrative* (West Sussex: Wiley-Blackwell, 2009), p. 102.

process.¹³ Following David Herman's approach to narrative situation,¹⁴ parenting books often present their advice through the first-person account of a 'dramatised author' – a position distinct from the textually constructed implied author who does not, by contrast, use the pronoun 'I'. In so doing, the text implies a reader who engages with the 'I' of the teller as the 'I' of this dramatised author; that is, one who recognises that the teller is not in fact a 'narrator' – a fictional creation generated by the actual author – but, rather, a persona of the author her/himself. Often written by professional 'experts' (psychologists, medical practitioners, etc.) the voice present within parenting books is therefore indistinguishable from the persona of the textually constructed implied author as an 'expert authority'. Parenting books also feature shifts in narrative situation through the presentation of personal testimony and case studies, whereby the 'I' speaker position is transferred, and the subject of that telling becomes a dramatised narrator – a speaker within the text functioning as a character-narrator. Parenting books therefore feature many instances of stories-within-stories as part of their overall narrative structure, and it is by the very nature of these narrative interactions that a communicative, and communal, author–reader relationship is created. The appearance of testimonials, stories, parables and myths as modes of instruction within parenting books cue readers to discern from their overarching moral, or endpoint, some form of 'real', concrete and applicable child-rearing advice. It is the ability of authors to reproduce – and, in their reproduction, continue readers' responsiveness to – specific elements of narrative that, in turn, secures the genre's continued production, dissemination and reception.

How a nonfiction text represents and constructs its version of reality aligns with the basic narrative element of 'worldmaking'.¹⁵ The way in which parenting books establish the 'real' world as the contextual blueprint for their narrative is by reference to real individuals and communities external to the text, and via a metacommentary of production – commentary about the parenting book's existence as a book. This appears both within the body text and the book's paratexts, such as the cover, preface, dedications, appendages and so on.¹⁶ The parenting book shares this characteristic of metacommentary with the self-help book or domestic conduct manual via a conveyed message that 'writers in the field of personal growth and self-improvement constitute a supportive community, one that rejoices in each new addition to the collective insights that draw them together'.¹⁷ Parenting books often present a self-reflexive acknowledgement of the genre and its material history, and

---

13  Herman, pp. 63–64.

14  David Herman's articulation combines the terminology of a number of narratological theorists to distinguish between the sender (author–dramatised author–[un]dramatised narrator) and the receiver ([un]dramatised narratee–narrative audience–authorial audience–real reader) of a narrative message. The implied reader is said to occupy both the authorial and narrative audience position simultaneously. See, in particular, Herman, pp. 63–74.

15  Herman, p. 105.

16  Gérard Genette defines paratexts as 'those liminal devices and conventions, both within the book (*peritexts*) and outside it (*epitexts*), that mediate the book to the reader'. See Genette, trans. Jane E. Lewin, *Paratexts: Thresholds of Interpretation* (Cambridge: Cambridge University Press, 1997), p. xviii.

17  Sandra K. Dolby, *Self-Help Books: Why Americans Keep Reading Them* (Urbana and Chicago: University of Illinois Press, 2008), p. 52.

place themselves within this literary tradition by their propagation of a 'metaculture of newness' – 'a desire to produce objects that, while not totally new, appear new enough to attract the interest of those who already have the old thing'.[18] Taken together, the text's recourse to external referents compounds for readers an intimate, communal relationship with not only a single parenting-book author, but also with expert authors and parents everywhere. The parenting book thus calls or interpellates its readers to adopt the position of self-reflexive parents, re-defining and understanding themselves as individuals and as a part of a collective community via the process of reading.

An analysis of parenting books focusing solely on their historical child-rearing content thus elides their potential to function as literary narratives that elaborate on the uses, function and trade in this literature, and on the parenting-book industry as an economic and commercial enterprise. Metacommentary pertaining to the physicality of the book and the external community of participants in its production perpetuate, in essence, the genre's social and cultural survival.

*A Closer Look at* Letters on Education *(1848)*

Scholarly attention to Hannah Boyd's work *Letters on Education* has generally originated from its bibliographic classification in John Alexander Ferguson's *Bibliography of Australia* as one of the first 'educational treatises'. Noted for its promotion of anti-establishment ideals regarding the home-schooling of children, Boyd's writing is viewed alongside a tradition of evangelical moral reform that emphasised the 'maternal duty' to home-educate, in particular, girls.[19] Its formalistic structure as a series of letters places this book within the sphere of acceptable female authorship prevalent at the time. By the close of the eighteenth century the epistolary form was transforming a once intimate 'feminised' mode of exchange into a public voice for mass consumption: 'the fiction of private correspondence was being dismantled … This transition from private expression to published property pulled the letter out of its fiction of individualism and complicated its "feminine" identity'.[20] Yet *Letters on Education* is, arguably, also one of the first Australian examples of domestically authored parenting literature, and analysis of the text in terms of its narrative features reveals a more subtle alliance with the vast corpus of parenting books in circulation in England and other colonies in the late eighteenth and early nineteenth centuries.

*Letters on Education* was the first publication of Irish-born governess and author Hannah Villiers Boyd. She migrated to the colony of New South Wales from Cork with her two children in 1842, following the breakdown of her marriage to author and physician Sir William Cathcart Boyd.[21] A Protestant woman, born into the Irish aristocracy, Hannah was

---

18  Greg Urban, *Metaculture: How Culture Moves Through the World* (Minneapolis: University of Minnesota Press, 2001), p. 74.

19  Elizabeth Windschuttle, 'Educating the Daughters of the Ruling Class in Colonial New South Wales, 1788–1850', *Melbourne Studies in Education* 22.1 (1980): 105–33.

20  Mary A. Favret, *Romantic Correspondence: Women, Politics and the Fiction of Letters* (Cambridge: Cambridge University Press, 1993), p.13.

21  For the only known biographical sketch of Hannah Boyd's life prior to migration see Robert Peterson and Sarah Paddle, Introduction, *Letters on Education: Addressed to a Friend in the Bush of Australia* (Sydney: R.C. Peterson, 1992), pp. 1–14.

to find what she later described in her second publication as a utopia, a 'New Jerusalem', in Australia.[22] *Letters on Education* was published by a small Sydney bookseller, W. & F. Ford of George Street, and printed by the then joint proprietors of the *Sydney Morning Herald*, Charles Kemp and John Fairfax. Whilst precise print-run figures are unknown, research suggests that the dissemination of this book was wide, with copies being distributed more than four hundred kilometres from the centre of Sydney to rural townships, including Walcha.[23] One can only speculate on the motives for Boyd's authorship. The book was most likely to be a self-promoted publication and its publishers selected for their experience in, and promotion of, religious sentiment. Moreover, the text exhibits Boyd's genuine desire to contribute to the self-education tradition in the instruction of mothers, with the proceeds of sale to be used in assisting the Irish poor (vi). The preface overtly emphasises the author's philanthropic conviction that

> if a perusal of this little book has the effect of arousing only *one* mother to the sense of the important position she holds in the scale of society, I shall feel myself amply repaid for my trouble. (vi)

In its advocating the use of phrenological principles – the study of skull shape and cranial development as an indicator of personality – the work could also be viewed as a contribution to the advancement of this scientific discipline, which was already a popular study amongst colonists.[24] Whatever the motivation, this book established Hannah Boyd's credentials as a noteworthy author of nonfiction.

*Letters on Education* is structured as a collection of seven letters, each written by Hannah Boyd and addressed to a Mrs Adam, a woman likely to be – as the title and biographical references in the text suggest – a 'friend in the bush': a mother residing in the interior of New South Wales. Each letter suggests to Mrs Adam different methods and modes of instruction by which she may home-educate her four children, who were isolated from established day schools and the ready society of other families. Unlike others situated closer to the vicinity of Sydney, she was unable to secure a live-in governess for her children. In Letter I, Boyd notes that she had advertised on behalf of Mrs Adam for a suitable governess, but none was willing to travel three hundred miles from Sydney, a distance which at the time was 'sufficient to terrify the most courageous, as it involves the idea of bad roads, travelling by mail cars, uncomfortable inns, and all the other annoyances attendant on a journey to the interior' (1).

---

22 Boyd, *A Voice from Australia: Or an Inquiry into the Probability of New Holland Being Connected with the Prophesies Relating to New Jerusalem and the Spiritual Temple* (Sydney: Robert Barr, 1851). Boyd published this book in an Australian edition (1851) and a second, rev. edition published simultaneously in London and Dublin (1856). There is also evidence of a third work prepared for the press in French and English, to be presented at the Paris Exhibition of 1855, entitled *Some Passages in the Life of a Governess*. This work was advertised in the *Sydney Morning Herald* on 20 and 24 March 1854, entreating persons desirous of procuring copies to submit subscription to publishers Waugh and Cox of George-Street, Sydney. Further research will be conducted in order to locate an existing copy.

23 Provenance information on an existing copy of the book suggests ownership by Sarah Jane Elliot of Winterbourne, Walcha.

24 Michael Roe, *Quest for Authority in Eastern Australia, 1835–1851* (Melbourne: Melbourne University Press in association with the Australian National University, 1965), p. 161.

The narrative situation of this work is complicated by the letter-writing structure of the text. Readers are led to inquire whether these letters were in fact written for a 'real' individual, Mrs Adam, or alternatively, exist as semi-fictionalised accounts or pure fabrication.[25] Although the preface notes that 'I have occupied a few leisure hours in writing the following letters' (vi), readers are left to question and judge the truthfulness of this authorial statement. Herman suggests that

> 'authentication' (or not) of particular situations and events as fictional facts depends not only on whether they are presented through first-person, third-person, or figural modes of narration, but also on the audience positions those narrative modes invite readers to occupy.[26]

The real reader must inevitably align, to some extent, with Mrs Adam in order for the advice to have some applicability to their own circumstances and predicament as a parent, and must be persuaded that the author's voice *is* the more experienced voice over and above their own natural instincts and inclinations. Thus Hannah Boyd, though the 'actual' or 'implied' author of her series of letters to 'a friend', functions within the text as the 'dramatised author' of *Letters on Education*. Occupying the position of a dramatised author, Boyd becomes visible in the text as the writer of her letters, as opposed to remaining the product of silent, textual implication as a mere implied author. In this way Boyd's first-person account confirms her position as both the knowledgeable advisor of Mrs Adam and the learned governess-cum-parenting-book-author. In addressing the implied reader of the letters, Mrs Adam, as 'You', the dramatised author equally addresses the implied readership of *Letters on Education*:

> You have not the temptations to sacrifice a great deal of time to society ... You have no lady neighbours to pay morning visits ... you are not obliged to give dinners to people who have plenty to eat ... you must be a 'keeper at home'. (3–4)

The direct, first-person address to the implied readership is thus not merely empathetic and convincing but, most importantly, authoritative. With her knowledge of child care aligned not so much with her experience as a mother, but rather with her affiliation amongst 'the paid teachers of the world' (9), the implied reader of *Letters on Education* is encouraged to adopt the position, alongside Mrs Adam, of pupil vis-à-vis the governess educator. Only after the process of reading the parenting book can the parent emerge as the 'new authority' – the competent educator of their own child. In Letter VII, the final letter and culmination of the book's instruction regarding religious education, the dramatised Boyd states that 'Now, as the little flock whom you have now an opportunity to instruct grow up to maturity ... you must do all you can to fulfil your duty as a "*teacher*"' (147).

---

25 Whilst R.C. Peterson goes to some length in his reprint to prove the historical existence of a family with similar genealogy to the Adams, namely the Morrice family of the Upper Murray, there is no conclusive evidence that Hannah Boyd was in fact acquainted with them. See specifically Notes in R.C. Peterson, ed., *Letters on Education*, pp. 3–4.

26 Herman, *Basic Elements of Narrative*, p. 73.

The separation of advice into discrete letters aids the actual reader in their use of the text as a manual of instruction; the contents page functions as a reference point for the various subject matters discussed, such as 'Letter II. On Teaching', 'Letter VI. Infant Education', and so on. This facilitates the actual reader's entering and re-entering of the text on separate occasions of reading. Each letter is interspersed with multiple excerpts from published works including poetry, autobiography, didactic treatises and fiction, as a means of illustrating the advice pertaining to the education and moral and religious upbringing of children. These passages often involve a shift in narrative situation: the 'I' speaker-position is adopted by a new voice, that of a dramatised narrator who has been selected by the author to be the subject of a separate telling. For example, Letter V, 'On Self-instruction', features excerpts from George Lillie Craik's *The Pursuit of Knowledge Under Difficulties: Volume II* (1842), whereby the dramatised Boyd notes, 'I shall give you another extract … which you can read as a preface to my hints' (87). Further to this, the book includes a fold-out lithograph of a selection of words (presumably handwritten by the actual author), from which the daughter of Mrs Adam may copy and practice her writing composition and grammar.[27] Together with the inclusion of poems, hymns and songs from which children can practise their singing and dictation, *Letters on Education* operates as a practical tool and physical parenting aid, with such peritextual devices as can prompt the actual reader to give life to the text in the real, external world. These textual features capture the notion of the parenting book as a significant material artefact in the lives of mothers, the inclusion of practical components within the parenting book promoting its longevity as a physical object.

The implied mother-reader is figured in the text as 'the keeper at home' (4), frequently likened to the biblical Eve. They are the ladies who 'eat the bread of industry' who are the mothers in the bush of Australia. As such, a distinction is drawn throughout the text between Australian and European mothers, the latter who 'have plenty of servants … and who consider themselves degraded by doing anything *unlady-like* … They prefer being only "ornamental"' (105). The implied readership is thus encouraged to 'keep looking forward' (8), observe the benefits of their position in a trying, new-found land, 'and we should in a few years teach the Europeans a practical moral lesson' (58). Together with the book's dedication to Mrs Anna Maria Macarthur of The Vineyard, the daughter of the then ex-Governor of New South Wales Philip King, and wife of pastoralist Hannibal Hawkins Macarthur, biographical references to 'real' external individuals canvass the 'new' community for which the book was intended: the white, migrant, rural mothers of Australia. In her dedication, the dramatised Boyd notes that Mrs Macarthur has 'with very little assistance from paid teachers, brought up a large family of daughters, who are both ornaments to their country and useful members of society, and who, in thus fulfilling her parental duties affords a bright example to the mothers of Australia' (iii). The depiction of Mrs Macarthur provides testimonial proof that the application of the book's advice is a step towards achieving similar parenting success. If we consider, however, that Mrs Macarthur did, in fact, employ multiple governesses – the most noteworthy being the author of Australia's first children's book, Charlotte Barton – we meet with the fictionality of parenting

---

27  The fold-out, appearing between pages 50–51, includes the insignia of J. Allan, a lithographer operating at 2 Hunter Street, Sydney.

books in their distortion of truths to achieve a more consistent, and persuasive, narrative. As an inherent aspect of advice writing, factual material such as the presentation of case histories and personal testimony buttresses the author's credibility, providing 'proofs that their analyses do touch empirical bases and their treatments do produce results in the real, tough, troubled world'.[28] The genre therefore rests on the assumption that readers interpret these statements as true: that they respond to the convention of identification through reference to real individuals and the real, external world.

The text compounds the socially prescribed role of motherhood as naturally bound to the domestic realm, and equally transposes such expectations upon the Australian mother. Yet whilst the nature of childcare advice and construction of the female subject are not novel or revolutionary aspects of the work, the mode of address for the Australian audience is itself evidence of a defining moment in the history of parenting-book production. For the first time the rural mothers of Australia were directly addressed by parenting literature specific to their individual circumstances and predicaments. If this period of the Australian book trade was indeed a time when 'one is entitled to suspect that the primary aim was not to satisfy – with taste and sensitivity – the special requirements of colonial readers but to dump excess stock',[29] then *Letters on Education* can be seen as a contribution to the 'New World', or new order, of the parenting book, responsive to the needs and demands of a real, historically specific, geographically defined reading public.

As an expression of the implied author's intention, the preface depicts the incidence of publication as a response to a gap in the market – the need for domestically published works educating mothers on how to raise and educate their children:

> I have frequently regretted that I could not recommend any one book which might be an assistant to a mother in this country, in the education of her children. Books written on this important subject for the use of European mothers, are not calculated for ladies so peculiarly situated as the mothers of Australia are, when they reside at a distance from town. I therefore thought, that as no more competent individual had undertaken the task of teaching them how to teach their children, I would do so myself. (v)

This self-reflexive metacommentary of the book's placement within a developing genre is yet another structural marker of the parenting book. The preface identifies the work as but one contribution to an already-existing genre 'for the use of European mothers'. The constant intertextual references to foreign-authored parenting books – such as the works of Hannah Moore, Sarah Ellis, Maria Edgeworth and John Stevens Cabot Abbott – and exhortations encouraging the practice and value of reading as a form of 'self-culture' are necessary constituents ensuring the book's placement within this specific generic tradition. As the dramatised Boyd states,

> Eve had no nice books to help her to instruct her children; whereas the Australian ladies have the experience of the old world, for nearly six thousand years at their command, if they will only read. (5)

---

28  Dillon, 'Fiction in Persuasion', p. 202.
29  Kirsop, *Books for Colonial Readers,* p. 11.

The idea that reading books, and parenting books in particular, is superior to the acquisition of simple advice from family and friends since it draws in 'the experience of the old world' points again to the materiality of the parenting book as an element of its omnipresence. The physical object creates for readers a shared community with the present, and also with the past, as a material artefact documenting the collective experience of 'family' and of 'parenting'. The ephemeral nature of the letter is thus transformed into something more permanent and substantial in its parenting book form – a durable medium that encourages its own circulation by and amongst women. In its metacommentary of production the work also makes reference to the realities of the Australian book trade; in particular, the relatively limited selection of books available to Mrs Adam and the need to 'send off' to England in order to obtain specific titles. The need for readers, women especially, to share and circulate their private stories amongst friends and neighbours is emphasised, as is an exhortation for the communal sharing of knowledge through the reading process. Her suggestions in each letter to Mrs Adam of specific practical, instructional works include a selection of titles widely available to the Australian readership at this time, such as the various tales authored under the pseudonym 'Peter Parley', and William Cobbett's *A Grammar of the English Language*, as well as titles by London-based religious publishers, including The Society for the Diffusion of Useful Knowledge and The Bible Society, whose productions readily featured amongst large consignments of books to the colony. The text further compounds the sense of a community of readers by imploring the implied readership to equally foster a love and appreciation for reading in the generation of the nation's children. If the daughter of Mrs Adam, and thus the daughters of Australian mothers everywhere, has 'the master key to the literature of England in her possession … She can in books find companions in prosperity, and friends in adversity' (12). It is a mother's duty to consider that 'your influence in the training of your children may have a serious effect on the future destiny of a rising country. And above all, consider that you are training souls for eternity' (8). The parenting book therefore functions as a guide and personified 'friend' in assisting mothers to this end. The text makes sure to reiterate the underlying objective 'that good books are the best teachers' (12) and that the writing process itself is a powerful medium in effecting cultural change: 'how important it is for parents to cultivate the moral sentiments of their children, before they put into their hands such a dangerous weapon as a pen' (37).

Nineteenth-century reviews of *Letters on Education* afford a means by which to gauge actual reader responses to the text, albeit the responses of a representatively select and limited section of the reading population. While mostly concerned with Boyd's employment of phrenological principles, a review published in the *Sydney Morning Herald* made particular mention of the 'rather desultory character' and 'digressive manner' of the 'numerous poetical extracts, which do not appear to be very appropriate', as well as Boyd's penchant for 'passing over many important things which we expected would have been carefully treated in a too perfunctory manner'.[30] This criticism of the work's formalistic features continues in the observations of contemporary commentators who view Boyd's 'openhanded approach to the use of sources' as a 'scissors and paste approach' that evidences

---

30   Review, *Sydney Morning Herald*, 29 December 1847. This review, appearing the year prior to the book's specified date of publication, appears to be based on the manuscript copy submitted to Kemp & Fairfax to be officially printed the following year.

both her 'limited formal education' and adherence to the convention of letter-writing as 'a more common private and female mode of exchange'.[31] However, Boyd's use of excerpts can be viewed as consistent with the narrative conventions particular to the parenting-book genre. The use of excerpts as exempla supports the overall problem–solution structure of instructional narrative, or rather the 'equilibrium–disruption–restoration' trajectory of typical narrative representation.[32] Moreover, the dramatised Boyd acknowledges a conscious use of this technique. In Letter III, directly following an excerpt of 'The Pebble and the Acorn' by American versifier Hannah Flagg Gould, she notes, 'This poem will enable you to explain to Fanny that fables, although not true themselves, are used as a means of explaining some moral truth to persons who like an amusing style of reading better than plain sermons or lectures' (55). The book's bibliographic record in G.B. Barton's *Literature in New South Wales* (1866) is perhaps evidence of the significance of Boyd's experimental approach in its attempt to exceed the generic boundaries of nineteenth-century parenting literature.[33] As early colonial readers brought with them expectations of 'traditional' works, Australian parenting books of a 'new' order can thus be seen to 'reset the system of generic classification'.[34]

With its focus on assisting rural mothers home-educate their children, *Letters on Education* depicts the efforts of female writers to forge an intimate author–reader relationship during this early phase in the history of Australian publishing. The structural and formalistic conventions which parenting books share allow such publications to exist not only as participants in a greater educative tradition, but also to generate a new and distinctive community in the development of literature by and for the emergent Australian parenting public. In analysis of the parenting book, one discovers that both the internal textual relationships functioning within the work, and the external community of writers and readers outside of it, are co-dependent constituents of the genre. In its propagation of the motif of child-expert author and mother as the nurturing caretakers of a growing nation, *Letters on Education* is thus suggestive of the continuing epistemological interdependency of the printed word and the social practice of parenting – the one always dependant on, and responsive to, the evolution of the other.

---

31 Sarah Paddle, 'Hannah Villiers Boyd and Colonial Culture', *Lilith* 5, (Spring 1988): 148–64 (154).

32 See Herman's account of Todorov's structuralist approach to 'prototypical' instances of narrative in *Basic Elements of Narrative*, p. 96.

33 George Burnett Barton, *Literature in New South Wales* (Sydney: Thomas Richards, 1866). Entry for *Letters on Education* appears in the 'Miscellaneous' section at p. 191.

34 Herman, p. 87.

# 13

## READING PUBLICS, WATCHING AUDIENCES: *LADY AUDLEY'S SECRET* IN NINETEENTH-CENTURY MELBOURNE[1]

Susan K. Martin

British sensation fiction regularly makes use of the colonies as a convenient zone for despatching and retrieving characters. What happens to such fiction when it is transported to Australia? Is a different community of readers produced by a novel when those readers are situated in the non-place of that novel? What happens to such communities when fiction is transformed and consumed in other forms? This chapter considers some of the ways in which sensation fiction was read and encountered in colonial Australia, using one of the most popular examples of the genre, Mary Braddon's *Lady Audley's Secret*,[2] in the most avidly consuming Australian city, Melbourne.

Historically, sensation fiction has been seen as alarmingly inclusive. The accusation levelled against Mary Braddon that she had 'temporarily succeeded in making the literature of the Kitchen the favourite reading of the Drawing room' suggests the dangerous class-crossing appeal of the genre.[3] The identification of these two physical domains implies that this was women's reading, but further evidence does not bear this out. In the bookshops and newspapers of colonial cities, readers of both genders were avidly acquiring, reading and discussing these texts. In the theatres a somewhat different audience was viewing versions and adaptations of them with similar effects. Colonial readers and viewers were 'insiders' because they identified as Britons concerned with the issues of gentility, morality and gender canvassed by sensation fiction. They were also 'outside' because of their distance from the metropolitan centre produced as the heart of culture and meaning within these texts, and because of the positioning of Australia and the colonies in works such as *Lady Audley's Secret* as the almost blank space into which characters disappear. Through reading, the colonial's distance is underscored, but also collapsed. Locality is asserted by the experience of a visit to Mullen's bookstore in Collins Street to jostle against other eager purchasers of the latest novel, or by reading in the margins of the serialised text: in the news, the advertisements, or the header of the newspaper. On the other hand, distance

---

1 Some sections of this chapter have appeared in a different form in Susan K. Martin and Kylie Mirmohamadi, *Sensational Melbourne: Reading, Sensation Fiction and* Lady Audley's Secret *in the Victorian Metropolis* (North Melbourne: Australian Scholarly Publishing, 2011).

2 Mary Elizabeth Braddon, *Lady Audley's Secret*, The Author's Autograph Edition (London: Simpkin & Co., [n.d.] Emory Yellowback series).

3 Walter Rae, review 1865, quoted in Andrew King, *The London Journal 1845–83: Periodicals, Production, and Gender* (Surrey: Ashgate, 2004), p. 32.

is collapsed by the standard textual experience of being interpellated into the imagined context of the narrative. James Belich contends that colonists saw themselves 'as denizens of a fragmented metropolis rather than a colonial periphery'.[4]

In the early 1860s, new fiction arrived in Australia direct from English ports to Melbourne via the Great [Southern] Circle route. *Lady Audley's Secret*, published in three-volume form in London in October 1862, would probably have been on sale in Melbourne by the end of that year. By July 1863, the arrival on the 'monthly' mail boat in Melbourne of the new 'cheap' single volume edition of the novel in quantity was immediately advertised by the main booksellers – Mullen's and Robertson's – and smaller concerns, most of them located in Collins Street east.[5] Annie Baxter Dawbin, in Melbourne in the winter of 1863, recorded in her diary for 28 June: 'I read "Lady Audley's secret", and Dr Russell's "My diary north and South" [sic]; and I am now beginning Seeman' [sic] "Mission to Viti".'[6] A frequenter of Mullen's (a 'piece of extravagance'), she had probably obtained her copy of Braddon there, along with the other reading, although she also borrowed from friends.[7] Her reading supplements evidence from the *Australian Common Reader* project that the community of sensation fiction readers was a diverse and overlapping one, that sensation fiction readers did not confine themselves to sensation fiction or 'women's fiction', and that not only women read sensation fiction.[8] Dawbin does not comment further on her reading of *Lady Audley's Secret*.

In the novel one 'hero', George Talboys, first appears on the ship returning from Australia, where for three years he has gone to make his fortune, leaving his wife and baby behind in England. He has a conversation with a fading governess coming home from Australia to her longtime fiancé, who shares her fears of how much in England may have changed during their absence. George's sketchy description to her of his life in Australia takes up two paragraphs of a 340-page novel: Australia is not a place in the novel so much as a plot element.

Whether Dawbin felt herself within a community of British readers to whom the Australia of the novel was a plot element, or whether she felt some divided identification – between British and Australian residency, let alone between the abandoned wife and the fortune-making husband – she does not share. She shared the colonial reader's displacement (reading in Australia, but as if from Britain), even if it felt odd to be in that antipodean plot element, with all those other Mullen's and Robertson's readers. She may have been impelled

---

4  James Belich, 'The Settler Revolution', keynote address to Australian Historical Association Biennial Conference, University of Western Australia, 6 July 2010, quoted in Penny Russell, *Savage or Civilised? Manners in Colonial Australia* (Sydney: UNSW Press, 2010), p. 108.

5  *Argus*, 15 July 1863, p. 7.

6  Lucy Frost, ed., *The Journal of Annie Baxter Dawbin: July 1858 – May 1868* (St Lucia: University of Queensland Press in association with the State Library of New South Wales, 1998), p. 336.

7  Frost, *The Journal of Annie Baxter Dawbin* (15 March 1862), p. 237.

8  Tim Dolin, *Australian Common Reader Project*, available at www.australiancommonreader.com/ [Accessed on 14 April 2011]. Sample searches of this database (which, oddly, has no records for Braddon's *Lady Audley's Secret* or *Aurora Floyd*) show mostly equal borrowing of other Braddon titles by male and female readers from libraries with mixed membership, and a variety of genres borrowed by these readers – a pattern demonstrated by Julieanne Lamond in 'Communities of Readers: Australian Reading History and Library Loan Records' in this volume.

to read the novel by another audience, though, and another community of respondents, a dramatic one.

The first Australian dramatic production of *Lady Audley's Secret* took place in Melbourne on Saturday 6 June 1863 at the Theatre Royal. In the mid 1860s, Melbourne had several thriving theatres. The Theatre Royal on Bourke Street was the oldest, operating more or less continuously since 1841, but there were at least four others,[9] some also named after London originals. The Theatre Royal was an entertainment complex of a very modern kind in the 1860s, incorporating the Royal Hotel and, upstairs from the theatre, the notorious Café de Paris, heart of bohemian Melbourne by some, perhaps inflated, accounts.[10]

The Melbourne production of *Lady Audley's Secret* commenced only three and a half months after the first London production, by William Suter, at the Queen's Theatre in February.[11] The colonial version demonstrates the rapidity and mobility of imperial cultural circulation. It was a 'local' adaptation by Julius Vogel, journalist, Melbourne *Argus* correspondent, and soon-to-be successful politician, who had recently emigrated from Victoria to New Zealand. The first performance of his version was in late April in Dunedin.[12] Within forty days this five-act extravaganza, its lead actors, and possibly its sets, were on stage in Melbourne. The transformation from novel to stage was, of course, largely about exposing the sensational to the senses, and the Melbourne *Argus* reviewer was careful to prefigure the visual experience for his readers: 'Several new scenes have been painted for this piece, and that representing Audley Hall and grounds, as seen from the limetree walk, was especially good'.[13]

The theatre district, and Melbourne itself, was a spectacle for the observing and participating crowd, in which the street and the people on it formed a moving theatre for the stroller, with the shops and all their temptations a coherent part of the 'performance'. For Waif Wander on Bourke Street on a Saturday night in 1869:

> a brilliant spectacle it still is ... On that last night of [the] week floods of light are pouring from door and from window ...

---

9 Ross Thorne, *Theatre Buildings in Australia to 1905*, vol. 1 (Sydney: Architectural Research Foundation, University of Sydney, 1971); Philip Parsons with Victoria Chance, eds, *A Companion to Theatre in Australia* (Sydney: Currency Press in association with Cambridge University Press, 1995).

10 See Andrew McCann, *Marcus Clarke's Bohemia: Literature and Modernity in Colonial Melbourne* (Carlton: Melbourne University Publishing, 2004), pp. 34–35.

11 This was on 21 February 1863, although Braddon appears to have approved George Roberts' (Robert Walters') adaptation which opened a week later at the St James' Theatre. See Kate Mattacks, 'Regulatory Bodies: Dramatic Creativity, Control and the Commodity of *Lady Audley's Secret*', *Interdisciplinary Studies in the Long Nineteenth Century* 8 (2009): 1–21 (9). Braddon and her publisher Tinsley sued Lacey – actually the publisher of both these versions. See also *Sydney Morning Herald*, 14 September 1863, p. 3 for reports of this action, and Robert Lee Wolff, *Sensational Victorian: The Life and Fiction of Mary Elizabeth Braddon* (New York: Garland, 1979), pp. 142–43, p. 440, note 77.

12 At the Princess Theatre, Dunedin, on 27 April.

13 Both performances starred Mr and Mrs Clarance Holt as Robert Audley and Lady Audley. The description of the scene in the *Otago Daily Times*, 28 April 1863, p.5: 'the Lime-tree Walk, with the well on one side, and the house seen through a vista of trees, is a really clever piece of scenic work' compared to that in the *Argus* quoted above suggest the possibility that some of the same scene flats may have been used. See *Argus*, 8 June 1863, pp. 4–5.

> Did the lamps not stand out independently, and the pavement width away from those blazing gasaliers, their lights would fade away into an insignificance unworthy of that broad street. But, stretching away down in brilliant star-like rows, and sweeping up the distant acclivity where Bourke Street West leaves the noble Post Office behind, and creeps away into the far distance, those brilliant lamps stand like dusky soldiers with radiant helmets guarding the wide thoroughfare, and the wealth-full emporiums that line its sides.
>
> ... such appetising confectioners' shops, with their tempting buns, and seed cakes ... But here is a jeweller's; is it within the power of woman to pass that array?[14]

Josephine Fantasia has pointed out that in Australia, as Michael Booth notes of England, theatrical spectacle echoed and represented the scenery and buildings of the imperial metropolis. The streets are full of human and commercial enticement and glitter: the move from the theatre to the street was only a transition between different versions of the staging of human drama and desire. The nature of Bourke street as a constantly changing consumer theatrical spectacle, an enactment of imperial wealth and change, must also have been enhanced by the constant turnover of theatre buildings, as they so regularly burnt down and were rebuilt.[15]

Marcus Clarke described 'Bourke-street at midnight [as] something very little better than the Haymarket (London) at two in the morning'. His vision of the theatre crowd is distinctive:

> Passing through the iron gates, we find ourselves in a large hall, open at one end to the street, and closed at the other by the pit and stall entrances to the theatre. The curtain has just fallen upon the piece of the evening, and the crowds from gallery, pit, and stalls are refreshing themselves before the farce. On each side are covered bars, where some twenty or thirty girls dispense, with lightning rapidity ... [drinks] which expectorating crowds of men and boys call for on all sides ... At the furthest table from the door sits a knot of government clerks ... That door leads to the 'ladies' refreshment room', but is known to its fast frequenters by another name. The women who assemble there are well dressed and orderly. They live for the most part in adjacent streets, paying a high rent for their houses, which are usually leased and kept in order by some old woman, who is too old

---

14 'Waif Wander' (Mary Fortune), 'Down Bourke Street' (1869), in Lucy Sussex, ed., *The Fortunes of Mary Fortune* (Ringwood: Penguin, 1989), p. 194. As W.W. approaches the theatre district the number of floozies seems to increase: 'Oh, bless us! do you see those chignons – those frizzes – those trains? Heaven help us with brains! Do you observe the eardrops, and the ribbons, and the glittering jet ornaments ... the smell of stale, inferior *eau de cologne*'? The approach to the Theatre Royal (and its attached bar) is more offensive still: 'We are passing the "Royal" now, at least we are being bodily hustled past it, and there is only one word – which I dare not write, you know – that can at all describe the odour with which you are so nearly poisoned', p. 196.

15 Josephine Fantasia, 'Entrepreneurs, Empires and Pantomimes: J.C. Williamson's Pantomime Productions as a Site to Review the Cultural Construction of an Australian Theatre Industry, 1882 to 1914', PhD thesis (Sydney University, 2007); Michael R. Booth, *Theater in the Victorian Age* (Cambridge: Cambridge University Press, 1991).

to attract; and the less public of them frequent the theatres more for their own amusement than with other designs.[16]

As Andrew McCann suggests, this is a gendered 'fantasy of the city' as a place apart from domesticity, 'an image of the city as a site of hedonistic pleasure for men who imagined that their own aesthetic impulses were antithetical to a respectable domesticity'.[17] The point of view here is male. The only female spectators described, the theatre-goers who pursue their 'own amusement', are prostitutes.

As with present-day cinema, there was substantial overlap between the audience for popular fiction and its adaptations, so one might expect the readership of the Victorian novel largely to be the audience of the play into which it was converted. My argument, however, is that there are some disjunctions between the Melbourne readers and theatregoers, and between the colonial and metropolitan scenes of reading and viewing – that the community of readers is neither coherent nor simple, even for a popular text perceived as breaking down boundaries and levelling distinctions. As Lynn Voskuil argues of sensation theatre audiences, there are several different, if intersecting, 'public spheres' experiencing and responding to these texts in their various forms.[18]

I want to suggest that, at least initially, there was a different audience for the sensation novels than for the dramatisations which followed them so quickly in Australia and the other British settler colonies, as they did in Britain. Particularly for women, ironically, the pleasures of looking – specifically women looking at women – were more available in the novel in 1863 than in the theatrical staging of sensation melodrama. For middle-class Melbourne women in the early 1860s, melodrama theatre was not respectable, and out of the time and price range of a lot of 'respectable' women of other classes. In a discussion of the full spectrum of female desire, relations, and particularly specular pleasures, Sharon Marcus has elaborated on the 'latitude accorded to female homoeroticism in an era when lesbianism was neither avowed as a sexual identity nor stigmatized as a deviant sexuality'. Marcus argues that Victorian society

> accepted female homoeroticism as a component of respectable womanhood and encouraged women and girls to desire, scrutinise, and handle simulacra of alluring femininity [and even] organized heterosexual femininity around women objectifying women.[19]

Although Marcus concentrates on the opportunities offered by fashion magazines, dolls and fiction, the theatre would seem to combine all these pleasures. In a discussion of an 1857 French fashion plate in which women are depicted at the opera, Marcus highlights

---

16 Marcus Clarke, 'Night Scenes in Melbourne: 1. Melbourne Streets at Midnight', in Laurie Hergenhan, ed., *A Colonial City, High and Low Life: Selected Journalism of Marcus Clarke*, (St Lucia: University of Queensland Press, 1972), pp. 101–2.

17 McCann, p. 31.

18 Lynn M. Voskuil, 'Feeling Public: Sensation Theater, Commodity Culture, and the Victorian Public Sphere', *Victorian Studies* 44.2 (2002): 245–74.

19 Sharon Marcus, *Between Women: Friendship, Desire, and Marriage in Victorian England* (Princeton: Princeton University Press, 2007), pp. 112–13.

the general point that fashion plates 'evoke a female world saturated by a tactile sensuality represented through carefully rendered drapery and studied contrasts' between soft fabric and hard, sharp objects.[20] The textual as well as textural access to this sensual world of women is discussed by Marcus, albeit in relation to *Great Expectations* and Pip's envious and desiring male gaze on the female world of Miss Havisham and Estella. She argues this is a text that 'reveal[s] a sartorial imagination that sees the world in terms of clothing and whose most telling glance registers even the most ephemeral characters' dress'. Miss Havisham's fetishisation of shoes and clothing, she suggests, is only evident because of the detail of Pip's gaze.[21] It is distinctive that the eroticised fashion image is of opera-goers, and *French* opera-goers at that. What was acceptable for French ladies was not necessarily acceptable for British women, and what passed for British ladies in Britain did not necessarily work for women at the furthest reaches of empire. In Charlotte Brontë's 1853 novel, *Villette*, the minute classifications of appropriate behaviour for genteel British and Continental citizens can be seen as a consolidation of a pan-British identity.[22] Some of the most crucial enactments of this centre upon the close observation of dress and/at the theatre, portrayed as a perilous site of gendered identification and desire.[23]

In Britain, Queen Victoria's endorsement of the theatre and theatre-going gradually legitimised drama as an art form and theatre as respectable, commencing perhaps with the first 'command' performance in 1848; but in Australia, still, by the early 1860s this respectability and acceptability had not entirely taken hold. In the more secure class situations of Britain, upper-class women could 'slum it' at the theatre. As Penny Russell has pointed out, however, a high level of maintenance and policing of boundaries was required by the Melbourne 'upper middle class' in the 1860s, and the small size of the colonial elite and its lack of recognition would have made such 'slumming' – an activity guaranteed by prior stability and security of class position – extremely risky.[24] Opera attendance had much more established elite class connections, even though in Melbourne, for instance, the performances by Lyster's company at the Theatre Royal necessarily included the same proximity to the hotel and bars as the less salubrious performances. According to Harold Love, in 1862, at least, opera remained an exception:

> it would appear that the company had begun to draw on a body of theatre-goers from the respectable middle class who in their earnest mid-Victorian way found moral and educational value in operatic performances while continuing to shun the legitimate stage with the possible exception of Shakespeare.[25]

---

20 Marcus, pp. 126–27.

21 Marcus, p. 181.

22 Kate Lawson and Lynn Shakinovsky, 'Fantasies of National Identification in *Villette*', *SEL* [*Studies in English Literature*] 49.4 (2009): 925–44.

23 This is most notable when the passionate performance of the actress Vashti is followed by a conflagration in the theatre, and the near crushing of Paulina, the proper English girl (whose name is Home) at a crucial point in the development of the romance narrative. Controlled Paulina replaces the ardent but repressed Lucy as the love interest for Graham Bretton. See Charlotte Brontë, *Villette* (London: Penguin, 1985 [1853]), pp. 338–44.

24 Penny Russell, *A Wish of Distinction: Colonial Gentility and Femininity* (Carlton: Melbourne University Press, 1994), pp. 54–63.

25 Harold Love, *The Golden Age of Australian Opera: W.S. Lyster and His Companies 1861–1880*

This is confirmed by the contemporary observations of British visitors, for whom Australia itself was often represented as theatre and spectacle to affirm the civilisation of the metropolitan centre. So Frank Fowler in *Southern Lights and Shadows* described the local theatre audience:

> The ladies, as already observed, are fond of the drama. They are addicted to blue dresses, red cardinals, straw-coloured gloves, and strained hair, embellished with two or three C's – aggravators they call 'em – running over the temple. Their voices are peculiar and unpleasant. They have a lisp, almost a sniffle, arising from the clouds of thin dust which particular changes of wind carry, like simooms, over the face of the country … I went one evening to see 'Hamlet' and was amused at hearing a lady remark, in a whisper, to her neighbour, 'Whoth Thakspere? I don't think much of hith play.'[26]

Fowler goes on to comment that this was a wealthy lady and relative of famous convict Margaret Catchpole,[27] and to observe the quantity of 'shirt-sleeves, babies, and pewter pots' in the pit, and that the upper boxes were full of prostitutes. Though Fowler's text is somewhat tongue-in-cheek, it reinforces the notion that respectable women (if there were any in Australia) did not attend the theatre in this period. This is backed up by other contemporary writers. In Henry Kingsley's *The Hillyars and the Burtons* (1865), for example: 'Haymarket at one o'clock in the morning after the Derby was not more hideous and revolting than the hall of the opera house at Palmerston', and this is aligned with Melbourne in the remark that the narrator has heard that

> Huskisson Street, Palmerston, and Bourke Street, Melbourne, have been purged with a high hand … [by] the respectable mechanics who wished to take Mrs. and Miss Mechanic to hear Catherine Hayes, without having their ears polluted by the abominable language of the Haymarket and Newgate combined.[28]

This purging *may* have opened up the opera (Hayes was a singer) for the lower middle classes, but even in the 1870s 'The Vagabond' (John Stanley James) was still commenting on the anomaly of the theatre bars:

> in the centre of this city of Melbourne exists a disgraceful, flagrant, heinous, scandal flaunting boldly and shamelessly in the face of decent society! – an

---

(Sydney: Currency Press, 1981), pp. 58–59: 'Whereas in the past it had been Lyster's practice to raise prices for Mozart, on the grounds that he would only appeal to the musically knowledgeable, he was now able to play *Don Giovanni* successfully at popular prices'.

26 Frank Fowler, *Southern Lights and Shadows: Being Brief Notes of Three Years Experience of Social, Literary, and Political Life, 1859* (Sydney: University of Sydney Library, 2002 [SETIS e-text]), p. 21.

27 Catchpole does not appear to have had any relatives in the colony, but she was frequently confused with Mary Reiby, and this may be the intended reference. See Joan Lynravn, 'Catchpole, Margaret', *Australian Dictionary of Biography*, available at adbonline.anu.edu.au/biogs/A010200b.htm?hilite=catchpole [Accessed 27 March 2011].

28 Henry Kingsley, *The Hillyars and the Burtons: A Story of Two Families, 1865* (Sydney: Sydney University Press, 1973 [facsimile edn]), p. 396.

outrageous insult to our wives and daughters! – an infamy hardly equalled in any civilized city in the world! – a reproach which should cover with ignominy those who instituted, and now profit by its continuance.[29]

This sustained proximity of unrespectable scum to theatre audiences may have continued to imperil the respectability of theatre-going in the colonies, at least for the most respectable of the respectable classes (upper-middle-class ladies). This leaves a smaller sensation audience of the non-respectable women readers and viewers – an overlap audience the critics were very exercised about, of course.

The conventions of melodrama and sensation theatre probably influenced the nature of Vogel's conclusion to his dramatisation of *Lady Audley's Secret* in 1863. It had a very similar melodramatic closing scene to that of Dion Boucicault's *The Octoroon*, on stage in Melbourne at the same time.[30] In the case of *The Octoroon*, the Melbourne production opted for the ending used on the American stage, in which the mixed-race heroine – the 'octoroon' of the title – dies so that no multiracial marriage is performed to disturb the audience. In the version ultimately rewritten for the British stage, this character, Zoe, is allowed to live, so that the marriage can take place.[31] Vogel's adaptation of Braddon's text has the problematic heroine take poison and die on stage surrounded by those who have wronged her in a tableau of remorse and forgiveness.

This restages the novel considerably, deleting the section where a rebellious and unrepentant Lady Audley is excised from Britain and deposited by Robert Audley, the narrative's main 'hero', in a lunatic asylum on the Continent. Lady Audley – Lucy, the former Helen Talboys – is problematic for a number of reasons. At the beginning of the novel she appears to be a perfect lady: blonde, beautiful, virginal, and accomplished. In the course of the narrative, though, she is exposed to be an acquisitive, murderous bigamist who has remarried for advantage and more or less abandoned her child, but who has so successfully performed her new role as to have duped almost everyone she encountered. When Lady Audley is finally exposed as Helen Talboys she declares herself mad – yet even this useful excuse is rendered doubtful within the narrative. She is not just a problem for the plot, however, but for a society that insists on an ideal notion of womanhood.

With *The Octoroon*, was it anticipated that Australian audiences, like the Americans, would be disturbed by the spectacle of a mixed-race marriage? Or was the heroine's death simply a less sensational acknowledgement that racial difference could not be so easily transcended by romance within the actual social and political context?[32] In *Lady Audley's Secret* the staged self-containment of an alarming sexual transgression – bigamy – which was actually quite common in the colony, may also have satisfied a particular need.

---

29 'Vagabond' describing the theatre vestibules, quoted in Paul McGuire, with Betty Arnott and Frances Margaret McGuire, *The Australian Theatre: An Abstract and Brief Chronicle in Twelve Parts with Characteristic Illustrations* (London/Melbourne: Oxford University Press, 1948), p. 132.

30 *The Octoroon* was playing at the Haymarket Theatre in June 1863 while *Lady Audley's Secret* was at the Theatre Royal.

31 John A. Degen, 'How to End "The Octoroon"', *Educational Theatre Journal*, 27.2 (1975): 170–78.

32 See Degen, p. 174.

The New Zealand reviewer of *Lady Audley's Secret* points out with satisfaction that in Vogel's Australasian adaptation George Talboys is overtly blamed for abandonment of his wife, something the colonial audience might have had more reason to criticise. In Australia and New Zealand, even more mobile populations, poor communication and distances between colonies frequently resulted in extremely long absences of spouses, and bigamy cases were regularly reported in the newspapers. Henry Finlay suggests that bigamy was a common practice from the earliest days of the colony, when convicts transported for seven- or fourteen-year sentences commonly formed new alliances in the belief (and sometimes the hope) that they would never be reunited with their original spouse. Perhaps this foundation, followed by the unsettling effects of the gold rushes – particularly in Victoria – led to more widespread disruption of marriage as well. Finlay notes frequent incidences of domestic violence, but also the popularity of 'bigamy based on the presumption of death' in cases of abandonment or separation.[33] In contrast to Vogel's version, in one popular 1863 London adaptation of *Lady Audley's Secret* George does not go to Australia at all but takes an 'appointment abroad' (in India) and sends for his wife repeatedly, so that all culpability falls on her.[34] In this version Helen/Lucy also had red hair, a form of visual coding, Jennifer Carnell points out, which 'further demonised Lady Audley.'[35] This is particularly interesting as this production, in a theatre on the Thames south bank, would most likely have catered to a working-class audience.[36]

When the Vogel production of *Lady Audley's Secret* was staged in Sydney in August 1863, local reviews also commented sharply on George Talboy's culpability, one referring to him as 'the wretched man, whose cruel and selfish abandonment has been the first cause of all her crime and misery'.[37] In this production, as the suicidal Lady Audley lies dying, there are mutual self-recriminations from George Talboys and his former wife, and mutual forgiveness from George and others for Lady Audley: a rather different ending to that in the novel. It is not hard to see how such an antipodean staging – of final reconciliation and forgiveness for abandonment and sins – might play well in the colonies. In addition to reunion and forgiveness, it represses and erases the obstacles and stains of criminality.

As one critic has pointed out, 'Australia remained a handy depot for extraneous spouses in bigamy fiction', and it reflected current British fascinations with marriage and contemporary scandal.[38] In the novel of *Lady Audley's Secret* the issue of abandonment might be seen as a commentary on marriage and marriage laws more generally, but the

---

33 Henry Finlay, *To Have But Not to Hold: A History of Attitudes to Marriage and Divorce in Australia 1858–1975* (Sydney: Federation Press, 2005), pp. 25–53, 29–30.

34 See C.H. Hazlewood, *Lady Audley's Secret*, act I (*Gaslight* e-text of 'adaptation first produced at the Royal Victoria Theatre, London, 25 May 1863', with Maria Daly as Lady Audley), available at gaslight. mtroyal.ca/ladyadly.htm [Accessed 13 December 2010]. Australia is not mentioned at all.

35 Jennifer Carnell, *The Literary Lives of Mary Elizabeth Braddon: A Study of her Life and Work* (Hastings: Sensation Press, 2000), p. 197.

36 Voskuil, 'Feeling Public', p. 252.

37 The Sydney review likewise comments on George Talboys' behaviour to 'the woman whom he has so shamefully abandoned': *Sydney Morning Herald*, 4 August 1863, p. 4; 7 August 1863, p. 4.

38 Jeanne Fahnestock, 'Bigamy: The Rise and Fall of a Convention', *Nineteenth-Century Fiction* 36.1 (1981): 47–71.

antipodean adaptations and reviewers focused on it as a particular issue. The 1857 British Matrimonial Causes Act did not alter the situation of women abandoned by their husbands, as Helen Talboys apparently is in *Lady Audley's Secret* – given that he did not contact her at all during his absence. Helen could wait for seven years, with a child to support, to see whether George reappeared, or she could take steps to support herself. She could have legally married again under this aspect of British law, although she would have been in just as much trouble when George turned up alive.[39]

Deserting husbands, if located, could be taken to court and charged to pay for the support of their wife and family, but this was an expensive and uncertain procedure. In Australia the unfairness of these arrangements was under discussion and amendment in the years before *Lady Audley* was published and staged. The *South Australian Advertiser*, commenting on debates in the South Australian Parliament in 1858, drew a picture of the vulnerability of wives:

> A woman of education and property marries a man who plunges into dissipation, squanders his own means, and then spends the last shilling belonging to his wife. Having deprived her of all resources he next abandons her to her fate, and tries his own fortune in another direction.[40]

The plot of *Lady Audley's Secret*, in which George Talboys is a 'good' man who leaves in order to gain support for his wife, is shadowed by the plot laid out here. As Helen/Lucy does not hear from him for 'three years and a half', his intent remains unspoken to her, and the possibility that he is the same sort of drunken, sponging man as her father is clear.[41] He disappears, in his narrative, to Australia and to the goldfields, site of domestic disruption and cause of widespread abandonment. In 1856 the Immigrants' Aid Society reported that 'almost one-third of the inmates at their institutional facility, the Immigrants' Home, were women and children "deserted by their natural guardians"'; and on various occasions and at other sites around Melbourne and Victoria this abandonment was attributed either to the diggings, or to the unsettled nature of work and family life in Australia.[42] After the passing of the British Matrimonial Causes Act, the parliaments of the Australian colonies discussed, and then progressively introduced similar acts across the following decade, commencing with South Australia in 1858 and Victoria in 1861.[43] As soon as the Bills were passed, they were back in the parliaments and the newspapers, being amended. In an 1862 parliamentary debate on reforming (again) the Divorce Act Amendment Bill in Victoria, John Pascoe Fawkner commented that such a Bill was 'absolutely necessary' because of the

---

39  See Finlay, p. 30. In the novel and the plays Helen Talboys chooses to change her name and her status to improve her prospects of employment: a single, childless, unmarried governess is more employable than one abandoned with an infant child.

40  *South Australian Advertiser*, 12 October 1858, p. 2.

41  Braddon, p. 22.

42  Christina Twomey, '"Without Natural Protectors": Responses to Wife Desertion in Gold-Rush Victoria', *Australian Historical Studies* 27.108 (1997): 22–46 (28).

43  Finlay, pp. 50–63.

'circumstances of the colony … There were many men who left their wives and families in great distress, and never thought of returning to them'.[44]

George's disappearance to Australia, then, might almost be code for desertion. The perceived prevalence of abandonment in Australia caused a rapid adoption by a number of states of forms of 'judicial separation', or divorce '*a mensa et thoro*', available after two years of 'desertion' which, while it did not enable remarriage, prevented the deserting spouse from committing various kinds of financial abuse. In Melbourne this Bill was debated extensively when it was first introduced in 1860, with the newspapers reporting, in their usual dramatic way, somewhat in the form of a playscript, the contributions of the various members.[45]

In the end, the Victorian Bill, which had initially been radical, passed in a conservative form with much of the debated British double standard reinserted.[46] The whole issue was played out in a number of public arenas. In the press, as noted, there were accounts of the lively Legislative Assembly debates and official records of the Supreme Court Bills, but also impassioned letters from deserted wives. One woman wrote, for instance:

> I was married but a short time when the man who swore to protect and be faithful to me commenced a career of dissipation and profligacy, and after squandering his means as well as mine, he left me penniless, dependent on friends and my own exertions for the support of myself and a young family.[47]

The following day, the Melbourne *Argus* – which carried the final report of the passing of the Divorce and Matrimonial Causes Bill 1861 – contained a full page supplement on the sensational British Yelverton case, a case of bigamy and deceit, set out like a literary supplement.[48] The progress of the divorce debates were accompanied through the newspapers by accounts of the 'desertion' of Mrs Tyers by the acting Chief Commissioner of Crown Lands and well known Gippsland identity, Charles James Tyers. These accounts became increasingly detailed: an initial order that Mr Tyers renew his financial support to his estranged wife despite his counter-accusations about her adultery caused a declaration by him to appear in the following day's paper that he would 'sue for a divorce, so soon as the bill now in progress through Parliament becomes law'.[49]

The sensation novels form part of this same conversation, exploring as they do the gaps in legal redress for individuals, particularly women in unhappy or disastrous marriages, and the ramifications of poor decisions. While the newspapers could report on the movements of the divorce debates, editorialise on the decisions, and even publish, if they wished, the

---

44  Finlay, pp. 70–80.

45  See *Argus*, 24 February 1860, pp. 6–7.

46  Finlay, p. 80.

47  *Age*, 21 February 1860, quoted in Finlay, p. 73.

48  The Yelverton case was a controversial and highly publicised bigamy case in which the wealthy Irish heir William Yelverton was accused of bigamy by Catholic Englishwoman, Theresa Longworth. The case exposed the irregularities of British marriage laws, where various versions of reading the marriage service and pledging marriage operated differently in different parts of the British isles. It divided supporters along class and religious lines. See Fahnestock, pp. 50–53; Supplement, *Argus* 16 May, 1861.

49  *Argus*, 27 April 1860, p. 4; 28 April, 1860, p. 5.

less commonly heard voices of abandoned and abused wives, sensation fiction, and its dramatisations, could more literally and extensively stage the scenarios and consequences of marital mistakes. While these were all enacted in the imperial theatre, in the courts, streets, homes, and presses of both England and the colonies, there were significant local variations.

In the 1860s, antipodean female pleasures of looking and consumption (some of it the consumption of the metropolitan centre, some of it the fantasy of imperial British readership) were enabled by the novel *Lady Audley's Secret*, however conservative the outcomes of that consumption. The staging of the novel offered different forms of looking and consuming to a different audience. The more foregrounded dramatisation of desertion in the colonies was topical and political. However, the tableau of remorse, forgiveness and, importantly, suicide also graphically removed the threat to the heart of the family represented not only by Lady Audley, but by the wider and more radical divorce laws proposed, and recently defeated, in the colonies.

This chapter has considered the republic of letters in relation to a range of reading publics. It takes up again the question of how the 'where' of reading situates the reader and the text. In this case the 'where' of the audience for sensation ranges from the antipodes to the metropolitan centre. It covers a very broad base, then, but it also cuts across various axes, in terms of the experience of the text available to private, drawing-room readers as compared to readers and spectators in public, in an audience which is part of the spectacle itself. The axes of class and gender also divide these experiences. I suggest that for a period, at least, private middle-class reading women formed an audience enjoying, potentially, different, secret pleasures in the text than public spectating viewers of adaptations of the same text, from which middle-class respectable women were likely to be excluded. The particular nature of, and restrictions on, public and private reading and viewing spaces in Australia inflected who sighted which texts, and when and how the texts were experienced. It is also worth remembering that *Lady Audley's Secret* was exported to Australia just a few years after the British Matrimonial Causes Act, and that extensive discussion of adjusted marriage laws in colonial parliaments and the press further recontextualised the representation of marriage in Braddon's novel and its stage adaptations.

# 14

## 'I Must Be My Own Director': Cynthia Reed, Elisabeth Lambert, and Reed & Harris, Publishers

*Jane Grant*

Travelling across New Mexico in 1958, writer Cynthia Nolan and her painter husband visited the English poet Al Alavarez, then staying in the house where D.H. Lawrence once lived. There, paying homage to Lawrence, Cynthia was struck by a familiar impulse to settle among the artists and writers who gravitated to Taos. 'At first because the country and the climate is so beautiful', she wrote in *Open Negative: An American Memoir*,

> one thinks how wonderful it would be to live in Taos or Santa Fe, or somewhere else in this State; but one has felt that way in other parts of the world and learned that it is not enough, and that whatever the charm or talent of individuals, small communities are fatal to those who do not enjoy communal intrigue, gossip, intimacy.[1]

In 1958 the alcoholic excesses of staying with George Johnston and Charmian Clift on the Greek island of Hydra were no doubt still fresh in her mind. The Nolans had spent most of 1956 on Hydra, living closely among a small community of Australian and British expatriate writers where Cynthia's need to tell the truth as she saw it had not gone down well. 'I get Frank even though I have the best intentions', she told friend and writer Pat Flower back in Australia, 'because everyone gives everyone their things to read and wants to know what they think ... and each in turn says Wonderful out of one side of their mouth, and Crap out of the other'. She clashed with Johnston, thought his latest novel *The Sponge Divers* (published in the US as *The Sea and the Stone*) 'a revolting rehash of Steinbeck and Hemmingway', and 'will not say what he wants to hear, that he is a brilliant writer'.[2] Taos, New Mexico, brought back memories of Hydra but she may well have been thinking about her brother and sister-in-law, John and Sunday Reed, and their Melbourne circle at Heide.

Scholarly interest in Heide has largely focused on the painters it produced, on the Reeds as art patrons, or on Sunday Reed as muse. Over the past thirty years its place in Australian cultural history has been territorially marked out by art historians Richard Haese, Janine Burke, Nancy Underhill and Patrick McCaughey.[3] What little critical attention has been

---

1  Cynthia Reed, *Open Negative: An American Memoir* (London, Macmillan, 1967), p. 22.

2  Cynthia Reed to Pat Flower, cited in Garry Kinnane, *George Johnston: A Biography* (Ringwood, Penguin, 1986), pp. 157–58.

3  Richard Haese, *Rebels and Precursors: The Revolutionary Years of Australian Art* (Ringwood: Allen Lane, 1981). Janine Burke, *Joy Hester* (Melbourne: National Gallery of Victoria, 1981); *Australian Gothic:*

paid to the publishing company the Reeds set up with Max Harris has tended to focus on their avant-garde journal *Angry Penguins* and the infamous literary hoax played upon them. In turn, the fictional Ern Malley has generated a seemingly endless stream of analysis and debate, in effect further decentring the publishing company and marginalising the writers it published.[4] While many would argue that Ern Malley and the painter Sidney Nolan are Heide's most significant stars, it is nonetheless curious that the scholars who have pored over the Reed papers (held in the State Library of Victoria) have overlooked the compelling literary correspondence that it contains. The letters between writers Cynthia Reed and Elisabeth Lambert and the publishers John Reed and Max Harris not only uncover two intriguing and long neglected Australian writers, but also a complex and fragile Australian wartime literary community stretching between Adelaide, Melbourne, Sydney and New York.

When in early 1944 Cynthia Reed wrote congratulating her brother John on becoming a publisher, ostensibly her letter was a peace offering to heal 'the bitterness which does and must come between us'.[5] For the past year, Cynthia had been living in Sydney with her young daughter and refusing all contact with John, who was dismissive of her talents and thought her neurotic. Born in 1908 into one of Tasmania's wealthiest families, Cynthia's trajectory was very different to that of her older lawyer brother, who married into the Establishment, settled in Melbourne and found his vocation promoting 1940s expressionist painters. Cynthia came late to writing. As a young woman in Melbourne she had experimented with painting, modern design and running a gallery before a radical departure to Chicago in 1935 led her to train to be a nurse – a career that would take her to London, wartime Paris and finally New York. Returning to Australia in 1941, two semi-autobiographical novels were published before her marriage to the painter Sidney Nolan in 1948, but it was not to be until the 1960s that Cynthia would find her true form as a writer with a series of unsettling nonfiction narratives of travel, creativity and marriage.

A month or so after renewing contact with her brother in 1944, Cynthia sent him a rough unfinished draft of her first novel, *Lucky Alphonse*, based on her nursing experiences. 'The result', Cynthia wrote to Reed, 'rings no particular bells, is ordinary, shows no genius – no I think you would not like it. It is not queer or surrealistic in the least'. Her writing, she concluded, 'will not rock the world'.[6] Cynthia would have been well aware of her brother's taste in contemporary literature and art through what she called the 'lectures' he had been delivering her for years. John Reed's intellectual framework was English rather than European, drawn from the anarchist, critic and champion of surrealism, Herbert Read, and the British New Apocalypse movement which was translating surrealism's exploration of the Freudian unconscious into poetry. Like Herbert Read, John Reed disapproved of

---

*A Life of Albert Tucker* (Milsons Point: Knopf, 2002); *The Heart Garden: Sunday Reed and Heide* (Milsons Point: Random House, 2004). Nancy Underhill, ed., *Nolan on Nolan: Sidney Nolan in His Own Words* (Camberwell: Penguin, 2007). Patrick McCaughey, ed., *Bert & Ned: The Correspondence of Albert Tucker and Sidney Nolan* (Carlton: Melbourne University Press, 2006).

4 For a detailed account of *Angry Penguins*, and of the Ern Malley hoax and subsequent trial see Michael Heyward, *The Ern Malley Affair* (St Lucia: University of Queensland Press, 1993).

5 Cynthia Reed to John Reed, undated, Reed Papers, State Library of Victoria, Melbourne.

6 Cynthia Reed to John Reed, undated, Reed Papers.

art serving a political end, a position that through the 1940s would lead him forcefully to denounce social realism. As an art critic, John Reed had therefore alienated a great many communist painters and writers. Now as a publisher and businessman pitching to the left and keen to garner the support of the communists, Reed's position was difficult and he trod carefully.

'Queer and surrealistic' was of course an easy dig at Max Harris' experimental novel, *The Vegetative Eye*, published by Reed & Harris in late 1943 and panned mercilessly by A.D. Hope in the autumn 1944 edition of *Meanjin*. Naturally Reed thought very differently about the first of the fifteen titles Reed & Harris would publish in their three years of operation. *The Vegetative Eye*, he told Harris, had convinced him of its author's 'power and genius'.[7]

John Reed was forty, his wife Sunday thirty-six and Harris twenty when they first met in 1941. A student at the University of Adelaide, Harris' working-class background was very different to the wealth and privilege with which John and Sunday Reed had been raised. Academic brilliance enabled him to win places at St Peter's College and the University of Adelaide, where he wrote poetry, fell under the influence of Herbert Read and founded the avant-garde journal *Angry Penguins*. A shared admiration for the English critic no doubt led John Reed to the poet and editor, although Harris' precocity and class conformed strongly to a type that attracted both the Reeds: key members of their small circle, Sidney Nolan, Albert Tucker and Joy Hester, were all in their early twenties and from lower-middle-class or working-class backgrounds. Through 1942 John Reed wrote regularly to Harris contributing his ideas on extending the magazine's literary focus to include visual artists, most pressingly his Melbourne protégées, and in May 1942 Reed was invited to become the art section editor.

It was on hearing the news in February 1943 that the young modernist poet had embarked on a novel that Reed wrote to Harris in Adelaide proposing a book publishing partnership which he and his wife Sunday would fund. To the twenty-three-year-old university student and struggling writer it must have seemed an extraordinary opportunity. By 1944 the partnership begun between Max Harris and John and Sunday Reed would expand to include the Reeds' painter protégé, Sidney Nolan. With the war easing restrictive overseas publishing conditions, which prevented simultaneous publication of books under contract to British or American publishers in Australia, Reed & Harris would look to publish work considered too radical for Australia's major publishing house, Angus & Robertson.

Reed & Harris appear not to have focused on fiction. In its three years of operation, the publishing company would only produce the two novels by Harris and Cynthia Reed, and two collections of short stories: *Drift* (1944) by Peter Cowan, and *The Courtship of Uncle Henry* (1946) by Dal Stivens. Its poetry list consisted of three slim volumes: *Night Flight and Sunrise* (1944) by Geoffrey Dutton, *Excellent Stranger* (1944) by Alastair Kershaw, and *A Second Summary* (1944) by Harry Roskolenko. Reed & Harris' strength lay in nonfiction titles which included: *Psychiatric Aspects of War* (1945), by Melbourne psychiatrist and socialist Dr Reg Ellery; *Ballet Crusade* (1943), the journey of Ballet Russe dancer Veletin Zeglovesky to Australia; and *Mo's Memoirs* (1945), the autobiography of comedian Roy

---

7  John Reed to Max Harris, 26 May 1943, in Barrett Reid and Nancy Underhill, eds, *Letters of John Reed: Defining Australian Cultural Life 1920–1981* (Ringwood: Penguin, 2001), p. 212.

Rene, ghosted by Elisabeth Lambert and Max Harris. Through such remarkable years of female literary production, when many left-leaning writers such as Katharine Susannah Prichard, Judith Wright, Jean Devanny, Dymphna Cusack and Kylie Tennant, among others, were being published, it is noteworthy that Cynthia Reed was Reed & Harris' only female author.

Although Reed & Harris advertised their titles as books, wartime paper shortage meant that other titles such as economist Bruce Williams' *The Socialist Order and Freedom* (1943), Reg Ellery's *Eyes Left! The Soviet Union and the Post War World* (1943), and politician Arthur Calwell's *How Many Australians Tomorrow?* (1945), an argument for postwar population expansion, were in fact cheaply produced essay-length pamphlets. Money was an increasing problem. Practices such as paying writers fifty percent of royalties, and Harris and Nolan a weekly wage, as well as maintaining a Melbourne city office, would prove to be a vastly more costly undertaking for the Reeds than supporting a handful of painter friends. Despite returns unequal to their debt, in 1944 Reed & Harris created two further salaried positions with the appointments of Elisabeth Lambert in Sydney and Harry Roskolenko in New York as their representatives. Reed, however, would find it impossible to translate an aesthetic shaped by intimate friendship and place to far flung writers with whom he had little close contact, not to mention the problems of national and international distribution and sales, and a four-cornered editorial partnership divided between Adelaide and Melbourne.

As Cynthia predicted, Reed was underwhelmed by *Lucky Alphonse*. In March he sent it off to Harris in Adelaide without identifying the writer, who went by the name of Hansen, as his sister. Harris was mildly more enthusiastic. 'What I saw had valuable patches', he told Reed, but 'she doesn't know how to construct a book … It doesn't drive on. Its tensions are slick conventions'.[8] The Melbourne publisher readily agreed: 'I'm afraid she won't do better than she's done'.[9]

Harris' criticism raises interesting questions about the novel's structure and plot. *Lucky Alphonse* does move rather clumsily between its hospital settings of prewar Chicago, wartime London and Paris, and finally New York, while the life Alphonse abandons in Australia and the failed love affair which first takes her to the United States and into nursing is only sketchily drawn. The real power of the novel lies in its detailed evocation of the rigours and isolation of nursing life, the interior workings of the hospitals, and the gendered constraints operating on nurses at a time when marriage meant forced resignation. In a novel that details draconian and abusive training practices, it is striking that Cynthia made no attempt to disguise the Catholic teaching hospital St Joseph's in Chicago, and St Thomas' in London, or that her editors did not insist that she do so. *Lucky Alphonse* is a polemic. Cynthia had set out to 'show that the whole profession of nursing is a superb one which is handled like shit'.[10]

Nonetheless, *Lucky Alphonse* engaged Harris enough to recommend publication. No doubt he calculated that the novel's references to Marxism and pro-Soviet stance would appeal to the left readership that Reed & Harris were aiming to attract, although it is the

---

8   Max Harris to John Reed, March 27 1944, Reed Papers.
9   John Reed to Max Harris, March 1944, Reed Papers.
10  Cynthia Reed to John Reed, undated, Reed Papers.

last section, set in New York's Payne Whitney Psychiatric Clinic in 1941, which, as he told Reed, interested him most. 'The reader is vitally interested not only in the social backbone of the psychiatric clinic but in the type and kind of patient, the human picture of the place'.[11] Cynthia would not be the only writer to take on the Payne Whitney as a subject, although, seen through the eyes of a nurse rather than a patient, *Lucky Alphonse* appears to offer a counter narrative to the dangers of psychiatry as explored by Mary McCarthy in *The Group* (1963). At the end of *Lucky Alphonse*, in contrast to a Europe 'blitzed and bombed and tottering'[12] and a grim and regimented English hospital system, the clinic's modernist architecture, central heating, swimming pools, decent food and 'scientific' recasting of delinquents as mad rather than bad, seems to promise a postwar utopia. And yet the novel's graphic descriptions of primitive pre-drug therapies – such as mummifying patients in wet towels and restraining them in baths for twenty-four hours – arguably cast doubt on the claimed humanity of the treatments, the scientific basis of psychiatry, and the utopia it heralds.

*Lucky Alphonse* was not the only unsolicited manuscript Reed & Harris received in the first six months of 1944. Frustrated by paper shortages and the censorship cuts imposed by Angus & Robertson, Marjorie Barnard sent Reed the manuscript of the dystopian futuristic novel *Tomorrow and Tomorrow and Tomorrow*, which she had co-written with Flora Eldershaw. Reed was typically dismissive. 'It is no masterpiece', he informed Harris, 'but on the other hand not lacking certain quite deep human and sociological flashes of insight'.[13] Whether Harris agreed with Reed's evaluation of a novel many critics would later praise highly is undocumented. While it seems unlikely that Reed & Harris would have been able to afford the cost of printing a novel that ran to 456 pages, other issues appear to have governed their failure to secure it. Reed insisted on joint editorial responsibility, although living in different cities made this impractical. Manuscripts were posted back and forth between Melbourne and Adelaide, slowing the process and forcing delays in a business built around deadlines, while urgent decisions were made by phone and telegram, adding considerable expense. Still a student, Harris' focus would also ebb and flow according to university demands. In July, Barnard wrote again to Reed in Melbourne, reminding him that she had been waiting nine weeks and requesting he return the manuscript, which was still in Adelaide. Three weeks later Barnard wrote again, this time 'demanding the immediate return of the MS'.[14]

The publication history of *Lucky Alphonse* raises further questions about the acumen of Reed & Harris. As an unpublished writer, Cynthia's expectations were decidedly unrealistic. She demanded a print run of 5000 and insisted on retaining the rights to overseas publication. It 'puzzled' Harris, in whose opinion '3000 would I think saturate the Aust market'.[15] Conceding her the overseas rights, Harris offered her a print run of 3000 for a book which, as he told Reed, he didn't think any good (Harris, it seems, was a better

---

11   Max Harris to John Reed, 27 March 1944, Reed Papers.
12   Cynthia Reed, *Lucky Alphonse* (Melbourne: Reed and Harris, 1944), p. 231.
13   John Reed to Max Harris, 9 May 1944, Reed Papers.
14   John Reed to Max Harris, 25 July 1944, Reed Papers.
15   Max Harris to John Reed, undated, Reed Papers.

critic than he was an editor). The publishing house worked very quickly to get its books out: Cynthia's incomplete manuscript was submitted in March and it went to the printers two months later in May. It was Harris who was responsible for negotiating the contract and editing *Lucky Alphonse*. Reed could not work with his sister. As he told Harris, 'the relationship between us is so extremely touchy that it is not possible to deal ... in normal terms'.[16]

'During the time I spent with you', Cynthia wrote to her brother, 'I think I had no idea what was going on inside me. It was quite impossible for me to enter deep conversations on art and people'.[17] The writer Michael Keon would later recall one particular dinner party at Heide in 1942, where Cynthia spoke only once to ask the painter Albert Tucker a question about the Australian Communist Party.[18] After five years of 'working with reality in all its sickest form'[19] as a nurse in Chicago, London, wartime Paris, and a psychiatric hospital in New York, she had returned to Heide exhausted and pregnant, her silence a manifestation of the depression she was experiencing at the time. And yet silence can also be an expression of resistance or scepticism.

Following the anarchist vision laid down by Herbert Read, Heide presented itself as a collective where ideas and approaches were arrived at consensually; although, as Albert Tucker recalled, in a group unequally divided by wealth, age and class, in reality consensus meant acceding to decisions made by the Reeds. When arguments turned into rows,

> Sunday would drift off to bed. She'd leave it to the boys to fight it out. And then John would go into the bedroom ... then he'd come out with what you could say was the policy on this particular issue ... this kind of thing happened repeatedly.[20]

More sophisticated and close to a decade older than the Reed coterie, Cynthia was disinclined to be told what to think. 'That I feel it is a good thing that forms of expression should be given an outlet and that it is fine that you are enabling people to express themselves and encouraging art forms yes', Cynthia wrote to John a year later:

> That I myself am as critical as you I kow [sic] but my approach to this is different. I wish for tolerance and understanding. I don't wish to be dogmatic and say sweepingly this is good, this is bad ... this or that person may or may not have genius.

When Reed accused her of working 'in opposition to our direction', Cynthia countered, 'I must be my own director'.[21]

---

16  John Reed to Max Harris, 11 May 1945, Reed Papers.
17  Cynthia Reed to John Reed, undated, Reed Papers.
18  Michael Keon, *Glad Morning Again* (EET: Watsons Bay, 1996), p. 101
19  Cynthia Reed to John Reed, undated, Reed Papers.
20  Robyn Hughes, interview with Albert Tucker, 14 February 1994, *Australian Biography: Extraordinary Australians Talk About Their Lives*, available at www.australianbiography.gov.au/subjects/tucker/interview4.html [accessed 12 October 2010].
21  Cynthia Reed to John Reed, undated, Reed Papers.

Cynthia's published work delivers a very different view of Heide and her place within it to that posited by commonly accepted history. In Janine Burke's biography of Sunday Reed, *The Heart Garden*, for instance, Cynthia is a minor character whose work and life are seen as peripheral to Heide, and whose influence and effect are narrowly confined to a specific time period and geographical location. Cynthia lived only briefly at Heide, although the correspondence between Cynthia and the Reeds in fact reveals an extensive and persistent intellectual interchange which lasted for more than twenty years. The view of Cynthia as peripheral fails to take into account her early influence on the Reeds when she was a curator in the 1930s, or the deep emotional complications between brother, sister and sister-in-law that would survive Cynthia's marriage to Sidney Nolan in 1948 and the breach it provoked.

The relationship between the sisters-in-law had always been complicated by Sunday's apparent need to be the centre of male attention and Cynthia's reluctance to play the submissive role. Living at Heide in 1942 irrevocably damaged Cynthia's opinion of Sunday. Ariel, Cynthia's portrait of Sunday Reed in her second novel, *Daddy Sowed a Wind* (1947), with her 'curiously unseeing eyes', is a study of moral blindness. After the birth of her daughter in May 1942, Cynthia became extremely ill and felt under increasing pressure to let the Reeds adopt her baby. She refused, but some years later the Reeds would succeed in adopting the child of their close friends, Joy Hester and Albert Tucker. Cynthia was also a witness to the early years of Sidney Nolan's affair with Sunday Reed. Nolan is portrayed by many as an opportunist who exploited the largesse of his benefactors, yet few have acknowledged the power imbalance between the very young painter and his much older and wealthy lover. Certainly Cynthia's portrait of Sunday suggests that she at least was troubled by the ethical questions posed by Sunday Reed's affair with Sidney Nolan, and her sexual and financial binding of the still very young painter. Later, after their marriage, in work that recorded the Nolans' travels, the Reeds and their beloved garden crop up as occasional oblique references: gardeners of people as much as of plants.

Some time in late 1942, Cynthia left Melbourne for Sydney where she bought a cottage in the northern suburb of Wahroonga. Despite ongoing illness, the burdens of single motherhood and a reputation for being difficult, she was far from isolated. She saw a lot of Labor politician H.V. Evatt and his artist wife Mary Alice Evatt; Maie Casey, art patron and wife of conservative politician Richard Casey; the writer Pat Flower; Syd Deamer, editor of the progressive *Daily Telegraph*; and the painter and designer Elaine Haxton. Other friends included designer Loudon Sainthill and his partner Harry Tatlock Miller (later manager of the prestigious London gallery, the Redfern), as well as curator Clarice Zander, her daughter Jocelyn, and son-in-law Carl Plate, the abstract painter and proprietor of the Notando bookshop in Rowe Street. Many of her friends were designers, an interest that dated back to the early 1930s, when she ran a gallery and design studio in Melbourne. Unlike her brother and sister-in-law, Cynthia rejected hierarchical divisions between art and design, and in the late 1940s would be a directing influence on future husband Sidney Nolan's business venture with Haxton and painter William Dobell into modern fabric design.

The 'witch trial'[22] of Max Harris was the major topic of conversation when Cynthia met Elisabeth Lambert in September 1944 at the International and Foreign Languages Bookshop in Martin Place. The intense dark-haired writer and the blonde libertine poet

---

22  Elisabeth Lambert to John Reed, 1 September 1944, Reed Papers.

would have made an interesting juxtaposition. Cynthia's views on the Ern Malley hoax and the subsequent obscenity trial are undocumented, but for Lambert the trial was 'a full scale attack on everything liberal and progressive'. As she reported to John Reed, 'I was holding forth on how the attack had been directed at you and Max', when Cynthia introduced herself. 'What a beautiful person she is. Such wonderful eyes'.[23] Reed replied: 'Am glad you felt that way about Cynthia. She has been so much knocked about it is a wonder any vestiges of her looks have remained'.[24] Although the face was yet to wear the ravages Patrick White so remarked on in *Flaws in the Glass*, at thirty-six Cynthia was strikingly more than conventionally beautiful. She often wore trousers which suited her tall elegant frame, and she smoked incessantly.

In 1944 Lambert was working as a journalist on the tabloid paper the *Daily Mirror* and living alone in a flat at Elizabeth Bay House while her husband, Patrick Terpening, was away fighting in Europe. Born in England in 1915, Lambert had arrived in Sydney via Jamaica at the age of nine where the family settled in Kensington. While her first poem 'Night Piece' was published in the *Sydney Morning Herald* in 1932, the young Lambert was also writing articles for the newspapers, defining herself as a feminist, and positioning herself politically to the left. An article she submitted to the *Sydney Morning Herald*'s Women's Supplement in 1935 employed the Marxist argument that women's economic emancipation would also liberate men. The following year, 'under the auspices' of the socialist Writers' League, Lambert delivered a lecture on the poet Christopher Brennan at Mooney's Clubrooms in George Street.[25]

By the mid 1940s Lambert was contributing anti-war poetry to *Angry Penguins* and the Melbourne journal *Comment*, and, with the help of Sydney feminist and designer Bessie Mitchell, had already published three books of her work. In an interview, Mitchell claimed to have set up Viking Press with the express purpose of bringing Lambert's verse into print.[26] Mitchell hand-blocked the illustrations and bound the volumes herself, publishing Lambert's first collection of poetry, *Insurgence*, in 1939. The following year Viking published Lambert's long poem, *The Map*, as a single volume. *The Map* was part of the 1940 'Prelude Series of Australian Poems', which also included *Kaleidoscope* by Dorothy Auchterlonie, *The Breaking of the Drought* by Harley Matthews, and *The Untramelled* by Elizabeth Riddell, which Mitchell intended to be set to music and performed as a ballet. Viking would publish Lambert's third collection *Poems* in 1943 before wartime paper shortages shut the company down.

In June 1944, when the Ern Malley saga was playing out in newspapers across Australia, Lambert seemed the obvious choice when Reed & Harris offered her the position as their Sydney representative. Together with the American poet and soldier Harry Roskolenko, then stationed in Sydney, she had edited a special edition of the Ern Malley poems which would shortly be published in the American journal *Voices*. As Reed outlined to her, they were looking for someone to persuade Sydney bookshops to stock their books, handle

---

23  Elisabeth Lambert to John Reed 18 September 1944, Reed Papers.
24  John Reed to Elisabeth Lambert, 19 September 1944, Reed Papers.
25  Notice, *Sydney Morning Herald*, 26 September 1936, p. 12.
26  'Woman Breaks New Ground', Women's Supplement, *Sydney Morning Herald*, 18 September 1939, p. 5.

publicity and to keep them informed about new writers. Lambert would be the company's ears and eyes in Sydney: it was a condition of her employment that she also join the Sydney branch of the Contemporary Artists Society, with whom Reed had a tense relationship, and report back to them on their meetings. In late June, when both Reed and Harris were still unclear as to the identity of the hoaxers, Lambert (correctly) informed Reed that the most likely suspects were James McAuley and Harold Stewart. And yet Reed had reservations about her. As he told Harris, Lambert's affair with Roskolenko and plans to return with him to America meant that she was a short-term investment. He was also suspicious: Lambert 'had jumped at the chance' to be the Reed & Harris Sydney representative 'with embarrassing enthusiasm'.[27]

Politically Reed thought Lambert 'cynical and unstable', and worried that she 'might prejudice us with serious left elements', noting in a letter to Harris that she had a 'strong admiration for Donald Friend'.[28] It is, however, unclear whether her admiration for the painter – whose politics were provokingly conservative, and whose work Reed dismissed as 'charm school' – was the sole evidence of the political instability he saw in Lambert. Reed in fact appears to have known very little about her. While Lambert and Friend most probably met in 1942 when he moved into Elizabeth Bay House (whose spiral staircase and wild parties the artist so memorably sketched), they would have intersected anyway through mutual friends and chief Reed & Harris antagonists, A.D. Hope and Harold Stewart.[29]

Lambert's cynical bohemia was very different to the cloistered atmosphere of Heide. Through the Malley trial her amusement at 'the policeman who didn't know what incest was but knew that it was wicked',[30] and flippant reportage that Goethe's *Faust* had been banned 'on the grounds that no one knew what other stuff that fellow Faust may have written',[31] would simply have irritated Reed. In July he sent her Reed & Harris' official statement on the hoax to be circulated in the Sydney press, spelling out their position that the poems were an expression of the poets' unconscious and greater than anything else they had ever produced. Certainly Reed would have been deeply shocked had he known Lambert thought the Malley poems 'delicious satire'.[32]

A great deal hung on Reed & Harris' 1944 Christmas list, which included *Lucky Alphonse* as well as Peter Cowan's short story collection *Drift*, although with Harris more than usually preoccupied by the trial, which ran through September into October, it fell to Reed to see to the printing. In October, Reed told Harris he had 'run into a bit of unfortunate trouble':

> the Chapter headings have got mixed up and it looks as though they will have to be altered right through the book, as page proofs have already been printed. It is

---

27  John Reed to Max Harris, 23 June 1944, *Letters of John Reed*, p. 326.

28  *Letters of John Reed*, p. 326.

29  As well as his merciless review of Harris' *The Vegetative Eye*, Hope had himself planned a hoax on *Angry Penguins*: see Heyward, pp. 113–17.

30  Elisabeth Lambert to John Reed, 11 September 1944, Reed Papers. The policeman in question was Detective Vogelsang: see Heyward, pp. 189–91.

31  Elisabeth Lambert to John Reed, 18 September 1944, Reed Papers.

32  Elisabeth Lambert Ortiz Obituary, *Telegraph* (UK), 6 December 2003, available at: www.telegraph.co.uk/news/obituaries/1448610/Elisabeth-Lambert-Ortiz.html [accessed 23 June 2010].

a bit of everybody's fault, including unfortunately the printer's and we will just have to get it out the best we can.[33]

*Lucky Alphonse* remained imprinted 1944, although it was not actually published until the following March, and it seems likely that the same mix-up happened with Cowan's book, as it too was delayed until the New Year. The loss of Christmas sales was a serious setback for the struggling publishers. Another debacle followed in May 1945 when fifty copies of *Lucky Alphonse* were posted to Roskolenko, now back in New York, and they never arrived.

While in Melbourne sales of *Lucky Alphonse* began slowly, they picked up after positive radio reviews from Vance Palmer and George Farwell, journalist and editor of the Communist literary journal *Australian New Writing* (1943–46). As Reed further reported to Harris, the manager of the Communist International Bookshop 'has taken a great fancy to it'.[34] Sydney was a different story. 'The Sydney position looks very bad, and the sales of Alphonse utterly ludicrous', Harris wrote to Reed in April. 'We must even involve Cynthia in peddling and pushing if 49 is all that can be sold there'.[35] It was Lambert who was responsible for publicity in Sydney and who now bore the brunt of the author's increasing frustration with her publishers. 'You don't know of course that Cynthia rang me when her book came out and was most beastly rude to me', Lambert told Reed. 'I was angry about it but knew she's been ill'.[36] It didn't surprise him, Reed replied: 'she seems to be chasing reviews for all she is worth'.[37] Despite her journalist contacts, Lambert appears to have done very little to promote *Lucky Alphonse*, and for both the book and the company it was in fact fortunate that Cynthia was 'chasing reviews' in a city that neither Reed nor Harris knew. She was in a position to call on her friendship with Syd Deamer, and in May when a strong review appeared in the *Daily Telegraph* by one of Deamer's leading journalists, Dick Hughes, sales markedly improved.

That May, Harris was in Sydney to begin work on the memoirs of the comedian Roy Rene, which he and Lambert were ghostwriting. *Mo's Memoirs* should have been a bestseller. While on the surface a book on the vaudevillian clown seems an odd choice for the serious-minded publishers, in the 1940s Rene's enormous popularity cut across class, political and educational divides; the middle classes flocking to be insulted by Rene's working class persona, Mo McCackie, just as they would a generation later to Barry Humphries' suburbanite, Edna Everage.

From Sydney, Harris informed Reed that:

> Cynthia provides an amusing side light. Apparently at a closer approach she seems impressed with my efficiency or something, and plies me with questions or seeks advice but alone seems to think she has a good find in me and that I have come over simply and only to sell Alphonse and to do the ground work for [her second novel] Lulu.[38]

---

33　John Reed to Max Harris, 5 October 1944, Reed Papers.
34　John Reed to Max Harris, 26 March 1945, Reed Papers.
35　Max Harris to John Reed, April 1945, Reed Papers.
36　Elisabeth Lambert to John Reed, 5 May 1945, Reed Papers.
37　John Reed to Elisabeth Lambert, 8 May 1945, Reed Papers.
38　Max Harris to John Reed, 28 May 1945, Reed Papers.

The Ern Malley court case had made Harris more anxious than before about potential legal action: his concerns for Cynthia's second novel centred on its harrowing description of an abortion and a possible backlash from the Catholic Church. In the end, Reed & Harris didn't publish 'Lulu'. Renamed *Daddy Sowed a Wind*, it would be edited by Syd Deamer and published by Shakespeare Head in 1947.

While the author amused her supercilious publisher, there is nothing humorous about her novel. *Daddy Sowed a Wind* looks back on her childhood and youth, and it is curious that John Reed even contemplated publishing it. Written in a period of intense depression, her portraits of her family, Sunday Reed and her erstwhile lover, the conductor Bernard Heinze, were uncompromising and possibly libellous. Hyacinth (a near anagram of Cynthia) is born into a wealthy Tasmanian family, to a neglectful mother and a father who rejects her, yet whom she adores. Moving to the mainland, Hyacinth falls in love with the social-climbing German immigrant musician, Claus Weinen. Unable to make up her mind to marry Weinen, and in search of an identity, she travels to England and Germany. On the return journey, a brief shipboard romance leads to pregnancy and, once home, a botched backstreet abortion and a mental breakdown. The discovery that her best friend, the socialite Ariel, has married Weinen is the final catalyst for Hyacinth's suicide.

The novel's use of memory and Freudian theory to shape the narrative, and its sudden shifts from third to first person, were far more stylistically experimental than *Lucky Alphonse*. Its catalogue of abortion, madness and suicide was a more savage rejection of utopia. Written through the first six months of 1945, the section set in Germany, with its description of the rise of Nazism, was based on Cynthia's travels in 1930, but it was also informed by the revelations of the death camps that were filling the papers. Reading *The Psychology of Fascism* (1943), Peter Nathan's Freudian analysis of authoritarian fathers, desire and fascism, was another influence on both her evocation of Germany and her study of her central character's Electra complex.

In America, Roskolenko, having heard nothing from Lambert for a number of months, and yet to hear that her husband had been killed in a plane crash, asked Harris to sound her out. 'Elisabeth antipathetical no hope',[39] Harris wired back. As Harris further revealed to Reed, Lambert's 'egocentricity' irritated him and he felt 'increasingly that she is less suited to our work'.[40] Some weeks later he complained again that Lambert had 'done nothing [on *Mo's Memoirs*] ... I imagine it will never be done ... Her interest is far more concerned with her affair with [Donald] Horne than with our work or with Patrick's death'.[41] Lambert would in fact meet her deadline, finishing it in time for the Christmas market of 1945, although it would be neither a critical nor a commercial success. If the review in the *Argus* is entirely to be believed, it was Lambert who did the bulk of the writing. Of Harris' contribution to a book hastily written and riddled with typographical errors, the reviewer pointedly noted that *Mo's Memoirs* had been 'slightly augmented and edited, slightly by Max Harris'.[42]

---

39  Max Harris to Harry Roskolenko, telegram, 20 March 1945, Reed Papers.
40  Max Harris to John Reed, 22 April 1945, Reed Papers.
41  Max Harris to John Reed, 21 May 1945, Reed Papers. Donald Horne (1921–2005) was a journalist, editor and academic, best-known as the author of *The Lucky Country* (1964).
42  '"Mo", New Guinea, Fiction', *Argus*, 19 January 1946, p. 11.

Under the weight of both debt and 'intimacy', the publishing house was already collapsing. In an effort to save the company, Harris moved briefly to Melbourne, but living and working in such close proximity to the Reeds only hastened its decline: Reed & Harris was formally and acrimoniously dissolved in November 1946. Harris, it seems, believed that the Reeds were withholding money owing to him as a partner. Of his departing shot that he would 'expose' the Reeds if they 'didn't do the right thing' and that he 'knew enough about' Heide 'to blow the whole show to bits', Reed replied that 'it places the final accent on our failure'.[43]

Lambert's affair with Donald Horne didn't last. In 1949 she left Australia for England and then America. Two novels, *The Sleeping House Party* (1951) and *Father Couldn't Juggle* (1954), followed. Marriage to a United Nations diplomat, Cesar Ortiz, enabled her to travel widely through Mexico, the Caribbean and Southeast Asia, reinvent herself as *Gourmet* food writer Elisabeth Lambert Ortiz, and capitalise on the new markets of cultural and culinary tourism opening up though the 1960s and 1970s. There are interesting parallels: Cynthia would also turn to nonfiction after her marriage, writing on Africa, the Subcontinent, Afghanistan and China in work that both mapped and critiqued the tourist trail.[44] In America and in England both writers would establish successful careers, but back in Australia, where the national identity of writers remained predicated on place and the definition of creativity was narrow, the nonfiction form these expatriate women adopted made it all too easy for literary history to forget them. While the correspondence of the Reed & Harris company goes some way to recovering these two Australian women writers, in documenting a far flung epistolary community – however fragile – the archive also reflects on the parochial weighting that has informed so much of the scholarship on Heide, and on Australian artistic and literary communities more generally.

---

43  John Reed to Max Harris, November 1946, *Letters of John Reed*, p. 430.

44  See, for instance, *One Traveller's Africa* (London: Methuen, 1965); *Open Negative: An American Memoir* (London: Macmillan, 1967); *A Sight of China* (London: Macmillan, 1969).

# 15

## 'Opposing All the Things They Stand For': Women Writers and the Women's Magazines

*Susan Sheridan*

Kylie Tennant recorded in a note on 17 January 1961: 'On Sunday I was offered 15 pounds a week to write a column for the *Woman's Mirror* – can I? – Irony that they want a "name" made by opposing all the things they stand for.'[1] Tennant had made her name as a twenty-three-year-old in 1935 with her prize-winning first novel, *Tiburon*, and by this time was an *éminence grise* in Australian literary life. She had established herself as a social critic, with her documentary novels of the Depression era, and as a professional career woman. Yet neither role was particularly visible or valued in the women's magazines of the era, which relentlessly pushed the view that woman's place was in the home, even though they also offered glimpses of the wider world of culture and politics, with substantial feature stories and sections on books and the arts – though nothing likely to create significant debate.[2]

While many women of Tennant's generation who published novels and poetry also wrote for money in magazines and newspapers, those who contributed to the women's magazines were entering into territory where they risked being discounted by their peers as less than serious artists. Dorothy Green, for example, a poet and an experienced journalist, was dismissive of women's magazines: although she wrote serious articles for the *Woman's Day* (a series on kindergartens), and for the *Australian Women's Weekly* (a series on poets),[3] she sneered at the latter's series on famous women (to which she also contributed) as the 'Famous Trollops series'.[4] Women's magazines did not even count as proper journalism, far less as real writing.

Yet the magazines' pages could provide a meeting ground for women writers and their readers, in the days before the advent of literary festivals and public readings. The *Woman's Mirror* obviously believed that its readers would recognise Kylie Tennant's name, just as a few years later both the Melbourne *Herald* and *Sydney Morning Herald* employed Charmian

---

1  Note dated 17 January, 1961, Kylie Tennant Papers, MS 7574, box 14, folder 86, National Library of Australia.

2  See Sharyn Pearce, 'Midcentury Australia: Women and Journalism in the 1950s', in *Shameless Scribblers: Australian Women's Journalism, 1880–1995* (Rockhampton: Central Queensland University Press, 1998).

3  Maurice Dunlevy, 'Dorothy Green the Woman', *Canberra Times*, 30 December 1967.

4  Dorothy Green to Clem and Nina Christesen, undated letter [mid 1950s], *Meanjin* archive, Melbourne University.

Clift as a literary 'name' to transform the women's pages from a repository for the social rounds into a location for good writing and controversial opinions. The third woman writer of the 1960s whose role in 'women's journalism' I want to consider here is Barbara Jefferis, who wrote a regular column in the *Australian Women's Weekly* as 'Margaret Sydney'. Each woman approached the issue of creating a community with her readers differently, using varying modes of address, and tackling differing subjects.

Kylie Tennant did, in fact, take up the *Woman's Mirror* offer, and her 'Kylie Tennant Says' column appeared weekly from 22 February until 5 August 1961. This magazine was one of the lesser lights in the grand era of women's magazines, when the *Australian Women's Weekly*, *Woman's Day* and *New Idea* were leaders in the field. The *Woman's Mirror* had been founded in 1924 by the *Bulletin* 'to serve every feminine interest', and Dulcie Deamer had been a regular weekly contributor under various pen-names.[5] In 1960 Frank Packer's Australian Consolidated Press bought both magazines, and gave the *Woman's Mirror* a new look under the editorship of Dawn James, a former *Weekly* feature writer.[6]

The *Mirror* at this time was comparable in size and price to the *Weekly* and, like it, paid contributors ten shillings and sixpence for letters chosen for publication. But the *Mirror* also invited readers to contribute to all its other sections – feature stories and fiction for example – and to submit paragraphs for regular features like 'Between Ourselves' and 'Have You Tried This?' It was, in effect, offering small job opportunities to women who aspired to write. Also like the *Weekly*, the *Mirror* assumed that its readers were interested in 'good reading'.[7] As well as including fiction by writers like Dorothy Sayers, Nicholas Monserrat and Ursula Bloom, the *Mirror* often featured a full-page colour photo of a scene of natural beauty, with a facing page of poems (in one example, by Shakespeare, Shelley and Kendall).

This was the context in which Kylie Tennant was introduced to her readers as the well-known novelist, children's playwright and winner of various literary prizes, as author of *Australia: Her Story* and, most recently, *Speak You So Gently* (about the formation of cooperatives among Aboriginal Australians in Cape York and the Torres Strait Islands). Readers were told that Tennant had lectured 'in Tasmania, Adelaide and Perth', suggesting perhaps that, although a Sydneysider, she had visited the outer states. In fact, although she had not published an adult novel for some years, Tennant's standing as a writer was at its height. Between 1957 and 1960 she had delivered Commonwealth Literary Fund lectures at many Australian universities.[8] In 1960 she had won the Children's Book Council Book of the Year Award for *All the Proud Tribesman*. As well, she worked as a publisher's reader for Macmillan, and had begun her career as a reviewer, mainly for the *Sydney Morning Herald*. Later in 1961 she was appointed a Member of the Advisory Board of the Commonwealth Literary Fund – its first woman member.[9]

---

5  *The Queen of Bohemia: The Autobiography of Dulcie Deamer*, Peter Kirkpatrick, ed. (St Lucia: University of Queensland Press, 1998), p. 83.

6  Brigid Griffen-Foley, *The House of Packer: The Making of a Media Empire* (North Sydney: Allen & Unwin, 1999), pp. 235, 237.

7  See Patrick Buckridge, 'Good Reading and the *Australian Women's Weekly*, 1933–1970', *JASAL* 1 (2002): 32–43.

8  See her *The Development of the Australian Novel* (Canberra: Canberra University College, 1958).

9  By 1961 she was the author of six novels for adults (since *Tiburon*, 1935), and two for children, as well

Was her name in fact 'made by opposing all the things' the women's magazines stood for? To a degree, it was: her social realist novels and outspoken views were not the usual stuff of women's magazines. But the scandal of 1952, when she was accused of being a communist in receipt of Literature Board funds, was well in the past by 1961, and indeed the Cold War atmosphere of the fifties was thawing. Social justice and environmental issues were given an occasional airing in the women's magazines, and the first faint stirrings of female discontent could be heard, as women began to return to the workforce after their postwar banishment to the home. As it turned out, 'Kylie Tennant Says' managed to touch on a range of social and political issues. But her sense of there being a great distance between her values and those of the magazine was not unreasonable. Like the other women's magazines, the *Mirror* rarely published fiction by Australian writers: it is unlikely that they would have asked for her fiction. But the offer of a column – at fifteen pounds a week, a good rate – came at a time when Tennant needed the money. Her husband, Lewis Rodd, was suffering deep depression after her confession of an affair, and the terrible injuries caused by his suicide attempt had forced his early retirement from teaching.[10]

'Kylie Tennant Says', accompanied by a photo of her smiling face, began to appear on 22 February 1961, in the first of the *Woman's Mirror*'s updated issues, which featured brighter colour and a modern font. According to Tennant's self-description in her introductory column, she is 'married to a schoolmaster, and has two children, Benison (13) and John (9)', and is 'interested in nearly everything from food to metaphysics but is unable to count. Her life is normally a state of mild desperation'.[11] Here, then, is Kylie's twist on the time-honoured tradition of the women's magazine speaking to its readers as friends: she is, indeed, wanted for her 'name' as a writer, and she will make a point of being interested in matters beyond the home, 'from food to metaphysics'. She is no model domestic manager, but rather chaotic.

The column generally consisted of four or five short anecdotes, some about domestic or garden matters, others making feminist points about such issues as the lack of equal pay, and yet others of broad general interest. Many have a humorous twist, and some are one-liners. The column has a title taken from the lead story. For example, the first is headed 'I still love the Yeti' and leads off with a story about Sir Edmund Hillary's discovery that the Abominable Snowman does not exist. How sad, writes Tennant; there is something poetic about the Yeti: 'we liked him because ... he was on his wild lone' and did not live crowded in with others. Such appeals to her readers' imaginations recur in other stories – one about the attractions of astrology (1 March), another which takes off from the astronomer Harlow Shapley's theory of life on other planets (8 March).

She took a few risks. Her jokes might have offended the respectable – for instance, her idea that forgers find fun in 'gypping' the public and also knowing that their work is so good (12 April). Some of her stories are gently subversive of the values of advertising and

---

as three collections of children's plays (published by Macmillan in 1950, 1955 and 1959). Her reviews for *SMH* began in 1954 and by 1957 they included reviews of White's *Voss* and Stow's *The Bystander*. The majority of her reviews appeared later than 1961. See 'Agent Details: Kylie Tennant', *AustLit*, available at www.austlit.edu.au/run?ex=ShowAgent&agentId=A(ND [accessed 3 January 2011].

10  Jane Grant, *Kylie Tennant: A Life* (Canberra: National Library of Australia, 2006), pp. 88–89, 90.

11  *Australian Woman's Mirror*, 22 February 1961, p. 11.

consumerism that the magazine depends on, and her comments on fashion are usually ridiculing (8 March, 9 August). In one column she tells of Trappist monks, baking bread for sale, who refused to use the slogan 'Baked in silence: too good for words' (22 February). In another she reports that the children's nagging has finally broken down her resistance to buying a television set (22 March).

Such references to her family and domestic circumstances are rare. There are a few garden stories – on keeping hens (26 April), and how to encourage butterflies (31 May) – but on the whole Tennant does as she promised, and keeps the issues broad. Several stories carry echoes of her Christian Science upbringing, such as an anecdote about receiving what you need by 'sending out a call' on the ether (19 April). She relishes stories that contradict popular racism, which read like examples of the power of positive thinking (15 March, 19 April). These 'spiritual' stories often have a political point: she tells her readers that Gandhi learned from women about passive resistance as a 'love force' (5 July). In another column she defends political lobbying by pressure groups as a continuation of the tradition of the Clapham Sect lobbying to end slavery, a practice they had 'learned from the Quakers and Dissenters' (19 July).

'Women's issues' appear in most of her columns. They range from the observation that when a woman is seen moving the furniture it's a sure sign that she feels out of control of her own life (5 April), through the idea that housewives are merely 'unpaid servants' (29 March), to the claim that they are 'heroic', 'salt of the earth' figures who put their family's needs first (26 April). She anticipates role reversal within families as more women join the paid workforce, but fears that increasing automation will delay the winning of equal pay for equal work. In the same column, she expresses the fear that women judges would be the 'bleak dominating type' who would impose harsher sentences than men (24 May). New jobs for women come to her notice: 'public relations' (17 May) and piloting planes (21 June). She pounces on anti-female superstitions, such as giving female names to hurricanes (why not call them Genghis Khan or Hitler?, she asks on 9 August) and miners' attempts to prevent her visiting a tunnel when she was being shown over the Snowy River Hydro-Electric Scheme (12 July).

There are fewer literary anecdotes than one might expect. On *Lady Chatterley's Lover*, she advances the view that Lawrence was a moralist, but not a genius (22 March). Noting the death of Jung – 'the falling of the last forest giant in the jungle of psychiatry' – she comments that 'between them, Freud, Adler and Jung destroyed the clear-cut boundaries between good and evil conduct', leaving only 'sick people' and 'ordinary citizens who managed well enough to mask their motives from themselves and other people' (26 July). Most interesting are her reflections on Jack Kerouac's *On the Road*. Quoting a passage on jazz from the novel, she writes:

> Even a square like me ... realises that Kerouac is writing well of his world of hopheads, beatniks, psychos and despair men ... Americans are not afraid of the beatniks' spiritual search. Their interest in violence is a creative interest.

'We must study this writing,' she continues, 'not with patronage but with understanding if we want to know where civilisation is going'. But, she adds:

this is possibly the most anti-feminine movement in hundreds of years. The beatniks' scale of values has no place for homes ... There is a heavy emphasis on the worthlessness of woman except as a source of pleasure. Otherwise they are a nuisance, dragging the beatnik down from his ecstasy of drink and drugs to a preoccupation with social safety and wage-earning.

She calls it a 'very masculine cult of denial' (3 May).

Over the six months of its brief existence, 'Kylie Tennant Says' became more and more outspoken on social justice issues. For example, she welcomed the establishment of the Institute of Aboriginal Studies (21 June), and commented on crime, punishment and insanity (24 May, 12 July), always favouring rehabilitation rather than retribution. She also commented on a wide range of ecological issues – the need for clean water (3 May) and air (16 August), problems of excess packaging (26 July), and space junk (2 August). Tennant was fiercely critical of the First World's high consumption of resources, and the hypocrisy of criticising high birth rates in the Third World (9 and 16 August).

In August 1961 the *Woman's Mirror* merged with another ACP magazine, *Weekend*, to form the new *Everybody's* – 'designed to appeal to the whole family', not just women. The new magazine had a disastrous first six months under the editorship of Donald Horne, who believed it had fallen between two stools, neither a women's magazine nor one of the 'salacious' men's magazines, which *Weekend* had been.[12] 'Kylie Tennant Says' survived the changeover by only three weeks. It is possible that she may have resigned as a result of her new duties for the Commonwealth Literary Fund Advisory Board, to which she was appointed in July of that year – an appointment that she may have seen as incompatible with the status of a women's magazine columnist.

While the *Woman's Mirror* disappeared, the *Australian Women's Weekly* went from strength to strength. Among its regular weekly features was the column, 'At Home with Margaret Sydney,' which had a very different style from Kylie Tennant's. All the stories were domestic – the title said it – and the approach was more personal, inviting readers into 'Margaret Sydney's' home and family. Barbara Jefferis's pen-name was that of an everywoman, not a famous individual. Her stories were connected to one another, so there was more continuity of theme and tone than with Tennant's bits and bobs. For instance, on 22 February 1961 – the same date as the first 'Kylie Tennant Says' in the *Woman's Mirror* – Margaret Sydney in the *Women's Weekly* talked about a dress allowance for her student daughter, her observations at Sydney airport (especially the contrast between young women's and men's style of dress), a story about her younger daughter protesting when she is not allowed to go out during the week, and two amusing anecdotes culled from her reading, about nineteenth-century London society.

Unlike Tennant, Margaret Sydney made her children (and husband, and the household cats) into characters in her stories. Her observations were lively but mostly confined to what she saw. Most of her reflections concerned the upbringing of three children, two girls and a boy, the eldest of whom had just started university: problems such as unchaperoned teenage parties, the need for swimming lessons, choosing school subjects, her son's strategies to avoid going to the dentist, and the younger daughter's despair about her looks.

---

12  Griffen-Foley, p. 237. *Everybody's* was published by ACP from 1961 to 1968.

She addressed her women readers as part of a community who like to share her reflections on the events of her life 'at home'.

Margaret Sydney's reading was limited. There were some historical tidbits about London society, or the history of tea drinking. One week there was a story about her admiration for the novels of Enid Bagnold (*National Velvet* and others), quoting her wise sayings – for example, that the demand for their children's gratitude is the unfairest of any that a parent can make (29 March). She reported that her favourite bedside reading were elaborate recipe books such as Elisabeth Ayreton's *The Good Pig*, from which she quoted a whole recipe (19 April). She often included recipes, and writes about giving dinner parties, something Tennant would never do. In a rare political comment, she reported that Sydney University had announced it will restrict entry from 1963 onwards, and expresses the view that Australia needs more universities (26 July). But she was interested in the changing roles of women, and later in the 1960s, as more stories appeared about married women taking on paid work, she offered a voice of reason in support.[13]

Readers would have had no idea that behind 'Margaret Sydney' was the professional writer and former newspaper journalist Barbara Jefferis, author of several prize-winning novels, one of which, *Solo for Several Players*, won the United States 'Best-in-Books' award in 1961 and was published in serial form in the *Weekly* later that year.[14] Jefferis wrote many radio plays and dramatised documentaries, and would later publish regular reviews in the *Sydney Morning Herald* and the *Australian*. She was a founding member and first woman president of the Australian Society of Authors. At this stage of her career, however, she was not a 'name' in the way that Tennant was. Her novels were published overseas and little noticed in Australia, and of course work for radio and TV was usually anonymous. Her job in 'At Home with Margaret Sydney' was to create a family and their stories, not to present herself – and indeed her 'family' does seem to have been largely invented.[15] The persona she creates for Margaret Sydney is an attractive one – a middle-class woman with a lively mind, who is engaged by her role as mother and wife but not defensive about it – but she is certainly not an intellectual like her creator.

There were two regular 'named' writers with columns in the *Weekly* at this time: Dorothy Drain and Ross Campbell. 'Ross Campbell Writes' was just as domestic in its focus as 'At Home with Margaret Sydney' and mostly humorous,[16] whereas Dorothy Drain's longer

---

13 Susan Sheridan, *Who Was That Woman? The* Australian Woman's Weekly *in the Postwar Years* (Sydney: UNSW Press, 2002), pp. 75, 113.

14 Her first novel, *Undercurrent* (1953) – published in the UK as *Contango Day* (1954) – had won joint second prize in the 1952 *Sydney Morning Herald* novel prize. See 'Agent Details: Barbara Jefferis', *AustLit*, available online at www.austlit.edu.au/run?ex=ShowAgent&agentId=A%2BM- [accessed 3 January 2011].

15 The older daughter doing science at university sounds a little like her daughter, Rosalind Hinde; but the characters, including two younger children, were invented. 'Margaret Sydney' was Jefferis' own pen-name, which she also used for her travel book, *The Happy Traveller* (Sydney: Angus & Robertson, 1970). Thanks to Rosalind Hinde for this information.

16 'His affectionate portrayals of family life in suburban Australia appeared in the *Australian Women's Weekly* and the *Sunday Telegraph* throughout the 1950s, 1960s and 1970s. Campbell also wrote on broader subjects for the *Bulletin*'. See 'Agent Details: Ross Campbell', *AustLit*, available online at www.austlit.edu.au/run?ex=ShowAgent&agentId=A%23$2 [accessed 3 January 2011].

column, 'It Seems to Me', ranged a little further afield. This column was a *Women's Weekly* institution, appearing from 1947 to 1963, as Drain was its 'most popular and recognised writer'.[17] Patrick Buckridge has drawn attention to her frequent reference to reading 'the classics', and she occasionally included some of her own verse. However, she did not range far from domestic and local matters, and rarely discussed political questions. Tennant's range of subject matter is not matched by any of the *Weekly*'s regular columnists.

It was not until 1964, when Charmian Clift returned after fourteen years living in London and Greece and was engaged to write a weekly column for the *Herald*, that a comparable range could be found in the Australian print media of the period.[18] Her editor wanted 'a writer, not a woman journalist', for, as he said, the daily press needed some '*real* writing, from a woman's point of view'.[19] So Clift, like Kylie Tennant, was hired as a name, a real writer, with a wide and free brief, to give readers good writing and controversial opinions.

The position from which Clift wrote – as an observer of Australian society who, because of her long absence, was both an insider and an outsider – enabled her to take a critical view, apparently without putting her readers offside. As her biographer Nadia Wheatley wrote:

> In the first six months, for example, she drew attention to the constructions of Australian social life; to the second-class status of women; to the ugliness and alienation of Australian architecture; and to the need for Australians to define their own identity through the establishment of their own film industry.[20]

Not only this, but her criticisms of Australia's role in the Vietnam War and the introduction of conscription by lottery for young men, were overtly political. Yet, despite widespread support for the American alliance at this time, Clift's column was immensely popular with its mainly middle-class readers. This gave her the power to offer her 'Strong Opinions' uncensored – though always in an even tone, and mixed with reflections on more personal matters. Her column's status was enhanced by high-culture associations, such as the specially drawn sketch by Russell Drysdale that accompanied her comments in support of the 1967 referendum to include Aboriginal Australians in the census.

Her motto – the same as for many a woman with unconventional views, at least before the reappearance of feminism – was 'Don't do it in the street and frighten the horses'.[21] Sharyn Pearce, considering the reasons for Clift's immense popularity with an audience of about one million, points out that she never wrote down to her audience, and varied confronting stories with light ones. 'Ultimately', she concludes, 'Clift projects an image of herself as a suburbanite like her readers, a woman caught up with similar routines, preoccupations and concerns', who 'perhaps had lived a more glamorous and exciting life

---

17  Buckridge, p.39.

18  Clift's column appeared in the Melbourne *Herald*'s *Weekend Magazine*, and was reprinted in the *SMH* Thursday Women's Section, from late 1964 until Clift's death in mid 1969.

19  Quoted in Nadia Wheatley, 'Introduction to Charmian Clift', in Wheatley, ed., *Trouble in Lotus Land* by Charmian Clift, (North Ryde: Angus & Robertson, 1990), pp. 2–3.

20  Wheatley, Introduction, p. 4.

21  Quoted in Wheatley, Introduction, p. 7.

than most, and was perhaps more cultivated' but whose social and political views were largely acceptable to them.[22]

Allowed about a thousand words per column, Clift was actually writing essays, not journalistic 'pars' like Tennant. In a letter to her London agent she wrote that, 'I have been making my own sneaky little revolution … by writing essays for the weekly presses to be read by people who don't know an essay from a form-guide, but absolutely love it'.[23] The essay form allowed her to use the personal tone she had developed in her two books about living in Greece – *Mermaid Singing* (1956) and *Peel Me a Lotus* (1959) – and to convey that sense of intimacy that is the hallmark of women's journalism. She was also adept at writing impersonally (or more objectively) about domestic issues, as Margaret Sydney did. In doing so, she managed to bridge the gap between the intensely feminised popular cultural space of 'the women's pages' and the larger public forum of print journalism. Clift addressed her readers as women – as women who could think.

She was indeed immensely popular. 'Within months of the beginning of the Clift column, hundreds of readers had written suggesting that it be published in book form' and two collections appeared, one in 1965 and the other in 1970, after her untimely death.[24] As an undergraduate, I was one of her fans, and her column had me thinking that I could escape what seemed to be my inevitable fate of becoming a school teacher, and become a popular and influential journalist instead (I was soon disabused of this idea by a tough old professional journalist, however). A woman writing a column in the women's section of the daily newspaper was, by then, a possible role model for an idealistic and educated young woman. Clift was a far cry from Margaret Sydney in the *Women's Weekly* or even Kylie Tennant in the *Woman's Mirror*. Clift showed that it was possible to write 'as a woman' about any subject under the sun, and to write personally about political questions.

Nevertheless Clift, like Tennant and other women contemporaries, feared that such writing would compromise her hard-earned place in the literary field. She saw herself primarily as a creative writer but she had published little fiction in the 1960s. Clift experienced an agonising conflict between continuing to produce her successful column and trying to complete her autobiographical novel, *The End of the Morning*.[25] By contrast, Tennant in the 1950s chose to present herself as a journalist, a hardworking professional who wrote for money – a persona that was incompatible with that of the creative writer. As she wrote to Dorothy Green in 1954: 'I believe you are a really creative person and you shouldn't bother with journalism at all' – and concluded her letter with a reference to finishing a book review, putting herself firmly on the side of journalism.[26] Green had published a critical article, 'The Novels of Kylie Tennant' in *Meanjin* in 1953, where she argued that Tennant's flaws as a novelist were to be explained by an unresolved conflict

---

22  Pearce, pp. 156, 179, 182.

23  Quoted in Wheatley, p. 4.

24  Wheatley, p. 12. The collections were *Images in Aspic* (London: Horwitz, 1965) and *The World of Charmian Clift* (Sydney: Ure Smith, 1970).

25  A tragic story told in Nadia Wheatley, *The Life and Myth of Charmian Clift* (Pymble: HarperCollins, 2001).

26  Tennant to Green, 2 July 1954, Dorothy Green Papers, MS5678, series 1.4, box 85, National Library of Australia.

between the journalist and the artist.[27] It was a conflict that both women believed to be insoluble. Later, however, Tennant saw this conflict as the product of changes in the literary field, rather than as a question of creativity: the move from writing to 'literature' had made it a jealously guarded preserve, with an exclusive canon.[28]

Such were the professional uncertainties of women writers. Their attitudes to their readers reflected the gap that they experienced between the feminised domestic sphere, where they lived their personal lives, and the public sphere, where they pursued their careers, and which made no allowances for women's difference. They could bridge this gap between public and private spheres for their women readers, but not for themselves. The conflict between their identities as women and as writer-intellectuals tended to separate them from other women. Tennant's attitude to other women remained ambivalent, like most of her generation of writers. In an interview in the 1980s she said that, although she would like to feel women were 'momentous matriarchs', many made a profession of being dumb 'because they think that men don't like clever women'.[29] Clift was not afraid to name male privilege when she saw it, and so was less inclined to blame women for their poses; but she consciously adhered to a more bohemian lifestyle than the vast majority of her contemporaries. Jefferis as 'Margaret Sydney' gave every appearance of being comfortable with her women readers, and her role in writing to them; but she was not writing as herself and, besides, she is remembered as one whose 'feminism was worn naturally'.[30]

Writing for the women's pages created a fragile community of women writers and readers, but it was so bound by the gendering of the domestic sphere that most writers remained ambivalent about it. Not until the advent of women's publishing was this community transformed into a positive counter-public sphere. As the influence of feminism spread, women were less and less likely to be wholly identified with the domestic sphere. By the late 1970s, as Sharyn Pearce points out, 'the Women's Pages had virtually disappeared from every major Australian daily and weekly paper, terminating the sex stereotyping which had existed in the Australian newspaper industry since its inception', and women journalists were free to cover a fuller range of topics.[31] In book publishing, Virago pioneered feminist publishing in London and, after Sisters established their publishing house and book club in 1978, other independent Australian women's presses like Sybylla and Women's Redress Press followed.[32] By the mid 1980s, commercial publishing houses were developing lists

---

27 Dorothy Green, 'The Novels of Kylie Tennant', *Meanjin* 12.4 (1953): 395–403, as paraphrased in Grant, *Kylie Tennant*, pp. 78–79. Grant discusses at length her 'creative inhibition' at this time of her life. Tennant offered another perspective on this conflict when she told a later interviewer that she wanted to be 'a particular kind of journalist' and had to do it in fiction in order to be successful: 'Kylie Tennant', in Giulia Giuffré, *A Writing Life: Interviews with Australian Women Writers* (Sydney: Allen & Unwin, 1990), p. 226.

28 Tennant, interview with Hazel de Berg, 8 December 1967, Hazel de Berg Collection (DeB 341, 342), National Library of Australia.

29 Giuffré, pp. 235, 236.

30 Judith Rodriguez, 'Barbara Jefferis Award 2011', *Australian Society of Authors*, available at www.asauthors.org/scripts/cgiip.exe/WService=ASP0016/ccms.r?PageId=10385 [accessed 21 April 2011].

31 Pearce, *Shameless Scribblers*, p. 189. Women's magazines continued to flourish, however.

32 See Louise Poland's ' "Sisterhood is Powerful": Sisters Publishing and Book Club in Australia 1978–85', *Script and Print*, 29.1–4 (2005): 276–89.

of women writers, producing anthologies of women's writing (such as *The Penguin Book of Australian Women Poets*, 1986) and reprinting colonial women's novels. This 'decade of the minorities', as Thea Astley called it, brought a 'moment of glory' for the woman writer, according to her contemporary, Elizabeth Jolley.[33] The idea of writing as a woman, and even writing to an audience principally of women, was embraced by increasing numbers of writers.

---

33  Gillian Whitlock, ed., *Eight Voices of the Eighties* (St Lucia: University of Queensland Press, 1990), p. xi.

# 16

## SEVEN WRITERS AND AUSTRALIA'S LITERARY CAPITAL

*D'Arcy Randall*

In the 1970s, Australia's thriving literary scene was typically associated with networks of male writers in such urban bohemian venues as Balmain in Sydney and Carlton in Melbourne. Yet as Australian literature continued to flourish into the 1980s and 1990s, one of its most successful communities turned out to be a group of women writers in the suburbs of Canberra. Founding members Margaret Barbalet, Sara Dowse and Dorothy Johnston began meeting in 1980 to critique their fiction. Suzanne Edgar, Marion Halligan, Dorothy Horsfield and the late Marian Eldridge joined later.[1] Dowse describes the meetings as 'electric with argument' (xvii). Members routinely disagreed with one another, but they did settle on a name: Seven Writers (xix).

All seven writers published fiction books and won prizes, including an Australian Capital Territory (ACT) Bicentennial Grant for their group anthology *Canberra Tales* (1988), later reissued as *The Division of Love* (1995).[2] Between 1980 and 1998, Seven Writers collectively published around thirty-two single-author books, plus scores of stories, essays and poems.[3] All received Literature Board grants or ACT Literary Fellowships. They reviewed Australian literature for major journals and newspapers, plus the Australian Broadcasting Corporation (ABC).[4] Behind the scenes, all were mothers and among them raised eighteen children.[5] Yet more importantly for my purpose here, Seven Writers unsettled their city of Canberra's reputation as a 'cultural desert'. Their degree of success in changing national attitudes remains questionable, but certainly Seven Writers and their effective 'sociability' improved Canberrans' own cultural capital.[6]

---

1  Sara Dowse, Introduction, Margaret Barbalet et al., *The Division of Love* (Ringwood: Penguin, 1995), pp. xiv–xvii. Subsequent page references are given in-text.

2  Margaret Barbalet et al., *Canberra Tales* (Ringwood: Penguin, 1988).

3  This approximate count comes from the individual entries for Barbalet, Dowse, Edgar, Eldridge, Halligan, Horsfield, and Johnston in the *Australian Women's Register*, published by the National Foundation for Australian Women (NFAW) and the University of Melbourne, and available at www.womenaustralia.info/index.html [accessed 6 January 2011]. It is approximate because several members published books prior to joining the group, or the group may have commented on a draft work that was published after they disbanded.

4  See individual entries in the *Australian Women's Register*; also 'The Best of Tomes for Canberra Writers,' *Canberra Times*, 28 December 1997, p. 20; plus CVs delivered in personal correspondence from Barbalet (11 December 2010), Horsfield (22 December 2010), and Halligan (20 December 2010).

5  Barbalet, Author Interview (AI), 15 December 2010.

6  Pierre Bourdieu, trans. Richard Nice, 'The Forms of Capital', in J.E. Richardson, ed., *Handbook of*

My interest in Seven Writers derives from my experience as Fiction Editor at the University of Queensland Press (UQP) from 1980 to 1989, where I worked with Eldridge and Halligan on their first two books.[7] Many UQP writers associated with networks like the Sydney Push, but Seven Writers was the first formally organised Australian women's critique group I had encountered. Their commitment and productivity impressed me. In the mid to late 1990s, however, Seven Writers suffered disruption and grief. Two of the members left Australia temporarily, and Marian Eldridge died unfairly young in February 1997.[8] By 1998, those remaining ceased formal meetings.[9] Nevertheless, if one includes the early group, Seven Writers lasted a remarkable eighteen years.[10] This duration is noteworthy given that members resisted unifying ideologies and aesthetics (xxi). Dowse's Introduction to *The Division of Love* relates Seven Writers' history, describes the raucous meetings, and discusses how members negotiated their group identity in public. Yet Dowse also portrays how the group affected her, as a writer working in solitude; clearly, she writes as a member of Seven Writers, yet does not speak for them (xxiii).

This chapter is a preliminary work of Australian literary history that extends Dowse's portrait of a writers' community that functioned extraordinarily well as a group. Using Dowse's Introduction as a foundation, I conducted online and oral interviews with remaining group members, then threaded together their disparate reflections and contextualised their success. Here, I examine three lines of inquiry. First, Seven Writers' endurance raises practical questions about how a group of literary artists could sustain momentum for nearly two decades. Their example also raises questions about the gender dynamics of Australian literary communities generally in the 1970s and 1980s, and the sociability of Seven Writers in particular. Finally, I outline Seven Writers' engagement with Canberra: how the city's 'myths' affected them, and how they responded as a group (xix). Along the way I suggest potential lines for further study.

*A Community of Writers*

In addition to being white women writers living in Canberra, each member brought to the group an education, a vast if various reading background and, even if she were new to fiction, some writing experience (ix–xi; xv–xvii). Dowse disputes the label of 'middle class', pointing out that three 'have been on welfare, and two are single mothers' (xix). Although they appear to have much in common, remaining members firmly resist identifying Seven Writers as a 'coterie' or 'school'.[11] Instead, they stress their distinct backgrounds, cultural experiences, and above all, aesthetic preferences.

---

*Theory of Research for the Sociology of Education* (New York: Greenwood Press, 1986), pp. 243–56.

7 D'Arcy Randall, 'Fiction Fast Forward: Fiction Publishing in the 1980s', in Craig Munro, ed. *The Writer's Press: UQP's First Fifty Years* (St Lucia: University of Queensland Press, 1998), pp. 112–27.

8 Barbalet, AI, 11 December 2010; Dowse, personal correspondence, 7 January 2011.

9 Robert Hefner, 'Seven Writers Led a Novel Existence', *Canberra Times*, 24 June 2006, p. 6.

10 'Seven Writers (1980–1998)', *Australian Women's Register*, available at www.womenaustralia.info/biogs/AWE2108b.htm [accessed 6 January 2011].

11 For Dowse, 'coterie' is 'a term that conjures up teacups and exclusiveness' (xix). Remaining members agree with Dowse that they did not 'constitute a "school"' (xxi): Barbalet, AI, 15 December 2010; Edgar, AI, 20 December 2010; Johnston, AI, 15 November 2010; Halligan, AI, 18 December 2010; Horsfield, AI, 30 December 2010.

Barbalet, Dowse, and Johnston first met in 1980 through mutual friends and soon began exchanging manuscripts (x–xi, xvi).[12] New to Canberra, Barbalet was the only published author: after receiving her MA in history from the University of Adelaide, she had published one social history and was writing another.[13] Aesthetic differences, and the challenges they bring to group critique, emerged quickly. Johnston was reading Gabriel García Márquez and struggling to cultivate magic realism in her own work.[14] Dowse, who grew up in the US and whose 'heroes' were James Joyce and John Dos Passos, was baffled by this project (xvi). Still, Johnston valued the small group's lack of a unifying aesthetic. She had belonged briefly to an aesthetically driven writing group in Sydney and 'didn't want to repeat that experience or format'.[15] For Dowse, the group compensated for the 'sociability of work' she had desperately missed after quitting a career in the public service (ix–xi). Barbalet's historical awareness of women writers may have added perspective.[16] Aesthetic freedom and intelligent companionship sustained the three until they began to publish their first books of fiction.[17]

After various incarnations, group membership settled in 1984, when Edgar, Eldridge, Halligan and Horsfield joined.[18] Individual views on language and literature made meetings more complex than ever. Barbalet explains that 'Marion Halligan had all her knowledge of French; Sara Dowse her sense of America; Dorothy Horsfield came from a strong tradition of journalism. We all wrote very differently'.[19] Some appreciated and tried postmodern writing; others resisted it.[20] Some longed to 'push the boundaries of fiction'; others fought for clarity.[21] Aesthetic differences – and defence of those differences – were foundational.

Seven Writers met once a month, on Sunday, at a member's house, where they discussed the work of one person. Meetings lasted for 'several hours', and discussion often continued through lunch. Each member received a full critique of her work approximately twice a year.[22] The workload – reading and critiquing the manuscripts for each meeting – was substantial, but even those with small children considered it 'manageable'.[23] Nearly all agree

---

12  An early version of the group also included Brenda Walker and Elizabeth Tombs (xv). Also Barbalet, AI, 11 December 2010.

13  Dowse (xv) and Barbalet, AI, 11 December 2010.

14  Johnston, AI, 15 November 2010.

15  Johnston, AI, 15 November 2010.

16  Barbalet, AI, 11 December 2010.

17  Sara Dowse, *West Block* (Ringwood: Penguin, 1983); Dorothy Johnston, *Tunnel Vision* (Sydney: Hale & Iremonger, 1984); and Margaret Barbalet, *Blood in the Rain* (Ringwood: Penguin, 1986).

18  See Dowse, pp. xiv–xv. Suzanne Edgar joined 'c. 1984', and she suggested that the group add Marian Eldridge and Marion Halligan (Edgar, AI, 2 November 2010). See also Horsfield, AI, 13 November 2010; Johnston, AI, 15 November 2010.

19  Barbalet, AI, 15 December 2010.

20  Edgar, AI, 2 November 2010; Horsfield, AI, 13 November 2010.

21  Barbalet, AI, 11 December 2010.

22  Johnston, AI, 15 November 2010.

23  Barbalet, AI, 15 December 2010; Horsfield, AI, 15 November 2010; Johnston, AI, 15 November 2010.

that no one led the meetings.[24] Edgar, however, took detailed notes at each meeting, and archived them.[25] Her initiative to record the discussions shows unusual organisation.

During the meetings, 'heated discussion' was 'the norm' (xxiii). Barbalet comments that, 'Members often disagreed about things; and were diametrically opposed ... I sometimes felt I had to struggle to be heard'.[26] Halligan insists that, 'We were polite; nobody said "Oh Marion, that's really bad", or anything like that ... [But] at the same time ... we tried to give them an idea when we thought things weren't working'.[27] Johnston says, however, that 'Heated discussion could be sparked by anything. It was something we came to allow each other – not having to be "nice." '[28]

One argument erupted over a draft of Barbalet's children's book, *The Wolf* (1991).[29] Barbalet recalls that:

> Some members questioned how un-Australian it felt, and suggested I make the wolf a dingo. One member asked where the ranger was, and why didn't he arrive and shoot the wolf. I wasn't sure that some members actually understood it.[30]

Another time, members disagreed about the format for *Canberra Tales*. Some suggested beginning each story 'with the same sentence', or including a Prologue, with 'all [our] characters taking a trip to the new Parliament House'.[31] Others, however, refused, citing 'artistic integrity'.[32] What is striking in both cases is not who said what about a draft or idea, but that the members brainstormed openly. Those free-flowing criticisms would have served as a preview for how an editor, or publisher's reader, could respond.[33]

Barbalet found Seven Writers 'enormously supportive and helpful.' She said, 'I used to hurry away from meetings desperate to get going on my own work again.'[34] Yet the idea of a group of writers working together for a generation raises the question of influence. Creative writers typically strive to attain that elusive entity known as 'individual voice', and fear that their 'voice' would be somehow compromised if they work with other writers.

In response to such questions, Dowse asserts that 'our mutual influence has been powerful, and all the more for being so subtle' (xxi). She cites Johnston's new appreciation for 'realism' and her own new love of 'language' (xxii). Others resist the idea that the group substantively affected their work. Johnston valued the 'attentive and critical audience', but found any 'tangible results ... almost impossible to define'.[35]

---

24  Barbalet, AI, 15 December 2010; Halligan, AI, 10 December 2010; Edgar, AI, 20 December 2010; Horsfield, AI, 15 November 2010; Johnston, AI, 15 November 2010.

25  Edgar, personal correspondence, 7 November 2010.

26  Barbalet, AI, 15 December 2010.

27  Halligan, AI, 10 December 2010.

28  Johnston, AI, 15 November 2010.

29  Edgar, AI, 20 December 2010; Barbalet, AI, 15 December 2010.

30  Barbalet, AI, 15 December 2010.

31  Dowse, AI, 19 November 2010.

32  Dowse, AI, 19 November 2010; Horsfield, AI, 30 December 2010.

33  Johnston, AI, 15 November 2010.

34  Barbalet, AI, 11 December 2010.

35  Johnston, AI, 15 November 2010.

Both Horsfield and Edgar state that the group primarily helped them with 'nuts and bolts', such as how to present dialogue, characterisation, and scene transitions.[36] Horsfield particularly appreciated the fuller discussions about craft. She recalls positing that 'No scene – no descriptive scene – was worth more than 500 words. We had a good discussion about that'.[37] Although Horsfield insists that 'the process of finding your own voice is done alone', she admits that Seven Writers 'helped to define what your voice might be'.[38]

That question of influence became frighteningly (or amusingly) theatrical for at least two members. In her introduction, Dowse describes herself writing, but the 'room of her own' is crowded with six writerly spirits:

> There's Edgar, perched on my bookshelf, taking careful note of where I place my commas; Eldridge has a quizzical expression, trying to go along with me, but wondering whether I'm making myself as clear as I could; Barbalet's shaking her head, telling me where to cut; Halligan, her face pressed to the screen, scrolls in vain for the imaginative bits; Horsfield has lit an exasperated cigarette. And there's Johnston, over by the window, laughing her head off. (xxiv)

Halligan experienced similar 'scary' episodes, with voices warning about 'adjectives' or 'long sentences'. But she reports that 'I'd either avoid those things or decide, quite defiantly, that they were what I wanted. So there was an ongoing conversation, real and virtual'.[39]

What happened 'around' the workshop was significant. Although the workshop was the core event, meetings included personal exchanges as well as what members call 'other business' or 'gossip'.[40] Yet 'gossip' in one century is literary history in the next. Edgar's notes show the conversation operating on three levels: personal matters, such as health, pregnancies, or relationships; the workshop; and 'other business', such as acceptances and rejections, what Australian works were doing well, what publishers were doing, and forthcoming events.

A sample of Edgar's notes from a meeting on 28 April 1996 shows the kinds of critiques exchanged (see Figure 1). Here, Edgar has submitted a story at the 'last minute', an exception to usual practice. Nevertheless, Halligan comments on 'how v[ery] readable and rhythmical it was'. The group discussed the issue of how a 'narrated story within a story' requires that the reader 'suspends disbelief and assists this narrative convention if the thing's done properly'. Then Eldridge introduces more pointed criticisms about the purpose, which 'temporarily floored SE [Suzanne Edgar]'; others question the ending, but offer 'praise for its pared down style, sinister tone.'[41]

The fuller note, however, also demonstrates the strategic importance, and emotional weight, of the 'other business' and personal exchanges. Edgar is rushing to meet a deadline

---

36 AIs: Horsfield, 15 November 2010; Edgar, 2 November 2010 and 20 December 2010; Johnston, 15 November 2010.
37 Horsfield, AI, 30 December 2010.
38 Horsfield, AI, 30 December 2010.
39 Halligan, AI, 10 December 2010.
40 Johnston, AI, 15 November 2010; Horsfield, AI, 30 December 2010.
41 Edgar, meeting notes from Seven Writers, 28 April 1996.

for the annual Max Harris Literary Award, a resonant goal for her because she had begun her career writing reviews for Harris. Personal and professional news blend as members discuss a wedding, two overseas trips, wrangling with an agent, and negotiations with the ABC. Edgar even sketches a group portrait: 'It was a superb sunny autumn day so DJ [Dorothy Johnston] spread a tarpaulin in her back yard and we all lounged out there for the workshop part of the meeting'. Eldridge, then in the last year of her life, appears 'very well and cheerful'.[42] Clearly, Seven Writers' success has brought with it accelerating demands of 'other business', new demands that could have been overwhelming for lives already brimming with joy, aspiration, fear, and shade.

When asked to account for Seven Writers' longevity, members – as usual – responded differently. Two stressed its practical usefulness in previewing work before publishers saw it; two its emotional support, particularly for the painful personal experiences they went through.[43] Halligan remarks that, 'in its heyday it was addictive [and that] its great strength was the way it kept me writing'.[44] Horsfield summarised many Seven Writers' practices that enabled this longevity:

> Keep the workshop closed; be practical – set an optimal number (seven was good); be very organised; have a schedule; don't be prescriptive; have a Chair take charge if the arguments get out of hand. Then cross your fingers and hope it works.[45]

Indeed, for Johnston, it was, overwhelmingly 'Luck. Serendipity. Luck. Timing. Shared focus on the task in hand. Luck. A lack of alternatives that measured up. Luck … '[46]

Seven Writers' timing was indeed fortunate. Publishers like UQP and McPhee Gribble were eager to publish original fiction from new Australian writers.[47] Eldridge, for instance, submitted her first manuscript to UQP at exactly the right time, 1983; she also benefitted from overseas interest in Australian fiction when the *New York Times Book Review* praised her second collection, *The Woman at the Window* (1989), noting its 'narrative brilliance'.[48] Eldridge – and Seven Writers along with her – could imagine a global readership. Meanwhile, they created an 'emotional' and 'critical' framework to house the very hard work it would take to reach those readers, with luck (xx).

---

42  Edgar, meeting notes from Seven Writers, 28 April 1996.

43  Barbalet, AI, 15 December 2010. See also Edgar, AI, 20 December 2010; Horsfield, AI, 30 December 2010.

44  Halligan, AI, 18 December 2010.

45  Horsfield, AI, 30 December 2010.

46  Johnston, AI, 15 November 2010.

47  Randall, pp. 112–27. See also Hilary McPhee, *Other People's Words* (Sydney: Picador, 2001), Chapter 4, pp. 127–68.

48  Randall, p. 120; Marian Eldridge, *The Woman at the Window* (St Lucia: University of Queensland Press, 1989); Carolyn See, 'Paperbacks: Flying Apart in Australia', *New York Times Book Review*, 29 April 1990, p. 26.

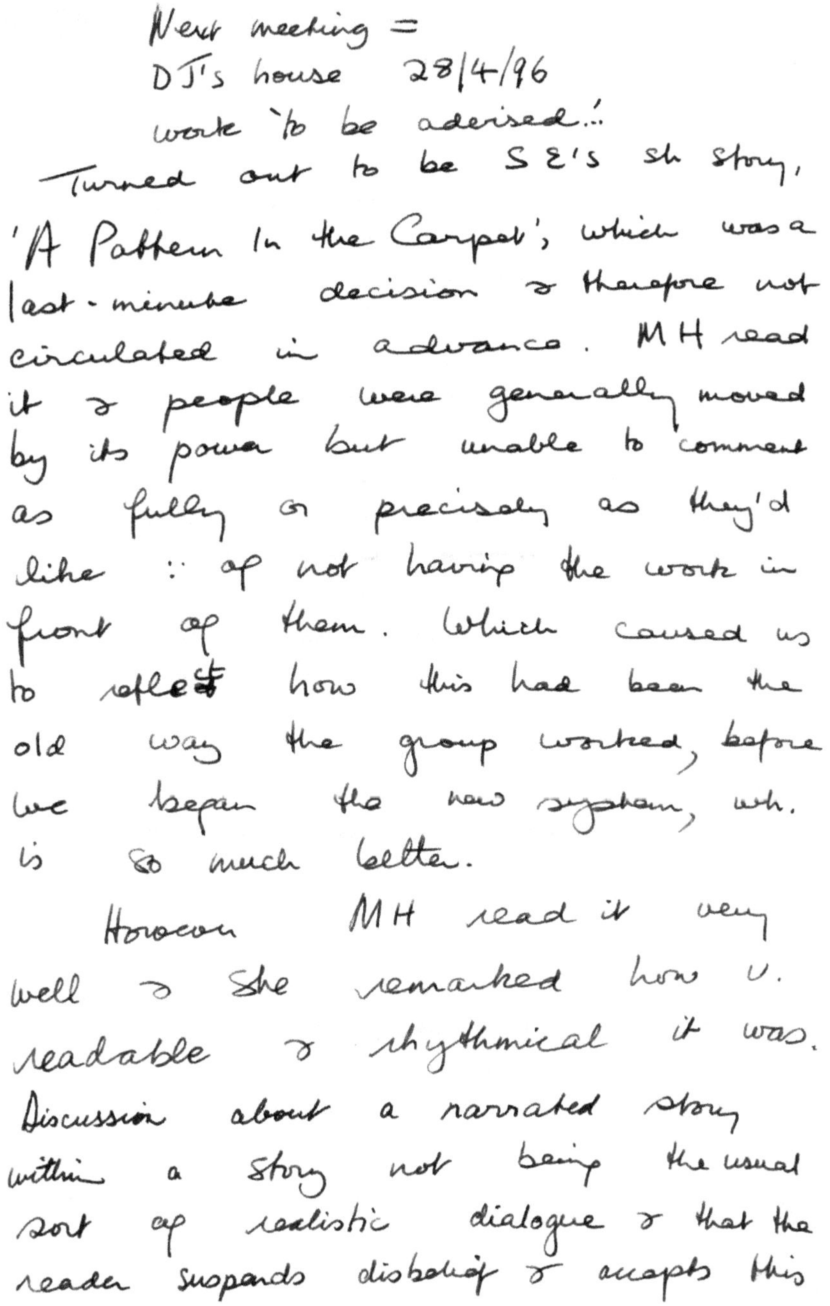

> Next meeting =
> DJ's house 28/4/96
> work to be advised...
> Turned out to be SE's sh story, 'A Pattern In the Carpet', which was a last-minute decision & therefore not circulated in advance. MH read it & people were generally moved by its power but unable to comment as fully or precisely as they'd like :: of not having the work in front of them. Which caused us to reflect how this had been the old way the group worked, before we began the new system, wh. is so much better.
>
> However MH read it very well & she remarked how v. readable & rhythmical it was. Discussion about a narrated story within a story not being the usual sort of realistic dialogue & that the reader suspends disbelief & accepts this

Figure 1. First page of Suzanne Edgar's notes from the meeting of 28 April 1996.

## 'We're Women'

Seven Writers' all-female membership and formal educations in the largely male canon raise the question of how they viewed themselves as an Australian women's literary community. At least three participated in the 1970s Woman's Liberation Movement and identified personally as 'feminists', but Seven Writers as a group resisted labels. Feminist identity was yet another topic for 'heated' discussion (xvii).[49]

Dowse relates a story of when a male writer asked to join the group. After a three-hour debate, involving fierce questionings of feminist identities, Seven Writers decided to remain as they were (xviii). This decision was explicitly gendered for some, though not for others. Some wanted to keep the group women-only based on their experience with mixed groups (xvii–xviii).[50] Others argued seven writers were sufficient, and adding another would strain the workload.[51] They never agreed on the gender argument, but workload concerns prevailed (xviii).

Yet when one considers the sociability of 1970s and early 1980s Australian literary communities generally, it is not surprising that original members built a women's group. As I noted at the beginning, males dominated most Australian literary communities in the major cities.[52] Canberra's poets' community at the Australian National University (ANU) seemed uninviting to young women writers like Barbalet. When she arrived in 1979, she discovered ANU's Poets' Picnic and 'well-known loose coteries of older, established writers' such as A.D. Hope, R.F. Brissenden and David Campbell. Yet she recalls that this very male tradition did not hold women in high regard. 'I never met any of them ever. Only later did I meet (and admire) Rosemary Dobson'.[53]

While established poets held picnics, new ones gathered at the pub. UQP, then managed by Frank Thompson, built its 1970s poetry and fiction lists from literary communities in Sydney and Brisbane. Roger McDonald describes the lively scene at the Royal Exchange Hotel in Toowong where, after work, Thompson held court 'among jugs of Fourex in the beer garden', coaxing first books from Rodney Hall, David Malouf, Tom Shapcott, and McDonald himself.[54] After working hours, Thompson conducted the vital 'other business' of building a productive literary community.[55] But McDonald also mentions the relative absence of women from such scenes; UQP's list at the time reflected this imbalance.[56] Again, Eldridge was fortunate. She submitted her first short story manuscripts over the transom just as UQP was proactively seeking new women writers to correct the bias.[57]

---

49  Barbalet, AI, 11 December 2010; Dowse, AI, 19 November 2010; Horsfield, AIs, 13 November 2010 and 22 December 2010.

50  Horsfield, AI, 15 November 2010; Edgar, AI, 20 December 2010; Barbalet, AI, 15 December 2010.

51  Barbalet, AI, 15 December 2010; Halligan, AI, 10 December 2010.

52  One exception was Melbourne, home to Sisters, Spinifex, and McPhee Gribble.

53  Barbalet, AI, 11 December 2010.

54  Roger McDonald, 'Imbibing Culture at the Royal Exchange', in Munro, p. 75.

55  See Frank Thompson, 'Creating a Press of National Value', in Munro, pp. 39–68.

56  See McDonald, p. 76, and Randall, p. 119.

57  Randall, p. 120.

Moreover, I suggest that the seven writers' shared experience as *mothers* influenced their sociability, or initial lack of it. By the early 1980s, women were visible in pub and literary lunches, but mothers – particularly working mothers – found them practically inaccessible. For example, Horsfield, who lived in Balmain at the time, could not mix with the Push because she was busy with young children as well as her job.[58] Seven Writers allowed both Horsfield and Johnston to meet at their own houses, and for all to schedule time away from family to build their identities as writers. At the time, Adrienne Rich's *Of Woman Born* (1976) had only recently exposed the absence of maternal voices in the literary canon.[59] Now, maternal scholarship and literature offers theoretical frameworks for examining how artistic combinations of creativity and procreativity can illuminate entire domains of human experience.[60] Dowse refers to the 'terribly creative period' she enjoyed after the birth of her fifth child: 'I lived on the pension and plunged into [writing], free to do so for the first time in my life. The baby was a joy and for most of the week I was on my own with him, writing and reading, and I owe him everything'.[61] Much more could be made of Seven Writers' contributions to maternal literature.

## *In the City That Must Not Be Named*

The seven writers were not originally from Canberra; all moved to the city from elsewhere. Johnston initially resisted for a year: 'I moved because my partner was offered a job in the press gallery and I worried, among other things, about whether I'd be able to write fiction in Canberra.'[62] Her new writing group offered hope, and then she discovered that much-maligned Canberra offered another benefit: 'I especially didn't want the burden of having to adopt or follow a kind of "writer's lifestyle", Canberra seemed blessedly free of this expectation.'[63] Yet Canberra's 'myths' of being 'pretty but soulless' did affect the group (xix), and their collective response demonstrates another way in which Seven Writers operated so effectively.

Into the early 1990s, Seven Writers gave public readings both as a group and individually (xviii–xix). In so doing, they 'set an example' that Canberra was, indeed, a place where imaginative writing could thrive.[64] *Canberra Times* literary editor Robert Hefner publicised them, commenting that in the late 1980s and early 1990s, 'Canberra was the literary capital of Australia, punching high above its demographic weight in literary scholarship and

---

58  Horsfield, AI, 30 December 2010.

59  Adrienne Rich, *Of Woman Born: Motherhood as Institution and Experience* (New York: W.W. Norton, 1976).

60  See Moyra Davey, ed., *Mother Reader: Essential Writings on Motherhood* (New York: Seven Stories Press, 2001); and Patricia Dienstfrey and Brenda Hillman, *The Grand Permission: New Writings on Poetics and Motherhood* (Middletown, CT: Wesleyan University Press, 2003).

61  Dowse, AI, 19 November 2010. See also interview with Sara Dowse, in Jennifer Ellison, ed., *Rooms of Their Own*, (Ringwood: Penguin, 1986), pp. 91–109.

62  Dorothy Johnston, 'Disturbing Undertones', *Griffith Review* 15 (2007), available at www.griffithreview.com/edition15/82-essay/171-johnston15.html [accessed 6 January, 2011]. See also Johnston, AI, 15 November 2010.

63  Johnston, AI, 15 November 2010.

64  Johnston, AI, 15 November 2010.

creative output'.[65] Inspired by Seven Writers' success, new writing groups sought advice; Dowse's Introduction to *The Division of Love* was written partly with such audiences in mind (xx-xxi). The presence of Seven Writers and the newer groups stimulated the government to support the literary arts. Moreover, Seven Writers worked to enhance Canberra's 'institutions' of cultural capital that supported local writers.[66] Dowse successfully encouraged the ACT Literary Award (now included in the ACT Creative Arts Fellowships); Eldridge helped establish the ACT Writers' Centre; and later Horsfield and Barbalet served on the ACT Cultural Council Grants Committees.[67]

Then Canberra's literary scene assumed global reach. Halligan volunteered with the Word Festival and quickly found herself installed as Chair.[68] Wenche Ommundsen and Rebecca Vaughn note that such festivals enable a valuable 're-entry into the social' for writers.[69] Yet they do so for publishers as well. Early Word Festivals established Canberra as a site to socialise with authors and to discuss manuscripts in a manner less awkward than correspondence. The Word Festival not only made it possible for me to meet Seven Writers, but it also presented Canberra as a literary location, a place where, as Halligan says, a writer can find 'fruitful narratives to explore … dark as well as light'.[70]

In Australian circles beyond the ACT, however, the 'imagined [literary] community'[71] still resisted 'Canberra'. Seven Writers had to argue that Canberra was 'a place for writers'.[72] Johnston wrote recently that the name 'Canberra' is 'a ubiquitous form of synecdoche in which "Canberra" elides to "Federal Parliament" – as in "Canberra to blame" – [which] makes it harder for anybody living outside to understand the place as a collection of citizens, or even to want to'. But she also elaborates on the force that, in the late 1970s, battled with no less than Eros to keep her at a physical distance from her partner in 'Canberra'. Despite the city's benefits, popular opinion maintains that:

> the city will somehow forever remain a stranger to passion and grief; that matters which fully engage the human heart will be shed at its borders – like a coat, if hearts were worn on sleeves, but more like an emptying of the spirit and a form of

---

65 Hefner, 'Seven Writers Led a Novel Existence'; Hefner's support is also mentioned in Edgar, AI, 20 December 2010.

66 Bourdieu, pp. 247–48. Bourdieu discusses the institutions of cultural capital in relation to 'academic qualifications', but prizes, fellowships, and grants also 'impose recognition' on the creative writer.

67 Dowse, personal correspondence, 21 April 2011; entry for Marian Eldridge, Australian Women's Register, available at www.womenaustralia.info/biogs/AWE2112b.htm [accessed 6 January, 2011]; Barbalet, personal correspondence, 21 April 2011; Horsfield, personal correspondence 21 April and 30 December 2010.

68 Halligan also served as Chair of the Literature Board of the Australia Council, 1992–95. Halligan, AI, 18 December 2010; personal correspondence, 20 December 2010.

69 Wenche Ommundsen, 'Literary Festivals and Cultural Consumption', *Australian Literary Studies*, 24.1 (2009): 19-34 (29). Ommundsen quotes from Vaughn's unpublished report on Adelaide Writers' Week (July 2004).

70 Halligan, AI, 18 December 2010.

71 See Benedict Anderson, *Imagined Communities: Reflections on the Origin and Spread of Nationalism*, rev. edn (London and New York: Verso, 2006 [1983]).

72 Halligan, AI, 18 December 2010; Johnston, AI, 15 November 2010.

voluntary evisceration. This activity, leading to a kind of death, spells death also to the creative imagination.[73]

For Seven Writers, publishing a collection of stories featuring the 'passion and grief' of Canberra's citizens provided one opportunity to address this challenge as a group.

All seven had been publishing short stories for some years when Edgar suggested that they create a group anthology.[74] They obtained a grant from the Australian Bicentennial Authority, and compiled the collection to publish during the Bicentennial Year (xvii). They had to fight for their title, *Canberra Tales* (1988). According to Johnston, their publisher thought: 'to include the word "Canberra" in the title would give the book the kiss of death. We argued back: hadn't Chaucer been a civil servant? Didn't *Canberra Tales* have a subtle, but resonant echo of *Canterbury Tales*?'[75] Unfortunately, when the anthology was reprinted in 1995, the publisher changed the title to *The Division of Love*.[76] Moreover, the new cover announced that the stories 'capture the essence of Australia's *urban* life', as if the suburbs for which Canberra is known should not be advertised. The blurb avoids naming Canberra at all, suggesting only that the writers 'penetrate the glittering surface of a city that is much more than a stamping ground for bureaucrats, diplomats and fat cats'. The cover image of a child, vulnerable and numinous, appeals. Thus, we leave Seven Writers still fighting the battle in the City That Must Not be Named.

Seven Writers' endurance as an Australian writing community drew from multiple factors. Members acknowledge luck: they wrote their first books when Australian literature was a growth industry, attracting local and international attention and government support. The meetings, however, prepared Seven Writers to capitalise on their luck when it arrived. Despite their differences, remaining members agreed that they followed no leader or unifying aesthetic and spent hours arguing. Paradoxically, these features may have strengthened their solidarity. Liberated from externally imposed standards, each writer held responsibility for developing her individual voice. Moreover, the group rigorously compelled her to defend – or reconsider – her aesthetic choices. Tempered by the rich sociability of the meetings, the critiques and arguments trained Seven Writers for negotiations with agents, publishers and reviewers. Seven Writers' acceptance of women as both writers and mothers, and willingness to accommodate the practical consequences, offered a necessary alternative to the literary pub. Australians' visceral resistance to 'Canberra' likely also sustained the group by presenting a clearly defined, if often unthinking, challenge.

Yet this initial investigation yields multiple questions. Given its long duration, Seven Writers' group dynamic must have changed, but how is not clear. Also, how their individual successes affected the group, for better or worse, remains obscure. More attention to Seven Writers' communication styles and sociability may reveal general traits that could benefit contemporary writing groups. Finally, Seven Writers' location in Canberra draws attention to the city's enduring repellant myth. Drawing from Halligan and others, Russell Smith

---

73  Johnston, 'Disturbing Undertones'.
74  Edgar, AI, 20 December 2010.
75  Johnston, 'Leaving Literary Canberra', *Canberra Times*, 12 January 2008, p. 11.
76  Johnston, AI, 15 November 2010; Barbalet et al., *The Division of Love*.

examines one manifestation of Canberra's 'uncanny place in the Australian imagination',[77] but much more critical work could be done to realise its worth as a storied city, and the investments of Seven Writers who helped to make it so.

*Afterword: Seven Writers Update*[78]

Margaret Barbalet worked in the Department of Foreign Affairs and Trade until the end of 2008, then moved to Sydney. She has continued to publish fiction, and is now working on a new novel.

Sara Dowse moved to Canada in 1998 where she edited the anthology *Reading the Peninsula* (2003) and began to paint and create digital prints. Several of her artworks were sold or hung in Canada and Manly. She returned to Australia six years ago and is back writing fiction.

Suzanne Edgar retired from the *Australian Dictionary of Biography* and shifted her attention to poetry. She joined another group (which includes men), and published a collection of verse, *The Painted Lady* (2006). She is now completing a second collection.

Marian Eldridge's death in 1997 was mourned by literary communities in Canberra and beyond. The Marian Eldridge Award, established to encourage new women writers, ran from 1998 to 2009.

Marion Halligan has published twenty books. In 2006, she was awarded an AM (Member of the Order of Australia) 'for service to literature as an author, to the promotion of Australian writers, and to support for literary events and professional organisations'.

Dorothy Horsfield published novels, a memoir, and numerous feature articles, most recently on genocide in Burma. She holds two MA degrees and recently received a three-year grant for her doctorate on contemporary Russia.

Dorothy Johnston continues to write fiction. With her series of crime novels, she has developed a new genre, 'Canberra gothic'. Her most recent novel is *Eden* (2007).

*Acknowledgements*

I would like to thank Margaret Barbalet, Sara Dowse, Suzanne Edgar, Marion Halligan, Dorothy Horsfield and Dorothy Johnston for their time and cooperation. I also wish to thank the Department of Chemical Engineering at the University of Texas at Austin for travel support.

---

77 Russell Smith, 'The Literary Destruction of Canberra: Utopia, Apocalypse and the National Capital', *Australian Literary Studies* 24.1 (2009): 78–94.

78 Compiled from individual entries for Seven Writers in the *Australian Women's Register*; Hefner, 'Seven Writers Led a Novel Existence'; Barbalet, personal correspondence, 11 December 2010; Dowse, personal correspondence, 8 January 2011; Edgar, personal correspondence, 27 September 2010 and 9 January 2011; Halligan, personal correspondence, 20 December 2010; Horsfield, personal correspondence, 20 December 2010; Johnston, 'Disturbing Undertones'; and Dorothy Johnston website, available at www.dorothyjohnston.com.au [accessed 6 January 2011].

Part 4

Unsettlements: Emerging Literary Communities

# 17

## 'Networking, Bumping into, Sucking up to, Catching up with, Meeting, Greeting, Chatting, Joking, Criticising': The Emerging Writers' Community as *Respublica Literaria*

Keri Glastonbury

This essay will consider the literary sociality of the Australian emerging writers' community in the era of social networking. My title quote is from Aden Rolfe's introduction to *The Reader: Volume 2*, the Emerging Writers' Festival's annual anthology. In his 'Notes from the Editor', Rolfe emphasises the discontinuous dialogue that such festivals foster within this community, where 'the social aspect manifests in discussion'.[1] This is something Damon Young also picks up on in his essay in *The Reader*, cautioning writers against getting too distracted:

> Literature can be a very cliquey industry, and it's true that handshakes and smiles help. But all the launches, seminars, festivals, parties and panels can be a serious interruption to writing, and a diversion from more enduring, enriching relationships.[2]

This wisdom aside, social interaction both on and offline is undeniably an increasing aspect of being a writer and the emerging writers' community operates as a participatory network of artist-run literary festivals (such as Newcastle's National Young Writers' Festival, Melbourne's Emerging Writers' Festival and the Format Festival's Academy of Words in Adelaide), a proliferation of literary bloggers (perhaps the best known is Angela Meyer's *Literary Minded* and numerous other DIY literary initiatives that are both semi-autonomous and enmeshed in broader literary culture.

While the phrase 'republic of letters' historically suggests more global networks, my focus remains on local iterations of literary community that may be read, nonetheless, as disrupting established conceptions of 'national' literature. Following the recent 'end of millennium' re-appraisal of Australian Literature (see Katharine Bode's 'Publishing and Australian Literature: Crisis, Decline or Transformation?'[3] for a good overview of these debates), the often practice-led resurgence by new generations of writers over the last

---

[1] Aden Rolfe, 'Notes from the Editor', *The Reader: Volume 2* (Melbourne: Emerging Writers' Festival, 2011), p. 5.
[2] Damon Young, 'Distraction', *The Reader: Volume 2*, p. 52.
[3] Katherine Bode, 'Pubishing and Australian Literature: Crisis, Decline or Transformation?', *Cultural Studies Review* 16.2 (2010): 24–48.

decade, many of whom are considered 'emerging writers', represents a recent wave of literary sociality. The activities of the emerging writers' community exceed analyses (such as Bode's) that remain heavily reliant on traditional publishing data, and may provide alternative models for negotiating and assessing the local literary field in terms of generational change. While the emerging writers' community is somewhat off the commercial and/or scholarly radar in terms of Australian literature, what might a focus on this networked small-scale community bring to contemporary reconfigurations of national literary culture?

If the historical Republic of Letters was more of a 'metaphysical' republic that transcended national boundaries across Europe and America in the late seventeenth and eighteenth centuries, and remained somewhat intangible in terms of representation, then our contemporary global Republic of Letters might look something like Randall Munroe's hypothetical 'Map of Online Communities' (Figure 1). If anything, this map suggests that we don't really know what's out there and is a visual representation of an 'imagined' twenty-first century community, given that, as Gerard Delanty argues, 'belonging today is participation in communication more than anything else'.[4] There are arguably more people playing with words now than ever before and communicating beyond face-to-face. Lately, it has been bandied about that if Facebook was a country it would be the third most populated, and you can see it in the top of the map (along with the Northern Wasteland of Unread Updates). If this is the broader social networking landscape, however, how are literary communities traversing it? Down in an archipelago above the Bay of Grammar Pedantry is a little island which has at its base the region for Writing/Poetry. Without the internet, but with pen, paper, letters and libraries, Enlightenment Republic of Letters scholars were in correspondence with one another, sharing hospitality, books and research. While this historically more 'highbrow' republic perhaps today has more in common with couch surfing and Wikipedia, the literary field – however provincialised – continues to engage with evolving *techne*.

In *The World Republic of Letters*, Pascale Casanova redeploys sociologist Pierre Bourdieu's idea of the literary field, which, even on a global scale she argues, continues to be highly stratified. In my article, 'The New Coterie: Writing, Community and Collective', Bourdieu's *The Rules of Art: Genesis and Structure of the Literary Field* also provides a useful schema in which to read some localised struggles over literary capital; in particular, those outlined in Mark Davis' *Gangland: Cultural Elites and the New Generationalism* (1997).[5] If, post-*Gangland*, the term 'coterie' became negatively associated with an elite group of cultural gatekeepers – the 'baby boomers' – it now seems counter-productive to dispense with ideas of coterie practice at a time when the idea of a monolithic or mainstream national literature may be breaking down and smaller 'non-elite' literary communities are forming. Retaining an idea of coterie practice deliberately draws on historical precursors and prevents any idealistic collapse, in contemporary terms, into envisioning the literary as having evolved into a democratised field. At a global level, in what Casanova calls 'international literary space', there 'are relations of force and a violence peculiar to them'.[6]

---

4  Gerard Delanty, *Community*, 2nd edn (London and New York: Routledge, 2009), p. 152.

5  Mark Davis, *Gangland: Cultural Elites and the New Generationalism* (St Leonards: Allen & Unwin, 1997).

6  Pascale Casanova, trans. M.B. DeBevoise, *The World Republic of Letters* (Cambridge, Mass., and

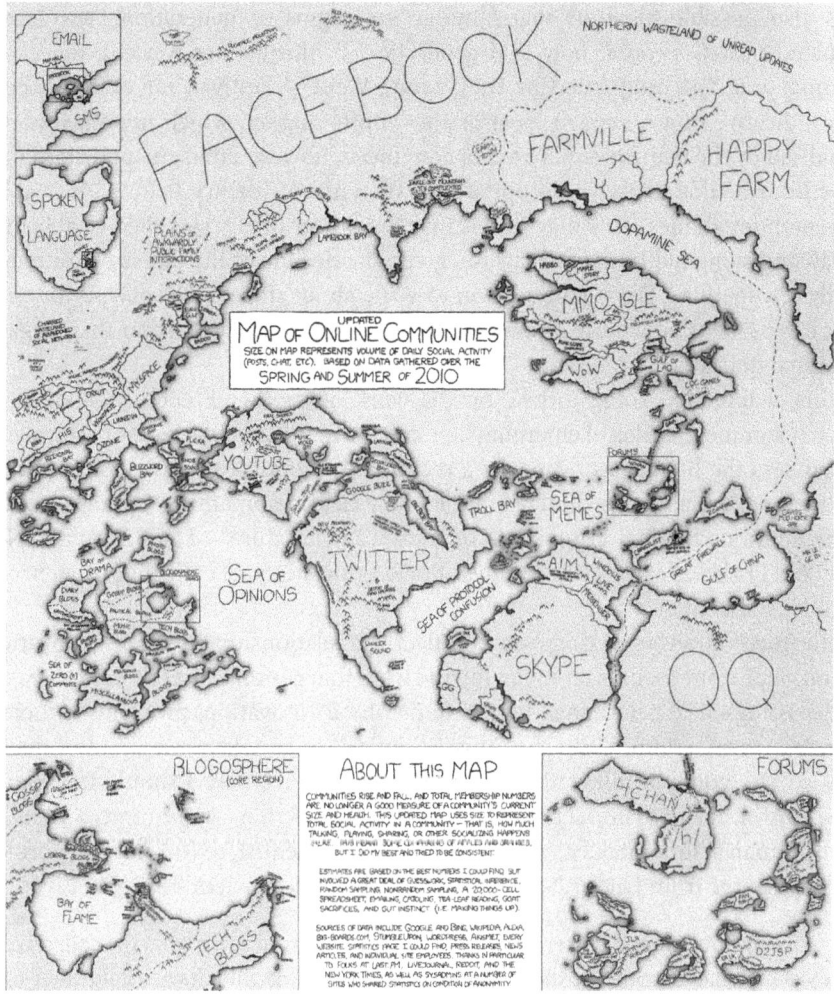

Figure 1. Randall Munroe, 'Updated Map of Online Communities', *xkcd: A Webcomic of Romance, Sarcasm, Math, and Language*. imgs.xkcd.com/comics/online_communities_2.png. Reproduced with permission from the artist.

So that, even on a local level, it is unlikely that '[l]iterary nepotism and cliquishness [will] be banished with the baby-boomers or any other generation, and [following Bourdieu] taste cultures [will] continue to prevail at all levels of the literary spectrum'.[7] The 'insider-trading' that Davis exposed in *Gangland* continues in the literary communities of subsequent generations, once the prestige of national broadsheets is substituted for zine fairs. As with the preceding baby-boomer literati, how you socialise arguably continues to be as important as how you write – or who and where you review.

---

London: Harvard University Press, 2004 [1999]), p. xii.

7   Keri Glastonbury, 'The New "Coterie": Writing, Community and Collective', *JASAL* (2010 *Special Issue: Common Readers and Cultural Critics*): 1–10 (3).

It is also possible to argue that familiar paradigms of 'generationalism' have been perpetuated post-*Gangland*, now that generation Y hipsters are wearing the cardigans. The annual zine fair programed by the Sydney Writers' Festival, for example, could be read as indicative of a tokenism towards the 'youth' market, which nonetheless remains marginalised by the mainstream. I am not convinced, however, that an oppositional model, apropos Bourdieu, is entirely appropriate for the current literary field in Australia, even along generational lines. This may be because the power of any so-called establishment is less totalising along old lines of exclusion, given the decline of the literary paradigm more generally – something Davis has gone on to write about since *Gangland*.[8] With emerging writers, it is perhaps now more a case of going where the energy is rather than engaging in oppositional politics.

In this chapter I'm going to take on the work of another French sociologist, Bruno Latour, to examine this idea of emerging literary communities/coteries more closely. Where Bourdieu sees the literary as primarily a recuperative 'bourgeois' taste culture prevailing over a hierarchical and two-dimensional literary field – something Casanova concludes with the continued global dominance of European literature – Latour's Actor–Network Theory (ANT) also allows for the tracing of new associations of collective existence within multidimensional networks.

While there is always a somewhat dialectical relationship between innovation and recuperation, Latour focuses on following the ways that communities of 'actors' reassemble beyond existing social paradigms: 'in situations where innovations proliferate, where group boundaries are uncertain, when the range of entities to be taken into account fluctuates'.[9] If I was strictly going to follow the Latourian ANT model, then I should now perform a detailed empirical and material tracing of the emerging writers' community and its human and non-human actors. Luckily, I'm not really a social scientist, so (for now) my project will somewhat diverge from Latour here, while honouring the spirit of his imperative:

> 'to follow the actors themselves' ... in order to learn from them what the collective existence has become in their hands, which methods they have established to make it fit together, which accounts could best define the new associations that they have been forced to establish.[10]

One of the central tenants of ANT is a flattening out or relativist reading of the social world. Considering our increasingly networked literary field, might a 'republic of letters', an aspirational social or community network built around communication (whether electronic or otherwise), provide a more contemporary model for our national literary culture? Melbourne's literary ecosystem, for example, ranges from zinesters on the streets to the Wheeler Centre for Books, Writing and Ideas. After postmodernism and the culture wars of the 1990s, what would an early twenty-first century literary 'enlightenment' project

---

8  See Davis, 'The Decline of the Literary Paradigm in Australian Publishing', in David Carter and Anne Galligan, eds, *Making Books: Contemporary Australian Publishing* (St Lucia: University of Queensland Press, 2007).

9  Bruno Latour, *Reassembling the Social: An Introduction to Actor-Network-Theory* (Oxford: Oxford University Press, 2005), p. 11.

10  Latour, p. 11.

look like? Perhaps a UNESCO City of Literature?[11] Indeed, in this instance, the 'ground up' sociality of the young and emerging writers' community in Melbourne was strategically co-opted into the city's literary 'brand', forged both in a globalised context and built around a local community (real or imagined).

This increasing focus in both practice and theory on collectivity and community also creates another dialectic tension, given the persistence of individual ideas of authorship within literary cultures. In their article 'Distributed Authorship and Creative Communities', Simon Biggs and Penny Travlou question 'the model of the solitary artist who produces artefacts which embody creativity as an ideal for achieving creative outcomes. Instead creativity is proposed as an activity of exchange that enables (creates) people and communities'.[12] In this model, ideas of individual authorship would be seen, at the very least, as a product of a network of associations: authors are, as individuals, subordinate to the logic of the literary architecture. Forty years on from Foucault's 'What is an Author?', the literary is still a distinct category: we still regard literary work differently in terms of authorship compared to, say, the contemporary collaborative writing example of Wikipedia, where writers are anonymous, inexpert and non-proprietorial.[13] But what could we learn by reading the Australian emerging writers' community, for example, as a kind of wiki or, to use another contemporary phrase, as a peer-to-peer community? This is not to argue that refiguring literary communities as social networks is invariably positive, but that literature's 'social capital' is increasingly diffused throughout communities of practice, something that will continue to change not only the material conditions of publishing (or circulating mediums), but appropriate reading and consuming practices.

The emerging writers' community is a vanguard in this respect and I suspect that part of my attraction to it is due to the fact that there are (at least by definition) no 'established' authors. This is not to say that it is strictly an authorless community of writers, and in fact the opposite may be the case, in that 'we [may] almost be at the point where [the] author-type is, in a Being-John-Malkovich kind of way, culturally overabundant'.[14] Sometimes, as I lay in bed at night suffering despotic delusions of grandeur, I imagine that I've been appointed Head of the Literature Board of the Australia Council. I imagine abolishing funding programs that support individual writers directly, whether established, developing or emerging (the current Australia Council funding rungs for individual writers). Or perhaps, when I feel like I should at least make a transitional concession, I'll just set up one category, for *sub*merging authors. My argument is that categories of national authorship have now proliferated beyond state support on the individual artist model, and the Board should instead focus on facilitating literary networks. I'm picking up on Latour here and his directive towards learning to feed off controversies:

> to be faithful to the experience of the social we have to take up three different duties in succession: deployment, stabilization, and composition. We first have to

---

11  Melbourne was appointed as the second UNESCO City of Literature in August 2008.

12  Simon Briggs and Penny Travlou, 'Distributed Authorship and Creative Communities', *ELMCIP (Electronic Literature as a Model of Creativity and Innovation in Practice)*, available at elmcip.net/critical-writing/distributed-authorship-and-creative-communities [accessed 28 July 2011].

13  See Dan O'Sullivan, *Wikipedia: A New Community of Practice?* (Farnham: Ashgate, 2009).

14  Glastonbury, p. 5.

learn how to deploy controversies so as to gauge the number of new participants in any future assemblage (Part I); then we have to be able to follow how the actors themselves stabilize those uncertainties by building formats, standards, and metrologies (Part II); and finally we want to see how the assemblages thus gathered can renew our sense of being in the same collective.[15]

Might some form of 'de-professionalisation' of authorship, more akin to the kinds of networks in the emerging writers' community, foreshadow similar realignments across the field of Australian literary practice?

The title of this book, *Republics of Letters: Literary Communities in Australia*, leads me to expect many deconstructions of the meaning of community, or what Jean-Luc Nancy would term *'being-in-common'*.[16] 'Community' is a contested term: on the one hand, by harking back to archaic origins, it is currently in vogue as a utopian antidote to contemporary social atomisation; and, on the other, critiqued by theorists such as Jacques Derrida as a mobilisation of exclusion and homogenisation. In her article 'Interrupting Mythic Community', Linnell Secomb writes that 'other theorists, however, have proposed a reformulation, rather than repudiation, of community, despite its troubling association with communal exclusions', and she cites the work of Benedict Anderson, Jean-Luc Nancy and Walter Benjamin.[17] At issue is the tension between the singular subject and the impossibility of a collective subject, or Nancy's *'Being Singular Plural'*, which, as Kate Fagan argues, 'is by one reading, a neat epithet for the collective networking of individuals that seems to take place on-line'.[18] Perhaps some kind of similar existential truce is necessary for ideas of literary authorship, which may remain tenaciously subjective, while at the same time being distributed across a creative network that no longer privileges the individual in the same way. If, speaking of the social scientist, Latour writes 'the acronym ANT (is a perfect) fit for a blind, myopic, workaholic, trail-sniffing, and collective traveler',[19] might this analogy equally apply to contemporary literary authorship?

As a 'republic of letters', Australian literary culture would consist of various local literary communities and transnational networks, as opposed to the conception of a national literature that has operated in the past, heavily derived from English, and later American, associations. If a 'republic of letters' still sounds somewhat utopian as a national literary model, then perhaps this reflects a return to something of the 'Enlightenment' philosophies of modernity, salvaged from beyond postmodernism's critiques. Yet, to return to Monroe's 'Map of Online Communities', it may be that the literary is somewhat saved from itself aspirationally, in the sense that it is but a tiny little peninsula in a sea of social networking. If the aim of *Republics of Letters: Literary Communities in Australia* is to explore 'a variety of

---

15  Latour p. 249.

16  Jean-Luc Nancy, *Being Singular Plural* (Stanford: Stanford University Press, 2000), p. 23.

17  Secomb, p. 86.

18  Kate Fagan, '"Scan My Glowing Interior/and Write Down What You See There": A Few Questions About Online Environments and Australian Poetry Communities', unpublished paper, Association for the Study of Australian Literature conference, Common Readers and Cultural Critics, Australian National University, 8–12 July 2009.

19  Latour, p. 9

networked relationships among writers, readers and texts, with an emphasis on processes of literary sociality that often elide or exceed the "imagined community" of the nation', then as the 'Map of Online Communities' shows, national boundaries may be imaginatively redrawn along other lines of communication. Rather than producing postmodern anxiety about popular culture and the decline of the literary paradigm, it is instead interesting to follow how the literary field, as defined by Bourdieu, is adapting to a broader networked environment, or open field. In this sense perhaps we are *all* emerging writers, as Gertrude Stein has argued:

> the whole crowd of you are contemporary to each other, and the whole business of writing is the question of living in that contemporariness ... That is what I mean when I say that each generation has its own literature.[20]

This is something Kate Fagan takes further, in extending Stein's imperative towards contemporaraneity: 'we could say that every generation of writers is charged with the task of finding its *community*'.[21]

Different dimensions of the literary may hold social ascendancy over time, but rather than the much touted 'end of Australian literature' debates that dominated millennium discourse, the literary field continues to adapt to contemporary conditions. To what extent this relies on the resilience of individual 'imaginations' is as much in terms of the social aspirations of both readers and writers: the 'literary', in other words, continues to have 'social capital' across the spectrum. To finish with Latour and to map recent Australian literary practice, perhaps 'controversies have been deployed' (the culture wars of the 1990s), 'uncertainties are being stabilized by the building of new formats, standards and metrologies' (networked media), as we wait to see 'how the assemblages thus gathered' are renewing 'our sense of being in the same collective'.[22] Might the loose-knit emerging writers' community, born somewhat of the episteme, and saved somewhat (despite itself) from capture by the apparatus of authorship, be read as an interesting barometer for the future of literary community in Australia?

---

20  Gertrude Stein, 'How Writing is Written', in Robert Haas, ed., *How Writing is Written: Volume Two of the Previously Uncollected Writings of Gertrude Stein* (Los Angeles: Black Sparrow, 1974), pp. 151, 54.

21  Fagan, n.p.

22  Latour, p. 249.

# 18

## AN UNSETTLED COMMUNITY: HARPUR'S CARNIVAL, HARRIS' ASSONANCE, MACKELLAR'S CODE

*Michael Farrell*

A textual community is conventionally defined as 'people ... brought together through a shared text, a shared set of texts, or a shared set of reading or writing practices'. Such a bringing together may be virtual, through online networks.[1] The concept of a virtual community extends Benedict Anderson's 'imagined community' beyond national boundaries. The community conceived of in this chapter is also conceptual, but not virtual. This community is also tied to the imagined one of nation, sharing what Anderson calls a 'horizontal comradeship'.[2] Katherine Russo riffs negatively on Anderson's use of 'imagined' in her book *Practices of Proximity: The Appropriation of English in Australian Indigenous Literature* (2010), when she refers to Australia's 'imaginary egalitarianism'.[3] In other words, who actually belongs?

The community I propose here is one of *texts*, not people: documents from the nineteenth and early twentieth centuries, distinguished by their *dis*interest in building a national literature, marked by conspicuous punctuation, and belonging (together) through non-belonging. I examine the trope of community in order to further network these disinterested texts, and 'negotiate' their 'differences'.[4] My argument draws on Philip Mead's recent *Networked Language: Culture & History in Australian Poetry* (2008). Mead writes that poetry 'has an after-life in subsequent and changing cultural contexts', and, in the chapter 'Unsettling Language', points to this 'changing context' by arguing that:

> Now, as the pressures of neo-liberal economics and globalisation are reshaping contemporary culture, the literary paradigm that played a central role in underpinning that Australian settlement is breaking up. One effect of this break-up is to allow us to recognise more clearly the kind of poetries that best support that previous model of a national Australian literature, and those that don't ... one of the first things it has to do is to come to terms with the *unsettling* difference

---

1 Kate Eichhorn, 'Sites Unseen: Ethnographic Research in a Textual Community', *Qualitative Studies in Education* 14.4 (2001): 565–78 (566).

2 Benedict Anderson, *Imagined Communities: Reflections on the Origin and Spread of Nationalism*, rev. edn (London: Verso, 2006 [1983]), p. 7.

3 Katherine Russo, *Practices of Proximity: The Appropriation of English in Australian Indigenous Literature* (Newcastle upon Tyne: Cambridge Scholars Publishing, 2010), p. ix.

4 'I move through the community of negotiated differences': Jan Idle, 'Walking to Work: Community and Contact', *Cultural Studies Review*, 16.2 (2010): 314–39 (332).

of Indigenous narratives of place and history and the plural knowledges of the multicultural present.⁵

My interest here is in the 'plural knowledges' of the past. And in the 'kinds of poetries … that don't [support settlement]': for example, prose and concrete poetries; poetries that suggest different beginnings than the triumph of an imported civilisation.

Returning to Anderson, he writes that the nation 'is imagined as a community, because, regardless of the actual inequality and exploitation that may prevail … the nation is always conceived as deep, horizontal comradeship'.⁶ I am not thinking here of mateship, of Lawson or Paterson, or the continuance of socialist inflection into the twentieth century, but rather pointing to works outside the literary canon, because of their aberrant style, or bad genre fit. These are works such as 'The Note to "Good Night"' by Charles Harpur; or Dorothea Mackellar's diaries, which have been read for their message rather than their form; or the 'Letter to Jim Bassett' by Norman Harris, which has been anthologised, but has scant reputation as a 'work', having stronger historical and political, rather than literary, affect. These texts, and others that are to the side of the oeuvres of recognised writers, often belatedly discovered in archives and introduced to Australia's waning literary culture, are what interest me. Though they are disparate in terms of form, diction, style, etc., they are all marked by their material rather than semantic resistance to the project of settlement (though, here, Harris' text is an exception). To call them 'outsider' texts has the wrong connotations: Mackellar and Harpur are surely 'inside' writers now, perhaps partly due to Harpur's struggle to create an Australian 'inside' during his lifetime. But these texts don't 'belong' to settlement's community, they do other work. As Jean-Luc Nancy writes, 'it is the work that the community does *not* do and that it *is* not that forms community'.⁷ I want to unsettle that community by bringing these texts in.

The texts that I consider in the following pages can be seen as having a shared place, an 'after-life': making room for themselves, as 'comrades' (*camarada*, room-mate in Spanish).⁸ Sharing, having in common, promotes a sense of belonging, and it is this attribute that is conventionally seen as defining community.⁹ Settlement assumes the belonging of some and denies the belonging of others. Michel Serres writes that culture is 'A spot of propriety or cleanliness, a spot of belonging': its constitution follows the exclusion, the expulsion of whatever belonged before.¹⁰ This constitution by exclusion is the theme or method of all three texts: Harpur's as a form of metacommentary on identity; Mackellar's as a privileged

---

5   Philip Mead, *Networked Language: Culture & History in Australian Poetry* (North Melbourne: Australian Scholarly Publishing, 2008), pp. 1, 400–1.

6   Anderson, p. 7.

7   Jean-Luc Nancy, *The Inoperative Community* (Minneapolis: University of Minnesota Press, 1991), p. xxxix.

8   J.B. Sykes, ed., *The Concise Oxford Dictionary of Current English*, 7th edn (Oxford: Oxford University Press, 1982), p. 194.

9   See, for example, Jono Bacon, *The Art of Community: Building the New Age of Participation* (Sebastopol: O'Reilly Media Inc., 2009), p. 7.

10  Michel Serres, trans. Lawrence R. Schehr, *The Parasite* (Baltimore: John Hopkins University Press, 1982), pp. 178–79.

member of the local gentry; Harris' most explicitly as a critique of settlement's exclusion of Aboriginal people. Yet my concern is not this thematics, but how the exclusion of these texts creates an ordered fantasy of normative verse, where experimentation, varying literacy, prose and concrete poetries don't exist. It is the unsettled or unsettling nature of these texts that makes them belong together.

It is not just texts by writers outside the English tradition that belong to this community of resistance, however, but also the writings of those accepted into the canon, such as Charles Harpur and Dorothea Mackellar. Recent *Macquarie PEN* anthologies also suggest an opening of the canon to include Indigenous writers like Norman Harris.[11] What follows is a reading of certain texts by these three writers in terms of a range of unsettling writing and/or editing practice.

A short, and surprisingly carnivalesque text of Harpur's, 'Note to the Song of "Good Night"' (1850) can be found in the slim edition of his work edited by Adrian Mitchell, but not in the larger, scholarly edition of Elizabeth Perkins.[12] This text, which reads like a prose poem, consists of three paragraphs. The first is explanatory, fitting with the title of the text. Harpur writes that he composed a drinking song after the memorable performance of another drinking song during a 'carouse'. The second paragraph is a reported anecdote, which quotes a policeman who wants racehorses that were 'acknowledged' to have 'performed … splendaciously' to '*go faster*' [Harpur's italics]. The third compares Harpur's desire for alcohol to that of the policeman's desire: Harpur 'cannot enjoy [it] at a moderate pace – he 'want[s] to see everything *go faster*'. Not at the sensible, hard-working pace of settlement, but at the wild pace of carnival. Here, Harpur unsettles his own text – deliberately disrupting and fragmenting the syntax as if the words in his head '*go faster*' than he can put them down: 'Hence accrues my peculiar peril: Sot respectably, like a prudent profess … I cannot. To *dram it*, like a tinker … me … sleep over it, would bloat m … me'. It mimics the slurring and wandering concentration of drunkenness. The paragraph and text conclude with a vow to stop drinking, the date '24th day of March, 1850' and a final phrase: 'God Help me!'

Like that of the policeman, Harpur's ' "licensed" (authorised)' poet behaviour has become that of ' "licence" (excess)'.[13] Rather than building up sentential steam, or aspiring to Romantic verse (examples of both can be found almost at random throughout Perkins' edition), it is the poetics of carnival – of transgression – that are foremost in the 'Note'. Perkins writes:

---

11 Harris' 'Letter to Jim Bassett' was included with another letter by Harris in Bain Attwood and Andrew Markus, eds, *The Struggle for Aboriginal Rights: A Documentary History* (St Leonards: Allen & Unwin, 1999), pp. 120–24. It is also included in Nicholas Jose et al., eds, *Macquarie PEN Anthology of Australian Literature* (St Leonards: Allen & Unwin, 2009), pp. 432–35; and Anita Heiss and Peter Minter, eds, *Macquarie PEN Anthology of Aboriginal Literature* (St Leonards: Allen & Unwin, 2008), pp. 25–28. My citations refer to the *Anthology of Aboriginal Literature*.

12 Adrian Mitchell, ed., *Charles Harpur* (South Melbourne: Sun Books, 1973), p. 134; Elizabeth Perkins, ed., *The Poetical Works of Charles Harpur* (Sydney: Angus and Robertson, 1984).

13 Peter Stallybrass and Allon White, *The Politics and Poetics of Transgression* (Ithaca: Cornell University Press, 1986), p. 34. The notion of the (Bakhtinian) carnival in relation to Harpur's text is derived from Stallybrass and White. See Introduction, pp. 1–20.

> Harpur believed he was innovative and original to the limits of poetic freedom, but his passionate respect for the tradition of the best English poetry circumscribed his creativity in form and technique. He would have shown a more truly creative genius had he produced poetry in which form and tone were more closely related to the milieu in which it was written, or to the ruggedness of his own mind.[14]

The 'Note' fulfils Perkins' criteria of being 'more closely related to his milieu' and 'to the ruggedness of his own mind'. Read in conjunction with the 'Note', both these characterisations suggest an outdoors 'milieu', such as the race track, or of the 'rugged' mountains of the 'pard'. Following the mimetic ellipses of the 'Note', Harpur writes: 'while to be as wild as I generally am when under its [strong drink's] influence – wild as a mountain pard, is nearly as low and brutal and far more perilous'. The 'Note' enacts the 'high and low' of carnival from one paragraph to the next, and in doing so as a literary conceit, proves itself not really low – nor really high.[15] So it appears that the *not* 'wild', but slow, slurring drunkenness that the poem mimes is not his own, but a performance of how others' drunkenness manifests. Unfortunately, we don't have a syntactical approximation of Harpur's 'wildness'. It is a wild text within the oeuvre of Harpur. But consider the figure he uses to illustrate wildness: 'as wild as a mountain pard'. Not only is it not a local reference, it is an archaic one (a 'pard' being an archaic term for leopard): a mannered, bookish one.[16] So while he says he must settle himself, must 'give up … the liberty of drinking', he both denies and affirms the use of the literary – foreign – simile. In the 'Note', Harpur enacts the 'catastrophe' of his life in speech; like the poet cited by Giorgio Agamben, he 'breaks his own dictation'.[17] Agamben writes in *The End of the Poem* that 'poetry and life … are united … in a medium. This medium is language'.[18] In the 'Note', Harpur represents his grapple with this, trying for the sake of his poetry and his life to bring them both under control. He is not 'a profess[or]' or 'a tinker', he is '*like* the Policeman' and 'wild *as* a mountain pard' [my italics]. He has no identity but the composing 'I'. But there is also identity in the ellipses of the 'broken' 'dictation': in the ' … me … ' and 'm … me'. It is at the point where he uses 'me' and the second broken 'm … me' that we lose the sense of these sentences. It is here that Harpur gives up the semantic. In her book *Punctuation: Art, Politics and Play* (2008), Jennifer DeVere Brody argues for the ellipse to be 'rethought as an active agent … the mark that hails the reader as a participant', that it is 'ambivalent, enigmatic, paradoxical – the presence of absence'.[19] Harpur performs self-obliteration in favour of punctuation and the reader, only to return 'as a mountain pard' denying 'Liberty' and calling on 'God'. Harpur's use of the word 'liberty' is ironic: his 'Note' represents him as being under compulsion and lacking control when drinking. If 'Life is what is made in speech and what remains

---

14   Perkins, Introduction, *The Poetical Works of Charles Harpur*, p. xxix.

15   Stallybrass and White, p. 3.

16   *Concise Oxford Dictionary*, p. 743.

17   Giorgio Agamben, trans. Daniel Heller-Roazen, *The End of the Poem: Studies in Poetics* (Stanford: Stanford University Press, 1999), p. 83. Agamben is discussing Italian poet Antonio Delfini.

18   Agamben, p. 93.

19   Jennifer DeVere Brody, *Punctuation: Art, Politics, and Play* (Durham: Duke University Press, 2008), pp. 71, 73.

indistinguishable from it and close to it,[20] this is Harpur's 'catastrophe' reduced to a 'Note' – it is the 'me' that is lost in elliptical speech, that mime, or 'm ... me'.

The rapid trajectory of the 'Note' moves from the community of drinking with friends, that Harpur describes as being a 'carouse [that] was the most kindly and harmonious affair of the kind that I ever participated in – and I wish therefore it had been *the last*' (the 'wish' implying that community has been lost) to being beyond community. He further alludes to community with regard to the policeman and 'his comrades'. From there the text moves to the breaking up of self, to be metamorphosed into a 'wild ... mountain pard', presumably outside comradeship, dependent on 'God['s ] help' as his final resort.

The 'Note' is far from 'traditional English verse'; but not so far from the French tradition, being contemporary with the prose poems of Charles Baudelaire.[21] Its prose form has made it a 'fugitive piece' within Harpur's oeuvre. It is such 'pieces', 'fugitives' from the law – and settlement – of English tradition, that interest me. Nicholas Jose writes – in the context of 'challenge[s to] convention and the status quo':

> Sometimes, combining terms that are unsettled and open to redefinition, Australian literature has a do-it-yourself quality ... This may explain the open enededness and formal indeterminacy of many of the most intriguing works. Australian literature can even seem to be a fugitive phenomenon.[22]

In the 'Note', Harpur abandons his verse models for a DIY approach. The performative aspects of the text contradict its ostensible status as merely a note on composition. Its exclusion from Perkins' edition emphasises its fugitive status; further, it enacts Harpur being on the run from himself; the success of his escape is ambiguous.

The assemblage of styles, Harpur's expressed strong feeling about his own drinking, and the mimetic, metastylistic syntax, distinguish the 'Note' from Harpur's accustomed modes. Its attention and dramatisation of prose rhythm both constitute poetic prosody while avoiding metre. Deleuze states in *Dialogues II* that 'desire concerns speed and slownesses', going on to say '*desire only exists when assembled or machined*' [Deleuze's italics]. In the 'Note' Harpur has 'constructed' his desire.[23] Yet Harpur's concluding invocation to God suggests another desire. Deleuze criticises the psychoanalytic construction of desire as a 'lack'. He states, on the contrary, that 'The process of desire is called "joy", not lack or demand. Everything is permitted, except what would come and break up the integral process of desire, the assemblage.'[24] Yet 'what would come and break up ... desire, the assemblage' is what Harpur calls on – that is, 'God'. It is God that Harpur appears to lack and desire; however, the paradox here is that God has been incorporated into the assemblage. If we read this as a textual rather than biographical plea, we may take 'God' as being an editor –

---

20  Agamben, p. 78.

21  Baudelaire 'inaugurated the genre in France' in 1862. See David Lehman, *Great American Prose Poems from Poe to the Present* (New York, Scribner, 2003), p. 13. Lehman's anthology includes earlier prose poems by Ralph Waldo Emerson (1839) and Edgar Allan Poe (1835), pp. 27–30.

22  Jose, General Introduction, *Macquarie PEN Anthology of Australian Literature*, p. 5.

23  Gilles Deleuze and Claire Parnet, trans. Hugh Tomlinson and Barbara Habberjam, *Dialogues II* (New York: Columbia University Press, 2002), pp. 95–96.

24  Deleuze and Parnet, p. 100.

but again the 'Note' is paradoxical: the plea for intervention is part of the contrivance – or assemblage – of the 'Note'. Harpur transgresses, through mimetic drunkenness, and by breaking the rules of normative grammar – yet by returning 'to his senses' at the end of the text (by dating it, and calling on God), Harpur demonstrates he has no need of God (or editor).

As noted, Norman Harris' 'Letter to Jim Bassett' (1927) is included in both recent *Macquarie PEN* anthologies of literature. Harris' text contains many of what would conventionally be considered spelling errors. This indicates contemporary editing practice: allowing the reader to negotiate spelling and grammatical differences – differences that evoke the writer, their time and culture. As theorist of the oral, Walter Ong, writes,

> when other dialects of a given language besides the grapholect [such as 'English'] vary from the grammar of the grapholect, they are not ungrammatical: they are simply using a different grammar, for language is structure, and it is impossible to use language without a grammar.[25]

Penny van Toorn argues against the 'cultural progress' model of Indigenous literacy, adding that there is a 'multitude of ways to practice literacy', and, grammar aside, Kevin Brophy has called Harris' writing 'worthy of Jonathan Swift'.[26]

'Letter to Jim Bassett' is an example of an editor's assemblage, as a note from Bain Attwood and Andrew Markus attests.[27] The 'Letter' as published consists of a letter as such, with an addition of 'Questions within the meaning on the Act'.[28] The 'Questions' also sign off in letter form. The 'Letter' doesn't begin with a conventional address, but commences, 'We have been looking out for you for some time now'. The addressee is first referred to in the second paragraph: 'Now, Jim, we are trying to get some of the natives and half-castes together'. There is a double sense of community here: of Jim's belonging with Harris' 'we', and of belonging to the group of 'natives and half-castes'. We don't know if Harris and Bassett share an Indigenous language, but they are forced to write in English to correspond.[29] Harris goes on to enumerate some of the prohibitions and exclusions faced by Indigenous people: 'He is not alowed in a pub, not to have a gun, not to camp on revers' (25). The theme of community here coincides with the formulation by Serres above in relation to culture: that its constitution follows the exclusion, the expulsion, of whatever belonged before. In other words, *non*-Indigenous community is constituted by Indigenous exclusion.

---

25  Walter Ong, *Orality and Literacy: The Technologizing of the Word* (London: Routledge, 2002), pp. 105–6.

26  Penny Van Toorn, *Writing Never Arrives Naked: Early Aboriginal Cultures of Writing in Australia* (Canberra: Aboriginal Studies Press, 2006), p. 9; Kevin Brophy, 'Aboriginal Voices Resist Colonial History' (review of *Macquarie PEN Anthology of Aboriginal Literature*), *Eureka Street* 18.13 (27 June 2008), available at www.eurekastreet.com.au/article.aspx?aeid=7823 [accessed 4 May 2011].

27  Attwood and Markus, p. 124.

28  Harris, 'Letter to Jim Bassett', in Heiss and Minter, pp. 25–28. All subsequent references are to this edition.

29  Mudrooroo, quoted in Russo, p. 55.

In his survey of twentieth-century Aboriginal literature, *Black Words, White Page*, Adam Shoemaker 'contend[s] that a fundamental relationship exists between the socio-political milieu and Aboriginal creative writing in English'; or, as Heiss and Minter phrase it, 'one of the persistent and now characteristic elements of Aboriginal literature – [is] the nexus between the literary and the political'.[30] My assumption is that an historical Aboriginal text will tend to be *un*settling: that however coded, however ironic, such texts are likely to bear the traces of a rejection of, and resistance to, settlement.[31] It is, in a sense, their job – as opposed (literally) to the job of settler texts, as indicated by Mead above.

Like Harris', many Indigenous texts are semantically explicit in their protest against settlement (as are, for a variety of reasons, a number of non-Indigenous texts). Shoemaker defends Aboriginal poetry against the charge of 'propaganda' in the following terms, 'No matter how obvious or how covert the socio-political dimension of this verse, it all expresses and reinforces a distinctive Black Australian world-view, highlighting pride, dignity and survival in the face of loss'.[32]

My poetic readings of ostensibly prosaic texts have a double aim: that of unsettling the excluding community of the Australian poem and of unsettling the cultural hegemony of the pragmatic. I argue that Harris *is* one of Mead's 'poetic artificers'.[33] Such poetry partisanship is not just for the sake of winning points for poetry, but in order to demonstrate the possibilities of insight that can be gained from such readings, and to test also the boundaries of criticism. How, then, does Harris' writing, its what we might call 'poetic literacy', argue for inclusion in the 'community' of poetry? I don't mean to reduce Harris' urgent and real political claims to an analogy, but to recognise that his letter's contribution to Australian literature is more historical. I begin with Harris' first sentence:

> We have been looking out for you for some time now but I don't think that you are much of a swimmer and I know that you haven't got a boat and now that the lakes are running you can't come per road or by water and perhaps not by train, so I don't expect to see you this winter. (25)

By noticing the length and the sentence's lack of punctuation, we might miss the way that the sentence's rhythm relies on the assonance of the 'er' sound. They constitute three instances of half rhyme, roughly equally distributed: 'swimmer', 'water', and 'winter'. These three are further linked by the assonance of the 'i' in 'swimmer' and 'winter', and the consonance of the 'w' and the 't' in 'winter' and 'water'. This community of like words, once

---

30 Adam Shoemaker, *Black Words, White Page: Aboriginal Literature 1929–1988* (St Lucia: University of Queensland Press, 1989), p. 6; Heiss and Minter, 'Aboriginal Literature', *Macquarie PEN Anthology of Aboriginal Literature*, p. 2.

31 See, for example, Gladys Gilligan's 'The Settlement' in Susan Maushart, *Sort of a Place Like Home: Remembering the Moore River Native Settlement* (Fremantle: Fremantle Arts Centre Press, 1993), pp. 13–21; and Michelle Grossman's commentary on this text in 'When They Write What We Read: Unsettling Indigenous Australian Life-Writing', *Australian Humanities Review* 39–40 (September 2006), available at www.australianhumanitiesreview.org/archive/Issue-September-2006/grossman.html [accessed 16 March 2011].

32 Shoemaker, p. 180.

33 Mead, p. 6.

established, suggests the belonging of two further 'er' words: the unusual use of 'per' instead of 'by', which points to the repetition of 'per' in 'perhaps'.

Examples in the 'Letter' where unconventional or misspelt words contribute to the letter's poetics are numerous. Regardless of his intent, Harris creates instances of rhyme and assonance, as well as further resonances of meaning, that a more conventional text would not. For example, Harris writes 'prohibiterd', again coincidentally using the 'er' sound, between two uses of the word 'Perth': 'I suppose you know Perth is prohibiterd around Perth for natives and half cast'. He makes an expressive pun: 'Last year in Parliament House they disgust where they should give halfcasts a vote or not', and truncates Aboriginee into the colloquial 'Abo.' for rhyming purposes: 'Now you see yourself where is the Abo. got a fare go.' As this leads directly on to a statement detailing where an Aboriginee can't go, the spelling of 'fare' suggests a ticket an Aboriginee can't buy. The disallowance: 'not to camp on revers' (25) suggests both the reserves where Aboriginal people were sent to, and the reverse Aboriginal people were suffering under settlement. More crucially, in the list of 'Questions' regarding 'the Act' (that has given Harris 'a headache thinking about', 26), and elsewhere in the 'Letter', Harris continually spells the word 'there' as 'their', supporting the statement-question 'The country belongs to him [the native]'? (27); the word 'as' also becomes the possessive 'has'. There is a persistent knowledge of dispossession in Harris' text that is not (cannot be?) known by Standard English texts.

That Harris has a flair for phrasing and an ironic sense of humour may be read in 'their was hell to pop over that', 'In the North has you know they were never given wages just work for a kick in the sturn and a little tucker such has it is', and 'What dose their food consist of, I bleave Billy Goats'? (25, 26, 27). The extent that Harris' language is style or accident (like the 'bleave' in relation to 'Billy Goats' as synthesis of 'believe' and 'bleat') is difficult to discern, pointing to the lability of language, which, in a settlement context, could be said to support the *un*settler – as well as Mead's 'assumption' quoted above 'that poetic language is always heteronomous and impure, and usually unstraightforward'.

Throughout the 'Letter' is a concern for the welfare of Aboriginal people throughout Western Australia. As a farmer, Harris embodies a contradiction to A.O. Neville's quoted pronouncement that 'it was no good giving natives land because they would not work it' (26). Harris writes, 'How are you getting on with your cropping, we haven't started putting any in yet. I was doing some rolling before that rain it settled the burn, although I set it alight last Sunday I may be able to plough it in' (27). But, in fighting for Aboriginal community, he is no supporter of settlement: settlement being dependent on the exclusion of Aboriginal people from the land. That Harris' text is as incendiary as, say, Henry Lawson's 'Freedom on the Wallaby', is articulated in his last line, 'Burn this when you are finished with it or send it back to me' (28).

Craig Dworkin, on reading the disruptive values of visual texts, writes:

> There is a strong temptation to recuperate the resisting and unsettling potential of 'noise' as a 'message' which can be absorbed into the very code it challenges, so that it can then be safely consumed by traditional hermeneutic strategies as simply another part of the message's 'meaning'.[34]

---

34  Craig Dworkin, *Reading the Illegible* (Evanston: Northwestern University Press, 2003), p. 49.

Code – or 'noise' – is always unsettling. Best known for her anthemic poem 'My Country', and its admission, 'I love a sunburnt country', the diaries of Dorothea Mackellar contain recurring lines of code.[35] The published diaries have been titled after her best-known line: *I Love A Sunburnt Country*. The coding of the diaries doesn't seem to belong to Mackellar's oeuvre – what do patriots have to hide? The editor of the diaries, Jyoti Brunsdon, describes the 'unforgettable moment [of] the discovery of the diaries', and a 'second [moment] came when I turned a page to find much of the entry for the next day in code'. She goes on to describe the process of deciphering Mackellar's code, and provides a key to the coding.[36]

There is poetry in Mackellar's diaries: in the shift between code and English – and in Brunsdon's edited version between bold and regular text. In other words, there is 'visual prosody': a sense of change that is not purely semantic (nor 'non-semantic', nor 'asemic').[37] Though for Mackellar the code has a practical purpose, it also perfectly expresses Mead's 'dissatisfaction with … the overly settled idea of the "ordinariness" of ordinary, or everyday language'.[38] In the diaries, Mackellar's coding disrupts the assured, conversational and everyday qualities of the typical entry. A paradoxically heightened consciousness of 'language' presents itself, consciousness of the word as made up of letters: a materialist poetics. To translate this – to break the code – is to lose the poetics. How might this 'noise' be communicated like a 'disease', as Dworkin recommends? Charles Bernstein records Veronica Forrest-Thompson's argument that: 'nonmeaningful levels [should] be taken into account, and that meaning be used as a technical device which makes it impossible as well as wrong for critics to strand poems in the external world', adding that '[t]he artificiality of a poem may be more or less foregrounded, but it is necessarily part of the "poetic" reading of any document … Content never equals meaning'.[39]

Brunsdon settles the question of Mackellar's artifice by dealing with the code in the introduction, as if it doesn't belong in the body of the text. Mackellar's code has been typeset in Brunsdon's introduction, but it challenges quotation: not all the symbols have equivalents in Microsoft Word. Brunsdon replaces Mackellar's code with deciphered, bolded English: the bolding reveals what Mackellar was hiding. There is no respect given to 'visual prosody'; rather, the use of bold type is what Ron Silliman calls a 'strateg[y] for consuming texts solely for their summarizable "content"'.[40] It tends to do this, but not completely, because the content of the diaries is the hiding of the hidden as much as the hidden itself. The bold type announces a differentiation (an exclusion) that gradually fades (in effect). The means of the hiding – the code – is, as I have said, dealt with in the introduction. No consideration is given to it as poetic material in its own right. The 'visual' prosody, however unintentional, is ignored, as can be seen by comparing the illustrative

---

35 Dorothea Mackellar, 'My Country', in John Kinsella, ed., *The Penguin Anthology of Australian Poetry* (Camberwell: Penguin Books, 2009), pp. 127–28.

36 Jyoti Brunsdon, Introduction, in Brunsdon, ed., *I Love A Sunburnt Country: The Diaries of Dorothea Mackellar* (North Ryde: Angus & Robertson 1990), pp. 15–16.

37 The term 'visual prosody' is Marjorie Perloff's. See *The Dance of the Intellect: Studies in the Poetry of the Pound Tradition* (Cambridge: Cambridge University Press, 1985), p. 110.

38 Mead, p. 5.

39 Charles Bernstein, *A Poetics* (Cambridge: Harvard University Press, 1992), p. 10.

40 Ron Silliman, *The New Sentence* (New York: Roof Books, 1989), p. 13. Quoted in Dworkin, p. 54.

photographs of certain diary pages in *I Love a Sunburnt Country* to their later transcriptions. Once deciphered, the text is treated as prose.[41]

Here are the first two coded entries of the published version: 'Florence came frightfully worried. **Her pretty maid Cayley has just had a child**' and 'Sat on the lawn and **smoked to keep the mosquitoes away**'.[42] This is from a diary written in January 1910. Mackellar was twenty-four and living at home: a life of both 'privilege' and 'restriction'.[43] The published text then, is to some extent unsettled, by interrupting what Silliman calls 'textual transparency'.[44] In thinking of this as an unsettled text, I am not referring to the semantic content, but to Brunsdon's representation of the content. In this instance, it seems that there is a direct correlation, however, between the content that Mackellar finds unsettling and its representation as code, and finally re-represented as bold. Though the propriety of the above entries – referring to unwed childbirth and smoking – has changed since 1911, other entries refer to Mackellar's relationship with a married man:[45]

> Thursday August 10
>
> … After dinner we talked. **He was worried about me, and I told him something of what was in my heart, for indeed there has been a great change in the last two days.** A relief, but rather exhausting …
>
> Friday August 11
>
> Got up earlier than usual … Felt quite reasonably well. Evening: Mrs Arthur Feez's and Mrs W. Collins' dance. A very nice one, and I loved it – what I had of it. Broke down at the 12th dance. Rather a stirring night. **He was upset because I love him**, and it upset *me*, and **I nearly kissed him, which would have startled things** a good deal. I never felt like that before – rather desperate – and yet not as miserable. Only he wouldn't believe me when I told him so.[46]

In her coding, Mackellar resists her implication in the settlement project: she is described as 'the first genuine Australian songster' in the *Commonweal*.[47] It denies her inheritance: 'all the historical, formal and linguistic categories necessary for its [Australia's] self-creation and development'.[48] Mackellar's invention could be considered a useless one in terms of settlement: as deceptive, sly, serving only a private purpose; alternatively it can be read as a form of diplomacy, affirming both community and – in egoistic miniature – the lies

---

41  See photographs on p. 14 of Brunsdon's Introduction of entries for 10 and 11 August 1911, compared to the edited versions on p. 84 of the *Diaries*.

42  Dorothea Mackellar, *Diaries*, p. 34.

43  Brunsdon, Introduction, *Diaries*, pp. 15, 16.

44  Dworkin, p. 54.

45  Mackellar, *Diaries*, p. 59.

46  Mackellar, *Diaries*, p. 84.

47  Brunsdon, Introduction, *Diaries*, p. 12. The description rivals that of Harpur, Australia's 'first authentic poetic voice'. See William Wilde, *Australian Poets and their Works: A Reader's Guide* (Oxford: Oxford University Press, 1996), p. 104.

48  Mead, p. 400.

told by the state. Through her poem 'My Country', Mackellar has a relation to Australia's national culture. In a sense, the code marks the diaries as homeless: they can't settle in Mackellar's 'privilege[d]' home – the 'restriction' is too great.[49] Mackellar's original diary unsettles reading through unsettling semantics, yet as Julian Wolfreys notes, 'Reading is an act of decoding'.[50] Reading Mackellar's poem, 'My Country', then, also involves decoding. Russo, for example, refers to the gendered aspect of 'My Country' as 'far from innocent and [functioning as] a metaphor for the relation between the masculine Australian settler and the conquered country', adding that 'the increasing replacement of past tenses [in Australian literature] may indicate a pattern of avoiding the past'.[51] The present tense of Mackellar's poem suggests that the 'streams', 'skies', 'mountains' and 'ferns' of Australia are naturally accompanied by 'cattle' and 'paddocks'. The 'love' that is expressed for 'My Country' is one of ownership rather than care: the poem ends, 'Though earth holds many splendours/Wherever I may die/I know to what brown country/My homing thoughts will fly'. Brunsdon describes Mackellar as a 'socialite': the lines are those of someone who travels the world, representing Australia.[52]

Bataille wrote that, 'Of poetry, I will now say that it is, I believe, the sacrifice where words are victims'.[53] If the coded words are victims in Mackellar's diary, the poetry they resemble is concrete. The visual emphasis of bold type in the published version evokes a concrete quality, but it is explicit in the original. Here is a sample, where a dash ( – ) represents 'A' and so on:

| A | E | G | H | I | O | S | T | U |
|---|---|---|---|---|---|---|---|---|
| – | \| | /\ | \\/ | \\ | / | = | \|\| | + |

Mackellar's code includes two punctuation marks: a small star for an exclamation; a small cross for a full stop. There is no differentiation between upper and lower case letters, so I follow Brunsdon in presenting the deciphered letters as capitals.[54]

'What makes me read this text as a Concrete Poem? ... What do I do when I read it as a Concrete Poem?' These are questions Claus Cluver asks in his article 'Concrete Poetry: Critical Perspectives from the 90s'. He adds,

> they are not easy to answer but seem crucial in assessing the status and achievement of Concrete poetry ... Among the many lessons I have learned ... from Concrete Poems is an understanding of the signifying potential of all the material aspects of the text.[55]

---

49  Brunsdon, Introduction, *Diaries*, pp. 15–16.

50  Julian Wolfreys, *Readings: Acts of Close Reading in Literary Theory* (Edinburgh: Edinburgh University Press, 2000), p. viii.

51  Russo, pp. 30, 31.

52  Brunsdon, Introduction, *Diaries*, p. 27.

53  Quoted in Dworkin, p. 192.

54  Brunsdon, Introduction, *Diaries*, pp. 16.

55  Claus Cluver, 'Concrete Poetry: Critical Perspectives from the 90s', in K. David Jackson, Eric Vos

These 'aspects' are what might be called, in Forrest-Thomson's terms, 'the "non-semantic" effects … contributing toward the "total image-complex" of the poem'.[56] Cluver writes: 'Everything concrete is nothing but itself. To be understood concretely a word must be taken at its word. All art is concrete which uses its material functionally and not symbolically'.[57] To define Mackellar's text as concrete poetry is not a definition that is easily settled. The code *is* 'material [used] functionally', but can it be said to consist of words at all? When the cipher obscures the Roman grapheme or letter, the text can only be 'read' as a line of (non-symbolising) symbols. In Mackellar's original, there is no clear demarcation of words. If we accept the definition of 'concrete', the boundaries of the text itself remain undefined. Is it only the code that is 'concrete'? What of the pages of (edited, at times fragmentary) everyday description? The question may remain unsettled. Mackellar's diaries are then doubly unsettled texts: there is the original that we can imagine in English, having been shown the code; then there is the published version, with its bold text, that we can imagine as cipher, and read, with the knowledge of the absent code, as if it were a meaningful loss. As a hybrid, Mackellar's diary is not, I suspect, unique: a mixed genre text of social diary and concrete poetry.

My reading suggests that Mackellar's diary belongs to the international text community of concrete poetry. We can also imagine a network of coded diaries speaking in keys. As a work by a nationalistically co-opted poet, the diaries transcribed in *I Love a Sunburnt Country* are interesting for the way in which they are constituted by an internal, textually explicit, exclusion and othering. We can think of this as a process of punctuation: the main body of the text punctuated by bolded/coded examples. In Harpur, ellipses (occurring not just between words, but also within the word 'me') mark the disintegrating effect of exclusion. In Harris, the use of question marks is notable. In the 'Letter' proper, question marks are not used: for example, 'thats rotten what do you say Jim', and 'thoes who dont pay what do you think ought to be done to them' (25, 27). But whether the 'Questions' were marked by Harris or by an editor, they mark the non-rhetorical nature of the 'Questions' themselves, the 'Why?', 'Who?', 'How?', 'Is?' and 'Do?' that Harris asks in relation to the treatment of Aboriginal people (27). And while Harpur and Mackellar are both writers of settlement-affirming texts,[58] these exceptions – Harpur's 'Note', and Mackellar's 'Diaries' – *perform* question marks. Punctuation marks, like the texts that give them material life, form a collectivity, a community: 'they can never appear "alone" '; but are in 'necessarily unstable and taut equilibrium'.[59]

---

and Johanna Drucker, eds, *Experimental – Visual – Concrete: Avant-Garde Poetry Since the 1960s* (Amsterdam: Rodopi, 1996), p. 279.

56  Quoted in Bernstein, p. 11.
57  Cluver, p. 278.
58  In Harpur's case see 'To the Lyre of Australia', Perkins, pp. 722–23.
59  Brody, p. 56; Nancy, p. xxxvii.

# 19

## THE BEGINNER'S GUIDE TO BEING AN AUSTRALIAN: JOHN O'GRADY'S *THEY'RE A WEIRD MOB*

*Lindsay Barrett*

John O'Grady's *They're a Weird Mob*, the pseudonymous memoir of immigrant Italian builder's labourer Nino Culotta, was published in November 1957; by the middle of 1959 the number of books sold had passed 200 000. As David Carter has noted, *They're a Weird Mob* sold more copies, more quickly, and over a longer period of time than any other Australian novel prior to Bryce Courtney, who, it should be remembered, was publishing in a greatly expanded market.[1] Also important in an appreciation of the reach of *They're a Weird Mob* is an element of its circulation that is impossible to quantify: the extent to which it was loaned out by purchasers to relatives and friends who did not generally buy books. This is a form of book distribution far from unique to *They're a Weird Mob*, but it is something worth bearing in mind in relation to this particular text, because it means that it may well have reached an audience as least as sizeable again as that which the official figures indicate.

*They're a Weird Mob* narrates the story of an Italian migrant's arrival in Sydney in the mid 1950s, speaking to the reader in first person and recounting how the protagonist, a journalist who has come to Australia to work on an Italian language newspaper that has subsequently folded in the course of his voyage out, is forced to take unskilled work as a builder's labourer. As it transpires, this is an activity to which this particular migrant takes like a duck to water, learning, primarily through his mastery of working-class forms of Australian English, to become both a builder and a culturally settled Australian in the process. The joke of course is that the book's author is not really the Italian 'Nino Culotta', but the Anglo-Celtic John O'Grady, a hoax effectively kept up as a marketing tool by both O'Grady and his publisher, Ure Smith, for the first few weeks after the book's publication. As David Carter has observed:

> the point of the novel depends (or appears to depend) upon the reader being taken in and reading the text as the true voice of an Italian migrant, at a second and more permanent level the joke just gets better when we can read the performance of this Italian voice.[2]

By the time of the appearance of *They're a Weird Mob*, Australia had undergone a decade of massive immigration, both from Britain and more significantly from northern

---

1 David Carter, 'O'Grady, John *see* Culotta, Nino: Popular Authorship, Duplicity and Celebrity', *Australian Literary Studies* 21.4 (2004): 56–73 (56).

2 Carter, p. 58.

and southern Europe. In terms of the creation of a context for John O'Grady's work, the social and cultural consequences of this demographic redesign of Australia were crucial. As Donald Horne put it at the time, Australians often seemed to assume that, since they left the world alone, 'it should do the same by them';[3] their politicians, though, albeit in a strictly controlled fashion, were doing their best to invite the rest of the world to Australia. As a result, for the first time in which any Australian alive could remember, the blanket cultural dominance of Anglos and Celts was being confronted on its own turf by new and different ways of being.

The great governmental paradox for Australia in the 1940s and 1950s was that, if it was to survive as a discrete entity independent of the rest of the world, it could no longer hold the world outside its borders. Postwar Labor Immigration Minister Arthur Calwell's plan, continued by the Liberal and Country Party coalition after it won government at the end of 1949, was to bring as many 'New Australians' to the country as possible, ideally from Britain and Ireland. Such, though, was Australia's need, in Calwell's words, to 'populate or perish', that he and his department were forced to make up the shortfall in British immigrants by turning to the refugee camps of north Germany and their population of 'displaced persons' from Estonia, Latvia, Lithuania and East Prussia. Ethnicity remained the key criterion, however: in fact, so dominant were the racial categories from which these non-English-speaking immigrants were selected, even former members of the Nazi SS could qualify as New Australians, provided they were prepared to lie a little about their past. And yet, it soon became obvious that not even this flow of 'Balts', as they were called, would be enough on its own to prevent Australia from 'perishing'. So in the late 1940s the New Australian category was expanded again, this time to include supposedly 'dark-skinned' peasants from southern Europe. As one woman from Trieste who applied to come to Australia in 1956 recalled, one of the best things about the Australian Government's screening process for migrants was that it 'made you proud to be white.'[4]

This is the Australia that *They're a Weird Mob* speaks to: a nation whose governing classes were engaged in remaking the actual human substance of the nation in such a way that it did not substantially differ from the form that already existed. This was a definitive act of social engineering underpinned by well-established twentieth-century governmental principles and practices. Yet it was intended purely as a form of social rather than cultural engineering: the nation would absorb the masses of new bodies it required, but not their ways of being in the world. As new subjects of a new nation, it was imagined that the postwar immigrants would leave their old identities behind in their old countries.

Between 1947 and 1951, an average of 17 000 Italians migrated to Australia each year.[5] Yet the racialised climate of resistance to southern Europeans that had led Calwell and the Department of Immigration to seek out northern and eastern Europeans as preferential migrants in the first place was given voice in a range of organs both forming and amplifying conservative public opinion in Australia, from the editorials of the *Age* newspaper to *Rev-*

---

3 Donald Horne, *The Lucky Country* (Ringwood: Penguin, 1964), p. 17.

4 Quoted in Brian Murphy, *The Other Australia: Experiences of Migration* (Cambridge: Cambridge University Press, 1993), p. 157.

5 Richard Bosworth, *Cop What Lot? A Study of Australian Attitudes towards Italian Mass Migration in the 1950s* (North Richmond: Catholic Intercultural Research Centre, 1986), p. 6.

*eille*, the journal of the New South Wales Branch of the Returned Services League (RSL). Italians, it was suggested, would not make good Australians, with explanations ranging from the assertion that they were all communists, to the fear that they were all gangsters armed with flick knives, to observations that their performance in the recently concluded war had been 'despicable and deplorable'. The RSL even went so far as to suggest that ex-soldiers of the German Afrika Corps would make better immigrants than 'some of those who have come here from the Mediterranean ports'.[6]

By the late 1950s, though, such conservative opposition to the Italian presence in Australia had begun to soften, and to O'Grady's credit he set out to produce a text designed to soften such opinions even further. O'Grady presented Nino Culotta as the very ideal of the postwar migrant: he is the New Australian who will eventually *become* Australian. And this is a task for which Nino proves well suited, because, despite that fact that he is from southern Europe, he is no peasant. In fact, he is a middle-class journalist from Milan, a sophisticated northern Italian with a trunk full of cultural capital that he can exchange for the affectations of an Aussie. In addition, Nino is tall and fair ('a big bloke' as the Australians he meets frequently observe), not some illiterate, undernourished agrarian worker, and this is a distinction O'Grady is constantly at pains to make.

Indeed, Nino looks down his nose at southern Italians the way narrow-minded Australians look down at him. In this way O'Grady uses a mechanism of displacement to open a sympathetic space for Nino in the intertwined hierarchy of race and class that existed in 1950s Australia. At one point Nino even intervenes in a dispute on a suburban train between a verbally aggressive drunken Anglo-Australian and a sober, knife-wielding Sicilian, relieving the latter of his knife, throwing it from the carriage window, and then punching him unconscious, along with the drunk. In the parlance of the Australians for whom the book is supposedly written, this is clearly having a bob each-way. And yet, as a narrative device, it works in terms of resetting the boundaries surrounding the central character, as it is an act which excludes both the peasant and the drunk in favour of the category of decent citizen, a category capable of including a range of ethnicities united not by origins but by actions, by a decent and civilised way of doing things.

Or, to take another example, as Nino's self-employed builder boss, Joe, instructs one of his other labourers when he leaves Nino with him or his first day of work: 'give 'im a go mate ... 'e'll be alright'.[7] This was the reality of populate or perish: if the nation were to survive the trauma of the massive influx of foreigners, then the newcomers, initially at least, would have to be given a fair go. Subsequently, Nino finds that if he has a go then he will be given a go; it really is that simple.

In *How to Do Things with Words*, J.L. Austin argues that the key aspect of language is its performative capacity. Rather than simply representing the world 'as it is', words possess a power generative of social action; in other words, they literally make things happen. In Austin's well-known example, the statement 'I bet you sixpence it will rain tomorrow' is

---

6 Bosworth, p. 6.

7 John O'Grady, *They're a Weird Mob*, 1957 (Sydney: Ure Smith, 1974), p. 35. Subsequent page references are given in-text.

not a description of a situation, it is an act (or at least it was when sixpences existed) that initiates an action.[8]

And this is a social fact that the Australian experience impresses upon Nino Culotta – journalist as he is and so familiar with the power of words – almost immediately upon his arrival. 'Kings Bloody Cross', answers a profane and surly cab driver when asked by Nino the name of the place at which he is being dropped off (15). Later on, while temporarily lost in the city streets, he is engaged in the following exchange with a policeman:

> 'Where do you live?'
> 'Kings Bloody Cross.'
> 'Keep using that language and you'll go to Central all right. Into a cell.'
> 'How can my language make me go to Central? It is good English language.'
> 'Are you fair dinkum?'
> 'No. I am Italian.' (57)

In the 1950s, Central – conversational shorthand for the area around Central Station – was the location of the main police lock-up in Sydney. With this example, as with many others, Nino finds that the gap between words and things can often be an unfathomable chasm. On an existential level, Nino's problem in the conversation quoted above is that he is both Italian *and* fair dinkum, yet, until he masters this peculiar new system of signification within which he is now immersed, these two identities will remain mutually exclusive. Austin's point about the productive power of words is perfectly illustrated by this vignette. Via this exchange, Nino has been shown in the starkest terms possible that his improper use of the colloquial literally has the power to take him to a place to which he has absolutely no desire to go.

Through encounters such as this, Nino learns quite quickly that it is words as much as deeds that are crucial to the process of becoming Australian. Not only do words possess the power to affect his physical position, they also possess the transformative power to reshape his identity. In fact, by the end of his first day's work he has successfully begun the process of cultural transformation to which the book is a testament. This is not so much because he has demonstrated that he can stand in the hot sun for hours digging trenches at the building site (even though this is a crucial demonstration of manliness and 'Australian-ness'), but because he is sharp enough to pick up and then put to use the linguistic tools he hears in action around him. On entering a pub for an after-work drink with his new mates, and asked by Joe what he will have, Nino answers: 'I reckon I could knock over a schooner'. The response is good-natured laughter all round, and Nino realises in an instant that, as far as his workmates are concerned, he has been 'accepted into their company' (44).

In analytical terms, and from a point of view particularly concerned with cultural history, we could say that this stress O'Grady places on the value of the Australian way of speaking embodies the creative power of the discourse of assimilation, in both its official and unofficial forms, in Australian society at the time. By the late 1950s, the expansion of the immigration program had pushed the old order of White Australia (founded along with the nation in 1901) beyond its structural limits. In 1958, Commonwealth officers stopped

---

8   J.L. Austin, *How to do Things with Words*, 2nd edn (Oxford: Oxford University Press, 1975), pp. 5–6.

administering the dictation test which had been the policy's fundamental tool of restriction since its inception. Within another decade or so, the entire White Australia policy itself had been quietly retired as Australia's official immigration strategy.

From the time European colonists took the landmass of Australia from its Indigenous owners until the middle of the twentieth century, the modern Australian nation had possessed a dominant form of racial coherence. It was British and it was white, and it could logically be defended on the basis of 'correct' and 'incorrect' racial types. But once the dominant notion of race began to be compromised by an ever-increasing expansion of the category of 'white' to include southern Europeans, language was forced to carry ever more of the burden of defining the preferred national type. Similarly, as the defining category of race (White) tied to language (English) became more and more unworkable as an administrative technology, so the cultural concept 'way of life' became increasingly crucial as a delineating marker. And this is why O'Grady has Nino testify that he cannot record the Australian language without also providing a record of the people who speak it, because, in a society no longer defined on the basis of racial homogeneity, way of life is now *the* indicator of what constitutes an Australian – with this way of life, in turn, only really made visible via a constant articulation and re-articulation of the language of which it is constituted.

In 1957 *They're a Weird Mob* was therefore launched into circulation in a nation that, for the previous six decades, had its racial and cultural integrity defended by a dictation test. Now, however, discrimination on the basis of language (as a default category for race) was no longer official policy; rather, it had been replaced by the idea of assimilation, a seemingly organic governmental response to the increasing numbers of foreigners within the borders of the nation. There was now no question that Australia needed to accept foreigners, but it was very much a reciprocal arrangement: as far as the opinion makers and policy planners were concerned, the foreigners who were invited in would need just as much to accept Australia.

Much of the discursive force of assimilation, as it is manifested in *They're a Weird Mob*, works through a choice of words as markers for a way of being in the world. Australian words, it would seem, really do have the power to make their speaker 'Australian'. And this, ultimately, is the message that Nino, pseudo-Italian-Anglo-Celtic-Australian, imparts to his readers. As he advises New Australians towards the end of his narrative: 'Mix with Australians, listen to them, work with them, and practice the secret sentences you hear, so that you can say them exactly as you heard them' (202).

It is difficult not to draw the conclusion from passages such as this that O'Grady was being at least a little ironic in his celebration of the virtues of the Australian way of life. But, again, O'Grady seems to have been backing more than one horse in this particular race, as the following stridently assimilationist statement from the book's conclusion attests:

> There are far too many New Australians in this country who are still mentally living in their homelands, who mix with people of their own nationality, and try to retain their own language and customs. Who even try to persuade Australians to adopt their customs and manners. Cut it out. There is no better way of life in the world than that of the Australian. I firmly believe this … He fears no one,

crawls to no one, and acknowledges no master. Learn his way. Learn his language. (204)

Had *They're a Weird Mob* been a novel of little impact, an obscure piece of working-class fiction that had sold only moderately, its significance as an object of culture would be principally as a curio. It was, however, anything but obscure; in fact, it was probably the most widely read, or at least widely disseminated, work of fiction ever published in Australia. Yet in relentlessly adhering to only one perspective in its account of the Italian-Australian immigrant experience of the 1950s, presenting this as a definitive account, and indeed amplifying this claim by purporting to speak with the voice of an actual immigrant, *They're a Weird Mob* embodied an aggressively one-sided narrative of the migrant experience. And within the climate of 1950s assimilationist Australia no real-life Italian immigrant was likely to come forward to present an alternative version of the story to Nino Culotta, as neither Australia's publishing industry, nor the overwhelmingly Anglo-Celtic reading public, could have supported such an author even if one had existed. In fact, it would be more than two decades before an Italian-Australian author produced such a book, *Paese Fortunato* (1981) – *Oh Lucky Country* (1984) – and inevitably, perhaps, in terms of the major transformations of the cultural landscape over this time, the author would be a woman: Rosa Cappiello.

At the peak of its phenomenal popularity, the closest approximation in textual form to any kind of counter argument to the assimilationist preaching of *They're a Weird Mob* appeared not in Australia but in Italy, and not in the form of a work of popular fiction, but in a single scene of a European art film. The narrative of Michelangelo Antonioni's masterpiece of 1959, *L'Avventura*, follows a group of friends as they search the coastal islands and towns of northern Sicily for a member of their party who has gone missing from a boating holiday. On a small and barren island, with night coming on and a storm approaching, they take shelter in a hut. Soon the occupant appears, a fisherman, who tells the three bourgeois Romans about how he has come back to the island after thirty years living in Australia. But these narcissists have no interest in his story: they ask him no questions about himself, or Australia, or the years he spent there; all they care about is the adventure of their search. Indeed the film's macho protagonist, Sandro, goes on to push the man around in the very same way that Nino pushes around the southern Italian he meets on the train in *They're a Weird Mob*.

Following the brief encounter with the fisherman, the narrative of *L'Avventura* moves on to mainland Sicily, leaving him on his island. We do not see him again and we learn no more about him. But this nameless fisherman is an infinitely more authentic migrant figure than O'Grady's fictional Nino, with all his exploitative humour. One of the hallmarks of Italian neorealist cinema, of which the younger Antonioni was one of the pioneers, was the use of non-professional actors in lesser roles, and this unnamed man from the Lipari Islands is clearly telling his own rather than an invented story. He had travelled halfway across the world, struggled and got by; and, even though he speaks nostalgically of his years in Australia, for some reason things there did not work out, so he returned to his Mediterranean home. Clearly, this ex-migrant did not follow O'Grady's orders to 'learn the way' of the Australian in order to 'get accepted by him', and thereby never leave the Promised Land.

Antonioni's fisherman was not alone in having his migration journey end where it started. In 1961 the Italian Government suspended its bilateral migration treaty with Australia – which had been in place for the previous decade – on the grounds that Italian emigrants were not receiving as good a deal in relation to assisted passage, access to welfare and so on, as were the 'favoured' migrants of northern Europe and Britain. Consequently, over the next few years ever greater numbers of Italians began to return home from Australia while fewer chose to make the trip out. In 1967 a new treaty was negotiated addressing the key issue in the Italian favour, and emigration numbers again began to rise.[9]

Given this context, the fisherman's story stands in direct contrast to that of Nino Culotta. Yet it is also limited as a retort to O'Grady's appropriation of an Italian speaking position. While this brief moment in *L'Avventura* does indeed provide an authentic voice to speak back to that of the inauthentic Nino Culotta, it does so in a textual context that is quite dissimilar to that of a populist novel, because it is an art film and so, by its very nature, a profoundly bourgeois text. Subtitled and released into Australian cinemas in the early 1960s as an archetype of the foreign film, the Cannes Film Festival Jury Prize-winning *L'Avventura* was screening to Anglo-Australians at the very same time that the nation was reading *Cop This Lot* (1960), O'Grady's sequel to *They're a Weird Mob* – but it is highly unlikely that the two texts found much common ground in terms of an audience.

One of the key tenets of the modernist text, both literary and cinematic, is an element of social and cultural critique; though in liberal capitalist democracies this has generally been a form of critique tailored to an audience possessed of enough cultural capital both to make sense of it and to desire it in the first place. As O'Grady famously said, Patrick White's *Voss* was a work he just 'couldn't understand'.[10] Similarly, even with subtitles, *L'Avventura* was still speaking a language unfamiliar to the majority of Australian fans of the populist O'Grady. Perhaps this is an inevitable consequence of the fact that a popular text will tend to be ideologically complacent in that, in order to achieve and maintain its popularity, in political terms it will always need to be in harmony with the status quo; hence the ongoing role, within the social and cultural experiences of modernity, of the avant-garde as an elitist, anti-popular force.

While O'Grady as Nino Culotta usurped the Italian migrant 'voice' for his mainly Anglo-Australian readers, this did not mean that competing voices were wholly absent from the circuits of local popular culture. They were just not speaking in English, but in Italian and, in one particular instance, in Calabrian dialect.[11] Salvatore Tripodi migrated from Palmi in Calabria to Melbourne in 1952, but did not enjoy the experience and returned home after a few years. Working in the oral story-telling tradition of the *cantastorie*, Tripodi recounted how the desire for economic advancement lured him to Australia and into a menial job in a suburban Melbourne glass factory. Yet despite the hype, all Australia seemed to offer the migrant was material wellbeing, and ultimately, for Tripodi, these economic advantages were of little consequence when compared to the greater riches of the friendly social environment back at home with family.

---

9 Murphy, p. 107.

10 Quoted in Carter, p. 62.

11 Thanks to Liliana Zavaglia for drawing my attention to this reference.

*Cantastorie*, or ballad-singing narration, is a mixture of humorous songs and anecdotes, and *Le Avventure di Salvatore Tripodi* found material form as a 45rpm record that circulated among Italians, particularly Calabrians, living in Melbourne and Sydney in the early 1960s. In a mixture of Italian, Calabrian and Australian English, Tripodi offered the sort of advice to his listeners that would have seen O'Grady and Nino Culotta fuelling their barbeques with his record: do not be tricked into thinking Australia was 'the land of milk and honey. Stay in your own homes and enjoy life with your little ones'.[12] Subsequently, Tripodi recorded further oral accounts of his Australian adventures for a Palmi record company, recordings that were still selling in the early twenty-first century.[13]

Tripodi's satirising of the Italian-Australian economic migrancy experience was very much in the long tradition of Southern Italian cultural mockery, exemplified perhaps by the translation of Goethe's iconic *Die Leiden von Junges Werther* into a Neapolitan puppet show in the early nineteenth century.[14] In this sense Tripodi's work formed an ideal counterpoint to O'Grady's *They're a Weird Mob*, but it is important to note that this was oral storytelling, not prose fiction, and that even within the dynamics of the popular culture of the time there were still strict delineations and boundaries regarding access to texts. O'Grady was writing for an audience that read English and was acutely sensitive to the nuances of written representations of their language, while Tripodi was recording for an audience that spoke both broader Italian and Calabrian dialect. Given the ethno-cultural dynamics of Australia at the time, these two groups were largely mutually exclusive, despite the presence of crossover figures like O'Grady's fictional Nino. Generally, New Australians knew all about *They're a Weird Mob*, but they also knew that it was a book about them, not for them. Meanwhile, the average Anglo-Australian, did not even have a clue that Salvatore Tripodi existed.

*They're a Weird Mob* is often credited with leading Anglo-Australians to an acceptance of New Australians, but while O'Grady's work may indeed have played some role in this development, it is far too narrow a text to deserve unqualified acclaim. Immigration succeeded and Australia grew and prospered not because of a patronising, conservative work of popular fiction by an imposter writer, but because of the countless personal struggles waged every day over decades by hundreds of thousands of nameless immigrants, the true heroes of postwar Australia: people like the fisherman in *L'Avventura*, the people who worked hard and built a complex multicultural nation in which respect for difference displaced the dead hand of assimilation.

Initially, the example of *They're a Weird Mob* leaves one in little doubt as to why conservative politicians like John Howard and Pauline Hanson spent the late 1990s expressing the desire to 'take Australia back to the 1950s'. The simplistic, assimiliationist landscape sketched out as the background to the antics of Nino Culotta really does depict a conservative utopia. In fact, the book's final two sentences see O'Grady's two-handed irony in full flight, with Nino thanking God for letting him be an Australian, and then speculating that perhaps God is in fact an Australian Himself (205).

---

12 Gaetano Rando, 'Expressions of the Calabrian Diaspora in Australian Writing 2004', *University of Wollongong Faculty of Arts Papers*, available at ro.uow.edu.au/artspapers/20 [accessed 15 March 2011].

13 See Rando, pp. 10–11.

14 Michael Hulse, Introduction in Johann Wolfgang von Goethe, *The Sorrows of Young Werther* (London: Penguin, 1989), p. 16.

Accept these New Australians, O'Grady seems to be saying, but do not accept them for what they are. Accept them if, and only if, they are prepared to become 'like us'. In terms of both style and content this message differs not at all from that trumpeted by John Howard forty years later. This is a paradox, though, because it is precisely to this period of great cultural uncertainty – of a massive twisting of the fabric of the nation, of struggle and debate over what it was that actually made an 'Australian' – that Howard and Hanson and their like dreamt of 'returning'.

Yet it never really was the way the dream would have us believe. The supposed golden years of the 1950s were in fact the very moment at which it became clear once and for all that the world was never going to 'leave Australia alone', and that Australia could never just shut the door and hope that the world would go away, even if this had been the guiding dream of Federation some fifty years earlier. Indeed, it was at this time that so many of the key decisions were made that have produced our contemporary globalised nation, with the decision to open up Australia to a diverse population from all over the world being perhaps the most important of them all.

If there is something truly significant about *They're a Weird Mob*, it is in its rendering of the speech of Anglo-Celtic working-class Australians. Indeed, it is remarkable that O'Grady manages both to capture and reproduce a genuinely oral idiom in a way that allows it to live and breathe, rather than blurring or reducing it. But this too serves ends that are ultimately quite conservative. The characters may work and strive, but they do so within a purely market-driven society: there are no trade unions, no government services, no tax officials; indeed, other than police, there are no organs of civil society of any kind within the pages of the book. Again, this is a remarkably selective rendering of the times, all the more so for the fact that it was written in the decade in which Menzies tried to eliminate communism from Australia's political canvas, and the Australian Labor Party split apart over the very same issue.

John O'Grady claimed that he was not really a writer of fiction, but a social commentator, and that his work was in essence 'reporting with exaggeration'.[15] In the end, however, the key point is that *They're a Weird Mob* is not an exercise in social commentary but an intensely ideological work of fiction. And, in this sense, it really is an exercise in persuasion: in persuading Old Australians that they should relax their xenophobia to some degree and accept New Australians, provided of course that they are worthy of being accepted; a judgment that in the last instance will always rest on the degree to which the foreigner in question is prepared to assimilate.

John O'Grady's astoundingly popular book was a cultural tool to help Anglo-Celtic Australians deal with this self-initiated invasion of the foreign. And this is really the crucial element that permitted the book to speak to such a massive audience. If the national subject had not been undergoing such a severe identity crisis as that which had been provoked by the postwar immigration program, then this particular text would never even have been written. Essentially, *They're a Weird Mob* is a guide to being an assimilated Australian, and in many ways it was simply a lifestyle book, albeit one that was a bestseller in an era before the lifestyle book had become mainstream.

---

15  Quoted in Bosworth, p. 13.

## 'HE LACKS ALMOST ALL THE QUALITIES OF THE NOVELIST': G.M. GLASKIN AND HIS AUSTRALIAN CONTEMPORARIES

*Jeremy Fisher*

Gerry Glaskin was quite a guy, and quite a writer. With a prodigious output across a range of genres, he wrote nine novels, a number of dramatic works, children's fiction, science fiction, romance and short stories. He was not a writer parsimonious with words. Even at school, Glaskin was known for his long essays. In his memoir *One Way to Wonderland* (1984) he writes:

> How often, when telling us the subject of an essay we must write, did Mr Constantine [the English teacher] insist that we should fill at least two pages of the ruled foolscap paper we used. 'But you, Glaskin,' he would inevitably add, 'must confine yourself to no more than ten!'[1]

Glaskin's writing owed much to his life's experiences. Even in fictional form, the majority of his works are closely modelled on events that happened to him. As we shall see, his was not an inconsequential life.

Gerry Glaskin was born in Perth on 16 December 1923. His parents struggled to make ends meet, even though, or perhaps because, they managed to have seven children, of whom Gerry was the eldest by some years. The boy was academically gifted and selected for a scholarship to study at the prestigious Perth Modern School, the alma mater of such prominent West Australians as H.C. Coombs, Kim Beazley Senior, Bob Hawke, Sir Paul Hasluck, playwright Alan Seymour, entertainer Rolf Harris, economist Ross Garnaut and businesswoman Janet Holmes à Court. The school was opened in 1911 as Western Australia's first public senior secondary school, and it remains Western Australia's only academically selective school today.

Glaskin began his writing there. As his confidence in his own abilities grew, he communicated with local writers in his first attempts at becoming a published author. He was in touch with West Australian writer Henrietta Drake-Brockman from this time:

> [Henrietta], after reading my first attempt at a short story when I was only fourteen [in 1937], said: 'Gerry, when I was fourteen I wrote a wonderful short story about Venice. You've chosen South America –' And now both of us write about the places we know.[2]

---

1  G.M. Glaskin, *One Way to Wonderland: Letters to a Penfriend in Europe* (Fremantle: Fremantle Arts Centre Press, 1984), p. 2.
2  Glaskin, *A Small Selection of Short Stories* (London: Barrie and Rockliff, 1962), p. ii.

This appears in the 'Dedication' to his *A Small Selection of Short Stories* (1962). Glaskin remained in contact with Drake-Brockman up until her death in 1968, and in 1971 he described her as 'a very close and dear friend'.[3] For her part, Drake-Brockman assisted the young writer in his career when she used a selection from his first novel *A World of Our Own* (1955) in a 1959 anthology.[4]

Glaskin left Perth Modern in 1939 when he was fifteen to take up a position as a trainee accountant and add to the family's modest finances. Two years later, at seventeen, he enlisted in the Royal Australian Navy. His first preference was for the Air Force, but they would not take recruits until they were eighteen. 'I thought it would be one way, perhaps, of helping to free Sjoerd', he wrote in *One Way to Wonderland*, referring to his Dutch penfriend, Sjoerd Steunebrink, with whom he would remain in contact until Sjoerd's death in October 1997.[5]

He was invalided out of the Navy in 1942 after being injured in an accident with a winch and a cable. His arms were severely wrenched, and he spent some time in hospital recovering. Indeed, Glaskin would suffer the consequences of this injury for the rest of his life. In hospital, he began sending stories out for publication. Since he could not use his arms, he dictated the stories to another patient who did not have the use of his legs. His first story, 'Got him!', was written in this way and published in the Perth *Western Mail*.[6]

In 1960, Glaskin returned to these events in his fourth novel, *A Lion in the Sun*.[7] When first offered to his publisher, Barrie & Rockliff, the narrator was titled Gerry M. Glaskin. However, the publisher would not support a literary device now quite common in fiction and 'could not cope with the blatant autobiographical, naïve, unsophisticated, know-all Australian persona in what purported to be a novel set in an exotic location', so the book was edited to be narrated by Geoffrey M. Graham.[8] In this book, set in Singapore on the edge of independence from Britain in 1963, Geoffrey Graham meets Bradley Chase in a hospital where both are recovering from battle service injuries. Geoff has lost the use of his arms in an accident on board a ship. Chase has been shot in the spine while flying his plane: his legs are paralysed and he is in a wheelchair. The narrative charts Geoff's attempt to distribute the author copies of a book of poems written by the missing, presumed dead, and once crippled Brad. The novel is also rich in describing the manner in which Geoff, with no use of his arms, and Brad, with no use of his legs, organise baths together in hospital. In reviewing the book some years later, Sylvia Marchant felt that the first person narrator was 'possessed of questionable standards, for the love of his life is obviously our hero'.[9] Sexual relationships in Glaskin's works were mixed and varied, though usually covert given the moral attitudes of his time.

Glaskin continued to write even after he finally managed to enlist, with some subterfuge given his injuries from naval service, in the Royal Australian Air Force (RAAF). He was

---

3 Glaskin, letter to G.C. O'Donnell, Chairman, Australian Society of Authors, 17 September 1971 (Australian Society of Authors).

4 Henrietta Drake-Brockman, *West Coast Stories: An Anthology* (Sydney: Angus & Robertson, 1959).

5 Glaskin, *One Way to Wonderland*, p. 149.

6 John Hetherington, *Forty-Two Faces*, (Melbourne: F.W. Cheshire, 1962), p. 228.

7 G.M. Glaskin, *A Lion in the Sun* (London: Barrie & Rockliff, 1960).

8 Carolyn Van Langenberg, 'Below the Surface' (letter), *Australian Book Review* 248 (February 2003): 5.

9 Sylvia Marchant, 'Lightweight Tales of Aussies Abroad', *Canberra Times*, 27 May 1995, C12.

then sent to Canada for crew training. He never saw active service in the RAAF, however, as the war in Europe ended as he was finishing his training and he was sent back to Australia.

His short story 'Sometimes It Wasn't So Nice' won third place in the 1946 Australian School of Journalism competition. The story concerns Joe, a sick bay attendant on a sinking ship, who has to leave his friend Andy to drown as Joe obeys orders from the Medical Officer. While the story maintains a conventional theme in terms of following orders and doing one's duty, there is a clear homoerotic undertone in the relationship between Joe and Andy. This is an early sign that Glaskin was never afraid to take on controversial themes and topics. Later, he would also experiment with technique and style, but in his early career his stories were conventional in voice and form.

Around this time, Glaskin also encountered the writer and school teacher, John Keith Ewers, another alumnus of the Perth Modern School.[10] Ewers was significant in the West Australian literary community. He was influential in the Fellowship of Australian Writers and wrote the first textbook for creative writing in Australia.[11] Gerry's mother had met Ewers when he acted as an air-raid warden in Perth during the Second World War. Ewers, an avuncular character in the small Perth writing world, advised Gerry to write while he was still young. Glaskin took that advice and soon met with some success. His manuscript for the book that would become *A World of Our Own*, which he wrote in a spurt in 1949 before he left to take up positions in Singapore – first with a motor firm, then as a stockbroker – shared the judges' commendation for the Commonwealth Jubilee in 1951.

Judging from what Glaskin wrote in an obituary, Ewers also appears to have encouraged him to leave Perth for Singapore,[12] though he returned home from time to time. He was back in 1955 and applied, successfully, for a £1000 Commonwealth Literary Fund Grant that year, but never took it up. Instead, he went back to Singapore, claiming he needed to work to earn money. But was this really the case? There is evidence that, on another fleeting visit in 1961, Glaskin apeared in court in Perth on a charge of wilful exposure. While he defended himself forcefully, he failed to convince the magistrate of his innocence.[13] 'Wilful exposure' was a common charge in those times for men caught soliciting other men at gay beats (although Gerry may just have been taking advantage of the local, illegal nude beach). Was a similar incident in 1955 responsible for Ewers sending Glaskin packing back to Singapore, despite his award? When in 2004 I spoke to Leo van de Pas, who lived with Gerry from 1968 until Gerry's death, he told me:

> He suffered from the tall poppy syndrome in Perth. He was resented for being successful, especially successful overseas. Gerry didn't get the Commonwealth Prize money because one influential person argued he didn't live in Australia.[14]

---

10  Glaskin, letter to G.C. O'Donnell, 17 September 1971 (Australian Society of Authors).

11  J.K. Ewers, *Creative Writing in Australia: A Selective Survey* (Melbourne: Georgian House, 1962).

12  Glaskin, 'So Long Keith Ewers', *Australian Author* 10.3 (1978): 30–33.

13  John Burbidge, 'Underexposed: Gerald Glaskin's Fiction', *The Gay and Lesbian Review Worldwide* (November–December 2007), available at findarticles.com/p/articles/mi_hb3491/is_6_14/ai_n29385790/?tag=content;col1 (accessed 3 March, 2010).

14  Interview with Leo van de Pas, 2004.

This influential person was identified as Ewers. But Ewers simply may have been saving Glaskin from himself. He had a reputation for assisting other authors.

Certainly Ewers was the epitome of respectability. As noted, he was prominent in the Fellowship of Australian Writers, becoming State President in 1938–39 and 1946–47, and was also involved with the Australian Society of Authors (ASA, founded in 1963) as Regional Vice-President for Western Australia. Ewers was also acquainted with Walter Murdoch, who had become the first Professor of English at the University of Western Australia in 1912, and its Chancellor from 1943 to 1947.[15]

Glaskin somehow missed falling within this respectable aura; Perth would never embrace him as a favourite son. He was living back in Singapore when his first book *A World of Our Own* was finally published in 1955.[16] *The Straits Times* recorded the publication of *A World of Our Own*, including a favourable quote from C.P. Snow and a photo of the 'stockbroker' author, on page 3 of its issue of 22 May.[17] The book also received a not unfavourable review in the London *Times*.[18] But the 1957 review in *Southerly* by 'H.H. & J.L.' was awful:

> overpraised [though by whom is not revealed] ... He lacks almost all the qualities of the novelist ... he has no natural gift ... His characters don't live or grow ... One hopes Mr Glaskin will seek, and find his right field, for his is not a book to dismiss too lightly. But it seems as though his talents do not lie in the direction of the novel.[19]

It seems in retrospect to be an attack on the person of the author rather than an objective assessment of the book. One wonders who H.H. and J.L. were, and why they were so unkind. Ewers reviewed the book in the *West Australian*[20] and later wrote of it: 'In spite of a certain exuberance of words and of situations, this first novel introduced a writer with an ability to create characters and to weave a closely integrated plot behind a superficially loose construction'. This was a kinder and more considered opinion than that in the semi-anonymous *Southerly* review.[21] The book was not a great success in Australia, but it sold 12 000 copies in the British hardback edition, another 15 000 in the Norwegian hardback edition, and 30 000 as a Norwegian paperback, establishing Glaskin's reputation as an Australian writer more successful overseas than in his own country.[22]

While he remained successful outside Australia, Glaskin continued to have difficulties with his image and reputation in his home country, to which he had returned in 1968, again taking up residence in Perth. This may well have been due to his frankness, abundantly apparent in the many letters he wrote. Such letters finally brought about the end of his relationship with Ewers. The pair fell out in 1971 over a dispute involving Nancy Keesing,

---

15 Brian Dibble, telephone conversation, 19 July 2010.
16 Glaskin, *A World of Our Own* (London: James Barrie, 1955).
17 'Stockbroker Writes Book', *The Straits Times*, 22 May 1955, p. 3.
18 *Times Literary Supplement*, 24 June 1955, p. 345.
19 H.H. & J.L., 'Australian Literature: Notes', *Southerly* 17.4 (1957): 237.
20 Glaskin, 'So Long Keith Ewers', p. 30.
21 Ewers, *Creative Writing in Australia*, p. 195.
22 Hetherington, *Forty-Two Faces*, p. 227.

who was then editor of the ASA's *Australian Author*, while Ewers was the Society's Regional Vice-President. The dispute involved an unsolicited article Glaskin had sent to the *Australian Author* in March, replying to one by Michael Page, publisher of Rigby. The article was provisionally accepted for the July issue by retiring editor Barrie Ovenden. However, it was mislaid during the changeover in editorship to Keesing. Keesing did not want to publish it, but wrote to Glaskin on 9 July apologising for the oversight and suggesting the article be shortened and then perhaps room could be found in the October issue. In her friendly and conversational letter she also indicated there would have been no room in the July issue anyway as she had to publish four obituaries (one for Kenneth Slessor). Unfortunately, this was not received well. Glaskin responded on 14 July, asserting that living authors were more important than dead ones and insisting his article be published as originally written. Ewers, founding Chair Dal Stivens, as well as the Chairman Gus O'Donnell, defended Nancy Keesing, but Glaskin was not to be mollified and resigned from the ASA. In a final letter to Gus O'Donnell on 17 September 1971, Glaskin quotes Ewers' defence of Keesing, then goes on to say:

> As you can see, my resignation did not bother him much, or not as much as his personal friendship with Mrs. Keesing; he did not wish to read my article; Mrs. Keesing, a poetess, did not wish to publish it and in any case, to me, has no qualification to 'be honest with me about it', and Mr. Page's publisher point of view is evidently of more importance than an author's.[23]

It was an odd way to treat an otherwise steadfast friend of nearly thirty years.

Glaskin rejoined in 1973 to embroil the ASA in a dispute with Angus & Robertson. His erstwhile A & R editor in London (A & R then had offices there), Felix Brenner, wrote on 18 April:

> although I think that Gerry is a very good writer, if undisciplined, none of my colleagues shared my opinion ... [A]fter his outburst we feel that we are busy enough and do not need another difficult author.[24]

There is some wonderment here. Since 1964, Brenner had been the partner of noted film critic David Shipman.[25] The two lived in Chelsea. Letters in the ASA's files reveal Glaskin had asked Brenner to be seconder for an application by Gerry's partner Leo van de Pas for a Commonwealth Literary Fund application. Brenner wrote on 12 April agreeing to be referee, but carefully avoiding 'any responsibility for publishing' van de Pas' proposed genealogical work. There are some indications of intimacy; Brenner signs off the letter with 'Bless you', and there is a colloquial reference to Glaskin's health. Eight days later he was returning all Glaskin's manuscripts to his agent. Was this a spat between queens? The Australians weighed in with the usual Glaskin putdown. A & R Publisher Richard Walsh,

---

23   Glaskin, letter to G.C. O'Donnell, 17 September 1971.

24   Felix Brenner, letter to literary agent David Bolt, 18 April 1973 (Australian Society of Authors).

25   Richard Cohen, 'David Shipman: Obituary', *The Independent*, 24 April 1996, available at www.independent.co.uk/news/people/obituary--david-shipman-1306512.html [accessed 20 July, 2010].

in Sydney, added on 6 June 1973: 'Gerry is too facile in his writing for his own good and an impetuous and difficult author for publishers to handle'.[26]

But Gerry had some literary form by this time. He had published nine novels, as well as a children's book (*A Waltz in the Hills*, 1961), a travel book (*The Land That Sleeps*, 1961) and numerous short stories. His books had also sold well in the United Kingdom and Europe, and he had been published in American editions. In most markets, except Australia, he was popular and also somewhat controversial: his themes were cutting edge. *A Minor Portrait* (1957, later republished as a paperback titled *The Mistress* which sold 75 000 copies[27]) features an adolescent boy seduced by an older woman. *The Beach of Passionate Love* (1961) is set in Malaysia and features interracial, underage sex. The pseudonymous *No End to the Way* (1965, credited to Neville Jackson), probably Australia's first overt homosexual novel, had done particularly well despite, or perhaps because of, its being banned from importation into Australia on first publication as a result of its overt homosexual narrative. The book was also published in an American edition (by McFadden-Bartell) and as a Corgi paperback, and ironically was Glaskin's most successful book. In January 1985 he wrote to Bill Larkins, then editor of *Australian Author*, to advise that *No End to the Way* had been reissued in a new Corgi edition after three reprints of the paperback edition in 1967 (twice) and 1968, following the original hardcover edition in 1965.[28] His publishers had recommended he use a pseudonym for it because they were concerned about his reputation. This book, written in sustained second person, is Glaskin's magnum opus. Few other books have used second person so consistently. The resultant tone of alienation, of an outsider looking in, fits perfectly with the subject of a gay man coming to terms with his sexuality in closeted times.[29]

In later years, Glaskin's reputation as a difficult author ensured that most publishers rejected his work out of hand, rather than face the prospect of a fiery relationship. Even when he was accepted for publication, he did not make it easy for his publishers. The small Western Australian firm of Fremantle Arts Centre Press (FACP) took on *One Way to Wonderland*, publishing it in 1984. Glaskin, probably quite rightly, was extremely critical of their distribution and marketing. He wrote a long, rambling letter to Ron Davies, then Western Australia's Minister for the Arts and responsible for funding of the press, criticising it:

> With over twenty publications, most of them into numerous overseas publications and translations, I regret to say that my dealings with the Fremantle Arts Centre Press have been the most difficult and distressing I have ever experienced. Indeed, I have never encountered anywhere near such off-hand treatment and incompetence.[30]

---

26  Richard Walsh, letter to G.C. O'Donnell, 6 June 1973 (Australian Society of Authors).
27  Hetherington, *Forty-Two Faces*, p. 228.
28  Glaskin, letter to Bill Larkins, 30 January 1985 (Australian Society of Authors).
29  Jeremy Fisher, 'When You is Me: Sustained Second-Person Narrative Voice in the Works of G.M. Glaskin and Peter Kocan', *Journal of Australian Writers and Writing* 1 (2010), available at www.australianliterarycompendium.com/journal/pdf/JeremyFisher.pdf [accessed 24 March 2011].
30  Glaskin, letter to Ron Davies, MLA, WA Minister for the Arts, 2 February 1985 (Australian Society

Glaskin's opinion was coloured by the fact that FACP was dragging its feet regarding commitment to publish his manuscript, 'Do Animals Go to Heaven?' He had received a letter from FACP on 16 January 1985, advising that this work would not be published in 1985. His furious letter to the minister followed within days, with copies to the ASA.

At the same time as this, Glaskin was battling Heinemann over the slow return of rejected manuscripts (they also rejected 'Do Animals Go to Heaven?'). On 6 February 1985, Glaskin wrote to Nick Hudson, then Heinemann Managing Director. He took exception to Heinemann classifying Barbara Ker Wilson's *Jane Austen in Australia* as an Australian book, then went on to conclude:

> Sorry, but some of you may some day get to respect authors and books, and perhaps even like them. After all, they have provided you all with very nice livelihoods, something few of us ever get back in return, nor can I see that we shall with attitudes such as yours, and those who choose to hide behind your coattails like [Heinemann editor] John Kerr ... So best wishes for a good life. Mine is now music and my beautiful beach.[31]

Glaskin continued to write, but his publishing career was effectively over. This did not stop him offering his opinion on matters related to his peers. In May 1985, he wrote to Robert Pullan, the new editor of *Australian Author*, to express his dislike of the new format of the magazine. He also expressed his views on the elevation of his fellow West Australian, Elizabeth Jolley, to the position of President of the ASA:

> I cannot see with her limited publication and time as a writer that she is the kind of person who can serve much purpose to the Society, let alone who can assume such a position when there are so many others known far more widely both in and outside Australia.[32]

Perhaps Gerry considered himself one of those others; but, in the light of such correspondence, his contemporaries chose to differ. He received a terse acknowledgement of his letter from ASA Executive Director Denise Yates, who advised it would be discussed at a meeting in six weeks time. There is no record of any further reply, but there is a lined foolscap page jotted with the dates of the many 1985 letters, phone calls and other contacts between Gerry and the ASA.

Later still, on 5 September 1985, Glaskin wrote to the then Chairman Ken Methold on a wide range of matters: copyright in China; the ongoing dispute with FACP; motions of his put to the Perth annual general meeting that had not been promulgated to members; and a final paragraph noting that he had

> not had a return call from Brian Dibble, which brings me to say that there are now a number of us who feel that his academic aspirations are too much in

---

of Authors).

31  Glaskin, letter to Nick Hudson, 6 February 1985 (Australian Society of Authors).
32  Glaskin, letter to Robert Pullan, 2 May 1985 (Australian Society of Authors).

diametric contradiction with the requirements of professional authors for him to
be a satisfactory representative for the State of Western Australia.³³

Brian Dibble had come to Australia from the United States to teach writing. He is now Emeritus Professor at Curtin University in Perth, author of *Doing Life*,³⁴ a biography of Elizabeth Jolley, and a continuing representative for Western Australia within the ASA.

Gerry Glaskin died fifteen years later on 11 March 2000, his last year a long, slow decline through which he was nursed and cared for by Leo van de Pas. Throughout his life he maintained long friendships and correspondences with other Australian writers, even though these were sometimes fractious. But he never seemed to fit in to the Australian literary community. It did not help that he was better known and more successful in Europe than most other Australian writers.

His sexuality may also have been considered problematic by Australian audiences. Unlike Patrick White, he did not have a 'companion' to suggest that he led a life akin to heteronormative monogamy until 1968, when Leo van de Pas came from the Netherlands to live with him. Even then, there was a considerable age gap, and though the two lived in separate but adjoining flats, they would have rattled the conventions of provincial Perth. They met in a gay bar in Amsterdam, and Glaskin asked Leo to come live with him within twenty-four hours of their meeting – so he was a fast worker when it came to matters of lust and the heart.³⁵ In *No End to the Way*, the narrator Ray Wharton also meets his Dutch lover Cor in a gay bar, though this one is in Perth. Van de Pas has told me that Cor was based on one of Glaskin's earlier lovers. In 1962 John Hetherington wrote that Glaskin, when in Australia (that is, before his return in 1968),

> nearly every afternoon … drove in his station wagon to Swanbourne beach, about two miles away [from his home], and walked on the sand alone for an hour or more, thinking out what he would write next day.³⁶

During at least one of these walks he was arrested for exposing his person, so there appears to have been more to his walks than just thinking. Sexuality and its various expressions is a significant feature of Glaskin's writing, as is his capacity for using his own life as material for his stories.

There was an intensity about Glaskin that could make him a staunch friend – his long relationship with Sjoerd Steunebrink is but one example – but could also make him appear abrasive. Brian Dibble certainly found him so when dealing with him on behalf of the ASA.³⁷ Yet Van de Pas, who spent over three decades with him, has a very different view of Glaskin, recalling that, 'over all those years I found Gerry to be warm, responsible, responsive and caring'.³⁸

---

33  Glaskin, letter to Ken Methold, 5 September 1985 (Australian Society of Authors).

34  Brian Dibble, *Doing Life: A Biography of Elizabeth Jolley* (Perth, University of Western Australia Press, 2008).

35  Fisher, interview with Leo van de Pas.

36  Hetherington, *Forty-two Faces*, p. 227.

37  Jeremy Fisher, telephone interview with Dibble, December 2010.

38  Leo van de Pas, 'Flaws, Not Only in the Glass', *Overland* 177 (2004): 74–76 (75).

# 21

## Anthologies and the Anti-republic of Australian Gay and Lesbian Poetry

*Ann Vickery*

Anthologies function as cultural cabinets in transforming poetry into muséal objects that indicate a particular set of values. Typically, such mapping has strongly marked and impermeable borders; anthologies become separate 'republics of letters' wherein each poem has democratic equivalency. At the same time, Andrew Michael Roberts suggests that anthology editors may seek to disrupt prevailing values by bringing attention to new groups in the poetic field.[1] Marjorie Perloff notes that in the United States a wave of minority communities began being anthologised in the 1980s, although poetry anthologies featuring women and African-American writers started being produced even earlier in the 1970s.[2] Underscored by the ideology that the personal was political, the focus of such anthologies was on claiming a voice for those marginalised or excluded in poetic formations.

This chapter examines how the unavowed nature of gay, lesbian, and queer communities finds expression in the genre of poetry, but also how it problematises the legislative role of anthologies. Indeed, editorial approaches towards the anthologisation of gay and lesbian poetry in Australia highlight a continuing resistance to representativeness and institutionalisation. While it is beyond the scope of this chapter to undertake a detailed comparative analysis, an investigation into the anthology history of Australian gay and lesbian poetries begins to reveal not only shared needs and attitudes between Australian and New Zealand gay and lesbian writers, and between gay and lesbian writers globally, but also quite culturally specific relations of sexuality to sociality and literary form.

With its focus on 'woman-identified' cultural production, the burgeoning feminist movement supported and was supported by lesbian poets. Yet there was still a struggle to vocalise *both* solidarity and difference. Eileen Myles has commented on her sense of invisibility as a lesbian poet when she arrived in New York in the 1970s:

> There wasn't a woman in that circle of poets, either, who could receive me and let me know I was heard. Alice Notley, who was married to Ted Berrigan, was there, and we were, and are, great friends, but she was a married woman and a mother and she was going to have a different life ... I made the model of what I needed

---

1   Andrew Michael Roberts, 'The Rhetoric of Value in Recent British Poetry Anthologies', in Jonathan Allison and Andrew Michael Roberts, eds, *Poetry and Contemporary Culture: The Question of Value* (Edinburgh: Edinburgh University Press, 2002), p. 101.

2   Perloff, Marjorie, 'Whose New American Poetry? Anthologizing in the Nineties', *Diacritics* 26.3–4 (1996): 104–23 (118).

there to be. I put lesbian content in the New York School poem because I wanted the poem to be there to receive me.[3]

A similar lack of identity could be found in Australia and New Zealand. Jill Jones notes that,

> Public lesbian and gay voices in poetry are a relatively new thing, so far as Australian poetry history goes. You would be looking hard to find anything other than the repressed, the presumed, the pronounless, the masked before the mid-1960s.[4]

And before editing the first anthology of gay New Zealand poetry, Jonathan Fisher recalls feeling

> as if I was working with a void. Certainly I knew many other poets, but as far as I could tell I seemed to be the only gay poet that was writing and being published in this country. I thought how wonderful it would be if there was a collection of New Zealand gay poetry that I could feel kinship to, but there was no such book and no major publisher had seemed interested in this as an idea.[5]

Gay and lesbian writing was largely undifferentiated from other writing of the sexual liberation movement. It would be featured predominantly in Australia in the 1970s in little magazines and independent presses, and most overtly in presses like InVersions, Nosukumo, and Wild and Woolley.[6] The first Australian anthology of gay and lesbian writing, *Edge City on Two Different Plans,* was published in 1983. It was followed by anthologies such as *The Exploding Frangipani: Lesbian Writing from Australia and New Zealand* (1990) and *Pink Ink* (1991). 2001 saw the first anthology of exclusively Australian lesbian poetry, *Sappho's Dreams and Delights*.[7] Only in 2009 would the first anthology specifically of both gay and lesbian Australian poetry appear with *Out of the Box: Contemporary Australian Gay and Lesbian Poets.*

---

3  Eileen Myles, quoted in Maggie Nelson, *Women, the New York School, and Other True Abstractions* (Iowa City: University of Iowa Press, 2007), p. 173.

4  Jill Jones, 'Going in Any Direction', in Michael Farrell and Jill Jones, eds, *Out of the Box: Contemporary Australian Gay and Lesbian Poets* (Glebe: Puncher & Wattmann, 2009), p. 20. Subsequent page references are given in-text.

5  Jonathan Fisher, Introduction, in Fisher, ed., *When Two Men Embrace: The New Zealand Anthology of Gay and Lesbian Poetry*, (Christchurch: Publishing Giant Press, 1999), p. 7.

6  Little magazines included *Compass* and *Imprint*. Wild and Woolley would publish titles such as *Fallen Angels* and *Invitation to a Marxist Lesbian Party*. Michael Hurley suggests that the dominant genres of lesbian and gay writing in the 1970s were 'nonfiction, coming-out stories, especially in student newspapers and university student orientation magazines; ephemeral, political leaflets; manifestoes; papers for the early national homosexual conferences; submissions to government departments by groups such as CAMP and Gay Task Force; and major educational material'. See Introduction, Kerry Bashford et al., *Pink Ink: An Anthology of Australian Lesbian and Gay Writers* (Redfern: Wicked Women Publications, 1991), p. 20. Subsequent page references are given in-text.

7  Beatriz Capello and Maralyn Rush, eds, *Sappho's Dreams and Delights: The Australian Anthology of Lesbian Poetry* (Earlwood: Bermac Publications, 2001). Volume 34 of *Stylus Poetry Journal* (2009) was a queer issue.

In contrast, *When Two Men Embrace: The New Zealand Anthology of Gay and Lesbian Poetry* and *Eat These Sweet Words: The New Zealand Anthology of Lesbian and Gay Poetry* were published a whole decade earlier in 1999. Jonathan Fisher and a lesbian collective of poets – Sue Fitchett, Marewa Glover, Cary McDermott and Rhonda Vickoce – separately edited their own volumes and the two volumes were then cling-wrapped and sold together in a pocket. As Sally McIntyre points out, the separate editing was a result of 'well-defined separate, but mutually supportive aspects of a desire to have a voice, to get the writing out there'.[8] At the same time, neither volume positioned itself as representative of either gay or lesbian poetry respectively. Indeed, as a mixed Pakeha and Maori collective, the lesbian editors were disappointed that there were not more contributions from Maori and Pacific Islanders, and editorial discussions broached issues of racism.[9] While the anthology was well received in the gay and lesbian community as well as by the mainstream press, a number of reviewers remarked upon the fact that the volume of lesbian poetry was almost twice as long as *When Two Men Embrace*. This discrepancy, the physical separation into two volumes, and a clear difference in tone – the lesbian volume tending more towards political critique and a celebration of sexuality while the gay one evoked a far greater sense of anxiety – may explain why the volumes now tend to be archived as distinct rather than joint anthologies.

While there are often analogies made between homosexual subcultures in Australia and New Zealand, it is evident that there are quite specific literary histories to be formulated, histories which showcase the variable tropological formations as well as the range of rhetorical and discursive strategies 'in which sexuality is not only embedded but conceived'.[10] Australian literary histories have, by and large, tended to elide issues of sexuality in relation to poetry, perhaps reflecting a broader tendency in the 1980s to collect them – as well as issues surrounding ethnicity and class – in the hold-all basket of the 'new diversity'. In their titles alone, the two 1999 New Zealand volumes feature performative acts that might be said to constitute a form of belonging. *Eat These Sweet Words* is a positive and sassily provocative invitation toward active participation by the reader, while *When Two Men Embrace* explicitly foregrounds sexual intimacy. Alternatively, Australian anthologies featuring gay and lesbian poetry tend to foreground the obscurity or subcultural elements that have informed some Australian gay and lesbian experience, and thus to render problematic the concept of a gay and lesbian community.

*Edge City on Two Different Plans* was published by the Sydney Gay Writers Collective. In his foreword, Dennis Altman argues that 'the idea of an identity based upon [homosexual] emotions and behaviour is ... comparatively recent', certainly the 'sense that one is part of a community ... has only come into being in our lifetimes'.[11] Yet while acknowledging the politicisation of homosexual experience into a 'gay' identity, the four editors of *Edge City* – Margaret Bradstock, Gary Dunne, Dave Sargent and Louise Wakeling – focus instead

---

8   Sally McIntyre, review, *Canta* 3 (17 March 1999).

9   Mark Pirie, review of *Eat These Sweet Words* and *When Two Men Embrace*, *JAAM: Just Another Art Movement* 12 (October 1999): 128–31 (130); Sue Fitchett, email to the author, 20 November 2011.

10  Lee Edelman, 'Homographesis', *Yale Journal of Criticism* 3.1 (1989): 189–207 (202).

11  Dennis Altman, Foreword, in Margaret Bradstock et al., eds, *Edge City on Two Different Plans*, (Leichhardt: Sydney Gay Writers Collective, 1983), p. 13. Subsequent page references are given in-text.

on an undoing of belonging and stability, featuring writing that demonstrates 'a sense of alienation, of frontiers crossed, of barriers set up and still to fall; of fringe-dwelling in rural and urban ghettoes', and poetry that exhibits affective responses – 'fear, danger, excitement' – that come with 'city living or the slow death of the (homo)sexual self' (16). In 'The City of Collective Memory', Dianne Chisholm suggests that gays, lesbians, and queers owe their emergence and continuing relationship to the world to the modern metropolis. As their 'habitation [is] primarily the inner city of big cities, where wreckage and renewal are most intense', the city, she argues, features in gay and lesbian writing as a central yet highly compromised image.[12] This problematising of social belonging in relation to the modern metropolis underwrites *Edge City*. For the four editors, it may not be a mapping of city sociability on two different plans – gay and lesbian, or straight and queer – but it may sometimes be many plans and sometimes none. The cover of their anthology significantly features an image of an almost melting Escher-esque city (one where stable perspective is undone), and the collection's title emphasises ex-centricity or marginality in relation to urban life.

A key element of a large city is the idea of a community of the anonymous. Scott Wilson argues that a 'queer community would be the community of those who do not have a community'.[13] He notes that as 'national communities in the West and elsewhere are overwhelmingly and, to varying degrees, prescriptively "heterosexual," homosexual relations call every community into question'.[14] Following the work of Lee Edelman, Wilson argues that what individual members of a gay and lesbian community have in common is a certain negative position in relation to straight society. He continues, 'The gay and lesbian community, if there were one, would be so much in excess of imposed, derogatory, appropriated, affirmed and invented definitions that it would perpetually exceed definition altogether'. For Wilson, gay and lesbian communities 'bare the arbitrariness and limitedness of particular communities, exposing the violence that polices and patrols those limits within the boundaries of the nation or the state'.[15]

I want to suggest that this idea of a queer community being predicated on an arbitrariness or even absence of community may find affinity with poetry's notorious obscurity. In *Infidel Poetics*, Daniel Tiffany argues that lyric substance allows for the existence of 'certain kinds of hermetic yet expressive communities, certain underworlds, within the social fabric'. He argues that the 'transitivity of the verbal enigma' 'reminds us of the possibility of communities that defy the seemingly inexorable logic of accessibility, universality, and transparency'.[16] So a poetics of obscurity offers a vehicle for unavowable communities such as those of gays, lesbians and queers, which are at once 'inscrutable and reflective, discontinuous and harmonious, solipsistic and expressive'. Indeed, Tiffany suggests that

---

12 Dianne Chisholm, 'The City of Collective Memory', *GLQ: A Journal of Lesbian and Gay Studies* 7.2 (2001): 195–243 (196).

13 Scott Wilson, *Cultural Materialism: Theory and Practice* (Oxford: Blackwell, 1995), p. 213.

14 Wilson, p. 208.

15 Wilson, p. 213.

16 Daniel Tiffany, *Infidel Poetics: Riddles, Nightlife, Substance* (Chicago: University of Chicago Press, 2009), pp. 10–11.

lyric obscurity becomes 'the very ground, or medium, of negative sociability'.[17] Rather than a community per se, it can engender a constellation, readers unified by expressive correspondences.[18]

A good example of how lyric obscurity may function as a compositional channel for enigmatic sexed being is the opening poem of *Edge City*, Javant Biarujia's 'A Un Javanais'. Not only creating his own language and identity but then combining it with French (as a poetics of mongrelism), Biarujia focuses on 'shadowy forms':

> they always come out silently and somehow beautifully
> the prostitutes and the underworld
> like certain species of plant which flower in the evening (19)

The 'prostitutes and the underworld' are part of the cityscape not visible by day, and largely unheard, but have some biospheric standing (are metaphysically material in the world). Like 'A Un Javanais', Kathleen Mary Fallon's 'Perfected' articulates nebulous desire through a blurring of the urban and nature:

> you have come up against me again
> as you do
> like a wet-slap-bang-in-the-face-fish
> I was walking down Central Tunnel
> the busker the slack offkey music
> my life you in my life sad effluent
>                     sad brown water (83)

Note the busker's music being 'slack' and 'offkey', the symbolism of the tunnel being walked down even as it is 'Central', and the water being effluent brown. All constitute a poetics of the shadowy and the unclear, providing ironic contrast to the title 'Perfected'. The sexual coding of 'fish' is transparent among a set of reading individuals as to be 'slap-bang-in-the-face'. Fallon foregrounds the 'illicit giggle,' the 'playful joke' and the 'old house' holding the 'tree to its face like a coquette's fan'. The social relations on display here are obscure but also an open secret. In 'For the Writer', Dave Sargent notes that if life fell into place 'as the structured characters before me./I'd probably lay down my pen forever' (179). Form is imbricated in the content of the secret and in what homosexual desire might feel like: ill-fitting, unstructured.

Appearing in 1991, *Pink Ink* was published by Wicked Women Publications and edited by Kerry Bashford, Mikey Halliday, Chris Jones, Peter Kerans, Leonie Knight, and Jan and Wendy Moulstone. It featured a number of writers who had appeared in *Edge City*, including Gay Dunne, Margaret Bradstock, Denis Gallagher, Kathleen Mary Fallon, Carolyn Gerrish and Louise Wakeling, but also introduced a host of new names, many of whom had found a publishing home in the little quarterly magazine *cargo*.[19] *Pink Ink* appeared in the final

---

17 Tiffany, p. 12.

18 Scott Wilson does note that '[h]owever chimerical and strategic the relation between gays and lesbians, such communities do exist in the practical form of crucial support institutions, at the very least' (p. 212).

19 *cargo* was a regular forum for gay and lesbian writing, although it would be joined by others like

year of the five year existence of *cargo*, which was edited by Laurin McKinnon and Jill Jones (as Jill Taylor), and which alternated between separate issues of gay fiction and poetry and issues of lesbian writing (with the exception of a combined gay and lesbian issue co-edited by Pam Brown and Sasha Soldatow).[20]

A number of gay and lesbian writers would publish under pseudonyms, Jones noting that she published as Angela Mysterioso and Dorothy Moore (in *cargo* and in *Pink Ink*). Many poems in *Pink Ink* reflect on invisibility or the pressure to conform to a normative heterosexual lifestyle, as illustrated in Margaret Bradstock's 'Selling Out':

> Thinking about the rain-forest,
> about heading north
> to the Rainbow Triangle,
> ringed by volcanic mountains,
> the roar of traffic
> hits you,
> sucks at your blood
> like infection,
> like a destructive love-affair
> you just can't do without.
> Running the red lights,
> programming the day ahead,
> you place the dream on hold,
> plug into the memory store
> of lead-light windows, superannuation,
> an almost nuclear family,
> & you know you'll never make it.
> The traffic snakes away,
> a grey, swollen river.
> This is the worst danger:
> the city's become home. (103)

It is the city that contaminates and overwhelms, and which exists in opposition to an ontological space of freedom and the ideal. As with Fallon's poem in *Edge City*, artifice and the organic run together as the urban noise of cars is as pathologically violent in its effect as love. In Catherine Bateson's 'Zoo Poem,' there is the sense of being enclosed or positioned by others' presumptions of 'natural' behaviour. The speaker notes how she and her lover

---

*Wicked, hell bent, Out*, and the *Journal of Australian Lesbian Feminist Studies*.

20  Interestingly, McKinnon's impetus to start *cargo* was very similar to Jonathan Fisher's desire to put together *When Two Men Embrace*: 'One of my initial motivations in working to construct *cargo*, was that I couldn't find enough material to read that was written by gay men. This is despite the fact that in the last few years there has been a very marked increase in the amount of printed material here, particularly from the United States and the United Kingdom. However, I became frustrated that little of this material related to my world'. See Editorial, *cargo* 3 (1988), n.p. In her opening Editorial, Jill Jones notes that she and McKinnon 'want to give lesbian and gay male writers a context for their work, whether it is explicitly about sexuality or about ... anything'. See *cargo* 2 (1988), n.p.

retreat when a gang of boys call one lioness washing another 'lesbians'. Such open jokiness contrasts against the silence of the speaker who continues:

> The lions are soft as cats or children's toys and
> boys will be ...
>
> We all know this story but let me tell it again:
> The woman had short hair. She wore jeans, a jacket, boots.
> She was carrying a can of petrol. The boys stopped her in the street.
> They made her pour petrol over her head ...
> That was in Boston, 1976.
>
> You cannot kiss with a mouth full of ashes. (266–67)

Even appearing gay or lesbian, or not performing 'proper' gender roles, involves risk and disciplining. Biarujia's moving elegy, 'Extract from Ra', mourns the AIDS-related death of Robert Gamble and highlights the elision between gay experience and the public world through a fractured poetic text that self-consciously draws attention to its own constructedness and obliquity, and which moves between free verse and multiple columns:

| | |
|---|---|
| it s not | *in* |
| a single spot | *the verb* to be |
| on a leopards | secrecy can be a |
| skin | stratagem |
| not a blotch | with smiles |
| of ink | for innocent enquirers |
| on a clean copy | and part estranged family |
| you can t infer the | it wouldn't be |
| your first secret | examined himself: |
| having to look right | *did I drain the* |
| having to look left | *same large cup* |
| at all the | *as he* |
| rules | |
| of the world | 3 |
| soon you shall | a year has unashamedly |
| stand between | passed |
| what I call | since you |
| the bell | faced the |

>           and                             M U
>
>           the bones                       S I C (185–86)

Again, there is the focus on animal imagery, but with multiple perspectives and narratives around the same event. Dorothy Porter's 'Extracts from "Thylacine"' foregrounds the impossibility of containing lesbian sexuality and its excess through language and traditional models of consumption:

> Like the gourmets in 'La Grande Bouffe'
>   I gorge till I bust,
>     a romantic appetite,
>   my language
>     garish, unlettered
>       as tunnel graffiti. (285)

In his lengthy introduction to *Pink Ink*, Michael Hurley cautions that categories of 'lesbian' and 'gay' writing suggest 'uniform bodies of work which can be claimed by homogenised readerships: the gay reader, the lesbian reader in a similar way to how "Australian" functions in "Australian literature"'. He notes, however, that 'in their quite separate beginnings', 'Australian' and 'lesbian' and 'gay' writing 'were assertions of minority cultures in the face of colonial and sexual hegemony – that is contesting a cultural dominant'. While that status of writing as gay and lesbian may come from reading against the grain of how individual writers see their own work, or how others have previously read them, they also register 'resistant performances in which there is a *refusal of definition by each other and wider social regulation*. In which "we" speaks myriad preferences' (13–14).

Hurley suggests that the history of publishing gay and lesbian poetry has been more 'fraught' than fiction due, firstly, to

> strongly masculinist traditions of criticism; secondly poetry's position at the heart of 'literary writing' and the protective manoeuvres which insulate it from perceived contamination; and lastly some strong colloquial voices that organise anglo-celtic, male heterosexuality at the centre of 'Australian' traditions'. (18–19)

Hurley points to the public and critical recognition of lesbian writing via literary prizes for 'new' and 'experimental' writing and by the mention of 'the lesbian voice' in *The Penguin Book of Australian Women Poets*. Yet he argues that there has never been the 'same demand for gay and lesbian writing as there has been for women's, multicultural and black material in the mainstream fiction and poetry publishing world' (22).

Indeed, it would take another two decades from when Hurley wrote in the early 1990s for the next anthology of gay and lesbian Australian poetry to appear. Like *Edge City* and *Pink Ink*, *Out of the Box* was published by an independent press, Puncher & Wattmann, though even its orange and white cover seems to echo the mainstream 'Popular Penguins' series. By choosing *Out of the Box* rather than the alternative *Paintbox* as a title, its editors Michael Farrell and Jill Jones emphasise movement and decontainment, reflecting the performative titles of the New Zealand anthologies, *When Two Men Embrace* and *Eat These*

*Sweet Words*. The editors decided to select poetry by gay and lesbian writers that did not necessarily have specifically gay and lesbian content, a decision that reflects the approach taken by the lesbian collective that edited *Eat These Sweet Words*. In 'Things Get Out' – his part of the shared introduction – Farrell argued that to denote something as gay or lesbian is not a 'subtraction but an addition', in the sense that it might extend the themes covered in the poetry (10).

As with other Australian anthologies of gay and lesbian writing, Farrell and Jones also decided to publish contemporary writing rather than assert a monumentalising tradition. Yet with *Out of the Box* appearing almost three decades after *Edge City*, many of the poems reflect the passing of time, an acceptance, even ease with the subject's fictive variants, and the integration of lesbian and gay sexuality within everyday life. Andy Quan writes of seeing in the youthful poet, 'the man I/would become blooming in the distance':

> I trampled those days, a lion, believed
> in myself with a ferocity that has since
> never been the same. They were days
> when self-knowing became real, a dented
> bud of a tulip infused with its own
> fragility and what it might reveal.
> I'd discovered *Great Men*. This late
> in the century, in so vast a country, so
> few gay poets. (74)

In 'A History Lesson,' David Malouf notes that, "These lives go other ways/than the documents intended' (32). Like Quan, there is a positive attitude of future possibility:

> But that is another story. Passed from mouth
> to mouth and not set down, it covers the facts, has a beginning and has survived
> its middle. Why shouldn't it end well? (33)

Jill Jones notes:

> And remember     edges of names
> past the established
>      and stolid
> past any eloquence of
>      the inherited.

And later in the same poem, 'The world can't be overwrought/anymore/like childhood' (99).

In her introduction, 'Going in Any Direction', Jones draws attention to the significance of gay and lesbian writing emerging in the 1970s out of 'shared households that comprised city living in many Australian capital cities prior to the yuppie property booms ... of more recent decades' (22). In *Out of the Box*, there is a sense of greater mobility, with Jones herself writing of the suburbs, while Martin Harrison engages equally with bush and cosmopolitan topographies. In 'shame & her sisters:', Keri Glastonbury demonstrates how the contemporary world blurs ontological categories of Being, such as the wild and domestic, and the sexual and philosophical:

>              instead her voice has a low growl
> a pitch
>              I'm learning to hear as ethical
> like an animal
> might be
>              the last wild thylacine probably shot
> in a chook pen
>
> this is the banality of her history (154)

Present-day experiences are always already known through previous representations. In the same poem, a trip to Christchurch is informed by Peter Jackson's film, *Heavenly Creatures* (1994), which itself focused on the city's notorious Parker-Hulme murder trial:

> another city of murders
>              neo-gothic as liquorice all sorts
> the scene
>              some kind of antipodean joust
>
> while
> she plays dead
>              on the floor (heavenly creature) (155)

As true crime has become reel time, this in turn informs a present moment and its 'affect de jour'. Sexual identity is framed through easy consumption, playfulness, and citationality. As Jill Jones notes, 'you can trace a doubleness, a slipperiness that could be said to characterize the queer life in the multi-gendered city' (27). She suggests that the poetry featured in *Out of the Box* has 'less about secret lesbian histories and desires than [there] may have been in the past', going on to argue:

> Whether these poets still work happily amongst metaphor and simile, as ways of thinking slant, or prefer self-conscious ironies, there is a questioning of positions, of the poet, of the text written, and, therefore, of the reader (24).

The anthology leaves the reader to find their own correspondences, whether it be through recitations of butch or less reverberant sexual identities, or even just a sense of tone that resonates. And while the anthology appears at a time when gay or lesbian marriage is still a controversial political issue, there is the possibility of change, even if it is rediscovery of a past that has been compositionally revised and can be known anew. As Pam Brown notes in her fabulous 'Peel Me a Zibibbo', 'you need to/choose/the "I'm feeling lucky" google option' (137). *Out of the Box*, along with its Australian precursors *Edge City* and *Pink Ink*, and similar New Zealand endeavours like *When Two Men Embrace* and *Eat These Sweet Words*, provides invaluable imaginaries of a non-republic, a space where constellations of being can form and fluctuate through the historically bound interstices of language and thought.

## 22

### 'ALL THE VILLAGE WAS RUNNING': SOME VOICES FROM YOUNG REFUGEES IN WESTERN SYDNEY

*Lachlan Brown*

I would like to begin with a story written by Stanley, a fifteen-year-old student at Lurnea High School, who was a refugee from the Congo. I remember Stanley because when I ran the writing workshop he was very quiet. He rested his head on his hands and his hands on the desk. He would not respond to questions beyond a nod or shake of his head. Yet at the end of the workshop he had written something remarkable:

> 1. The time that war broke out in the Congo everyone was running. The time that I was running I saw a pregnant woman have been shot in the stomach. Everyone feel ... Oh oh.

> 2. The time that war broke out in the Congo all the village was running. The time that I and my brother were running we saw a pregnant woman have been shot in the stomach on the way. We all feel like crying. The thing that you have seen you cannot forget it easy. It will be like a printed book in my mind.[1]

Stanley read this story to the rest of his cohort at the end of the day, his low voice barely reaching the walls of the demountable building in his school in Sydney's southwest. But for those of us listening at the time, his words were compelling and heartbreaking, as he recounted experiences utterly removed from most middle-class Australian suburban upbringings. Later I learnt from Stanley's teacher that this was the first time he had shared information about his life in the Congo. Since that day, he has written other works, including a play that he performed himself. He was also on the panel at the launch of *Westside Jr. Vol. 2: Violence* where he read this original story and confidently answered questions from the floor.

This chapter attempts two things. Firstly, I would like briefly to map out some of the networks, the organisations and individuals who came together in order that refugees like Stanley could be given a chance to express themselves, to tell their stories and to have their writing published. Secondly, I would like to consider the published writing in more detail, examining the kinds of sociality and positioning that the works in *Westside Jr. Vol. 2: Violence* exhibit. I will consider the techniques involved in writing about trauma, as well as the kinds of displacements and replacements seen in the works. I am doing this as someone

---

1 Michael Mohammed Ahmad, ed., *Westside Jr. Vol. 2: Violence* (Bankstown: Bankstown Youth Development Service, 2010), p. 34. All subsequent references to this work are given in-text.

who was involved in the project, both as a workshop facilitator and a subeditor. Therefore, whilst I may not be the most impartial person to speak about this collection of writing, I have come to know this work thoroughly and am continually challenged by these pieces and the remarkable individuals who produced them.

The scene for this project was set in 2009 when Eric Brace, a project officer from the Australian Literacy and Numeracy Foundation, approached Bankstown Youth Development Service (BYDS) in order to enlist their help in running a series of workshops throughout high schools in Western Sydney under the umbrella of Refugee Action Support (RAS). The RAS program had been initially set up 'to provide effective support for adolescent refugee students as they grapple with the language and literacy demands of the classroom'.[2] Its usual mode of operation included recruiting and training tertiary education students to work with adolescent refugees in tutorial settings within classrooms across greater Western Sydney and the Riverina. Funding came from the federal government Department of Education, Employment and Workplace Relations. To complement the ongoing work of the RAS tutors, BYDS was asked to run a series of drama and creative writing workshops across schools with significant refugee populations in Western Sydney. Importantly, BYDS had, at this time, developed a stable of emerging young actors and writers, which gave it a pool of people who could relate relatively easily to younger students from the area.

Seven high schools were selected from the west and southwest of Sydney, and each had either a dedicated program for refugee students or a large number of refugee and migrant students within the wider school population. BYDS sent along eight workshop facilitators to each school, including actors and writers. Beginning on 19 November at Lurnea High School, and finishing on 30 November at Fairvale High School in Fairfield West, each four-hour workshop held between fifteen and forty students. The workshops started with drama games and a forum theatre performance where students watched a play on bullying or violence before being encouraged to step into the situation themselves, taking on certain dramatic roles with the aim of producing different outcomes. The second half of the workshops involved creative writing groups facilitated by artists and writers from BYDS. Here students discussed styles of writing and read previous editions of *Westside Jr.* (a community journal of writing from school students). Next, students were able to spend half an hour writing their own works on the theme of violence with the help of writing facilitators. At the end of visiting all the schools, BYDS selected and transcribed students' works for publication by the BYDS team in *Westside Jr. Vol. 2: Violence*. A documentary film about the workshops was launched at refugee week at Blacktown Library and has since been shown at various refugee events and film festivals around New South Wales. The volume of writing was itself launched in 2010 at the This is Not Art (TINA) Young Writers' Festival in Newcastle. At the launch, Eric Brace was able to bring a group of students from Lurnea public school. These students were given video cameras to document their trip and the launch. Two of the students were on the panel that day and answered questions about their writing alongside members of BYDS. Eric Brace has since taken *Westside Jr. Vol. 2: Violence* and used it within a variety of settings, in particular using the publication as a way

---

2  Australian Literacy and Numeracy Foundation, *Refugee Action Support: Assisting Young Refugees Make a Successful Transition into Australian Schooling*, 2009–2010, available at alnf.org/Pages/programs/refugee-action-support [accessed 14 August 2011].

of inspiring other students to begin writing. He has also taken class sets to Tennant Creek where teachers in training have used them with Indigenous students.

It is worth pointing out that there were thus a number of networks in play here to bring these stories to light. There were very faithful teachers who work with intensive English programs and with refugee students across high schools. There were funding bodies like the Australian Literacy and Numeracy Foundation, who attempt to run programs like RAS that cut across the normal boundaries and structures of education. There were arts organisations like BYDS, who often got their funding from running workshops in schools and who have a particular aesthetic that involves an emphasis on writing the local, or writing works that are true to the uniquely multicultural existence of living in the south of Western Sydney. It was this combination of educators within the department, extra governmental support and a local arts organisation that made this program so successful. For example, in many cases a program like this might involve approaching a major established poet or novelist who has written about migration. This writer might be taken to one school to talk to a couple of hundred students who then try to write some of their own work. But in this part of the RAS program, by using local emerging artists as facilitators, BYDS was able to run workshops that were relevant and not intimidating. This is not to downplay the strength of the artists BYDS used: there were actors who had played on Australian television, writers who had been published in major journals, and poets like Fiona Wright, whose work has appeared in three consecutive volumes of Black Inc.'s *Best Australian Poems* from 2008–10. But these artists were young. They were keen. They loved the area. And they could be employed for little money.

One of the key issues that arose from the 2009 RAS workshops involved the writing of trauma. The *Westside Jr. Vol. 2: Violence* publication is, therefore, a cutting-edge example of some of the techniques that young writers employ when dealing with excruciatingly demanding content. This was evident in a number of the titles and opening lines of the pieces that position the writer as witness, which also indicated the difficulty of describing first-hand experiences. These included titles such as, 'I Have Seen Things that You Have Never Seen' (83), and opening lines like, 'I have seen and heard thing … I can't describe' (74). Stanley's piece on the Congo closed with a similar statement: 'The thing that you have seen you cannot forget easy. It will be like a printed book in my mind' (34). This self-consciousness about the act of writing, the acknowledgement of a disjunction between experience and language, primarily stems from the harrowing subject matter of the work. *Westside Jr. Vol. 2: Violence* includes first hand experiences of war, the death of loved ones, beheadings, mutilation, infanticide, the discovery of dead bodies in backyards, natural disasters, the fear of being murdered, and the experience of displacement.

In one moving example, a student wrote two works. The first was a paragraph about a woman finding a litter of kittens under a house and suffocating them in a polythene bag. The mother cat searches but cannot find her babies. The second work is a poem about immense devastation wrought by the 2004 tsunami in Sri Lanka. As the waves arrive, children are buried under the sand where they were playing. The poem's last stanza sees mothers crying for their lost children (85). What can young writers do with such particularised moments of trauma? What can they do with the sheer scale of the destruction wrought by wars and natural disasters? On the one hand, these stories seem to resist detailed analysis. They are testimonies to hardship and struggle that press a certain ethical demand onto the reader. It is difficult not to weep as one reads them. On the other hand, many of these works benefit greatly from an examination of their structures and themes. For example, in the two stories introduced above, the juxtaposition of maternal grief is vital to understanding just how a local instance of suffering might relate to a universal concern. Hence it is worth sensitively exploring some of the ways that the students use language to deal with trauma in *Westside Jr. Vol. 2: Violence*. This is not to subject the writers to unwanted appraisal or scrutiny, but in order to better appreciate the subtle contours of their work.

As one approaches the pieces in the volume, it is clear that repetition is one of the key techniques that students employ in representing responses to traumatic events. For example, a student from a school in Sydney's west writes: 'Hello, my name is Achol and I live in Sydney. I sit alone in the cold empty classroom with no one beside me but my sad shadow. Lonely I stand. Lonely I stand' (15). A younger student on the cusp of becoming a teenager sums his life up this way: 'I was born in blood and live in blood and die in blood. Is it fair? Why, why everyone likes which just got blood in it of human's heart' (20). In a one line piece a student expresses their frustration: 'I am comfuse. I crack my scalp. Nothing to work out. Anger! Anger! Anger!' (42). Similarly, an untitled poem reads, 'War/an immoral world./Blood of Ocean/Ruin Ruin Ruin' (44). Not only does this repetition create an almost tactile sense of frustration, but it also demonstrates one way of writing trauma and violence for those not brought up with English as a first language. For these writers, emphasis may not and cannot necessarily come through linguistic variation or elaboration. Rather, it is the repetition of words and phrases that brings out the horror of each experience. This refusal to over-elaborate not only gives these works a kind of gravitas, but it leads to powerful rhythms; for example, in this untitled poem about a father's journey to Australia:

> My dad came by boat
> he left us when I was little
> he travelled many countries
> he only told me that
> when he was coming to Australia
> he travelled by boat their boat
> was small and they had many
> people on the small boat
> it took him 28 days and night
> they didn't have much food and
> water to eat or drink because
> the boat was small and
> there was many people on the
> boat so they didn't have food
> to eat when they
> were on boat the waves were
> all over the boat after
> 28 days they took him
> migration camp after

> 2 or 3 year my dad told
> to migration people that
> my family is left in Afghanistan
> in war I want my family
> to come here in Australia
> because I don't
> want them to be there
> in war in Afghanistan after
> 5 to 6 year then
> we went to Pakistan and my dad
> came there too and brought us to
> Australia. (75)

Here the repetition corrals the reader into the very space that the father has occupied in his cramped journey to Australia. Yet with each iteration the boat assumes increasing importance, desperately rocking its way through the work's irregular lines. It is the rhythm of this repetition that the poet and workshop facilitator Fiona Wright gestures toward in her own personal response to an incident from one of the RAS workshops:

> The kid is quiet. I close his book and ask about his father and he says he came by boat and it took thirty days and there wasn't enough water. He says the ocean came over the sides and it took thirty days and it was three years until he saw his sons again. He says that he was sick when he came by boat and the ocean came over the sides and then he's quiet and I give him back his pen. The kid says that his English is not good and he does not know what to write.[3]

Wright's reflection of the repetition in this boy's story portrays its urgency and sense of frustration, the difficulty involved in its telling. '[H]e is angry' and 'biting on his lip' as he writes, she tells us later.

If the majority of the pieces in the volume give a very direct account of certain traumatic experiences or events, there are a few which are more sophisticated in the way they deal with the theme of violence. Some use third-person narration and focalise experiences through characters. Others attempt to write the stories of friends in the first person. One piece includes a baby demon who accidentally drowns a baby lion. At the end of the work, the student has written, 'Sorry. Not about violence' (34). Another chilling piece takes on the persona of a sadist who is abused by bullies and an alcoholic father. The abused narrator then speaks about how he or she looks for weaker things to hurt. Here the short sentences help to build a menacing tone:

> And when I go to school school gangs attack me. They're not students. They're gangs. They always bash me. No reasons. They hit me and laugh. Sometimes, they've got some urine on my face. But I'm quiet. I don't say a word. This is my school life. And after school. I'm looking for weak something. Something is weaker than me. I'm looking for it. Children, old people, animals … When I

---

[3] Fiona Wright, 'Writing about Violence', unpublished, 2010.

> find it, I'm just hitting them. I have no reason. I'm just bashing them. Then I feel happy. (51)

Of course, I am making a big assumption here that the student in question is adopting a persona, rather than writing about a personal experience (the work ends with 'This is my life. Wild life'). But in any case, the clipped sentences, the immediacy of the present tense, and the disturbing voice indicate a series of creative choices that work together effectively. This is breathtaking for a work completed in half an hour by a student whose first language is not English. A girl from Iraq wrote an equally well-constructed piece with a different tone, and she spoke about it at the launch of the volume. In it she psychologically interrogates the act of catching a butterfly and callously pulling off its wings:

> One day I've seen a butterfly. The butterfly was flying and I've seen her so happy. The black, red and yellow colours were bright into my eye. So I ran after her and caught her. I took off her wings and let her sad walking one the floor. How violence was am I?
>
> I woke up today morning and I looked at the window directly, I'm just imagine why I can't fly like the bird? If I can fly like the birds, I'll be free and loosefoot. Am just thinking why I broke butterfly wings. (35)

The questions in this piece are extremely effective, allowing the writer to take one of the simplest of childhood acts and stand back to examine it. This is a creative consideration of violence that comes in from the side, as it were. And so it stands alongside those horrific and stark statements of witness, offering another way of thinking through violence. In my own interviews with this student, it is plain that her experiences of the Iraq war include some very disturbing events. But here she chose to write about a butterfly, a small and yet profound act of violence that opens a window onto larger concerns.

As the editorial team began to draw these pieces together for publication it became evident that many students were self-editing their work in unique ways that were often related to their inability to express the magnitude of what they were writing about. In one piece the student has crossed out certain words, searching for the right way to express what he has experienced: 'HELP! I was sitting under a tree, waiting for someone to pick me up from the rain of ~~river of blood wars blood~~ bombs' (20). For this student the extent of what he has experienced could not be poured into the tiny vessels of the English language.

This led to what was perhaps the most controversial of the editorial decisions in the volume. The editor Mohammed Ahmad, in consultation with others, decided to transcribe each page including the strike-throughs where they were legible. His argument was that each strike-through spoke powerfully about the inability of language to convey the trauma that refugee students have experienced. Or, as he puts in it his introduction:

> When my colleagues and I went back to transcribe and edit the material, we found the 'errors'; the unconventional use, and misuse of grammar and words, the strike-throughs, just as fascinating as the writing itself. (8)

It must be said that the inclusion of these strike-throughs does make *Westside Jr. Vol. 2: Violence* a much more interesting collection to read and study. They point to the enormity of trying to wrap language around experience. They fit with the workshop goals of moving beyond the binary of correct/incorrect English use that can paralyse students from non-English speaking backgrounds. Yet the addition of these strike-throughs raises ethical issues, including the fact that, in a very real sense, the editors of the volume could be charged with not allowing students to speak in the voices that they have finally chosen. In fact, one could argue that the editors have actually reversed the intentions of the authors in this respect, undermining the meaning of the typographical strike-through by including the very words that should have been omitted. This is surely important in a volume such as this, as the work so often functions as a kind of witness or testimony. In this way the decision also subtly changes the function of the pieces and the relationship between editor and author. Instead of these stories existing as vehicles of expression, a vital witness to voices that would otherwise remain unheard, they run the risk of becoming editorial curios to be examined by those who know better than what each student has written.

Despite these reservations, however, the inclusion of the strike-throughs offers remarkable moments in the reading experience of a number of works. In one story the main character, Ron, asks the question 'why ~~I~~ am here?' (42). The struck-through 'I' fits the sentence beautifully, perhaps indicating something about the fading self. Or consider this untitled poem:

> I have seen and heard things ~~you~~ I can't describe.
>
> People screaming
>       blood everywhere
>       baby crying
>       men with weapons
>       soldier killing young children
> women with pregnance getting harassed.
>       War between two countries
> Young men at the age of 12 is carrying guns.
>
> ~~Before this thing happened the world was peaceful~~
>
> Kid cry for food to eat because of the starvation.
> Men hunting for food in the bush. (74)

Here the change of 'you' to 'I' may well have been a simple error, but the play between the two pronouns speaks something about the nervous and possibly fraught relationship between the author and reader. The personalising impulse ('this is my story') is even more important when one considers the remainder of the poem, which contains a list of atrocities, images of blood, violence and crying children. Like many of the works in the volume, this poem struggles to articulate the overwhelming nature of the things that have been experienced. Furthermore, the second struck-through section could be read as an indication that certain forms of violence blot out all hope for a peaceful world. That is, even the memories of better times cannot force their way into the poem. So what the strike-throughs give us is a way of thinking about how young people can write about the unthinkable and unpresentable. And whilst I am still unsure about the ethical implications of such a move, it does provide a fascinating insight into some of the issues surrounding the writing of traumatic events.

Compounding the issues that surround the representation of trauma and violence was the fact that for most students English was a second language, something unsteady and untameable, particularly for the older students. It is difficult enough to speak about some experiences in one's mother tongue. But when you are asked to do so in a foreign place, using a foreign language, then the problems intensify. As Sneja Gunew notes in *Framing Marginality*:

> The term 'migrant', as pointed out above, conjures up subjects whose presence in the dominant culture is merely temporary, and whose orientation is towards a past nostalgically conceived of as a lost motherland and mother tongue. This precariousness is further signalled by such widely used bureaucratic terms as NESB (non-English speaking background), an exclusionary acronym which indicates an insecure hold on the only language which is the measure of linguistic competence in Australia, namely English.[4]

Many of the schools we visited have their own acronyms for programs for refugee and newly arrived students. For example, one school used IEC for Intensive English Class. RAS is itself an acronym that can possibly function in the exclusionary way that Gunew describes. The sponsorship of the program by the Australian Literacy and Numeracy Foundation also meant that the program was directed toward improving English literacy outcomes. Here we see, perhaps, one limitation of the kinds of networks that made the program possible. Because of them, students' creative voices were ostensibly limited to the language of the dominant culture. In my own experience, however, workshop facilitators did actually *encourage* the use of students' first languages. Yet only some students took up this suggestion. Of course this meant that students sometimes made references to the problems and achievements of learning English. In the documentary about the program, one girl spoke movingly about her progress in language learning. Statements like, 'Now I'm happy cause I can speak English better than nothing', or 'I improve my English a lots', also portrayed something of the way that self worth is tied to knowledge of the dominant language group. But some of the most interesting pieces are less self-conscious about their use of irregular forms. This was a marked feature of the workshops, encouraging students to value their own expressions in English when so often they do not think of themselves as writers worthy of any kind of publication. For example, one of the pieces, titled 'My Poem,' starts the first five of its six stanzas with the words 'I'm scare' (12). It is such a strong piece precisely because of its combination of striking similes and its non-standard forms of English, which give it a really innovative and moving voice:

---

4  Sneja Gunew, *Framing Marginality: Multicultural Literary Studies* (Carlton: Melbourne University Press, 1994), p. 7.

> I'm scare when I was in the jail
> They keeping me like a dirty dog.
> The bars was cold like a ice
>
> I'm scare when I'm in the dark.
> The walls are bleeding like a rain
> The tree is Free and walking like a human
> but why can I . ?
>
> I'm scare when I was at bed.
> I saw a shadow
> it spring like a cheetah.
>
> I'm scare when my mum was really sick.
> Her head is like a basketball with no hair.
> Cancer is spring fast like a water.
>
> I'm scare when my husband is gonna dead.
> I feel like I gonna be a window.
>
> He's smile is like a man from the heaven
> He's skin is smooth like a table. (12)

This piece works because the workshops focused on students being less inhibited when they write. For most of these students, writing practice involves being marked on correct English. Here, however, we were able to develop different ways of writing, different standards for written expression. As one student noted in an interview, 'Now I got many ideas what I can do … Firstly, before that, I just think that I am dumb. Now I know that I can do really much work.'

Another important aspect of many pieces in *Westside Jr. Vol. 2: Violence* is the way that the young writers depict the act of refugee or migrant displacement and replacement. I do not wish to pursue this in great detail here except to make three brief points about how these themes appear in the volume. Firstly, the journal contains many examples of what one might call 'classic' refugee or migration stories, which follow the structure of: i) a nostalgic description of a peaceful time; ii) the introduction of violence and unrest; and iii) the move to Australia, sometimes via an intermediate location. This is not to say that all these three elements exist in every story. Some works focus in more detail on the time of peace or the details of war. Interestingly, though, there are many pieces that make an abrupt turn when the narrative moves to Australia. In fact, it is almost as though the writers ran out of time (which could have been the case) or were unwilling to spell out in detail how their move to Australia occurred. Here are some examples of the final lines of such pieces:

> [after speaking about the war in Iraq] In 2008 we arrived in Australia. I'm steady now and I hope my life to get better in this country. (25)
>
> [after speaking about a neighbour in Iran who was forced to marry her cousin because she was caught talking to a boy] But I prefer now when I come to Australia. (33)

> [after speaking about someone helping a family escape an attack in Africa] When the attack was calming down, we had to go back to where we lived to get water, food, cooking equipment and after six month we returned to our homes and after a year or two we came to Australia. (59)
>
> [after speaking about a girl and her parents fleeing the Taliban] After a few years they came into a ship. (87)

The strange narrative acceleration – even a kind of prolepsis – in each of these narratives is worth considering. Firstly, it signals a sense of displacement. That is, these young writers can find no connection between their old lives in Iraq, Africa or Afghanistan and their new existence in Australia. In their narratives they cannot easily link these two spheres. But additionally there may be a hesitation to speak about journeys to Australia, particularly within a certain governmental and societal atmosphere which is disproportionately anxious about asylum seekers, illegal entry and boat people. One cannot say that these students have been directly intimidated into not speaking about their journeys, but their reticence may be symptomatic of a kind of 'border security' culture that discourages any disclosure of how they got here.

Secondly, linked to this narrative acceleration, it is fascinating to note that there is a marked ambivalence towards Australia in these stories. Readers get a sense of this in the above cluster of quotes, which are circumspect in their expectations and guarded in their praise. In another story, one student speaks about witnessing a fight and ends the piece with, 'If I in my country I should help the old man' (17). We do get some endings which read, 'Australia is a country of multiculture and no one teases other races' (15), or, 'Now when I come to Australia I feel safe and in Australia I feel like I am in heal' (65). But there are also more decidedly defensive responses, such as this closing sentence: 'The only thing, I made sure before I came to Australia was that I will never assimilate myself into Australia society because I am Indian and want to maintain my Indian culture and tradition' (53). Again it is worth thinking about what this ambivalence might signify, particularly within school contexts, where students are required to sing the national anthem and make other increasingly overt shows of patriotism. That one student would use the word 'assimilate' is of immense significance when we consider how refugee students see themselves in relation to an Anglo-European conception of Australian society in this period. That this student would take a stand against this kind of assimilation therefore says a great deal about the difficulties involved with this paradigm.

Thirdly, following on from this ambivalence toward Australia, in the writing of displacement and replacement it is helpful to explore the ways in which some of these pieces attempt to establish an identity for the self precisely through the medium of creative writing. Indeed, two pieces in particular strike me as defiant and urgent in their tone, trying to speak clearly from within an identity that is under pressure. In the first, an older Afghani teen writes about the proud history of his country, before lamenting the appearance of the Taliban and the Americans as 'the two snake[s]' on a mission of destruction:

> Afghanistan was the country of the Nobels.
> The country of Jalal Aldin, Firdowsy and
>        Hafiz.

> People around the world came, for learning.
> But that was before the Talibans and
> > Americans.
>
> Then the two snake started to start their
> > mission.
>
> There came the war and violence.
> There came the separation of child and
> mother.
> There came ME out of Afghanistan, my
> > beloved mother. (78)

The ending of this poem is notable because of the way that war, violence, and parental separation are made to accumulate with the repeated 'there cames', so that the final line proclaims the birth of the poet, arising from the labour pains of his beleaguered homeland. There is a kind of postcoloniality at work in the defiant tone of the poem. Here the pointed retelling of Afghanistan's history, destroyed both by Islamic fundamentalism and the 'mission' of the civilising West, leads to the very violence that brings a young refugee to Australia from his mother country. This is not exactly the kind of hybridity that Ashcroft, Griffiths and Tiffin describe, where time gives way to space;[5] nor does it house the more problematic ethical dilemmas that Gandhi thinks hybridity may bring.[6] Yet there does seem to be a declaration of self-identity here which pushes away from a certain binary (which in the eyes of the writer is really no binary at all), thereby establishing the author's identity out of the very violence that has destroyed Afghanistan.

A second piece in the collection stakes a similar claim in terms of identity, opening with a poignant line from a Tamil author: 'This is not a story or it is not a poem. It's just some lines of my country, a telling of a boy' (86). Once more there is a remarkable intertwining of country and identity, an awareness that one's individual status is tied up with the fate of one's people. The stark tone of this piece, the author's attempt to opt out of what he perceives as the artificial act of writing stories and poems, makes this a moving witness to the experience of a persecuted people. Each calm statement builds the list of charges and moments of injustice that the writer feels he must expose. Importantly, the Sri Lankan government is never named beside the generic 'they say', and even the 'we' is withheld until the last sentence. Identity appears only in the final section – 'All of this happen because we are Tamil' (86) – indelibly marked by persecution and violence. What we see here, in the writing of two refugees, is not only the kind of self-fashioning one would expect from any young writer, but the way that this is set into wider political struggles with a sense of pride and urgency – and the way these things in turn must always and already overshadow any sense of Australian nationality and citizenship, together with those sets of 'values' that are required by or promoted by the government at any given time.

---

5  Bill Ashcroft, Gareth Griffiths and Helen Tiffin, *The Empire Writes Back: Theory and Practice in Postcolonial Literatures*, 2nd edn (London: Routledge, 2002 [1989]), pp. 32–36.

6  Leela Gandhi, *Postcolonial Theory: A Critical Introduction* (Crows Nest: Allen & Unwin, 1998), p. 136ff.

When Stanley spoke of his memories in that demountable classroom, he may not have envisioned the distances that these memories would travel. In a sense, this chapter has merely scratched the surface of these texts and the background to their production. But as Australia becomes home to increasing numbers of refugees, more and more stories like this will be shared. So when students 'hear the voices of bombs' (25) it is vital that we hear their voices. Or when a student is confronted by an 'ARMY TANK' (102) we must ensure that this testimony confronts others. Publications like this one provide a place for the creative voices of those who have been displaced. They are, in a sense, the 'printed books' of those memories that our country, and indeed the world, should not forget.

# Distance

*Bonny Cassidy*

### *Nearing Cobar, Undoing*

From an eroded dip by the highway, comes a chain of gobbling birdcall. I watch feet moving around our midday fire, scattering clumps of curled leaf litter into new positions; and worry that we are interfering with something. I take a wander, further out into the clearing, to remind myself that we are simply rearranging and shifting shapes. These elements are always on the verge of becoming their opposites: here, old bits of timber are so dry that they have come to resemble water; long ribbons inscribed with deep flows from end to end. The wood looks like the spores of a sea, blown away to propagate itself elsewhere.

How strange, then, that we have come to talk about tropes of metonymy and metaphor as aesthetic constructions, when it's plain to see that wood is water, a bough is a creek. After all, literature works that way: its connections and communities of ideas, works, eyes, hands and sounds are just malleable elements. Unfixed, they fly away from their maker and settle in the mind of the reader like so many grains of sand can suddenly form a break, or even a dune. Boneless, writing is an echo until an audience replies and cuts across its call.

Even the ants at my feet, carrying splinters of bread, are undoing the great disintegrating metonymy of scale. They lead to a vertebra punctured by tides. I no longer touch bones with trepidation; I like to hold the vertebra deep and tightly closed in my palm, feeling the vitality still in its warmth, in its cavity where insect webs quiver. Stand here like this, in the clearing; listen, and you'll hear the distant rush of wheels, or a wave spreading through treetops and jumping the road, rolling down to a dense mound of granite pebbles rising from the soil. We are living with echoes; the earth is simile.

### *White Cliffs*

As we cross the marshy fields around Wilga Station, and the prehistoric seabed at White Cliffs, a flock circles overhead: herons, black across the wings and white beneath, drawing webs that fade into uninterrupted blue. They put me in mind of Jennifer Rankin's poem 'Earth Hold', with its sudden bird:

> My slow fingers close about.
> This pod. Seed and pod.
> Squat brown seed-pod. Closing about.

> Wrapped inside the mud-bed.
> Mangroves. Mangrove tree and root.
>
> Oyster and shell.
>
> Now it is the grey heron.
> Now my white ibis flies.
>
> This warm morning's sun.
> This valley folding away.
> Sea-glare.
>
> And thin houses. Weather-whitened.[1]

And, as though manifested by the poem, the grey heron – alone as usual – appears. Its heavy, startled sweeps lift it low over the saltbush.

It's not the first time that Rankin's imagery has surfaced far from her poetry's coasts and islands. The work suggests that there is a deeper element in those littoral places. In another of Rankin's poems, 'Seasonal Move', a shedding tree not only leads to soil, but also further down to the water table, where 'scraping apart the sweet-matted needles/I find earth. Hard and cold'.[2] On the road through to Tilpa, the only sound is the tide of wind through desert oaks, and the floor of needles on silky, orange soil. But the herons indicate that the sea and cliffs once here are now inching up through these groves.

If earth can collapse our sense of time's scale into a place, so a poem can overturn perspective. While Rankin's poems alight on patches of earth and the objects found there, they also sail like the heron over great distances. Their panoramas are able to account for the shifting arrangements in a place comprised of several others. Even when they seem to speak of ocean, they are aware of the more complex realities of time and space. Reading her poem 'Earth Count', I feel its words chasing us from high above the dried rivers:

> At the centre the sea has dried up.
> Earth itself is burning away out there.
> Now I speak a subterranean language
> burrowing in beneath the ground.
>
> Moon mix
>
> and dust scratches back off the walls
>
> she-oaks are dying
>
> tropical palms needlessly making desert-shade.[3]

---

1 Jennifer Rankin, 'Earth Hold', in Judith Rodriguez, ed., *Jennifer Rankin: Collected Poems* (St Lucia: University of Queensland Press, 1990), p. 45.

2 Rankin, 'Seasonal Move', *Collected Poems*, p. 23.

3 Rankin, 'Earth Count', *Collected Poems*, p. 53.

Ghost gums are flourishing in the Darling River's absence, marking its sharp banks. Plains flank the riverbed, gradually developing low and gentle hills. Their profile is a bristle of sparse marks, a threadbare mane of round acacias and stiff, bright wax. When the earth is lightly tipped by these rises, I can see that it's evenly spotted with green-grey puffs of saltbush. The country becomes aerially orientated and one-dimensional: the heights formed of cracked rock; the rock crumbling into slopes; the slopes reducing to pebbled soil. Eventually, the hills plateau to such a low line that they are once again barely distinguishable from the plain. The only way across is up.

*Crossing the Border*

The outlines of silver outcrops are neatly broken off, as their diagonal pipes of stone turn into air. They point out of New South Wales, over into South Australia, toward a stretch of warm and taut earth, furred by grass. A lip appears over the plain: the crest of a fat, slow, embryonic wave – its edge rubbled with pockets of foam, forever peaking to a break. To the south, more rugged ranges begin to dive up from the horizon. I don't know whether they are meteoric craters or volcanic rims: the earth surrounding them has calmed into smooth, crafted oceans of soil.

I am thinking more about the conundrum of representing space in language, and particularly the community of attempts upon its solution. On his first visit to this area, the painter Hans Heysen (1877–1968) remarked how difficult it was to paint clear space. If Heysen struggled to realise his desire for clear space, the colonial painter John Glover (1767–1849) saw good reason to fill it. Critic John McPhee writes that Glover's work is obviously 'witness to a new land' and 'emphasises that we also have a responsibility to look at [the land] closely and to read its symbols'. It was imperative for Glover that his landscapes identified 'the particularities of the trees and their distribution'. This view prioritises orientation and form over composition, which we might associate with drawing rather than painting. As McPhee explains, Glover's 'veracity can be ascribed to his early self-instruction, which consisted of sketching the countryside'.[4] Calling me back to poetry, Glover's habit is reminiscent of the notational, highly localised mode adopted by William Wordsworth and John Clare, and quite unlike the hybridised landscapes created in the work of Australian colonial poets such as Henry Kendall and Charles Harpur.

In turn, I look at the border country and see, manifested like the heron, the language of space in Fred Williams' (1927–1982) inland-scapes. As Paul Carter observes, they find expression through the creation of 'a grammar in a visually chaotic or grammarless nature'. To do this, Carter notes, Williams desired an 'underdetermined' landscape.[5] Compared to Australian painters before him, Williams was tremblingly efficient with three or four landmarks – wiping from the work's ground the minutiae that Heysen and Glover found important. It could be said of Williams that, like Glover, he set out to 'sketch' the You Yangs of southern Victoria: even in painting, Williams is drawing the ground as located points and positions. Perhaps Williams struggled with Heysen's problem of clarity some fifty years later than he, in places far from here. Are Williams' minimal crescents of paint and etched

---

4  John McPhee, 'A Stranger in This World', *Australian Financial Review*, 21 November 2003, pp. 4–5.
5  Paul Carter, *The Lie of the Land* (London: Faber, 1996), p. 363.

twitches the residue of a draughtsman's impulse to flag a location; or do they clear common ground all the way from Geelong to the Pilbara?

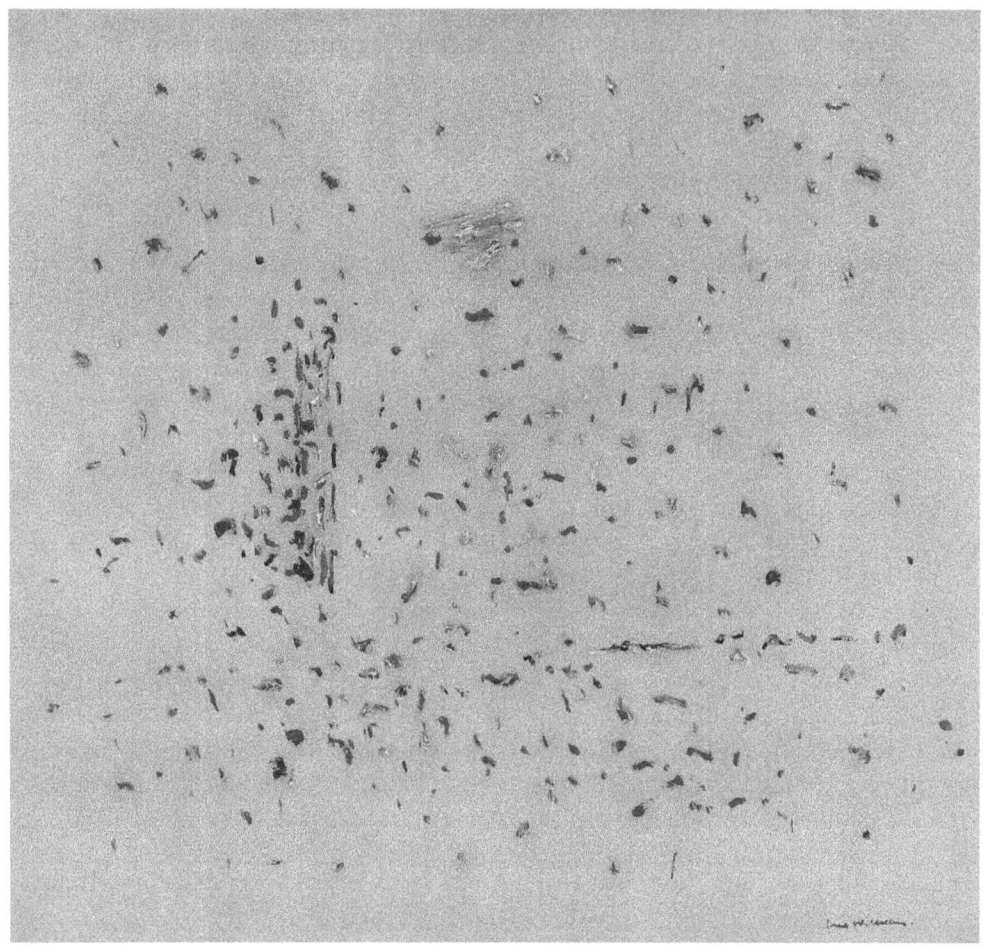

Figure 1. Fred Williams, *You Yangs Landscape*, 1966, oil on canvas (91.6 x 98.4 cm). Gift of Rudy Komon, 1969, Newcastle Art Gallery collection. © The artist's estate courtesy Lyn Williams.

The line on the etching plate or canvas encounters the line on the page or screen: how easy it is to find plentiful words and images that wrap around a place or flow over it without restraint. The challenge of representing space, on the other hand, is between pressed, faceless ridges and poetry's economy; and in whether or not three or four words are capable of bristling at our feet and colouring those distant creases. In the spattered plateaus around Broken Hill, there's a grammar in being here, by this outcrop; or there, close to that circle of saltbush. In reading place, Williams was reading those painters before him; both marking and erasing a line that connected their problems as artists.

Are the possibilities in the expanse of canvas so very different to the printed page, or can we see a shared lineage of painting and poetry that deals with the problem of space? 'You try a middle distance that remains/distant', writes Barry Hill in his poem 'Some Centre: Nolan/Thomas'. Placing enjambment before the ultimate 'distant', Hill creates an open edge: the way Rover Thomas' compositions are bordered within the edge of the canvas. A wash of white, emerald green or deep navy is laid down and lurks at the outer edges of a painting as if the top design has been haphazardly stamped onto it. The final painting, then, is an arbitrary enclosure of the wider subject matter and its line: 'All gives way to ground/shadow of ground, a pick of blues', writes Hill.[6] The work is floating and drifting over the fixed surface, rather than sticking to it. Line moves on and in. As Hill puts it:

> 'The shade from the hill comes over and talks in language'
> *Rover Thomas*
>
> because it must.
>
> And because shade is
> and language is
>
> one black ball
> folded into the shade
> you can hear the black ball talking.
>
> You can walk this way
> and come over into language.
> You can walk this way
> and come over into shade.
>
> The language comes over
> the shade comes under[7]

Having crossed the borderline, we are among red ridges hung with treeless cliffs. Williams' solutions to the problem of 'interior' drew a new line, a transfer of gestural energy, between painters as culturally distinct from one another as Rover Thomas and Sidney Nolan. Both, like Williams, are able to read locality in order to depart from it. The picture space is opened and turned outwards like an unfolded carton. Rather than being marked, it is clothed in tones and sometimes textures like Thomas' ochre stains. His earth is an equilibrate field in which terrestrial surfaces possess shifting overlays more usually associated with cloud.

From tone comes complexity: the thickening and thinning that happens between layers of paint, and a surface that has been smoothed down. In a mail plane north of here, on 28 June 1949, Nolan began his desert series; focusing on bringing fresh yellow and green tones through the red surfaces, mixing PVA with dry pigments to create washes, then

---

6 Barry Hill, 'Some Centre: Nolan/Thomas', *As We Draw Ourselves* (Melbourne: Five Islands Press, 2008), p. 31.

7 Hill, 'Some Centre', p. 33.

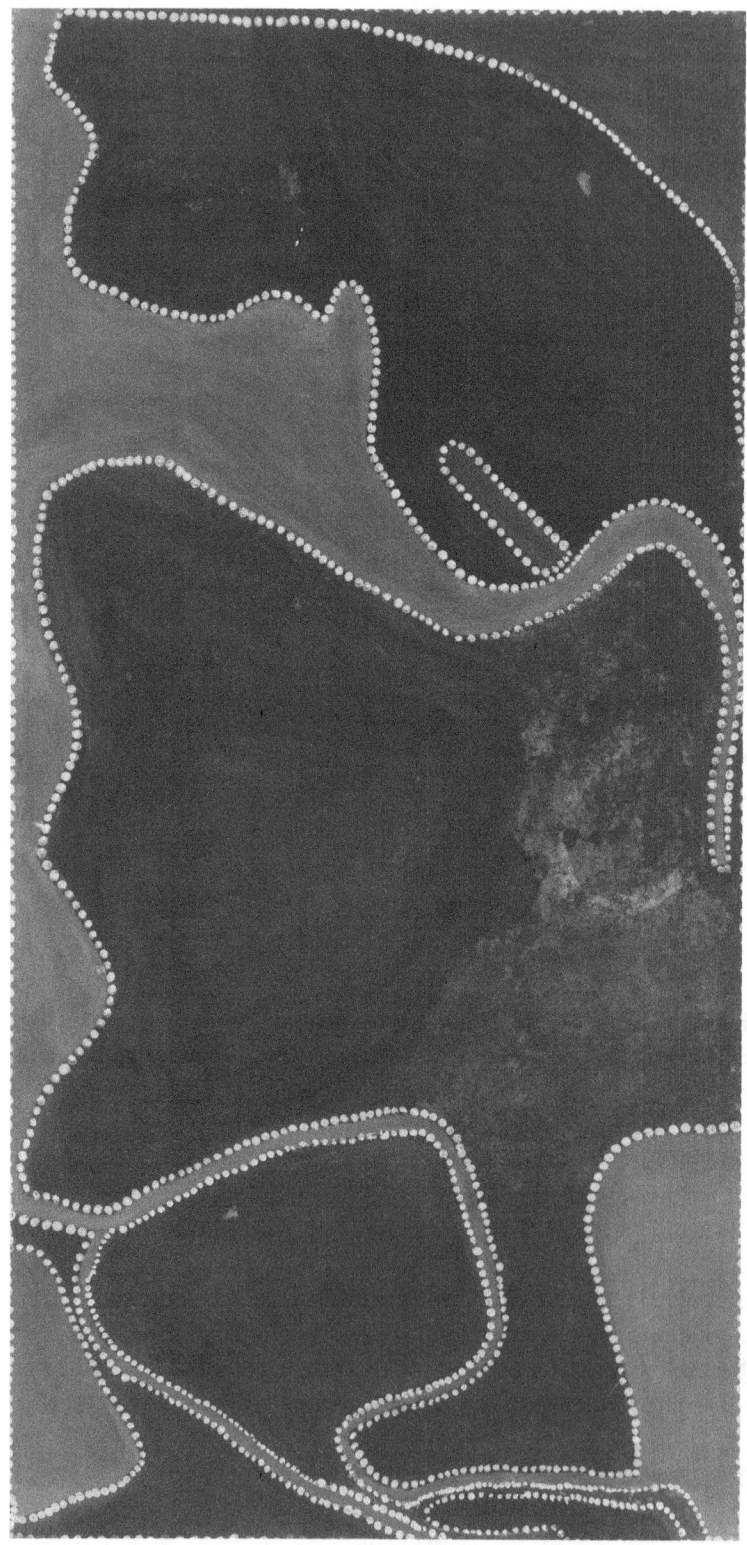

Figure 2. Rover Thomas (Joolama), *Lurinjipungu (Clara Springs)*, 1984, natural pigments and binders on plywood (90 x 180 cm), National Gallery of Australia, Canberra. Purchased from Gallery admission charges, 1984. © The artist's estate courtesy Warmun Art Centre.

scraping this back with a cloth. By going so deep through the soil profile, Nolan's desert series appears to find blankness; yet this blankness is comprised of substance. The brush is used to drag a wind current into fast-drying paint. Giving the canvas evolution and wear. Clearing evidence of particularity.

For this space is not only an inland line: painters of the East Kimberley such as Thomas work with even expanses, too. In the bubbled white bordering and pale cream of his dim earth tones, there's the inkling of subterranean wetness. How often, from our plane windows, are unmarked earth and water seen from above. From there, they cease to compose maps and begin to build layers. These are not only earth lines: at Cooktown and Fraser Island, Nolan developed a sense of distance through fathoms and light rays. Working with the vocabulary of ink, his nocturnal swamps find green and blue within black, and lose drips along the way. The paint coagulates to a murky lagoon into which the scratched legs of a bird, *Great Heron* (1949), dissolve. Nolan's broad tug of cloth across the canvas echoes the mopping motion of calligraphic hair brushes. In the salt glare of his Burke and Wills series, and even in the straining folds of his desert works, Nolan anticipates the forms of Antarctica.

Nolan's Antarctica series is, as Rodney James puts it, 'quite literally black and blue ... wiped to the "bare bones"' with knife and comb.[8] The rubbed, plastic surface of *Headland (Antarctica I)* (1964) has the appearance of oily feathers – laden and intricate, yet dry and damaged. James points out that the generic titling of the series – in which the evasive repetition of 'Antarctica' becomes tantamount to 'untitled' – was Nolan's way of liberating both the viewer and himself from the novelty of the unfamiliar place and from a fixed experience of it.[9] Nolan's written notes were used to aid his later process, in a kind of negative practice that then wiped the page clean. 'These mental images, like words', writes James, 'would become sublimated in the physical act of painting'.[10] Following his trip to Antarctica, Nolan's painterly act was mostly undertaken in a London studio, far from the deserts and tundra of its source. And so the painter steps away from a responsibility to the landmark, as if ice peaks might just as likely appear among that other tundra, in central Australia.

Down the Barrier Highway, alert pink gums begin to fill the plain, which undulates about their roots. Paper silhouettes drying into gluey creases, the high rock walls are layered one upon another. A man walks the railway like an insect stalking beneath the ranges. I imagine the regular rhythm he can hear, and then it comes: blocks of green and rust, blue, and a stripe of yellow; and, inside that sound, a tangle of motion between the carriages as they cut across my view of sooty shrubs and the dirt-streaked, chalky apex of a hill. Snatches of purpling lines rip across the hill, hovering with cool detachment until, at last, the train moves ahead and the man is left walking, as if backwards. At the level of his feet, the plateau's eroded profiles form miniature versions of the ranges: little cliffs of soil cropping away into

---

8 Rodney James, *Sidney Nolan: Antarctic Journey* (Melbourne: Mornington Peninsula Regional Gallery, 2006), p. 11.

9 James, p. 18.

10 James, p. 16.

shadows, and shallow pits in the banks of bare creeks. To his eyes, the slopes spray down to iron soil. Distantly, it is covered by grey lawn, and in one of the paddocks he sees a fallen roll of wire unscrolling from a cylinder to a cone, becoming a shell the size of a wombat, worn to its spidery core.

After I read Hill's poem I run a bath in the motel room and roll my hands under the water. On the edge of desert, I realise that I had nearly forgotten what it was to stand on a boulder and look through bands of water, down to sand or weed. But I have remembered enough to know that the cold earth in Rankin's poem is not, in fact, impenetrable. When I read, it reverberates with other images and places, and the page seems to tremble. As if enacting these odd networks of affective connection, her poems burrow up and down; they spiral through layers, like the wombat in her final major sequence, 'The Mud Hut':

> Mud cracks
> the skull's temple cracks
>
> wombat stretches inside his burrow inside the earth
> he loosens himself his skin gliding easily on the head-bone
> the thin white bone of the skull that picks its way out
> hard and thin against this dry earth
> these burrows deep and always winding
> up now and out he leaves [11]

As the poem breaks down the telluric profile, it cuts through air and time:

> Yet this is earth-tremor country
>
> and in these crumbling walls new cracks
> shuffle and reshuffle the light.
>
> Now the roaring draws closer.
> The walls twist and split.
> And the distant clatter of the train
> drowns in itself at last
> as the earth takes itself back.
>
> I crawl through these remnants
> this diligently worked entrance
> this exit dug by the wombat.[12]

Given that things dive into soil, as well as out of it, I wonder if I've been looking at earth the wrong way. While there is a 'surface earth quality', Rankin once told an interviewer, it is not a blank floor of soil or quite what painter John Olsen calls 'the void'. Rather, by 'going into the desert, going into any desert, it's sort of like getting under the earth: there's

---

11  Rankin, 'The Mud Hut', *Collected Poems*, p. 108.
12  Rankin, 'The Mud Hut', p. 110.

always limestone caves under the earth, there's always this cool room in the dark hut'.[13] Its stalactites and stalagmites create what appears to be a space without gravity, in which verticality stretches in two directions. Seeping through stone, rainwater creates these expanding pockets and, above them, a floating floor. That, perhaps, is the reader's ground.

*Reading as Burrowing*

Outside of Peterborough, with its lemony scent of pepper trees and the red-dusted steps of a grand bluestone Federation Hall, abandoned stone cottages slump in the paddocks. We pass the unsealed entrance to a signed property, *Rankine*. I think of Rankin's 'dark hut' – a place of comforting relief, but one without solid walls. I look at the eyes of a cottage, through to the lush green and orange of the hills in the back of its mind.

From a long way off, the Southern Flinders Ranges are tightly blushed. They resemble distant, blue mountaintops that I once saw from a train in France. It passed dark red vegetation, dry and fresh like the carpet of lavender leaves that have cropped up here. That rusty shrub continued over to the west of France, around the Neolithic limestone caves of Périgord. Heading into the Vézère valley, hawks cruised over pastures and the train ran alongside undergrowth where rabbits, mice and squirrels went. The valley opened suddenly at Les Eyzies de Tayac – a corridor of white and grey cliffs, bulging over their bases. In 'Hotel Cro-Magnon', titled for the motel at Les Eyzies, poet Clayton Eshleman describes these walls as 'the abyss of everywhere', of 'dead/fresh stone,/air/pervasive cenotaph'.[14] Inside them, the sounds of the valley were distant and muffled. They held something in; and something out. It was already chill, and I kept encountering a feeling of moving underwater. The river itself worked fast to clear obstacles out onto its banks. When, at sunset, I emerged onto the rooftop of the town's famous prehistory museum, nothing and everything appeared to move. A golden limestone shelf curved around toward troglodyte houses, which rose out of the stone like growths under skin. It was Dante's first Cornice of Purgatory, engraved with images of Pride: 'So there, with livelier likeness, due to skill/Of craftsmanship, I saw the whole ledge graven/Where, for a road, it juts out from the hill'.[15] Above my head, the lip of the cave reeled upward, the ceilings of the human structures melted into it, stuck for good. A silent and stormy sun glossed the valley, and the thick river still flowed speedily into evening; at its bottom, cream sand stepped into great fingers. As the light dropped, I trailed into the Abri Pataud with a school excursion, and the kids' droning warmth sharply brought out the lines of a little, pallid ibex protruding from the lining of the cave, horns turned in a whip of triumph.

*Wilpena Pound*

In the early morning, the sky is ripped thin, but still the cloud keeps coming from behind

---

13 Jennifer Rankin, interview with Hazel de Berg, 2 March 1978, Hazel de Berg Collection (DeB 1083), National Library of Australia. Permission to quote from this material kindly granted by David Rankin.

14 Clayton Eshleman, *Hotel Cro-Magnon* (Santa Rosa: Black Sparrow Press, 1989), p. 125.

15 Dante Alighieri, trans. Dorothy L. Sayers, *The Divine Comedy: Purgatory* (London: Penguin, 1955), p.158.

the nearby range. I watch it from the house we are renting, where two birds are nipping back and forth out of a red gum until one takes off into the range, gone into that backlit shape. As the sun draws warmth out of the rock, I see the raised cicatrices of the range. Its lit face is shot through with vein-rich blue, purple and orange; its darkened wall is dormant.

*Gasps and fibrillations* – the oaks bring the phrase back to me from a Stephen King audio book we've had playing in the car. I make my way over the floodplains of wildflowers to get a better look at the cliffs beyond Wilpena Pound, but the ground is strewn with pieces of the two rock faces. The burning red stone is porous and sparkling, ready to crumble; whereas the shadow shale is more constant – if it cracks, the block shatters, flaking off in egg-like boles. Black oaks nod. Long forgotten pods open at their tips. Their needles twitch and circle. A group of three trees passes the wind from one to the next, feeling it a little then flicking it off. The open lattice of dead branches crawls with ants and pellets. It's breaking into twigs, matches, splinters. Every now and then I hear a zip or jangling keys, but it's something else.

The crags at the top border of the Pound are ten or so tablets leaning upon one another. In fact, there are twenty-six in total, named the ABCs. Each slab's truncated trajectory into the air is a phantom limb, its original scale somehow visible. The ABCs are the roots of a Precambrian era range that edged the downfold of rock into the Pound's basin. To the Adyamathanha peoples, a group encompassing Nukunu, Pankarle, Kuyani and other languages, the creation serpent woke to drink the gorges dry, leaving the depression of the Pound behind him. Returning with a swollen belly, he vomited lichen and pissed waterholes. In the dry Wilcolo Creek, I sink into small bricks of brown and purple shale scattered by the crumbling ABCs. Along with shit-coloured sandstone, these lozenges compose the lower hills and slopes of the Pound's floodplain. Six-hundred million year-old Ediacara fauna are stored in both the quartzite and shale: jellyfish, segmented worms, sea pens and *Dickinsonia costata*, fossilised into a fanning round of lines like a periwinkle, radiating out into a sea that has now gone into the sky. What words will be left for the range of letters to form, when it has finally eroded down to earth? A full, flooding current lifts up the folding chair and bobs me away downstream.

*Standing/Looking/Moving*

In the sixties, American experimental psychologist James J. Gibson developed his theory of ambient optics. According to this thesis, human cognition is formed by the consolidation of individual sense data into public perceptual knowledge. We attain this knowledge, he argued, by piecing together data not from one point in space, but from our own multiple, motile places or positions. Not only do we use constantly shifting perspective, but we also work with an assumption that parts of a place – what's over the precipice, behind the boulder or past the horizon – are invisible or insensible to our own body. In this way, one person's positional placements will and will not resemble another's, and both will come to share or exchange perspectives of a surrounding environment.

What our perceptual knowledge ultimately agrees upon is that objects, as well as places and events, are environments in which things intersect. According to Gibson, our senses tell us that the earth is one big nest. Through 'paths of possible locomotion', Gibson suggested, we constantly reassess the world. 'We perceive that the environment changes in some respects and persists in others ... We perceive both the change and the underlying non-change'.[16] I am sitting in the Wilcolo, that rain of shale talking at my ankles, and I am looking up and I am looking down.

*Inside*

It is possible that several bodies and minds have, as though outside of time, responded to an unchanging problem of Australian space. The problem remains; pondering it, I walk and drive around it, gathering the collective memory of other artist's views. Charles Buckmaster's 1971 poem, 'Wilpena Pound', speaks of the enclosure of the downfold, to have 'first noticed that we were/inside'; and to turn, seeing:

> Sunset. To the west, etched
> in a sky of all colour – a lone tree against the light:
>
> and to the north, the Pound: a circle of fire.[17]

Buckmaster's sky takes us through the passage from the Pound, north into the first ranges. Its last light flashes onto a long web, which drifts toward me then washes over. The light pulls over the faint lines that separate element from element, material from material; over the forgetting of the line itself; over the very notion of forgetting. As it reaches me, I have almost remembered it all.

*Writing Out*

Yesterday, a flat brown cloud pushed across Mount Little and passed us in the streets of Hawker. A local history describes a colossal dust storm in the nineteenth century, during which pastoralists watched magpies and sparrows leave the sky and huddle, together with families and their stock, inside dwellings. Today, windless, the air of the plateau is moved by flies and stalking emus. But the earth finds other ways of moving itself, grinding away beneath us. A recent tremor, we're told, sent livestock fleeing the local properties.

At Sacred Canyon, the Adyamathanha set aside the human hair string that they used to weave story patterns, and took up chisels to peck in Panaramitee style at a break in the southern wall of the ranges. Like chiselled work found around the Australian coast, these animal and linear designs could be 40 000 years old. Descendents of the rock tribes tell that they were created by ancestral beings, but their symbolism within the original ceremonial laws of this place of caves and waterfalls has been buried in time.

At the top of a dry creek bed flanked by a straight avenue of gums, the canyon sits about one storey high. Shale tablets slip away underfoot, displacing each step with the next. The entrance walls are long, vertical palings of red stone balanced in a precarious frieze. At shoulder height, I spot two circular designs for rockhole or waterfall. They are head sized and picked out with single lines. As I slip deeper into the canyon toward the signed water,

---

16 James J. Gibson, *The Ecological Approach to Visual Perception* (Boston: Houghton Mifflin Company, 1979), pp. 17–18.

17 Charles Buckmaster, 'Wilpena Pond', in Simon Macdonald, ed., *Charles Buckmaster: Collected Poems*, (St Lucia: University of Queensland Press, 1989), p. 124.

the corners of its corridor lock the next bend out of sight. I step up to the first, empty rockhole and as my foot leaves the loud shale, I hear a sound running below. My ear tunes in to a low, even murmuring above the canyon. The closed bend faces me, and I hesitate; I'm not sure why I want to clamber here, through empty sinks that must be so rich when water comes to touch them. The droning carries on. I am about to crunch back into the creekbed when I see the shadows of insects against a rock at my feet; and then a swarming in front of it, as hornets draw themselves out of a mouth in the grey limestone. I recollect the bees in a prose poem by Rankin called 'Koan':

> I make a mental note as the bees crawl out of the mud walls. They are using the crack from the tremor. This interests me. They are crawling into and out of the crack … I search their wall. I search the crack they enter. I search remembering the trenches I have built remembering the pines. And the notches.[18]

There are more designs at the first sink, this time higher on the flat red wall. They seem to be a series of rockholes, and a pair of the inverted horseshoe shapes that denote a cave or sacred site – and, in a different hand, '1867'.

The singing drone carries on through the canyon, and I notice that a second nest of hornets is turning beneath these higher engravings. The nest's opening is positioned to shield the inner rockhole: no longer red flint but grey limestone that swims up into arcs as smooth as a sea mammal, as smooth as fat. I slip over the lapping tones of grey on grey, its whorls chunking off into jade and blue chips. Climbing up over a causeway, I emerge onto the floor of an enclosed place walled by more flint. Jagged, chaotic ladders form around a scorched cave that lies deep behind what will again be the mouth of a raging waterfall. Lichen and noon sun glint, and I can already see the gathering of people messing about under a rush of chalky rain.

My hands and feet slide away; I wish I hadn't come. Writing this, I wish it once again, but feel instead that my mistake is only more deeply re-inscribed. I imagined that writing could smooth together lives and places; that the grammar of human expression could intersect to make a persistent and unchanging view of space.

I sense the dry creek at the canyon's entrance waiting to take in my steps; and the hornets down below, invisible under the soft limestone, filling up the canyon floor and ready to flood out into the passage.

*The Sea Outside*

Wind brings a high-tide boom against the ridge and we turn to see the falling wave; realising, in the same moment, that we've been teased. When the water pulls out then falls a second time, I turn again and feel trapped by my impulse. From the top of this thin spine, at 566 metres, we can just glimpse Lake Frome posing as a mirage. Its miles of salt appear to be a sandbar across the horizon; several days in from the island coast, and many metres below sea level, it's the beach we can hear behind and ahead.

Water's memory is everywhere between the empty gorge walls: in the dense, trampled mud that's still soggy and deep when its surface cracks, and in the waterfall runnels

---

18  Rankin, 'Koan', *Collected Poems*, pp. 28–29.

streaked with absent rapids. Trickling and dripping are somewhere, invisibly. As we go further through the halls of the gorge, we find dried debris wrapping itself urgently around the trunks of white gums. Imitating the line of water that once was, some of the gums lie at full stretch. When I try photographing some of these, their line does not come; instead, it springs out of their roots in the sliding shale and waits for when the rain will carry it along the creek's course. The wind's memory of wetness is even more distant but, nevertheless, it carries from the south to flap about our heads.

The night before, a young German astronomer had brought a nebula into the view of the observatory telescope, spreading his arms to the night air and speaking of *this mess* – this mass of ice, fire, and dust particles that cloak an absorptive nebula, shielding it from light. If this morning's gorge were wet, it would pool at Stubbs Waterhole where I clamber and slide over boulders parked in the silt. They're milky blue, with a random grab of smoothed pebbles protruding from their strange, set sea: tillite, a conglomerate formed when glacier drives a rock forward, forcing it to collect other fragments in its path. The tillite is held together by a rumour of water, caught in the blue-grey tone of the parent rock. It's the same colour Nolan used for under-painting in the Antarctica series – as flat as sea washing over ice, and as deep as the constellations lodged in it. When the ice dissolved, the boulders fell into ocean mud and stuck where they are; and when the tillite garden ends, we are in a shallower place. Low tides have pressed themselves against tablets of quartzite, leaving indented ripples that cast shadow stripes in the spring sun.

In the serpent's time, the organisms of this place had not yet developed shells. Instead of skeletons and eyes, there were mounds of soft tissue that travelled over the slime bed of the inland sea, new shapes everywhere. The slime took their imprint, and sealed them in sediment. Their creeping, trickling movement seeps through and runs beneath art and language.

We have just crossed the Murray River at Paringa, when I see motion down in the willows by the eastern bank – slow and soft, and now still – a grey heron. Only as the car climbs the hill can I glance back and see what it sees: the bones of the river, its cliffs dropping down to a white mess. The heron stands where the river runs into a milky whirlpool. The bird is a vortex, in Ezra Pound's sense – not the visual idea of repose, but now, a concentration of the river's real motion in bones and muscle, and an event that both receives and generates a line of energy in the water.

In the scrub around the citrus farms of the Murray, the malleefowl hen builds a mound over one metre high by kicking together earth and leaf litter. Inside the mound, she incubates her eggs, and goes about habits of sedimentary life. Her terrestrial structure, a form of permanence and return, diverges from the aerial domesticity and nomadic or migratory departure with which we like to associate birds. A nest, of course, is homely, but it's not an enclosure. When the malleefowl sits or stands atop her mound, the dwelling has not only a biological and protective function, but also a territorial and defensive one. On top of the mound, she is positioned exactly half way between ground and nest levels. The bird is able to survey her environment with an elevated perspective, but not with the horizon view or aerial breadth seen from a nest. Her height, in fact, matches the average human eye-level. The malleefowl knows the burden of gravity – the binding of time – for even the skyward bird must return to ground.

To be held to the earth is to take in the entire periphery of places; and writing, like painting, is also bound by this line. In *The Linguistic Moment*, J. Hillis Miller describes the peripheral tradition that surrounds language. For Miller, 'each text is seen as referring to some still earlier text' and the poetic text is positioned in a burrow:

> Each is like a thousand borrowed atoms dancing in the air or like stone made of minute, once-living fragments agglomerated ... Each poet's precursors are present, whether or not he knows it or wishes it, in the intimate texture of his material, in the words he must use to speak or write at all, there in the language like tiny fossils in the builder's stone.[19]

From there, revelling in the bind of gravity, the poet discovers an infinite community of distance and scale. Her grammar cannot be original, but she finds a language of perspective in events of texture and surface and motion.

---

19  J. Hillis Miller, *The Linguistic Moment: From Wordsworth to Stevens* (Princeton: Princeton University Press, 1985), p. 113.

## Contributors

LINDSAY BARRETT is a member of the Writing and Society Research Centre at the University of Western Sydney. He has written on a range of aspects of Australian cultural history, and is the author of *The Prime Minister's Christmas Card: Blue Poles and Cultural Politics in the Whitlam Era* (Power Publications, 2001).

LACHLAN BROWN is lecturer in English and creative writing at Charles Sturt University, Wagga Wagga. His 2009 PhD dissertation, completed at the University of Sydney, examined the poetry and prose of Kevin Hart. Lachlan has run writing workshops in a number of high schools across Sydney with the Redroom Company and Bankstown Youth Development Services. His own poems have appeared in such journals as *Southerly*, *Heat*, *Mascara* and *Westside*.

PATRICK BUCKRIDGE is professor of literary studies in the School of Humanities, Griffith University. He has published widely on Australian literary history and the history of reading, and is currently working on a study of Australian reading culture during the interwar period, and a history of the publishing house of Harrap.

DAVID CARTER FAHA is professor of Australian literature and cultural history at the University of Queensland. He is a contributor to *Paper Empires: A History of the Book in Australia 1946-2005* (University of Queensland Press, 2006), *The Cambridge History of Australian Literature* (Cambridge University Press, 2009), and author of *Dispossession, Dreams and Diversity: Issues in Australian Studies* (Pearson, 2006).

BONNY CASSIDY is a poet and writer who has taught creative writing, English and Australian literature, and written on Australian poetry and poetics. She was co-editor of *The Salon Anthology of New Writing + Art 2005-2007* (non-generic, 2007), and is the author of the collections *Said To Be Standing* (Vagabond, 2010) and *Certain Fathoms* (Puncher & Wattmann, 2012). She was President of Sydney PEN in 2009-2011.

MICHELLE DE STEFANI is a PhD student in the Department of English, Communications and Perfomance Studies at Monash University. Her research interests include Victorian literature, histories of childhood and book history.

ROBERT DIXON FAHA is professor of Australian literature at the University of Sydney and a judge of the Miles Franklin Literary Award (2004-2009). His most recent books are *Photography, Early Cinema and Colonial Modernity: Frank Hurley's Synchronized Lecture Entertainments* (Anthem, 2011), *The Diaries of Frank Hurley 1912-1941* (Anthem, 2011), co-edited with Christopher Lee, and *The Novels of Alex Miller: An Introduction* (Allen & Unwin, 2012).

MICHAEL FARRELL is a poet with an interest in early Australian experiment. He has published articles on Ned Kelly's 'Babington letter' and *Waltzing Matilda*. Recent publications include *thempark* (Book Thug, 2010), *thou sand* (Tinfish, 2011) and *open sesame* (Giramondo, 2012).

JEREMY FISHER is senior lecturer in writing in the School of Arts at the University of New England. He came to this position in 2010 following thirty-five years' experience in the Australian publishing industry as editor, publisher, indexer and author and, most recently, as executive director of the Australian Society of Authors. His writing has been published in India and translated into Vietnamese, and his most recent book is the novel *Music from Another Country* (Fat Frog Books, 2009).

KERI GLASTONBURY is a poet, essayist and lecturer in creative writing at the University of Newcastle. She researches contemporary cultures of writing, publishing and criticism in Australia post Mark Davis' *Gangland: Cultural Elites and the New Generationalism* (1999).

JANE GRANT has a PhD in English from the University of Sydney. She is the author of *Kylie Tennant: A Life* (National Library of Australia, 2006) and is currently working on a history of Melbourne University's English Department under Professors Maxwell, Goldberg and Felperin.

PETER KIRKPATRICK is senior lecturer in Australian literature at the University of Sydney. He is the author of *The Sea Coast of Bohemia: Literary Life in Sydney's Roaring Twenties* (2nd edn. API Network, 2007), and co-editor with Fran De Groen of *Serious Frolic: Essays on Australian Humour* (University of Queensland Press, 2009).

JULIEANNE LAMOND is lecturer in English at the Australian National University. Her research focuses on Australian literary culture and reading history around the turn of the twentieth century.

SUSAN K. MARTIN is associate professor in English and associate dean of research for the Faculty of Humanities and Social Science at La Trobe University. She teaches Australian studies and Victorian literature, and publishes on nineteenth and twentieth century Australian literature and culture. Her books include *Reading the Garden: The Settlement of Australia*, with Katie Holmes and Kylie Mirmohamadi (Melbourne University Press, 2008), and *Sensational Melbourne: Reading, Sensation Fiction and* Lady Audley's Secret *in the Victorian Metropolis*, with Kylie Mirmohamadi (Australian Scholarly Publishing, 2011).

PHILIP MEAD is the inaugural chair of Australian literature at the University of Western Australia. His book *Networked Language: Culture & History in Australian Poetry* (Australian Scholarly Publishing, 2008) won the 2010 New South Wales Premier's Prize for Literary Scholarship. He has co-edited, with Brenton Doecke and Larissa McLean Davies, *Teaching Australian Literature: From Classroom Conversations to National Imaginings* (Wakefield Press, 2011).

KYLIE MIRMOHAMADI is a senior research associate in English at La Trobe University and research associate on the ARC-funded Cities of Words project. She is the author, with Susan K. Martin, of *Sensational Melbourne: Reading, Sensation Fiction and* Lady Audley's Secret *in the Victorian Metropolis* (Australian Scholarly Publishing, 2011).

NICOLE MOORE is the author of *The Censor's Library* (University of Queensland Press, 2012) and co-author with Marita Bullock of the *Banned in Australia* bibliography (AustLit, 2008). She is contributing editor for 1900–1950 to *The Macquarie PEN Anthology of Australian Literature* (Allen & Unwin, 2009) and coordinator of the English program at the University of New South Wales, Canberra.

FIONA MORRISON is lecturer in the School of English, Media and Performing Arts at the University of New South Wales. Her most recent book is *The Selected Prose of Dorothy Hewett* (University of Western Australia Press, 2011). She is currently working on Christina Stead's American novels.

D'ARCY RANDALL was born and educated in the US, but during the 1980s she lived in Brisbane, where she was senior editor at the University of Queensland Press. She there worked with Marian Eldridge and Marion Halligan on their first books. After returning to the US, she founded the journal *Borderlands: Texas Poetry Review* and began a teaching career at the University of Texas at Austin.

JOAN SHELLEY RUBIN is professor of history at the University of Rochester. She received an AB *magna cum laude* in American history and literature from Harvard University in 1969 and a PhD in American studies from Yale University in 1974. A Guggenheim Fellow, she is the author of three books: *Constance Rourke and American Culture* (University of North Carolina Press, 1980), *The Making of Middlebrow Culture* (University of North Carolina Press, 1992), and *Songs of Ourselves* (Belknap Press, 2007). She is also co-editor of *A History of the Book in America, Volume 5: The Enduring Book* (University of North Carolina Press, 2009).

SUSAN SHERIDAN FAHA is adjunct professor of English and women's studies at Flinders University. She has published widely on women's writing, feminist cultural studies and Australian cultural history. Her latest book is *Nine Lives: Postwar Women Writers Making Their Mark* (University of Queensland Press, 2011).

CHRISTINA SPITTEL received her PhD from the University of Freiburg for a thesis titled 'Based on a True Story: The Great War in Australian Novels, 1914–2008'. She is a visitor at the University of New South Wales, Canberra, and a research manager at the Australian National University. Her work has appeared in *Book History, Australian Literary Studies,* and the *Journal of Contemporary History*.

ANN VICKERY is senior lecturer in literary studies at Deakin University. She is the author of *Stressing the Modern: Cultural Politics in Australian Women's Poetry* (Salt, 2007) and *Leaving Lines of Gender: A Feminist Genealogy of Language Writing* (Wesleyan University Press, 2000). She co-authored *The Intimate Archive: Journeys through Private Papers* (National Library of Australia, 2009) with Maryanne Dever and Sally Newman.

JAN ZWAR recently completed a PhD thesis at Macquarie University on 'Cultural Value and Books in Public Debate in Australia, 2003–2008', which involved cross-disciplinary research between the departments of Economics and English. Her research interests include the economics and marketing of cultural goods and services and changing contemporary readerships.

# Index

## A

Aboriginal literature  148, 228–229, 232–234, 269
*Advertiser* (Adelaide)  19, 24, 180
*Age*  58, 240
Anderson, Benedict  31, 80
  *Imagined Communities*  227–228
  *The Spectre of Comparisons*  72
*Angry Penguins*  107, 184–185, 190. *See also* Harris, Max
Angus & Robertson  185, 187, 253
  *Australian Poetry* anthology  104
*Argus*  20, 173, 181, 193
Arnold, Matthew  42–43
asylum seekers  53–55, 62–66. *See also* refugees
Australasian Book Society (ABS)  113
Australasian Home Reading Union (AHRU)  17–25
  *Australasian Home Reader* (*AHR*)  23–25
*Australian*  58, 64, 200
Australian Broadcasting Corporation (ABC)  205, 210
Australian Common Reader (Database)  35–36, 38, 172
*Australian Literary Studies*  140
Australian Society of Authors (ASA)  200, 252–253, 255–256
*Australian Women's Weekly*  195–202. *See also* Jefferis, Barbara

## B

Barbalet, Margaret  205, 207–208, 212, 216
Beckett, Samuel  119, 153–154
Book-of-the-Month Club  5, 7–9
Bourdieu, Pierre  85–86, 220, 222
  *The Rules of Art*  220
Boyd, Hannah Villiers  164–165
  *Letters on Education*  159, 164–170

Braddon, Mary
  *Lady Audley's Secret*  171–175, 178–182
Bradstock, Margaret
  'Selling Out'  262
Brisbane  39–45, 51
  'Red Flag' riots  41
*Brisbane Courier*  42, 44
Buckridge, Patrick  35
*Bulletin*  28, 101, 106–107, 196

## C

Canberra  205–206, 212–215
*Canberra Times*  58, 213
cantastorie  245–246
  *Le Avventure di Salvatore Tripodi*  246
Carter, David  30, 35, 88, 91, 141, 222, 239
Casanova, Pascale  74, 85–87, 95–98, 129–130, 141–145, 154–155. *See also* republic of letters
  Greenwich Meridian of literature  89, 155
  literary space  71, 78, 80, 90–91, 95, 100, 142–143, 220
  *The World Republic of Letters*  71, 85, 108, 142–143, 153–154, 220
  world republic of letters  108, 142–144, 155
censorship  41, 92
Ciardi, John  10–11
Clarke, Marcus  174–175
Clift, Charmian  183, 195–196, 201–202
coding  235–238. *See also* decoding
Cold War  13–15, 125, 130, 197
Commonwealth Literary Fund  199, 251, 253
communism  44, 107, 115–117, 124, 126, 185, 192, 197, 241, 247
Conrad, Joseph  95
*Courier Mail*  58
Cousins, Norman  10–11
Culotta, Nino. *See* O'Grady, John

## D

*Daily Telegraph* 54, 189, 192
Dale, Leigh 140–141
Damrosch, David 30, 74, 141
  *What is World Literature?* 71, 141
Dante Alighieri 151–153
Dante Alighieri Society 40, 51
Davis, A.H. (Steele Rudd) 27–28, 32, 37
Davis, Mark
  *Gangland* 220–221
decoding 236–237. *See also* coding
Desiderata 86–95, 97–98
Dimock, Wai Chee 71, 81–82
  *Through Other Continents* 80
Dolin, Tim 29, 35–36. *See also* Australian Common Reader (Database)
Dowse, Sara 205–209, 214, 216
Drain, Dorothy 200–201
Drake-Brockman, Henrietta 249–250
Dunne, Gary 260–261
During, Simon 136, 141–143

## E

Edgar, Suzanne 205, 211, 215–216
Eggert, Paul 29
Eldridge, Marian 205–206, 210, 216
  *The Woman at the Window* 210
Erskine, John 5–7
*Everybody's* 199
Ewers, John Keith 251–253
  *Creative Writing in Australia* 251

## F

Facebook 137, 139, 220. *See also* Zuckerberg, Mark
Factiva 56–60
fascism 50–51, 106, 123
Federation, Australian 18, 75, 77, 108
Fellowship of Australian Writers 101, 251–252
feminism 79, 134, 190, 198–199, 200–203, 212, 257
Fisher, Jonathan 258–259, 262
Franklin, Miles 75
  *Laughter Not for a Cage* 74
Franzen, Jonathan 127–128, 131, 134–136

Fremantle Arts Centre Press (FACP) 254–255
Furphy, Joseph 74–79
  *Such is Life* 74–78, 80, 82

## G

Gelbin, Gertrude 116, 123, 125
German Democratic Republic (GDR) 115–120, 124–125
Giles, Paul 72–74
Glaskin, Gerry 249–256
Great Books movement 4–9

## H

Halligan, Marion 205, 208, 216
Hall of the Muses 44–48, 101
  *The Muses' Magazine* 39–40, 47–51
Hanson, Howard 11–15. *See also* verse speaking choir
Harpur, Charles 229–232
Harris, Max 101, 107–108, 184–189, 192–193. *See also* Angry Penguins; Jindyworobak movement; Reed & Harris
  *The Gift of Blood* 107
  *Mo's Memoirs* 185–186, 192
  *The Vegetative Eye* 185
Harris, Norman 229, 232–234
Hart-Smith, William 104–105. *See also* Jindyworobak movement
Heide Circle (Melbourne) 183–184, 188, 191, 194
Herman, David 163
Hewett, Dorothy 113, 117, 124–126
  *Bobbin Up* 113–122, 125
  'The Times They Are a'Changin'' 124
Hill, Barry 283, 286
Hope, A.D. 103, 106, 185, 191, 212
Horne, Donald 193–194
Horsfield, Dorothy 205, 209–210, 216
Hudson, Flexmore 103–104. *See also* Jindyworobak movement
Huggan, Graham 72, 100, 141
Hurley, Michael 264

## I

imagined communities  24, 26, 31, 73, 76–77, 104, 142, 214, 220, 225, 228. See also Anderson, Benedict
immigration  239–241, 244, 247. See also White Australia policy
Ingamells, Rex  99–108, 110–111. See also Jindyworoback movement
  *Conditional Culture*  97
  *Gumtops*  111
  'Kuark's Mockery'  108–110
  *The Gangrened People*  105

## J

James, Henry  74–75
Jarrell, Randall  127–128, 131
  'An Unread Book'  130–135
Jefferis, Barbara  196, 200–203
Jindyworobak movement  99–105, 107–111. See also Ingamells, Rex; Harris, Max; Hart-Smith, William; Hudson, Flexmore; Mudie, Ian
  *Venture*  97, 103–104, 107
Johnston, Dorothy  205, 207–208, 210, 216
Jones, Jill  264–265
Jose, Nicholas  72, 229, 231

## K

Keesing, Nancy  252–253
Keneally, Thomas  65–66
  *Another Country* (with Rosie Scott)  34, 57, 62, 65–66
  *The Chant of Jimmy Blacksmith*  99
Kevin, Tony
  *A Certain Maritime Incident*  55, 57, 62, 66
Kinsella, John  146, 154–155

## L

Lambert, Elisabeth  184, 186, 189–194
  *Father Couldn't Juggle*  194
  *Insurgence*  190
  *The Map*  190
  *Mo's Memoirs*  185–186, 192
  'Night Piece'  190
  *Poems*  190
  *The Sleeping House Party*  194

Latour, Bruno  222, 223–224
  Actor–Network Theory (ANT)  222, 224
libraries  30, 32–38
*Library Quarterly*  34
Lindsay, Norman  88, 90, 92
literary canon  3, 5, 7, 9, 29–30, 89, 94, 127, 142, 203, 212–213, 228–229
literary communities  8, 10, 85, 100, 106, 137, 184, 194, 212, 219–220, 222–224, 227
literary sociability  3–4, 7–8, 10–11, 15–16, 18, 25, 220, 228–229, 231
Literature Board of the Australia Council  197, 205, 214, 223
Lyons, Martyn  18, 21, 24

## M

Mackellar, Dorothea  229, 235–238
*Macquarie PEN Anthology of Australian Literature*  53, 62, 65–68, 72, 229, 232
Malley, Ern  99–100, 107, 184, 190–194
Manne, Robert
  *Sending Them Home* (with David Corlett)  55, 57, 67
Mares, Peter
  *Borderline*  54–56, 59–60, 66–67
Marr, David
  *Dark Victory* (with Marian Wilkinson)  54–56, 58–59, 61–67
Mead, Philip  99–100, 112
*Meanjin*  101, 107, 124, 185, 202
Melbourne  171, 173–177, 176, 205, 222
modernism  89, 93–96, 100, 138, 185, 245
Montgomery, H.H. (Bishop)  17–21, 25
Moretti, Franco  71, 144–145
Morris, Meaghan. See also social networking
  'Grizzling about Facebook'  139–140
motherhood  167–170, 213
Mudie, Ian  101, 103, 105–106. See also Jindyworobak movement
  *The Arunta*  110

## N

Nancy, Jean-Luc  224, 228
national literature  28, 71–74, 77, 80–82, 86, 91, 155, 219, 227
Neville, A.O.  112, 149, 234

*New York Times* 14, 127, 131, 135
Nielsen BookScan 54–55, 59, 65
Nolan, Cynthia. *See* Reed, Cynthia (later Cynthia Nolan)
Nolan, Sidney 184–185, 189, 283
   *Headland (Antarctica I)* 285

## O

O'Grady, John 247
   *They're a Weird Mob* 239–247
online communities 220–221, 224. *See also* social networking

## P

Palmer, Nettie 90, 99
parenting books 159–164, 168–170
Parés, Luis Amadeo 43–46, 49–51
Pawley, Christine 31, 34–35, 36–37
*The Penguin Book of Australian Women Poets* 204, 264
postcolonialism 82, 141, 277
postmodernism 138, 151, 207, 222, 224
Praed, Rosa 38
Preece, John 87–88, 91–93, 95, 97–98
Prichard, Katharine Susannah 115, 186
   *Coonardoo* 92
provincialism 73, 77–79, 80, 82, 90, 94, 153

## Q

queer communities 257–260, 262–263, 266
queer literature 257–259, 264, 266
   *Eat These Sweet Words* 259, 266
   *Edge City on Two Different Plans* 258–261, 264–266
   *The Exploding Frangipani* 258
   *Out of the Box* 258–259, 264–265
   *Pink Ink* 258, 261–262, 264, 266
   *Sappho's Dreams and Delights* 258
   *When Two Men Embrace* 259, 262, 264, 266

## R

Rankin, Jennifer
   'Earth Count' 280–281
   'Earth Hold' 279–280
   'Koan' 290

'The Mud Hut' 286–287
readers 3, 5, 7, 13, 15, 25–26, 37–38, 91–92, 137, 169, 171–172, 175, 200, 203
Read, Herbert 184–185, 188
reading 3, 5–6, 15, 18, 30–37, 71, 77, 80, 82, 145, 237, 264
Realist Writers Groups 113, 115
Reed, Cynthia (later Cynthia Nolan) 183–184, 186–190
   *Daddy Sowed a Wind* 189, 192–193
   *Lucky Alphonse* 184, 186–188, 192
   *Open Negative* 183
Reed & Harris 185–187, 190–192, 194. *See also* Harris, Max; Reed, John; Reed, Sunday
Reed, John 183–185, 187–191, 194. *See also* Reed & Harris
Reed, Sunday 183, 185, 189. *See also* Reed & Harris
Refugee Action Support (RAS) 268–269, 271
refugees 62, 268–269, 275–278. *See also* asylum seekers
republic of letters 54, 98, 182, 219–220, 224, 257. *See also* Casanova, Pascale
Richardson, Henry Handel 78, 93, 96
   *Maurice Guest* 74–75, 78–80, 82
Roskolenko, Harry 186, 190–193
Rourke, Constance 4, 6
Rudd, Steele. *See* Davis, A.H. (Steele Rudd)

## S

*Saturday Review* 5, 11
Scott, Kim 146, 148, 154–155
   *Benang* 146
   *Kayang & Me* (with Hazel Brown) 146–148
   *That Deadman Dance* 146–147, 149, 155
Seven Seas 114, 116–117, 119, 121–122, 125–126
Seven Writers group 205–210, 215
   *Canberra Tales* 205, 208, 215
   *The Division of Love* 205–206, 214
Smith, Zadie 139–140. *See also* social networking
social networking 137–139, 144, 155, 161, 219–220, 222–223, 224, 227. *See also* Facebook

Southerly  65, 101, 252
Spivak, Gayatri Chakravorty  81–82
Stable, Joseph Jeremiah  41–43
Stead, Christina  75, 129, 131, 135
   *For Love Alone*  127
   *Letty Fox: Her Luck*  127
   *Salzburg Tales*  97
   *The Man Who Loved Children*  127–136
Stephensen, P.R.  106
Suarez, Michael  32–33
Sydney  205, 268–269
*Sydney Morning Herald*  58, 165, 169, 190, 195–196, 200

## T

Tardent, Henri Alexis  43–45, 48–49, 51
   *I Fiddled the Years Away*  44
Tennant, Kylie  186, 195–196, 198–199, 202–203
   *All the Proud Tribesman*  196
   *Australia: Her Story*  196
   'Kylie Tennant Says'  196–198
   *Speak You So Gently*  196
   *Tiburon*  195
theatre  174, 176–179, 182
Thomas, Rover (Joolama)  283–285
   *Lurinjipungu* (*Clara Springs*)  284
Thorpe Bowker Media Mx database  56
transnationalism  73–74, 77. *See also* world literature
trauma  269–272, 274
Tucker, Albert  188–189

## U

University of Queensland Press (UQP)  210, 212

## V

van de Pas, Leo  253, 256
verse speaking choir  8–15
Virago  125, 203

## W

Webby, Elizabeth  28–30
*Weekend*  199
*West Australian*  252
*Westside Jr. Vol. 2: Violence*  267, 269–270, 275
White Australia policy  239–240, 243. *See also* immigration
White, Patrick  256
   *Flaws in the Glass*  190
   *Happy Valley*  98
   *Riders in the Chariot*  99
   *Voss*  245
Whitman, Walt  11–13, 15
Williams, Fred
   *You Yangs Landscape*  281–282
*Woman's Day*  195–196
*Woman's Mirror*  195–197, 199, 202
Woolf, Virginia  92–94
world literature  30, 71, 73, 77, 81–82, 87, 97. *See also* transnationalism
World War Two  104, 130

## Z

Zboray, Ronald  33, 36
Zuckerberg, Mark  139–140. *See also* Facebook

www.ingramcontent.com/pod-product-compliance
Lightning Source LLC
Chambersburg PA
CBHW062136160426
43191CB00014B/2304